THE GEOGRAPHIES OF AIR TRANSPORT

The Geographies of Air Transport *provides a timely and incisive overview of the socio-economic, cultural and environmental ramifications of commercial aviation and aeromobility. An international array of contributors expertly interweave theoretical and empirical perspectives to provide a global analysis of this key industry.*

Brian Graham, University of Ulster, UK

The Geographies of Air Transport *is a significant work, with an assemblage of well-respected authors covering the comprehensive landscape of aviation geography. Commercial aviation is evolving at nearly jet speed, and this book explains and analyzes historical and contemporary developments with clarity and intelligence.*

Paul Stephen Dempsey, McGill University, Canada

This seminal text provides a truly original and global perspective on the key developments which have occurred in air transportation in the most dynamic period of contemporary globalization and societal change. The world experts assembled not only offer new and unique insights into commercial aviation, but also present case studies from all regions of the globe, including the emerging markets. This book is a must read for all scholars of aviation and policy, and the 'movers and the shakers' of the air transportation industry itself!

Jonathan V. Beaverstock, University of Bristol, UK

T0304151

Transport and Mobility Series

Series Editors: Richard Knowles, University of Salford, UK and Markus Hesse, Université du Luxembourg and on behalf of the Royal Geographical Society (with the Institute of British Geographers) Transport Geography Research Group (TGRG).

The inception of this series marks a major resurgence of geographical research into transport and mobility. Reflecting the dynamic relationships between socio-spatial behaviour and change, it acts as a forum for cutting-edge research into transport and mobility, and for innovative and decisive debates on the formulation and repercussions of transport policy making.

Also in the series

Innovation in Public Transport Finance
Property Value Capture
Shishir Mathur
ISBN 978 1 4094 6260 6

Hub Cities in the Knowledge Economy
Seaports, Airports, Brainports
Edited by Sven Conventz, Ben Derudder, Alain Thierstein and Frank Witlox
ISBN 978 1 4094 4591 3

Institutional Barriers to Sustainable Transport
Carey Curtis and Nicholas Low
ISBN 978 0 7546 7692 8

Daily Spatial Mobilities
Physical and Virtual
Aharon Kellerman
ISBN 978 1 4094 2362 1

Territorial Implications of High Speed Rail
A Spanish Perspective
Edited by José M. de Ureña
ISBN 978 1 4094 3052 0

The Geographies of Air Transport

Edited by

ANDREW R. GOETZ
University of Denver, USA

LUCY BUDD
Loughborough University, UK

LONDON AND NEW YORK

First published 2014 by Ashgate Publishing

Published 2016 by Routledge
2 Park Square, Milton Park, Abingdon, Oxfordshire OX14 4RN
711 Third Avenue, New York, NY 10017, USA

First issued in paperback 2016

Routledge is an imprint of the Taylor & Francis Group, an informa business

British Library Cataloguing in Publication Data
A catalogue record for this book is available from the British Library

The Library of Congress has cataloged the printed edition as follows:
The geographies of air transport / [edited by] Andrew R. Goetz and Lucy Budd.
      pages cm. -- (Transport and mobility) Includes bibliographical references and index.
   ISBN 978-1-4094-5331-4 (hardback) 1. Aeronautics, Commercial. 2. Transportation geography. 3. Economic geography. I. Goetz, Andrew R. II. Budd, Lucy. III. Series: Transport and mobility series.
  HE9774.G46 2014
  387.7--dc23

                                                                            2014010312

ISBN 13: 978-1-138-24557-0 (pbk)
ISBN 13: 978-1-4094-5331-4 (hbk)

Contents

List of Figures

The Geographies of Air Transport

List of Tables

Notes on Contributors

Peter Adey is Professor of Human Geography at the Department of Geography, Royal Holloway, University of London. Peter is Programme Director of an interdisciplinary MSc on Geopolitics and Security, and Chair of the Social and Cultural Geography Research Group of the RGS-IBG. He has published on the contours and cultures of mobility and aviation security, most notably in *Mobility* (2009), *Aerial Life* (2010) and the edited collections *From Above: War, Violence and Verticality* (2013) and the *Handbook of Mobilities* (2013). His new book *Air* is currently forthcoming for 2014.

Khaula A. Alkaabi is Assistant Professor and Chair of the Geography and Urban Planning Department at the United Arab Emirates University (UAEU). Her research interests include the geography of air transportation and regional economies, tourism and urban development. She has published two co-authored articles in *Journal of Air Transport Management* and *Journal of Transport Geography*, and a book chapter in *Aviation and Tourism: Implications for Leisure Travel*, published by Ashgate. She has presented several papers at the annual meeting of the Association of American Geographers (AAG), Air Transport Research Society (ATRS) and other local conferences.

John T. Bowen, Jr is Associate Professor in the Department of Geography at Central Washington University, USA. He earned his PhD in Geography at the University of Kentucky and has taught at universities in the United States and Singapore. For several years he also worked for Singapore Airlines. His research has emphasized topics related to air transportation, including the role of aviation in economic development, airline industry liberalization in Asia and the changing geography of commercial aircraft production. His book *The Economic Geography of Air Transportation: Space, Time, and the Freedom of the Sky* was published by Routledge in 2010.

Lucy Budd is Senior Lecturer in Air Transport in the School of Civil and Building Engineering at Loughborough University in the UK. Her PhD, obtained in 2007, explored the multiple and contested geographies of airspace and she has a long-standing interest in commercial aviation. Lucy's research has appeared in a variety of media and publishing formats, including in the journals of *Political Geography*, *Environment and Planning A*, *Mobilities*, the *Journal of Transport Geography* and *Transactions of the Institute of British Geographers*. She is currently researching global social perceptions of air travel and airport expansion.

Keith G. Debbage is Professor of Geography at UNC-Greensboro with research interests in air transportation, tourism and urban economic development. He is the author of numerous research publications in book chapters focused on air transportation and tourism, contracted reports and various academic journals including *Annals of Tourism Research*, *Journal of Air Transport Management*, *Journal of Transport Geography*, *Policy Studies Review*, *The Professional Geographer*, *Regional Studies*, *Tourism Management*, *Transportation*

Quarterly, and *Urban Geography*. He co-authored a book with Dimitri Ioannides titled *The Economic Geography of the Tourist Industry: A Supply-Side Analysis* with Routledge.

Ben Derudder is Professor of Human Geography at Ghent University's (Belgium) Department of Geography, and Associate Director of the Globalization and World Cities (GaWC) research network. His research focuses on the conceptualization and empirical analysis of transnational urban networks in general, and its transportation and production components in particular. His work has been published in leading academic journals and he has co-edited a number of books on this topic, including a recent edited volume entitled *International Handbook of Globalization and World Cities* (Edward Elgar, 2011, with P.J. Taylor, F. Witlox and M. Hoyler).

Frédéric Dobruszkes is a lecturer at the Free University of Brussels (ULB) and the head of the Brussels-based Interuniversity Centre for Mobility Studies. He is also the Vice President of the Brussels Regional Commission of Mobility. He has an MA in Geography (1995), an MA in Transport (1996) and a PhD in Geography (2007) from the Free University of Brussels. His main research interests relate to transport geography and policy. His current focus is mainly on the dynamics of the European air transport industry and on airline/high-speed rail competition.

Kurt Fuellhart is Professor of Geography in the Department of Geography and Earth Science at Shippensburg University in Pennsylvania, USA. His research focuses on regional economic analysis and aspects of global air transportation including multiple airport regions, links with the urban hierarchy, and Australasia.

Andrew R. Goetz is Professor in the Department of Geography and the Environment and a faculty member in the Intermodal Transportation Institute at the University of Denver, USA. He has co-authored two air transport books: *Denver International Airport: Lessons Learned* and *Airline Deregulation and Laissez-Faire Mythology*, as well as numerous publications on topics including the geographic effects of airline industry policy, airport planning, economic development, globalization and sustainability. He received the 2010 Edward L. Ullman Award from the Association of American Geographers for significant contributions to transportation geography.

Anne Graham is Reader in Air Transport and Tourism at the University of Westminster. Anne has been involved in the teaching, research and consultancy of air transport for over 25 years and has developed two key research interests. The first is in airport management, economics and regulation. Her other research area is the analysis of tourism and aviation demand and the relationship between the tourism and aviation industries. Her latest books *Managing Airports: An International Perspective* (fourth edition) and *Airport Marketing* were both published in 2013. Anne is also Editor-in-Chief of the *Journal of Air Transport Management*.

Paul Hooper is Chair of Environmental Management and Sustainability and Head of Enterprise Development in the Faculty of Science and Engineering at Manchester Metropolitan University. He leads efforts to increase enterprise activity across the faculty. His teaching and research interests are in the areas of environmental management, corporate environmental and social responsibility, carbon accounting and management, and aircraft noise communication. Much of his work over the last 15 years has been focused on the air transport industry as part of the Centre for Aviation, Transport and the Environment.

Stephen Ison is Professor of Transport Policy in the School of Civil and Building Engineering, Loughborough University. His primary research interest is in the area of transport economics and policy, focusing specifically on air transport issues. He has published over 200 refereed journal and conference papers in the area of transport and is the author/co-author/editor of six books. He is the editor, with Lucy Budd, of the book *Low Cost Carriers: Emergence, Expansion and Evolution*, published by Ashgate, April 2014.

Weiqiang Lin is a doctoral postgraduate at the Geography Department of Royal Holloway, University of London, with concurrent affiliation to the National University of Singapore. His research interests converge on issues of mobilities, in particular, air transport, airspaces and migration in Asian contexts. In 2010, he won the Wang Gungwu Medal and Prize for best thesis at the National University of Singapore. He has published in a diverse range of edited volumes and peer-reviewed journals, including *Cultural Geographies*, *Environment and Planning A*, *Geoforum*, *Mobilities* and *Political Geography*. His current work seeks to unravel the socio-cultural aspects of airspace-making in Southeast Asia, and engages in 'alternative' theorizations of mobilities.

Gustavo Lipovich is a specialist in air transport geography. He is a researcher in the Transport and Territory Programme and a lecturer in Transport Geography at the Universidad de Buenos Aires (Argentina). He holds a Master's in Urban Economics (UTDT-Argentina) and a Doctorate in Geography (UBA-Argentina). He is mainly interested in the relationship between air transport and economic development. Gustavo was one of the founders and former President of the Ibero-American Network of Air Transport Research (RIDITA). He has worked as a consultant, as an assessor in Aerolíneas Argentinas, as a member of Aeropuertos Argentina 2000 Board of Directors – representing the National State shares participation – and at present is the President of the National Airport Authority (ORSNA) of Argentina.

Kevin O'Connor is Professorial Fellow in Urban Planning at the University of Melbourne and at the School of Geography and Environmental Science at Monash University. His research explores the links between the economy and the growth and internal structure of cities. Recent activity has involved an analysis of logistics; the current focus is upon the role of airports in city development in the Asia-Pacific region. In 2011 he was invited to give the Fleming Memorial Lecture in Transportation Geography at the annual meeting of the American Association of Geographers. He is currently an associate editor of the *Journal of Transport Geography*, responsible for papers submitted from Asia-Pacific and Africa. He uses results of his research in the debate about the strategic development of Melbourne, involving extensive contact with print and electronic media, along with briefings to professional groups, government and private firms. This involvement has been recognized in major awards from the *Planning Institute of Australia* and the *Urban Development Institute of Australia*.

Christopher Paling is a senior researcher and project manager at Manchester Metropolitan University. He returned to academia in 2012 after 11 years working for the Manchester Airports Group as an environmental manager. He works within the University's Centre for

Aviation, Transport and the Environment (CATE), a research group within the Department of Environmental and Geographical Sciences. His research and teaching is focused on the environmental sustainability of air transport and the implications of a changing climate upon aviation.

Gordon Pirie has researched, taught and published about various elements of transportation in Africa, including the geographies and geopolitics of air transport there. His two books on British imperial civil air transport and travel (Manchester University Press) examine the makings and meanings of intercontinental air transport in the 1920s and 1930s. Gordon's current research is on the history of airports in South Africa. He is presently Deputy Director of the African Centre for Cities at the University of Cape Town.

Tim Ryley is Senior Lecturer in Transport Studies within the Transport Studies Group, School of Civil and Building Engineering at Loughborough University in the UK. A geographer by background, his research focuses on the environmental aspects of transportation and covers a range of air transportation topics including air travel demand and airport surface access. Dr Ryley has published a range of academic and industry transport publications including *Transport and Climate Change*, a book he co-edited and published in 2012.

Callum Thomas is Chair of Sustainable Aviation at Manchester Metropolitan University. He returned to academia in 1998 after 13 years in the aviation industry. He is internationally known within the industry and has been an advisor to the UK Government and the EU on aviation and the environment and sustainability issues. He was responsible for establishing Manchester Airport's Bird Control Unit and Environment Department. His expertise involves the sustainable development of aviation, environmental constraints upon airport growth and the impact of airport operations on local communities.

Sean Tierney writes and teaches about transportation, energy and cities. Interest in the airlines began with an examination of how Southwest Airlines influences intra-metropolitan airport competition. Other airline studies have ensued as have broader transportation-related questions. New areas of research are focusing on how cities are fusing economic prosperity and environmental resilience, with a specific emphasis on the arrangement of enduring things like mobility options, natural amenities, and cultural features. He is currently Adjunct Professor in Geography at the University of Denver.

Frank Witlox is Professor of Economic Geography at the Department of Geography, Ghent University. He is also Visiting Professor at ITMMA (Institute of Transport and Maritime Management, Antwerp), and Associate Director of GaWC (Globalization and World Cities, Loughborough University). Since 1 August 2013 he has been Honorary Professor in the School of Geography at the University of Nottingham. His research focuses on sustainable mobility issues, business travel, city logistics, globalization and world city-formation, polycentric urban development and locational analysis of corporations. He has published widely on these topics in leading academic journals. With Ben Derudder he co-edited *Global Cities – Vol. III: Infrastructures for Cities in Globalization* (Routledge, 2013).

Acknowledgements

Andy and Lucy would like to thank Richard Knowles for his encouragement in pursuing this book project, as well as Tony Budd, Stephen Ison, Markus Hesse, Katy Crossan and all of the individual contributors to the volume.

Acknowledgements

Andy and Lucy would like to thank Richard Knowles for his encouragement in pursuing the book project, as well as Tony Budd, Stephen Holt/Matheus Press, Katy Crossan and all of the individual contributors to the volume.

The Geographies of Air Transport: An Introduction

Lucy Budd and Andrew R. Goetz

In 1957, 30 years after its launch as a scheduled passenger and air mail carrier and in anticipation of the inauguration of their new fleet of jet-powered Boeing 707 and Douglas DC-8 aircraft into commercial passenger service, Pan American World Airways unveiled a new corporate identity. Designed by New York architect Edward Larrabee Barnes and his associate Charles Forberg, the airline's new logo featured a royal blue globe inscribed with white parabolic lines of latitude and quickly became a graphic ambassador for a new age of mass global aeromobility in which distance, that once great obstacle to human movement, had apparently been overcome (Zukowsky 1996). The simple motif invoked notions of speed, unhindered travel and global domination (at least in commercial aviation terms) and implied that Pan Am's passenger and cargo networks encircled the earth (see Eisenbrand 2004).

The new logo quickly permeated international public consciousness and helped Pan Am develop into one of the most highly-regarded and widely-recognized global travel brands of the 1960s and 1970s.[1] Yet, in addition to promoting new and unfettered global trade and travel opportunities, Leslie (2005: 70) contended that the airline's revised logo also 'symbolized the dissipation of the local into the abstract ether of global travel' and the 'elimination of recognizable land forms and places in favour of a mathematical representation of navigation and capital'. As such, Pan Am's logo neatly encapsulates the complex debates surrounding the extent to which continued processes of modernization and globalization – which have been facilitated and accelerated in no small part by the invention of the airplane – have necessitated the rethinking of traditional geographical concepts of space and place in an increasingly interdependent world of mass mobility and the degree of cultural homogenization that this has, or has not, effected (see Sassen 2000; Castree 2003; Ley 2004). Like other global networks of communication and mobility, including transcontinental railways, mobile telephones and the Internet, air travel binds ostensibly the 'global' and the 'local' together in complex, unpredictable and often unexpected ways as international time/space relations are selectively distorted and continually rearranged in response to changing market demand, the introduction of new technology, the nature of international political relations and the dynamic structure of global capitalism.

Since the Wright brothers' first successful heavier-than-air powered human flights in December 1903, successive developments in aerodynamics, propulsion, avionics, navigation and material sciences have enabled aircraft to fly progressively further, faster, longer and higher, emancipating humankind from the confines of an otherwise terrestrial

---

1   The Pan Am mystique of the period was captured well in the 2002 movie, *Catch Me if You Can*, about a con artist who masqueraded in several prestigious occupations, including as a Pan Am pilot.

existence. In response to the commercial opportunities and national security threats this new technology of the air posed, a plethora of international regulations were introduced between the 1910s and the mid-1940s in an attempt to manage this newfound aerial mobility. The introduction of these new political and regulatory interventions, combined with continued technological innovations in aircraft performance and airline business practices during the latter half of the twentieth century, enabled air transport to progressively reconfigure human understandings of presence, absence, and proximity. In so doing, aircraft have come to embody notions of socio-economic progress and modernity and have shaped the fashions, attitudes, styles and mobility patterns of the twentieth and early twenty-first centuries. However, as a direct result of facilitating the routine global mobility of nearly 3 billion passengers and over 50 million of tonnes of airfreight every year, commercial air transport has resulted in acrimonious political debate and generated a range of challenging socio-environmental externality effects, the potential severity of which are only now starting to be appreciated. Given its multifarious and highly dynamic social, economic, political, cultural and environmental dimensions, commercial air transport offers geographers and other social scientists a fascinating platform from which a complex array of physical, human and cultural phenomena can be explored.

From Geography to Geographies of Air Transport

This edited volume contributes to the existing and burgeoning literatures on global air transportation by providing pluralistic and detailed theoretical and empirical analyses of contemporary patterns and processes of commercial air transport and aeromobility. In so doing, it updates the seminal contributions of Eva Taylor (1945), Kenneth Sealy (1957, 1966) and Brian Graham (1995) to geographical studies of air transport. The volume is international in scale and commercial in scope, focusing solely on the patterns, processes and socio-economic, cultural and environmental implications (at a variety of spatial scales) of revenue-generating passenger and cargo air transport services rather than military or general aviation.[2] Furthermore, while we appreciate the fundamental importance of the physical environment, including geomorphology, geology, climatology and atmospheric science, to the safe and efficient provision of air services, the location of airports and the orientation of runways, this is not our primary concern.

Since the publication of Graham's *Geography and Air Transport* in 1995, new commercial aircraft, including the Boeing 747-8, 777, and 787 and the Airbus A380 'Superjumbo' have entered regular commercial service. New airports have been constructed and existing ones dramatically expanded to handle the near-three billion passengers who fly around the world every year. A plethora of new airlines, including full service operators such as Abu Dhabi-based Etihad, and low cost carriers including easyJet (UK), Air Asia (Malaysia), and Gol (Brazil) have taken advantage of an increasingly deregulated and liberalized international operating environment to establish new air services and introduce new passenger service innovations and airline products into the marketplace. New multinational airline alliances, including STAR, oneworld and SkyTeam, have been established, major carriers have merged, and once familiar names in global aviation, such as Ansett Australia, Continental

---

2 Refers to all non-commercial common carriage and non-military aviation including the operation of corporate jets, personal aircraft, flight training, flying clubs, agricultural spraying, aerial surveying and other private activity.

Airlines, Olympic Airways, Swissair, SABENA, TWA, and even Pan Am, have ceased trading owing to bankruptcy or mergers.

In addition to dramatic changes in the airline operating environment, the last 20 years have also seen the emergence of growing public awareness of commercial aviation's negative environmental externality effects; rising appreciation of the socio-cultural diversity and plurality of global air transport mobilities; and the introduction of increasingly stringent international border controls, security interventions and passenger screening protocols for reasons of defence and national security. As a result, the patterns, processes, socio-spatial implications and user experiences of twenty-first century commercial air transport are, we would argue, already very different from those of the late twentieth century.

Contributions to the Volume

By bringing together 21 leading scholars in geographic air transport research, this volume offers a unique insight into the key developments that have occurred in the field of air transport geographies over the last two decades and the implications that they have had for geography and geographers. Excluding the introduction and the conclusion, the volume contains 14 chapters that have been written by the leading global authorities on air transport geographies. The first part contains eight chapters that offer a systematic or thematic human geographic analysis of some of commercial aviation's principal attributes, including its historical, cultural and geopolitical dimensions. The second part of the volume, in contrast, contains six chapters that examine the regional geographies of air transport in North America, Europe, Asia-Pacific, Latin America, the Middle East and Africa.

In Chapter 1, Lucy Budd examines the historical geographies of air transport. Uniquely, she focuses not only on the history of the development of heavier-than-air powered flight but also on the historical development of geographical approaches to the study of air transport. Alighting on key issues surrounding the introduction of new aircraft types, the use of aircraft in peacetime and war, the development of air transport regulation, and the effects of what Adey (2010) and others have termed a growing global culture of 'airmindedness', the chapter reveals how evolving popular and academic discourses of commercial flight have shaped geographical thought, theory and practice from the early years of the twentieth century to the present.

Issues of geopolitics and the evolution of global regimes of air transport regulation are introduced and then critically analysed in Chapter 2. Here, Keith G. Debbage provides a detailed and highly engaging account of the complex global geopolitics of air transport provision and regulation. Despite the inherently 'global' nature of air transport operations and policy initiatives towards air transport deregulation and liberalization, the chapter details the extent to which the current international regulatory regime fundamentally shapes the geography of air transportation provision. Crucially, he identifies and articulates the inherent tensions that currently exist between more liberal 'Open Skies' approaches to air service operations and the more traditional protectionist stances.

In Chapter 3, John T. Bowen, Jr provides an authoritative account of the global economic geography of air transport. In it, he demonstrates how passenger and cargo air transport services both drive and are driven by global economic development and how this has resulted in marked spatial inequalities in air service provision and access to flights. The development of Low Cost Carriers (LCCs), the reasons for and implications of the formation and consolidation of three main global airline alliances – Star, oneworld and

SkyTeam – and the role of new aircraft technology in reshaping the global contours of the industry are also discussed in detail with reference to a wealth of statistics and valuable commercial insights.

The discussion of the economic geographies of air transportation is followed in Chapter 4 by an innovative examination of the complex social and cultural geographies of air transport. Given that the study of air transport addresses the large-scale and often international movement of people, goods, capital and knowledge around the world it is only right that people are put at the heart of geographic inquiry into air travel. Drawing on their extensive expertise, Peter Adey and Weiqiang Lin document the development of a new corpus of research on air travel mobilities that embraces the embodied social and cultural dimensions of mass aeromobility. They critically examine the cultural construction of airspace as the interface between land and sky and alight on key issues surrounding the corporeal experiences of 'entubulation' in commercial aircraft cabins and offer exciting opportunities for developing future research avenues in creative aeromobilities.

In recognition that air transport not only offers new ways of becoming and being mobile in the modern world but also imposes a range of negative externality effects, Tim Ryley in Chapter 5 examines the range of commercial aviation's environmental externalities at local and global scales. In addition to detailing the impact of air transport operations on local airport communities in terms of acoustic burden, the deterioration in local air quality resulting from aircraft and surface access transport and perturbations to the global climate caused by high-altitude engine emissions, he details some of the management interventions that can be used both at airports and by aircraft en-route to minimise or mitigate some of aviation's environmental impact.

Of course, air transport could not function without the provision of supporting infrastructure that facilitates a change of mode and movement type between the ground and the air. As the physical interface between land and sky, the importance of airports to the safe and efficient provision and operation of air transport services worldwide cannot be overstated. In Chapter 6, Anne Graham and Stephen Ison provide a compelling and densely resourced account of the spatial provision of global airports and the changing global patterns of airport traffic worldwide. They examine the reasons for and implications of the changing management styles and regimes of world airports (many of which are now private and often foreign-owned enterprises that derive most of their revenue from non-aeronautical sources) as well as the links between global airport expansion, economic development and environmental impacts.

In Chapter 7, Ben Derudder and Frank Witlox explore the spatiality of global air transport service provision and the key (and changing) role and position of cities in air transport networks. Drawing on the findings of a detailed analysis of SABRE airline computer reservations data, they demonstrate the continued primacy of world cities in the air transport network and detail the effects of changing global regulatory, policy and economic environments to the stagnation and potential decline of once-important mega-hubs and the rapid rise of mega-airports in the industrializing economies of the Middle East.

Given the rapid development of air transport infrastructure and growing passenger demand in rapidly industrializing countries and the net increase in flights, passenger numbers and environmental impacts this will entail, Chris Paling, Paul Hooper and Callum Thomas examine, in Chapter 8, the challenges and prospects for improving commercial aviation's environmental sustainability. In particular, they show how promoting aviation's sustainable development within the existing global regulatory regime is often fraught with difficulty, not least because emissions from international aviation were excluded from the Kyoto Protocol on climate change.

Part II of the volume presents six chapters that offer detailed analyses of the geography of air transport in the six key world regions. Given the importance of the United States to the history of powered flight and commercial aviation, Chapter 9 by Sean Tierney provides an in-depth examination of the North American airline industry. The chapter offers critical insights into the form and function of the pre- and the post-deregulation era air transport market as well as commenting on the creation of hub and spoke networks, the emergence of LCCs and the response and restructuring of the industry after the 9/11 terrorist attacks.

Chapter 10, by Frédéric Dobruszkes, moves across the North Atlantic to give detailed consideration to the changing geographies of air transport provision in Europe. In it, he explores the growing provision of air services on the continent, the impact of liberalization and LCCs on patterns of air service connectivity, and discusses the importance of public service obligation routes in supporting flights to remote communities that would otherwise not be commercially viable. Crucially, he demonstrates that the dramatic changes that have occurred since European liberalization have not yet ended and he highlights the potential implications of the creation of a so-called European Common Aviation Area which would incorporate neighbouring countries and expand the geographic extent of the European Union's air transport market.

The third regional analysis, by Kevin O'Connor and Kurt Fuellhart is presented in Chapter 11. O'Connor and Fuellhart exploit their extensive knowledge of air services in Asia-Pacific to explain how the varied physical geography and topography of the region (which stretches east from Pakistan to New Zealand and south from Japan to Australia), combined with varied patterns of economic development and air service deregulation have shaped the historical development and contemporary networks of flights. Using OAG (Official Airline Guide) data they examine the hierarchy of airports and the spatial concentration of air services within the region and debate the extent to which growing consumer demand for flights within certain countries will change patterns of air services within the region.

Another world region which is experiencing net growth in air transport demand is Latin America. In Chapter 12, Gustavo Lipovich explores the geographies of commercial aviation in the continent. In it, he reviews the historical development of air transport in the region, highlights the principal airport hubs and leading origin/destination pairs and explores the impacts that recent policies of air transport liberalization and airline and airport privatization have had on the provision and delivery of air services. He notes, in particular the recent evolution of the Latin American airline market and the strategies that the principal airlines have adopted in response to the changing regulatory and economic environment.

Chapter 13, by Khaula Alkaabi provides a ground-breaking analysis of the geographies of air transport in the Middle East, a region that is experiencing dramatic growth in consumer demand for air travel but which has all-too-often been overlooked in existing studies of air transport geography. Her chapter details the historical evolution of air transport in the region before turning its attention to the corporate strategies and network structures of the region's major airlines. She also comments on the recent rapid rise of airports in the region, explains how the Middle East is strategically positioning itself as the global transfer point between east and west, and comments on the implications of the on-going development of major new mega-airport hubs in Dubai, Doha and Abu Dhabi.

The final contribution in this section is Chapter 14 by Gordon Pirie which brings the geographies of air transport in Africa into sharp relief. Drawing on his unparalleled research and knowledge of aviation within the continent, he shows how colonial Africa, despite occupying a significant place in the overseas ambitions of European airlines in the late 1920s and 1930s, nevertheless remained a relative 'backwater' in terms of global aviation growth post-1945 and remains the world's smallest air transport market. However, though currently small in terms of relative global revenue passenger kilometres, the potential for growth in the region is considerable. The chapter describes the development of African airlines, the challenges of operating services within the continent as well as the main intercontinental and continental routes.

The final, concluding chapter, by Andrew R. Goetz and Lucy Budd, draws together the key themes that have emerged from the volume and speculates on future directions for geographic research into air transport. We hope that *The Geographies of Air Transport* will not only offer a valuable insight into contemporary patterns and processes of commercial flight and current geographical approaches to the study of commercial aviation worldwide but also that it will help to firmly cement the study of air transport as an important field of geographic inquiry and inspire further theorization and empirical investigation into a highly significant yet controversial component of contemporary society.

References

Adey, P. (2010) *Aerial Life: Spaces, Mobilities, Affects.* Chichester: Wiley-Backwell.

Castree, N. (2003) *Place: Connections and Boundaries in an Interdependent World,* in Holloway, S.L., Rice, S.P. and Valentine, G. (eds) *Key Concepts in Geography.* London: Sage, pp. 165–185.

Eisenbrand, J. (2004) *Dining Aloft,* in von Vegesack, A. and Eisenbrand, J. (eds) *Airworld: Design and Architecture for Air Travel.* Weil am Rhein: Vitra Design Stiftung gGmbH, pp. 212–229.

Graham, B.J. (1995) *Geography and Air Transport.* Chichester: Wiley.

Leslie, T. (2005) The Pan Am Terminal at Idlewild/Kennedy Airport and the Transition from Jet Age to Space Age. *Design Issues* 21(1): 63–80.

Ley, D. (2004) Transnational Spaces and Everyday Life. *Transactions of the Institute of British Geographers* NS29(2): 151–164.

Sassen, S. (2000) Specialities and Temporalities of the Global: Elements of a Theorisation. *Public Culture* 12(1): 215–232.

Sealy, K.R. (1957) *The Geography of Air Transport.* Londo: Hutchinson University Press.

Sealy, K.R. (1966) *The Geography of Air Transport.* 2nd Edition. London: Hutchinson University Press.

Taylor, E.G.R. (1945) *Geography of an Air Age.* London: Royal Institute of Economic Affairs.

Zukowsky, J. (ed.) (1996) *Building for Air Travel Architecture and Design for Commercial Aviation.* Munich: Prestel.

PART I
Thematic Approaches

Chapter 1
The Historical Geographies of Air Transport

Lucy Budd

Aviation is a question which affects the development, happiness, and peace of the entire world. When, with the growing speed of aerial transport, we shall be able to dine in New York one evening and in London the next; when no part of the earth's surface, however remote, is more than a week's journey from London by air, then I think we may say that the coming of this aerial age will do more for the world than any other invention or discovery man has ever made.

Mr Claude Grahame-White, British aviator and aeronautical engineer, in a
lecture to the Royal Aeronautical Society, London, 19 February 1919

The arrival of the aerial age at the beginning of the twentieth century marked a new era in modern world history. The invention of practical heavier-than-air powered flight provided a new way of moving around the earth and introduced new kinaesthetic experiences of being mobile. In the 110 years since the Wright brothers' first successful heavier-than-air powered flights in December 1903, continued developments in aerodynamics, propulsion, avionics, navigation, and material sciences have enabled the construction of progressively larger, safer and more reliable civil aircraft which can fly further, faster, longer, higher, more efficiently and at lower financial cost than ever before.

These technological innovations in aircraft performance, combined with regulatory reforms and the emergence of new airline business models, lowered the monetary cost of airfares and facilitated a dramatic expansion in passenger numbers worldwide, particularly after 1945. In the year of the world's first scheduled international passenger service in 1919, only a few dozen passengers took to the air. By 2012, the figure was 2.8 billion (ATAG 2012). As a consequence, major international airports have gone from handling 50 or fewer passengers a day in the mid-1920s (Dierikx and Bouwens 1997) to tens and even up to hundreds of thousands a day by 2012. Providing the capacity and landside and airside infrastructure to support this level of aerial mobility has necessitated the dramatic (and often controversial) expansion of airports and aviation support facilities around the world.

As significantly, perhaps, the growing availability of – and increased access to – safe and affordable commercial air transport has been responsible for reconfiguring global cultural understandings of presence, absence and proximity. For those with the financial and personal means to access it, air travel has promoted the rapid normalization of a new form of transnational mobility and the creation of an increasingly 'air minded' society (on which see Adey 2010). Yet, as numerous scholars have been quick to highlight, the spatial and socio-demographic distribution of commercial air services and airline passengers is highly uneven, and routine access to air travel remains the exception rather than the norm for the majority of the world's population. Certainly, and as later chapters in this volume will show, air travel's dynamic distortion of international time/space relations brings particular groups of people and places closer together in both time and space, but this process is highly selective and marginalizes those who are not integrated into the global space of air traffic flows.

In the early years of commercial flight in the 1920s, air travel was expensive and unreliable. Nevertheless, it was portrayed as being daring, fashionable and exciting and quickly became the mobility mode of choice for society's most affluent and privileged elite. Almost from its inception, powered flight embodied notions of geopolitical power and modernity and over the course of the twentieth and early twenty-first centuries, civil aviation has influenced the fashions, attitudes, styles, mobility patterns, trade flows, geopolitical relations, business practices and migration movements of virtually every nation on earth. The practices and infrastructures of commercial air travel quickly entered the lexicon of everyday social interaction and airports have become familiar features of our cultural landscape. However, as a consequence of facilitating international connectivity and global socio-economic interaction, aircraft and airports have become a target of terrorist activity and the focus of growing environmental concern about noise, local air quality, and climate change.

Unsurprisingly, the rapid emergence, expansion, evolution and socio-economic and environmental implications of air transport have rendered it a subject of considerable scholarly attention and debate. Worldwide, a large corpus of academic papers, narrative histories, technical compendia, aeronautical biographies and illustrated anthologies detail the planes, the pilots, the people, the processes, the places and the flights that are considered central to conventional historiographies of both civilian and military air transport. Crouch (2003), Edgerton (2013) and Hamilton-Paterson (2010) are among those who have provided valuable insights into the complex interplay between developments in military and commercial aviation while Adey (2010), Cwerner (2009), Davies (2011), Dierikx (2008), Graham (1995), Pascoe (2001, 2003) and Wohl (1994, 2005) have critically examined the impact of changing inter/national economic imperatives, geopolitical relations, cultural discourses, technological priorities and regulatory regimes to the development of twentieth- and early twenty-first-century commercial air transport. Indeed, the scale and scope of the existing trans-disciplinary body of academic literature on air transport is such that arguably few aspects of air transport's development remain unexplored.

Rather than risk replicating existing accounts, this chapter adopts a different approach which seeks to examine the implications that evolving popular and academic discourses of human flight have had for geographic thought, theory, and practice. In order to reveal the complex interactions between the geographic history of air transport and the history of aviation geography as a distinct sub-discipline of academic inquiry, this chapter is divided into two principal sections. The first identifies key moments in global aeronautical history while the second discusses the implications that the developing global commercial air transport system has had for the discipline and practice of geography.

The Geographic Histories of Air Transport

As numerous aviation scholars and historians have rightly observed it is impossible to determine, with any real degree of accuracy, when the story of aviation begins. While most concur that heavier-than-air powered flight dates back only as far as 1903, historical evidence suggests that humans have been actively trying to 'conquer' the air since before the middle of the third century BC. Although gravity proved to be a formidable obstacle for centuries, historical evidence shows that the idea of flight has captured human imagination since ancient times, with many cultures and civilizations containing mythical or religious accounts of winged creatures carrying people up into the heavens.

In Greek mythology, Icarus and his father Daedalus attempted to escape exile in Crete by attaching feathers to their arms with beeswax in order to fly. While Daedalus eventually reached safety, Icarus famously ignored his father's warnings and flew too close to the sun, melting the wax that held the feathers in place and causing him to plunge to his death. Despite this and other cautionary tales, imitating birds remained popular with early would-be aviators, and numerous deaths and injuries were attributed to over-enthusiastic 'birdmen' attaching wings or sails to their arms and jumping from tall platforms or hillsides.

In the thirteenth century AD, the English Franciscan philosopher, Roger Bacon, postulated that flying was theoretically possible if air could be made to support a craft in the same way as a boat floats on water. However it was not until the late eighteenth century that lighter-than-air (or aerostatic) flight by means of hot air balloons became a viable technology (see Holmes 2013). While tethered and free-flying balloons afforded a new aerial perspective of the planet, they lacked propulsion and an effective means of directional control. Although dirigibles (airships) partly addressed these limitations, they were slow and cumbersome and a series of fatal accidents irrevocably damaged public confidence in the new technology. Continued experiments by proponents of heavier-than-air machines, including Sir George Cayley in England and Otto Lillenthal in Germany, demonstrated the viability of gliders which, in turn, soon enabled the development of powered heavier-than-air craft.

According to most conventional historiographies of air transport, the modern aerial age commenced at 10.35 am on 17 December 1903 on the windswept sand dunes at Kill Devil Hills, near Kitty Hawk, North Carolina, when Orville Wright successfully took off and flew for 12 seconds before landing. Although only covering a distance of 120 ft, the flight marked 'the first in the history of the world in which a machine carrying a man had raised by its own power into the air in full flight, had sailed forward without reduction in speed, and had finally landed at a point as high as that from which it started' (Wright 1913: 12). Despite scepticism in certain media and scientific establishments, news of the flight quickly reached Europe and aspiring aviators began building, and crashing, numerous aircraft in an attempt to emulate Orville's success. On 25 July 1909, the French aviator, Louis Blériot, became the first person to successfully fly across the English Channel in a heavier-than-air aircraft. However, amid public excitement at his achievement, the flight posed challenging questions about the right of an aircraft from one state to access the aerial space above another (see Debbage, Chapter 2, this volume).

As long as a pilot took off, flew within the confines of a state's navigable airspace and landed within its national borders there was no problem but international flights threatened the territorial integrity of individual nation states. This situation resulted in one of the longest and most acrimonious debates in aeronautical politics as each country sought to cede as little and seize control of as much airspace as possible while maintaining control over their borders for reasons of defence and national security (see Petzinger 1995). One of the earliest attempts at airspace regulation occurred in 1900 when the French government proposed that a code governing international aerial navigation should be formulated after German balloons made a series of unauthorized flights over French territory (Millichap 2000). By 1901, debates were focusing on the extent to which a state's sovereignty extended vertically into the air (Dierikx and Bouwens 1997). However, while national claims to land and adjoining seas had been common since Roman times, national claims to airspace were entirely new concepts and international agreement was not immediately forthcoming (Butler 2001).

Countries with rapidly expanding aviation interests, including Great Britain and the United States, initially advocated complete freedom of the skies and opposed any bureaucratic interventions (other than those which would secure their aerial hegemony) while other nations advocated a strict system of national control. The mutually incompatible geopolitical positions held by the British and the French governments were such that attempts in Paris in 1910 to bring international air services under unified control were largely unsuccessful (Veale 1945).

In 1911, the British government passed the British Aerial Navigation Act which declared that all of Great Britain's airspace (including that of her overseas colonies and dominions) was sovereign territory and therefore inviolable (Butler 2001). This protectionist stance frustrated commentators who considered it 'absurd to conceive of air travel and air transport in terms of national boundaries and local systems of control' and warned that such bureaucratic interventions would only impede aviation's long-term development (Burney 1929: 142).

Although individual states increasingly sought to protect themselves from the threat of aerial attack through the provision of hastily formulated aerial legislation, aviation was being publically promoted as an instrument of global peace and unity. In the 1910s and 1920s regular international air meets, races, competitions and flying demonstrations were held at venues across Europe and North America to engender public interest in flight and stimulate aeronautical innovation (see Wohl 1994 and Demetz 2002). The early pilots and entrepreneurs quickly recognized the commercial potential of air travel and, in 1914, the world's first passenger air company, the Tampa Bay Line, began operating commercial services in Florida. Although the flights only lasted a few months, they demonstrated that aircraft could be used to transport paying passengers. Nevertheless, despite being promoted as instruments of peace and commerce, aircraft were also being developed as weapons of war and tools of state aggression and oppression.

Aircraft were first employed in a military campaign by Italian forces in what is now Libya in 1911 and, since then, have evolved to fulfil a variety of specialized military roles including surveillance, reconnaissance, troop conveyance, aerial interception, medical evacuation and the delivery of explosive ordnance. The use of aircraft during World War I (see Kennett 1999) demonstrated the importance of states maintaining absolute control over their airspace. This fundamental shift in the spatial geographies of military engagement highlighted the obsolescence of old geopolitical paradigms that were literally grounded in the conventions of two-dimensional terrestrial geography (Graham 2004). Indeed, the use of sophisticated aerial weaponry, military satellites, unmanned surveillance drones and fighter aircraft in contemporary global conflicts demonstrates the continued strategic and tactical importance of achieving and maintaining aerial supremacy (see Williams 2010, 2011a and 2011b for a detailed discussion of the geographies of contemporary military airspace and aerial operations).

By the end of 1918, the need to reconstruct Europe's shattered economies and enshrine the growing miscellany of national air transport regulations into a series of internationally-binding agreements became increasingly acute as the world's leading aeronautical nations, including Britain, France and the United States, all vied for aerial supremacy (Butler 2001). With serviceable aircraft suddenly available after the Armistice, demobbed pilots began organizing themselves into air companies to operate these aircraft on a commercial basis (see Sampson 1984).

In August 1919, the world's first scheduled international passenger flight left London's Hounslow Heath aerodrome for Le Bourget airfield outside Paris. The flight demanded not only technical expertise but also political agreement and there was concern that international reluctance on behalf of some states to allow foreign aircraft to enter their territory would unduly restrict civil aviation's development. An attempt at resolving this impasse, while creating the economic conditions that would foster future growth, was attempted in Versailles in 1919.

The right of individual countries to claim sovereignty over their aerial territory was formally enshrined in Chapter 1 of the Paris Convention of 13 October 1919 and signed by the delegates of 26 Allied and Associated Powers (Veale 1945). Signatories agreed that 'every power has complete and exclusive sovereignty over the air space above its territory', including that of its overseas colonies (cited in Lissitzyn 1942: 366). However, this right was granted on the understanding that aircraft from all contracting states would enjoy 'freedom of innocent passage' through the airspace of other contracting states (cited in Butler 2001: 9). This new regulatory regime enhanced prospects for more closely-connected European empires and profoundly shaped the global geographies of post-1919 air transport.

In a bid to capitalize on aviation's growing public awareness and stress its utility to the development, maintenance and policing of Empire, Great Britain and other Imperial nations sought to demonstrate their aeronautical capabilities and expand their sphere of territorial and cultural influence through the medium of flight (see Pirie 2009 and 2012). Countries without extensive overseas empires also actively sought to develop international air services in an effort to compete on the global stage and demonstrate their technological prowess and economic aspirations (Davies 1964).

The outbreak of World War II in 1939 temporarily disrupted the development of commercial aviation. In Great Britain, all civil flying was banned and attention focused on developing new aeronautical technologies that would confer military advantage (Edgerton 2013). New engines, aircraft control systems, radar surveillance and communications equipment were developed and, soon after the war ended, were installed on commercial aircraft. However, despite the rapid technological advances that had occurred during the early 1940s, the world's leading aviation superpowers held radically different views about how post-war commercial air transport should develop. An important step in securing the necessary political consensus occurred in Chicago in 1944 at a conference that was attended by the representatives of 52 states, excluding Germany (ICAO 1944).

Although the majority of delegates agreed that every contracting state had complete sovereignty over its airspace, some countries were unwilling to grant extensive access rights to foreign aircraft. US proposals for 'open skies' across the Atlantic and unrestricted competition were thus rejected by Great Britain and other European nations who sought to protect their fledgling domestic aviation markets from US competition using a strict system of bilateral regulation (Dobson 1985). Despite the incompatibility of these two strategies (see Dobson 1998, 2012), the Chicago Conference did produce two important documents: the 1944 International Air Transport Agreement and the International Air Service Transit Agreement. These agreements established a series of 'freedoms' of the air that would enable states to reciprocally negotiate traffic rights by exchanging bi- and multilateral air service agreements and led to the formation of the International Civil Aviation Organization (ICAO), a United Nations body that was responsible for regulating technical competence and civil aviation safety standards around the world. With this new international regulatory framework in place, post-war commercial airlines were able to expand their overseas operations.

The introduction of new faster and longer-range piston-engined civilian aircraft in the mid-1940s established new standards of passenger comfort and service and enabled airlines to expand the scope of their passenger operations within the confines of their existing national regulatory regimes. US carrier Trans World Airlines commenced regular transatlantic flights between New York and Paris in February 1946 while Pan American World Airways inaugurated the world's first round-the-world service in June 1947 (Sampson 1984). In May 1952, the world's first jet-powered passenger aircraft, the British-built de Havilland Comet 1, entered commercial service with BOAC (British Overseas Airways Corporation) on the airline's London to Johannesburg route and immediately cut the journey time between the two cities from days to hours. Despite a series of fatal accidents that were caused by metal fatigue, the Comet demonstrated the utility of jet propulsion for commercial aircraft.

Although the first generation of civilian jet aircraft only initially comprised a very small proportion of the world's total commercial aircraft fleet, the cultural allure and superior speed and operational performance of the new machines meant that airlines were keen to add them to their fleets. By the late 1950s, new higher-capacity and more fuel efficient aircraft, including the Boeing 707 and Douglas DC-8, were becoming available. These aircraft, which could transport over 100 passengers in safety and relative comfort across the Atlantic Ocean in under eight hours, stimulated growing consumer demand for flight. Airlines were quick to promote the advantages of jet flight in their marketing strategies and the resulting advertising copy (see Figure 1.1) created and reinforced the apparent desirability of a 'jetset' lifestyle. The development of even higher-capacity and more fuel efficient wide-bodied aircraft, including Boeing's 747-100 'Jumbo Jet' in the 1970s which were powered by new high-bypass turbofan engines, lowered the monetary cost of airfares still further and brought air travel within the financial reach of more people.

The inauguration of supersonic Concorde flights by British Airways and Air France in 1976 marked the most extreme manifestation of air travel's ability to compress time and space. Travelling at twice the speed of sound and at an altitude from which her passengers could view the curvature of the Earth, Concorde symbolized the accomplishments and the aspirations of an increasingly affluent and aeromobile world. Yet while Concorde shrunk the temporal duration of journeys between London, Paris and New York to new extremes for a privileged and wealthy few (the fastest transatlantic crossing from New York to London by a British Airways Concorde took 2 hours 52 minutes and 59 seconds in February 1996[1]), the oil crises of the 1970s and growing environmental concerns about the impact of sonic booms and stratospheric engine emissions meant that only 14 airframes entered commercial service and the majority of passengers flew in sub-sonic machines.

In addition to transforming passenger experiences of flight, the increased size, speed, range and weight of the new post-war commercial jet aircraft necessitated the radical redevelopment and expansion of airports. Runways were lengthened and strengthened, terminal buildings expanded, approach roads widened and new handling facilities constructed to cope with vastly increased volumes of passengers and bags (Pearman 2004). However, growing global demand for, and an increasing reliance on, air travel made aircraft and airports an attractive target for terrorists. Rising incidents of aviation terrorism during the 1960s and 1970s resulted in the progressive tightening of security regimes, which obliged passengers to spend increasing amounts of time waiting in the terminal (Sweet 2009). In order to capitalize on the ancillary revenue streams these captive, bored and/or anxious travellers presented, airports began to diversify their service offering and provide a growing range of retail concessions and cultural diversions in passenger terminals (see Gordon 2004).

The deregulation of the US domestic aviation market in 1978 had profound implications for airlines, airports and passengers. The removal of tariff-setting legislation and greater

---

1   British Airways (2013).

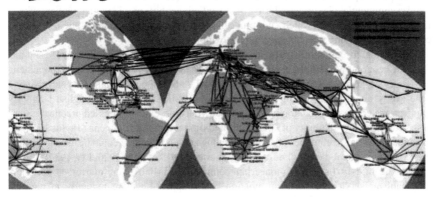

Figure 1.1   A British Overseas Airways Corporation (BOAC) advertisement from 1961 emphasises the spatial extent of routes served by the airline

Note: At the time, the airline was operating jet and propeller-powered aircraft to over 100 destinations on six continents.

Source: Image reproduced by kind permission of British Airways' Speedbird Centre.

freedom of market entry and exit caused incumbent carriers to restructure their operations around key hubs and allowed new entrant airlines to compete on price with the established operators (Petzinger 1995). The new competitive environment depressed airfares and stimulated increased passenger demand for flight. Similar policies have subsequently been adopted in other world regions from the 1990s onwards in an attempt to replicate US deregulation's economic success (see Budd and Ison 2014). In the European Union, air passenger transport services were progressively liberalized through three packages of measures which were ratified in 1987, 1990 and 1993 (with full liberalization occurring from 1 April 1997). The resulting combination of increased liberalization, globalization and competition has stimulated unprecedented consumer demand for flight, changed patterns of global connectivity, altered consumer expectations and experiences of flight and profoundly influenced geographic thought, theory and practice. It is to the history of air transport geography as a distinct sub-discipline of geographic practice that the chapter now turns.

The Historical Geographies of Commercial Air Transport

Air transport, like other forms of surface and maritime mobility, exists to facilitate the efficient movement of people and goods between geographic locations and involves the complex interaction of physical and human environments. As Willis Lee of the US

Geological Survey remarked in one of the earliest publications on the geography of flight, 'The airplane opens a new world to the geographer' (1920: 310) and the development of regular commercial air services during the twentieth century provided geographers with a fascinating platform from which a multitude of physical, social, geopolitical, environmental, economic and cultural phenomena could be explored.

Yet despite the inherently 'geographic nature' of air transport (Vowles 2006: 18) and the fact that geography had 'long addressed the nature and organisation of human movement across distant spaces' (Zook and Brunn 2006: 472), geographers initially had surprisingly little to say about the emerging discipline of aeronautics. The earliest English language publications concerning geography and civil air transport either addressed practical issues associated with the suitability of landing grounds and weather phenomena (Taylor 1919) or examined how new techniques of aerial surveying and photography could be used to further the geographic method (Woodhouse 1917; MacLeod 1919; Moffit 1920; Lee 1922).

By the mid-1920s, when pioneering commercial airlines were starting to develop long-haul air services, articles on aviation began appearing more regularly in popular and professional geography journals. Some documented the success of pioneering long-distance flights (Walmsey 1920; Byrd 1925) while others described the development of air services in different world regions (Hildebrand 1924; Wilcox 1930) or debated the strategic geopolitical importance of aviation to the maintenance and administration of Empire (Sykes 1920; Dowson 1921). Professional and enthusiastic amateur geographers alike also wrote about the practical utility of flight and explained how aircraft enabled explorers and adventurers to reach areas that were inaccessible by land and view both foreign and familiar places from a new and elevated vantage point. A series of pioneering long-distance flights resulted in the publication of a corpus of work that detailed how individual places looked from the air (Grosvenor 1924; Dargue 1927; and Van Zandt 1925) and described the discovery of peoples and places that were previously unknown to Anglo-American geography (Street 1926; Byrd 1930; Goddard 1930; Light 1935).

Yet in addition to participating in and describing a new era of aviation-enabled geographic exploration and encounter, geographers were also well placed to assess the strategic geopolitical and economic importance of proposed new air routes (Mitchell 1921; Steffansson 1922). However, the limited scale and scope of the early air services meant that a distinctive geographic discourse of *commercial* flight arguably did not emerge until after World War II when developments in aircraft technology and changes in international regulation shifted attention towards studies of transnational aviation and the formation of early transcontinental airline networks (Plischke 1943; Hinks et al. 1944; Spoehr 1946; Pearcy 1947; Pearcy and Alexander 1951, 1953). In particular, geographers were keen to emphasize the time-saving (or distance-shrinking) effects of these flights, a phenomenon anticipated by Darley in 1939 when he suggested that future transoceanic air services would ultimately render the Atlantic Ocean only a day wide.

The rapid post-war development of civil air transport necessitated the creation of a new word to describe the emerging sub-discipline of air transport geography, and a range of awkward amalgamations, including 'atmography', 'pneumography', 'aerography' and 'airography', were proposed (Possony and Rosenzweig 1955). Despite the lack of terminological consensus, the 1940s represented an important decade in the development of aviation geography. Professional geographers, including Lawrence (1942), Renner (1942), Van Zandt (1944), Taylor (1945), Balchin (1947) and Huntingdon (1947) all published influential works that highlighted the geographical nature of flight and examined the complex interactions between air transport and physical and human geography at a variety of sites and scales.

The quantitative revolution of the late 1950s and early 1960s stimulated the publication of a new corpus of work that examined the network attributes of global airline operations, airport connectivity and air routes. In the United States, Taaffe (1956, 1959, 1962) pioneered research into the description and visualization of the spatialities and connectivity of US passenger airlines while Kish (1958) demonstrated the primacy of Moscow in the USSR air network by means of an isochrone map based on flight times to and from the Soviet capital. In Great Britain, Stamp (1950) discussed the effect of airfields on the landscape while Sealy (1957) explored the geographies of airport location, global aviation regulation, and the regional characteristics of air transport operation in his seminal work, *The Geography of Air Transport*.

The 1960s witness a diversification of geographic research into air transport. Warntz (1961) examined the effects of atmospheric pressure systems on the routing of transatlantic flights while Donne (1964) explored the implications of the introduction of jet aircraft on patterns and processes of air travel. Towards the end of the decade, issues of airport capacity and runway provision were increasingly dominating political agendas and geographers responded by examining the multifarious dimensions of airport planning at a variety of scales (see Sealy 1966, 1967, 1976).

By the mid-1970s, the introduction of Concorde and wide-bodied passenger jet aircraft had raised the issue of aircraft noise around airports (Adams 1971) and the political vacillations and controversy surrounding the choice of site for London's third civilian airport ensured that issues of airport location, development and externality effects were firmly placed on the geographic research agenda (Adams 1970; Sealy 1970; Hoare 1974; Pepper, 1980). Geographers also became alert to the possible network diseconomies that may result from there being insufficient airport or airspace capacity available to handle future demand (Hay 1973). Significantly, and in addition to quantitative studies of airport capacity and air service provision, a few geographers also began exploring the human experiences of flight. Borgstrom (1974), in particular, examined the behavioural geographies and affective experiences of commercial flight, a theme more recently developed by Budd and Adey (2009), Adey (2010), Budd (2011a) and Millward (2008).

The deregulation of the US aviation market in 1978 had sudden and profound implications for airlines and consumers, and geographers were well placed to discuss the changes in air service provision that this regulatory reform had enacted (see Smith 1981; Farrington 1985; and Tierney, Chapter 9, this volume). The 1990s saw a substantial increase in geographic research on commercial aviation, a phenomenon Vowles (2006) attributed to the combined effects of the Internet and easier access to empirical data, the founding of dedicated transport geography journals and an increased awareness of the implications of airline deregulation. Some of this research focused on the business strategies of individual airlines (Debbage 1994; Graham 1995; Raguaraman 1997) and changing patterns of air service connectivity (Smith and Timberlake 1995) while others explored aspects of airport development, economics and location (O'Connor 1995; O'Kelly 1998; Graham and Guyer 2001; Caruana and Simmons 2001).

The increasing availability of airline route information on the Internet, combined with developments in cartographic representation and statistical computation, enabled geographers to describe and visualize the evolving twenty-first-century airline network in increasingly innovative ways at a variety of spatial scales (see Bowen 2002; Burghouwt and Hakfoort 2002; Derudder and Witlox 2005; O'Connor 2003; Zook and Brunn 2006).

Through mapping the network attributes of global airlines and airport hierarchies, geographers demonstrated how policies of deregulation and liberalization have fundamentally changed the spatial configuration of airline networks (see Burghouwt et al. 2003; Bowen and Leinbach 1995; Goetz 2002; Goetz and Graham 2004; Goetz and Sutton 1997). While much of this work concerned scheduled passenger networks, attention also turned to the hitherto largely under-reported geographies of airfreight (Bowen et al. 2002; Bowen 2004).

Within the last 10–15 years or so, inspired in part by the cultural and mobilities turns in the social sciences (see Urry 2000), geographers have also begun to examine the multiple social and cultural dimensions of air travel. As a result, commercial aircraft and airports are increasingly being theorized not just as technological formations for moving people from A to B but also for their role in creating new social practices, experiences, and spaces. In this respect, research by Adey (2004a, 2004b, 2006, 2010, this volume), Adey, Budd and Hubbard (2007) and Cresswell (2006) into the diversity and sociality of air travel and Caprotti (2008, 2011), Budd (2011b) and Millward's (2008) work on cultural representations of past aeromobile regimes are advancing new research agendas for social and culturally-informed geographies of air transport.

Paralleling the growth in these social and cultural approaches to air transport geography is research that addresses broader aviation policy and management issues such as international tourism (Page, 2005), environmental impact mitigation (Budd and Budd 2013) and the human health implications of global air travel (Bowen and Laroe 2006; Budd et al. 2009; Warren et al. 2010). This literature offers a counterpoint to more conventional quantitative studies that have traditionally dominated air transport geography.

Conclusion

At the start of the second decade of the second century of powered human flight, the discipline of geography is exhibiting a growing awareness of the rich socialities and spatialities of air travel. It has taken inspiration from other disciplines from both within and beyond the social sciences and, as a result, it is now equipped with a diverse repertoire of empirical and theoretical approaches that aid in the identification, visualization and critical analysis of the dynamics of global commercial aviation. However, in reflecting on over a century of air transport geography, it is necessary to recognize the academic blindness and occlusions in both the historical and contemporary knowledge base. Certainly, until relatively recently, the geography of air transport has been predominately written by white male academics working in the global north and west who, perhaps out of necessity, have focused on selected issues of national strategic and/or commercial or competitive importance. As a consequence, it has only been within the last decade or so that alternative geographies of historical and contemporary air transport are being articulated that draw on a wide range of disciplinary approaches and expertise. Far from diluting the discipline, these new contributions have the potential to enrich and enhance geographic understandings of air transport and, in turn, lead to exciting new avenues of research. Certainly, recent examinations of airspace and the spatial politics of the sky (Williams 2011a) and the geographies of the flightdeck (Budd and Adey 2009) and the passenger (Adey 2010; Budd 2011a) indicate the richness and the diversity of the field.

Understanding the historical geographies of air transport is vital to comprehending the present and helping to inform the future of air transport. One of the most pressing issues facing future generations of air transport geographers is the extent to which it is possible (or indeed desirable) to reconcile aviation growth with commitments to reducing aviation's environmental impact. At the time of writing, it is hard to imagine a more challenging yet more important research agenda than that of identifying and evaluating the various combinations of technological innovations, procedural mechanisms, behavioural incentives and policy interventions that might constitute a policy of socially and environmentally sustainable aviation. Here, it is salient to return to, and reflect on, the words spoken by Mr Claude Grahame-White in 1919. Dozens of transatlantic flights a day fly between London and New York in as little as seven hours and virtually all the world's airports are within 24 hours flying time of each other. Whether the 'aerial age' has indeed done 'more for the world than any other invention or discovery man has ever made' is a moot point, but few would doubt air travel's wide ranging social and geographic significance.

References

Adams, J. (1970) Westminster: The Fourth London Airport? *Area* 2: 1–9.

Adams, J. (1971) London's Third Airport: From TLA to Airstrip One. *Geographical Journal* 137(4): 468–493.

Adey, P. (2004a) Secured and Sorted Mobilities: Examples from the Airport. *Surveillance and Society* 1: 500–519.

Adey, P. (2004b) Surveillance at the Airport: Surveilling Mobility/Mobilising Surveillance. *Environment and Planning A* 36: 1365–1380.

Adey, P. (2006) Airports and Air-Mindedness: Spacing, Timing and Using Liverpool Airport 1929–39. *Social and Cultural Geography* 7(3): 343–363.

Adey, P. (2010) *Aerial Life: Spaces, Mobilities, Affects.* Chichester: Wiley.

Adey, P., Budd, L.C.S and Hubbard, P.J. (2007) Flying Lessons: Exploring the Social and Cultural Geographies of Aeromobility. *Progress in Human Geography* 31(6): 773–791.

ATAG (2012) *Aviation. Benefits Beyond Borders.* Geneva: Air Transport Action Group.

Balchin, W.G.V. (1947) *Air Transport and Geography.* London: Royal Geographical Society.

Borgstrom, R.E. (1974) *Air Travel: Toward a Behavioural Geography of Discretionary Travel,* in Eliot Hurst, M.E. (ed.) *Transportation Geography Comments and Readings.* New York: McGraw-Hill, pp. 314–326.

Bowen, J. (2002) Network Change, Deregulation, and Access in the Global Airline Industry. *Economic Geography* 74(4): 425–440.

Bowen, J. (2004) The Geography of Freighter Aircraft Operations in the Pacific Basin. *Journal of Transport Geography* 12(1): 1–11.

Bowen, J. and Laroe, C. (2006) Airline Networks and the International Diffusion of Severe Acute Respiratory Syndrome (SARS). *The Geographical Journal* 172(2): 130–144.

Bowen, J. and Leinbach, T. (1995) The State and Liberalisation: The Airline Industry in the East Asian NICs. *Annals of the Association of American Geographers* 85: 468–493.

Bowen, J., Leinbach, T. and Mabazza, D. (2002) Air Cargo Services, the State and Industrialisation Strategies in the Philippines. *Regional Studies* 36(5): 451–467.

British Airways (2013) *Celebrating Concorde.* Available at: www.britishairways.com/travel/history-concorde/public/en_gb [accessed: 1 July 2013].

Budd, L. (2011a) On Being Aeromobile: Airline Passengers and the Affective Experiences of Flight. *Journal of Transport Geography* 19: 1010–1019.

Budd, L. (2011b) Selling the Early Air Age: Aviation Advertisements and the Promotion of Civil Flying in Britain. *Journal of Transport History* 33(2): 125–144.

Budd, L. and Adey, P. (2009) The Software Simulated Airworld: Anticipatory Code and Affective Aeromobilities. *Environment and Planning A* 41: 1366–1385.

Budd, L. and Budd, T. (2013) *Environmental Technology and the Future of Flight*, in Budd, L., Griggs, S. and Howarth, D. (eds) *Sustainable Aviation Futures*. Emerald.

Budd, L., Bell, M. and Brown, T. (2009) Of Plagues, Planes and Politics: Controlling the Global Spread of Infectious Diseases by Air. *Political Geography* 28(7): 426–435.

Budd, L. and Ison, S. (eds) (2014) *Low Cost Carriers: Emergence, Evolution and Expansion*. Farnham: Ashgate.

Burghouwt, G. and Hakfoort, J.R. (2002) The Geography of Deregulation in The European Aviation Market. *Tijdschrift voor Economische en Sociale Geografie* 93(1): 100–106.

Burghouwt, G., Hakfoort, J.R. and van Eck, J.F. (2003) The Spatial Configuration of Airline Networks in Europe. *Journal of Air Transport Management* 9(5): 309–323.

Burney, C.D. (1929) *The World, the Air, and the Future*. London: George Allen and Unwin Ltd.

Butler, D.L. (2001) Technogeopolitics and the Struggle for Control of World Air Routes, 1910–1928. *Political Geography* 20(5): 635–658.

Byrd, R.E. (1925) Flying Over the Arctic. *National Geographic*, 519–532.

Byrd, R.E. (1930) The Conquest of Antarctica by Air. *National Geographic*, 127–227.

Caprotti, F. (2008) Technology and Geographical Imaginations: Representing Aviation in 1930s Italy. *Journal of Cultural Geography* 25(2): 181–205.

Caprotti, F. (2011) Visuality, Hybridity and Colonialism: Imaging Ethiopia through Colonial Aviation, 1935–1940. *Annals of the Association of American Geographers* 101(2): 380–403.

Caruana, V. and Simmons, C. (2001) The Development of Manchester Airport, 1938–1978: Central Government Subsidy and Local Authority Management. *Journal of Transport Geography* 9: 279–292.

Cresswell, T. (2006) *On the Move: Mobility in the Modern Western World*. London: Routledge.

Crouch, T.D. (2003) *Wings: A History of Aviation from Kites to the Space Age*. New York: W.W. Norton and Co.

Cwerner, S. (2009) *Introducing Aeromobilities*, in Cwerner, S., Kesselring, S. and Urry, J. (eds) *Aeromobilities*. London: Routledge, 1–21.

Dargue, H.A. (1927) How Latin America Looks from the Air. *National Geographic* 450–502.

Darley, J.M. (1939) The World that Rims the Narrowing Atlantic. *National Geographic*, 139–142.

Davies, R.E.G. (1964) *A History of the World's Airlines*. Oxford: University Press.

Davies, R.E.G. (2011) *Airlines of the Jet Age: A History*. Washington, DC: Smithsonian Institution Scholarly Press.

Debbage, K. (1994) The International Airline Industry: Globalization, Regulation, and Strategic Alliances. *Journal of Transport Geography* 2: 190–203.

Demetz, P. (2002) *The Air Show at Brescia*. New York: Farrar Straus Giroux.

Derudder, B. and Witlox, F. (2005) An Appraisal of the Use of Airline Data in Assessing the World City Network: A Research Note on Data. *Urban Studies* 42(13): 2371–2388.

Dierikx, M. (2008) *Clipping the Clouds – How Air Travel Changed the World*. Westport, CT: Praeger Publishers.

Dierikx, M. and Bouwens, B. (1997) *Building Castles of the Air Schiphol Amsterdam and the Development of Airport Infrastructure in Europe, 1916–1996*. The Hague: Sdu Publishers.

Dobson, A. (1985) The Other Air Battle: The American Pursuit of Post-War Civil Aviation Rights. *The Historical Journal* 28(2): 429–439.

Dobson, A. (1998) The USA, Hegemony, and Airline Market Access to Britain and Western Europe, 1945–96. *Diplomacy and Statecraft* 9(2): 129–159.

Dobson, A. (2012) Canadian Civil Aviation 1935–45: Flying Between the United States and Great Britain. *The International History Review* 34(4): 655–677,

Donne, M. (1964) The Revolution in Air Communications. *The Geographical Magazine* 37(6): 435–447.

Dowson, E.M. (1921) Further Notes on Aeroplane Photography in the Near East. *Geographical Journal* 58(5): 359–370.

Edgerton, D. (2013) *England and the Aeroplane: Militarism, Modernity and Machines.* London: Penguin.

Farrington, J.H. (1985) Transport Geography and Policy: Deregulation and Privatisation. *Transactions of the Institute of British Geographers* 10: 109–119.

Goddard, G.W. (1930) The Unexplored Philippines from the Air. *National Geographic*, 310–343.

Goetz, A.R. (2002) Deregulation, Competition, and Anti-Trust Implications in the US Airline Industry. *Journal of Transport Geography* 10: 1–19.

Goetz, A.R. and Graham, B. (2004) Air Transport Globalization, Liberalization and Sustainability: Post-2001 Policy Dynamics in the United States and Europe. *Journal of Transport Geography* 12(4): 265–276.

Goetz, A.R. and Sutton, S.J. (1997) The Geography of Deregulation in the US Airline Industry. *Annals of the Association of American Geographers* 87: 238–263.

Gordon, A. (2004) *Naked Airport A Cultural History of the World's Most Revolutionary Structure.* New York: Henry Holt and Company.

Graham, B.J. (1995) *Geography and Air Transport.* Chichester: Wiley.

Graham, B.J. and Guyer, C. (2000) The Role of Regional Airport and Air Services in the United Kingdom. *Journal of Transport Geography* 8: 249–262.

Graham, S. (2004) Vertical Geopolitics: Baghdad and After. *Antipode* 36(1): 12–23.

Grahame-White, C. (1919) Transcript of a lecture given to the Royal Aeronautical Society, 'Commercial and Pleasure Flying', Central Hall, Westminster, 19 February 1919.

Grosvenor, G.H. (1924) America From the Air. *National Geographic* 84–92.

Hamilton-Paterson, J. (2010) *Empire of the Clouds When Britain's Aircraft Ruled the World.* London: Faber and Faber.

Hay, A. (1973) *Transport for the Space Economy.* London: Macmillan.

Hildebrand, J.R. (1924) Man's Amazing Progress in Conquering the Air. *National Geographic*, 93–122.

Hinks, A.R., Tizard, H., Cobham, A. et al. (1944) The Geography of Post-War Air Routes Discussion. *Geographical Journal* 103(3): 93–100.

Hoare, A. (1974) International Airports as Growth Poles: A Case Study of Heathrow Airport. *Transactions of the Institute of British Geographers* 63: 75–96.

Holmes, R. (2013) *Falling Upwards: How We Took to the Air.* Harper Press.

Huntington, E. (1947) *Geography and Aviation* reprinted in Taylor, G. (ed.) (1951) *Geography in the Twentieth Century.* London: Methuen, pp. 528–542.

ICAO (1944) *Convention on International Civil Aviation Done at Chicago on the 7th Day of December 1944.* Available at: www.icao.int/publications/Documents/730_orig.pdf.

Kennett, L. (1999) *The First Air War, 1914–1918.* Simon and Schuster.

Kish, G. (1958) Soviet Air Transport. *Geographical Review* 48: 309–320.

Lawrence, C.H. (1942) *New World Horizons: Geography for the Air Age.* New York: Duell, Sloan and Pearce.

Lee, W.T. (1920) Airplanes and Geography. *Geographical Review* 10(5): 310–325.

Lee, W.T. (1922) *The Face of the Earth as Seen From the Air: A Study in the Application of Airplane Photography to Geography.* New York: American Geographical Society.

Light, R.U. (1935) Cruising by Airplane: Narrative of a Journey Around the World. *Geographical Review* 25(4): 565–600.

Lissitzyn, O.J. (1942) International Air Transport and National Policy. *Studies in American Foreign Relations, No. 3.* New York: Council on Foreign Relations.

MacLeod, M.N. (1919) Mapping from Air Photographs. *Geographical Journal* 53(6): 382–396.

Millichap, R.J. (2000) *Airline Markets and Regulation* in Jarrett, P. (ed.) *Modern Air Transport Worldwide Air Transport from 1945 to the Present.* London: Putnam Aeronautical Books, pp. 35–52.

Millward, L. (2008) The Embodied Aerial Subject: Gendered Mobility in British Inter-War Air Tours. *The Journal of Transport History* 29(1): 5–22.

Mitchell, W. (1921) America in the Air: The Future of Airplane and Airship. *National Geographic* 339–352.

Moffit, F.H. (1920) A Method of Aerophotographic Mapping. *Geographical Review* 10(5): 326–338.

O'Connor, K. (1995) Airport Development in South East Asia. *Journal of Transport Geography* 3: 269–279.

O'Connor, K. (2003) Global Air Travel: Towards Concentration or Dispersal? *Journal of Transport Geography* 11: 83–92.

O'Kelly, M. (1998) A Geographer's Analysis of Hub-and-Spoke Networks. *Journal of Transport Geography* 6(3): 171–186.

Page, S. (2005) *Transport and Tourism Global Perspectives.* 2nd Edition. Harlow: Pearson.

Pascoe, D. (2001) *Airspaces.* London: Reaktion Books.

Pascoe, D. (2003) *Aircraft.* London: Reaktion Books.

Pearcy, G.E. (1947) The Air Age: Fact or Fantasy? An Evaluation of the Global Air Transportation Pattern. *Journal of Geography* 46(8): 304–312.

Pearcy, G.E. and Alexander, L.M. (1951) Pattern of Commercial Air Service Availability in the Western Hemisphere. *Economic Geography* 27: 316–320.

Pearcy, G.E. and Alexander, L.M. (1953) Pattern of Air Service Availability in the Eastern Hemisphere. *Economic Geography* 29: 74–78.

Pearman, H. (2004) *Airports: A Century of Architecture.* London: Laurence King.

Pepper, D. (1980) Environmentalism, the 'Lifeboat Ethic' and Anti-Airport Protest. *Area* 12(3): 177–182.

Petzinger, T. (1995) *Hard Landing How the Epic Contest for Power and Profits Plunged the Airlines into Chaos.* London: Aurum.

Pirie, G.H. (2009) *Air Empire: British Imperial Civil Aviation, 1919–1939.* Manchester: Manchester University Press.

Pirie, G.H. (2012) *Cultures and Caricatures of British Imperial Aviation. Passengers, Pilots, Publicity.* Manchester: Manchester University Press.

Plischke, E. (1943) Trans-Arctic Aviation. *Economic Geography* 19: 283–291.

Possony, S.T. and Rosenzweig, L. (1955) The Geography of the Air. *Annals of the American Academy of Political and Social Science* 299: 1–11.

Raguraman, K. (1997) Airlines as Instruments for Nation Building and National Identity: Case Study of Malaysia and Singapore. *Journal of Transport Geography* 5(4): 239–256.

Renner, G. (1942) *Human Geography in the Air Age.* New York: Macmillan.

Sampson, A. (1984) *Empires of the Sky: The Politics, Contests and Cartels of World Airlines.* London: Hodder and Stoughton.

Sealy, K.R. (1957) *The Geography of Air Transport.* London: Hutchinson University Library.

Sealy, K.R. (1966) *The Geography of Air Transport.* 2nd Edition. London: Hutchinson University Library.

Sealy, K.R. (1967) The Siting and Development of British Airports. *Geographical Journal* 133(2): 148–171.

Sealy, K.R. (1970) Links with the Outside World. *The Geographical Magazine* 42(8): 591–597.

Sealy, K.R. (1976) Airport Strategy and Planning. *Theory and Practice in Geography.* Oxford: Oxford University Press.

Smith, D.A. (1981) Americans Take to the Air. *The Geographical Magazine* 53(4): 245–249.

Smith, D.A. and Timberlake, M. (1995) Conceptualising and Mapping the Structure of the World System's City System. *Urban Studies* 32(2): 287–302.

Spoehr, A. (1946) The Marshall Islands and Transpacific Aviation. *Geographical Review* 36(3): 447–451.

Stamp, D.L. (1950) British Food and British Homes. *The Geographical Magazine* 22(12): 504–512.

Steffansson, V. (1922) The Arctic as an Air Route of the Future. *National Geographic* 205–218.

Street, S.C. (1926) The First Alaskan Air Expedition. *National Geographic,* 498–552.

Sweet, K.M. (2009) *Aviation and Airport Security. Terrorism and Safety Concerns.* 2nd Edition. Boca Raton, FL: CRC Press.

Sykes, F.H. (1920) Imperial Air Routes. *The Geographical Journal* LV(4): 241–262.

Taaffe, E.J. (1956) Air Transportation and United States Urban Distribution. *The Geographical Review* XLVI: 219–238.

Taaffe, E.J. (1959) Trends in Airline Passenger Traffic: A Geographic Case Study. *Annals of the Association of American Geographers* 49: 393–408.

Taaffe, E.J. (1962) The Urban Hierarchy: An Air Passenger Definition. *Economic Geography* 38(1): 1–14.

Taylor, E.G.R. (1945) *Geography of an Air Age.* London: Royal Institute of International Affairs.

Taylor, G. (1919) Air Routes to Australia. *Geographical Review* 7: 256–261.

Urry, J. (2000) *Sociology Beyond Societies: Mobilities for the Twenty-First Century.* London: Routledge.

Van Zandt, J.P. (1925) Looking Down on Europe. *National Geographic,* 261–326.

Van Zandt, J.P. (1944) *The Geography of World Air Transport.* Washington, DC: The Brookings Institution.

Veale, S.E. (1945) *To-morrow's Airliners, Airways and Airports.* London: Pilot Press.

Vowles, T.M. (2006) Geographic Perspectives of Air Transportation. *The Professional Geographer* 58(1): 12–19.

Walmsey, L. (1920) The Recent Trans-African Flight and its Lesson. *Geographical Review* 55: 263–270.

Warren, A., Bell, M. and Budd, L. (2010) Airports, Localities and Disease: Representations of Global Travel during the H1N1 Pandemic. *Health and Place* 16(4): 727–735.

Warntz, W. (1961) Transatlantic Flights and Pressure Patterns. *Geographical Review* 51(2): 187–212.

Wilcox, H.C. (1930) Air Transportation in Latin America. *Geographical Review* 20: 587–604.

Williams, A. (2010) A Crisis in Aerial Sovereignty? Considering the Implications of Recent Military Violations of National Airspace. *Area* 42(1): 51–59.

Williams, A. (2011a) Reconceptualising Spaces of the Air: Performing the Multiple Spatialities of UK Military Airspaces. *Transactions of the Institute of British Geographers* 36(2): 253–267.

Williams, A. (2011b) Enabling Persistent Presence? Performing the Embodied Geopolitics of the Unmanned Aerial Vehicle Assemblage. *Political Geography* 30(7): 381–390.

Wohl, R. (1994) *A Passion for Wings Aviation and the Western Imagination, 1908–1918*. New Haven: Yale University Press.

Wohl, R. (2005) *The Spectacle of Flight Aviation and the Western Imagination*. New Haven: Yale University Press.

Woodhouse, H. (1917) Aeronautical Maps and Aerial Transportation. *The Geographical Review* 4(5): 329–350.

Wright, O. (1913) How We Made the First Flight. *Flying* 2(11): 10–12, 35–36.

Zook, M.A. and Brunn, S.D. (2006) From Podes to Antipodes: Positionalities and Global Airline Geographies. *Annals of the Association of American Geographers* 96(3): 471–490.

Chapter 2
The Geopolitics of Air Transport

Keith G. Debbage

In an era of increasingly open markets and globalization, the international air transportation industry remains one of the most regulated and byzantine sectors of the world economy. The geopolitics of this regulatory regime can substantially manipulate and shape the geography of air transportation. According to Doganis (2010: 2), 'any understanding of the economics of the industry must start with the regulatory framework which circumscribes and constrains airlines' freedom of action'. One of the themes of this chapter is to articulate the fundamental tension that drives the geopolitics of air transport on the global stage. It will be argued that two regulatory regimes exist based on a liberal 'open skies' approach versus a more traditional, protectionist perspective, although the chapter will also stress that, in practice, this is not a simple twofold division.

Sovereignty and the 1919 Paris Convention

Aircraft have the unique ability to fly over and *potentially* disregard natural and cultural barriers, and so, air transportation is not just about the movement of passengers and cargo, it is also about geo-politics, regulation and power (Butler 2001; Shaw and Sidaway 2010). In this sense, nation-states have a vested interest in the development of the international air transportation industry, particularly regarding the state's ability to control its borders. As a result, a dense framework of political, economic and regulatory institutions have evolved that fundamentally shape international air transportation (Duval and Macilree 2011; Duval 2008). In developing a 'politics of mobility' research agenda, Cresswell (2010) recently invoked several key questions regarding the geopolitics of material movement: Who moves furthest? Who moves fastest? Who moves most often? Although the answers to these questions are partly linked to the machinations of the global economy – where, not surprisingly, the New York–London route is one of the busiest air passenger markets in the world – they are also directly related to the regulatory apparatus that governs origin – destination flows at the national and global scale.

Much of this regulatory legacy can be traced back to the 1919 Paris convention which established that nation-states have sovereign rights to the air-space above their territory (in large part for national security reasons). Such an action elevated airline traffic to the level of a national resource that governments protected in the interests of national welfare. In the aftermath of World War I, many European nations clearly understood the national security imperative after a decade under the potential shadow of German Zeppelins (Butler 2001). That said, it would not be until 1944 that the Chicago Convention established an over-arching and enduring framework for the regulation of the international air transportation industry.

It should be noted here that although the rest of this chapter will deal with the geo-politics of commercial aviation, both the Paris and Chicago Convention protocols also helped shape concepts of aerial sovereignty as it related to military airspace, although this area of air transportation geography remains under-researched and under-theorized (Budd 2009; Williams 2011). Such a dearth of research in this area is unfortunate, because the vertical geopolitics of military air space can speak to the manner in which nation-states project power across space. Such a perspective might include a god's eye view of targeting and surveillance from above (Graham 2004) but also an analysis of how states 'look upwards' through the implementation of air defence practices (Williams 2013).

In a post 9/11 world, where drones such as the much publicized Predator and Reaper Unmanned Aerial Vehicles (UAVs) utilized by the US military can strike terrorist targets anywhere in the world, geographers need to be more actively engaged in better understanding how these military spaces are contoured and manipulated. Williams (2010: 57) has gone so far as to suggest that we may be facing a crisis in aerial sovereignty. She argues that we are potentially 'witnessing the chronic decline of the sanctity of aerial sovereignty, as strategies of security and securitization increasingly enacted by powerful states enable them to violate and render contingent sovereign airspace with continued impunity'. Adey et al. (2011: 183) echo this view when they suggest that 'there is a pressing need to uncover and illuminate the critical geographies of the aerial view and the politics of verticality, especially when that view is utilized to target people, infrastructure and technologies for destruction'. Although it is clear that a geo-politics of military spaces is slowly emerging and crucially important, it is not the primary purpose of this chapter. With that said, we can now return to the primary narrative and discuss in more detail how the 1944 Chicago Conference outlined the essential geo-political parameters of commercial aviation.

The 1944 Chicago Conference and the 'Freedoms of the Air'

As World War II drew to a close, world leaders began to focus on establishing an institutional framework capable of nurturing international trade and commerce. To that end, the groundwork was laid for the establishment of the United Nations, the Bretton Woods Agreement, the International Monetary Fund, and the World Bank. In addition, there was a clear understanding that the fledgling aviation industry was directly linked to the facilitation of international trade and commerce. Consequently, pressure emerged to establish a coherent legal framework for the emerging international airline industry (Butler and Keller 1994; Doganis 2010; Kasper 1988; de Murias 1989).

In 1944, the Chicago Conference on International Civil Aviation was convened to develop an acceptable legal framework for the international operation of airlines. Two conflicting approaches emerged. The United States had emerged from World War II with its territory largely unscathed and with a relatively well developed airline industry and thus advocated a free-trade, laissez-faire approach towards air transport. By contrast, the United Kingdom and most other European nations were more protectionist, in part because their civil airlines had been severely damaged in the war. Because these conflicting views could not be reconciled, the Chicago Convention could not come to a multilateral agreement on the three key issues of traffic rights, tariff control and capacity. However, the principal 'freedoms of the air' that underpin present-day air travel agreements and fundamentally influence the contemporary geography of air transportation were initially defined in Chicago and these included the following traffic rights:

- **First Freedom**: the right of an airline of one country to fly over the territory of another country;

- **Second Freedom**: the right of an airline to stop in another country for refuelling/ maintenance reasons but not to pick-up or drop-off passengers or cargo;
- **Third Freedom**: the right of an airline to carry passengers or cargo from its own country to another country;
- **Fourth Freedom**: the right of an airline to carry back passengers or cargo from a foreign country to the country in which the airline is registered;
- **Fifth Freedom (or 'beyond rights')**: the right of an airline to carry passengers or cargo between two foreign countries provided the flight originates or terminates in the country in which the airline is registered (e.g. US-based United Airlines flying from Chicago to London and on to Frankfurt).

It should be noted that any city-pair market (e.g. New York–London) is essentially a combination of the third and fourth freedoms (i.e. the outbound and return flight segments) while the fifth freedom is highly controversial and less common not least because there are always three countries involved in the frequently protracted negotiations. Four additional 'so-called' freedoms have emerged since the Chicago Conference and although they rarely feature in any global regulatory agreements there are increasing signs that these 'new' freedoms may become less exceptional in the future – a point to which we shall return later in the chapter. These additional freedoms include:

- **Sixth Freedom**: the right of an airline to carry passengers or cargo between two countries via the country in which the airline is registered (e.g. Emirates Airlines carrying passengers between London and Singapore via its Dubai hub). In some ways, sixth freedom rights are simply a pair of third/fourth freedoms although they are invariably more difficult to negotiate since they involve three different nation-states.
- **Seventh Freedom**: the right of an airline to operate 'stand alone' service between two foreign countries entirely outside the territory of the home state of the registered airline (e.g. American Airlines operating a route exclusively between Mexico City and Rio de Janeiro). It should be noted that seventh freedom rights are more commonly exchanged for cargo-only services and are much less common for passenger services.
- **Eighth Freedom (or 'consecutive' cabotage rights)**: the right for an airline to pick up and set down passengers or freight between two domestic points in another country on a service that originates or terminates in the home country of the registered airline (e.g. Delta Airlines operating a route from Atlanta to Paris and then Marseilles).
- **Ninth Freedom (or 'stand-alone' cabotage)**: the right for an airline to fly between two domestic points in another country without continuing service to the home country of the registered airline (e.g. British Airways operating a route between Paris and Marseilles exclusively within France without a tie back to the United Kingdom).

The participants at the 1944 Chicago Conference were only able to agree on the mutual exchange of the relatively rudimentary first and second freedoms while no agreement was reached on the crucial third through fifth freedoms which essentially facilitated the exchange of 'real' commercial traffic rights between countries. Furthermore, the sixth through ninth freedoms were neither discussed nor fully defined in the Chicago Convention. As a result, no equivalent maritime 'freedom of the seas' agreement for aviation emerged out of Chicago. Instead of regulating the international airline industry on a multilateral basis, each country was left to negotiate generally restrictive nation-to-nation bilateral aviation agreements through a series of international air service agreements. The shortcomings of the Chicago Conference subsequently spawned over 2,500 bilateral aviation agreements during the post-World War II era that overly complicated and fundamentally dictated and constrained the geography of air transportation (Butler and Keller 1994).

It should also be noted that the International Civil Aviation Organization (ICAO) – an inter-governmental United Nations agency – was established at Chicago to co-ordinate technical and operational standards and practice worldwide. Over time, these standards have been adopted by virtually all countries so, unlike the shipping sector, there are very few 'flags of convenience' in air transportation. One reason for this is the fear of ICAO sanctions so the end result is that 'no major international airline can enjoy a competitive advantage by operating to airworthiness standards below the generally acceptable level' (Doganis 2010: 28).

Regulatory Regimes and International Air Service Agreements: The Transition from Restrictive Bilaterals to 'Open Skies' Accords

In the aftermath of the Chicago Convention, it was inevitable that international air transportation and the related traffic rights (or 'freedoms of the air') would be governed by a network of bilateral air service agreements. Much of this was predicated on the recognition at Chicago that each nation state had exclusive sovereignty over the airspace above its territory but it was also linked to the requirement that each airline should have a nationality by being registered in just one particular state (the so-called 'nationality clause'). The nationality or ownership clause ensured that aircraft from one nation-state had to obtain special permission from another nation-state to operate an international flight segment and this was usually codified through a bilateral air service agreement.

Underlying all bilateral aviation agreements has been the principle of reciprocity and the fair and equal exchange of rights between countries although, in practice, this has frequently proven problematic when the pair of countries involved are very different in size and with host airlines of varied strengths. According to Kasper (1988), the 1946 US–UK bilateral or Bermuda I agreement acted as the intellectual foundation for all subsequent bilaterals. The Bermuda I agreement (so named because the US and UK governments negotiated the bilateral in Bermuda) emerged as the 'standard model for air service agreements between many other countries' (Wheatcroft 1994: 19). Although each bilateral agreement tends to vary with regard to content, the essential regulatory issues in Bermuda I were generally covered by clauses dealing with the specification of routes, the designation of specific air carriers, ownership and control issues, capacity and tariff matters, and various confidential 'memorandums [sic] of understandings' between the two nation-states. Most bilaterals severely constrained the range of cities served by the airline industry and controlled the output or production of each airline through various capacity controls (e.g. number of seats, flight frequencies).

The Bermuda I bilateral also approved the International Air Transportation Association (IATA) as the primary institution through which international airfares would be mediated. IATA was founded in Havana in 1945 as an airline lobby group that essentially acted as a counter-weight to the ICAO which largely represented government interests. According to Doganis (2010: 36), 'there can be little doubt that IATA was effectively a suppliers cartel, whose object was to maximize its members' profile by mutually fixing the prices at which they sold their services'. Through the bilateral framework, IATA was able to effectively set airline fares and cargo rates worldwide, thus, minimizing the possibility of price competition.

Although many bilateral agreements in the post-World War II era reflected the protectionist attitudes of the prevailing national governments, the Bermuda I agreement was the first bilateral to accept the concept of fifth freedom rights or 'beyond rights' first enshrined in the Chicago Conference. Because of the large size and strength of the American market in 1946, the US was able to aggressively negotiate 'beyond rights' out of London to Amsterdam, Berlin, Budapest, Copenhagen, Frankfurt, Helsinki, Leningrad, Moscow, Munich, Oslo, Stockholm, and Vienna, plus Beirut, Calcutta, Delhi, Karachi, and many other cities. The generous granting of fifth freedom rights to US-designated carriers was one of the major issues that led the UK government to push for a re-negotiated bilateral that led to the 1977 Bermuda II Agreement. The UK achieved important gains in Bermuda II by increasing the number of US cities served from 9 to 14 including Atlanta, Dallas-Fort Worth, Houston, San Francisco, and Seattle while the US gave up many of its fifth freedom rights beyond the UK.

The Bermuda II agreement marked a watershed in US air transportation policy in the North Atlantic market. The 1946–1977 Bermuda era that had been marked by a series of restrictive bilateral negotiations came to a close and was replaced with a radically different 'open skies' approach in late 1977. In a 1978 Annual Report to Congress, the US Civil Aeronautics Board (CAB) stated that:

> The renegotiated US–UK bilateral agreement is the LAST episode in the history of restrictive markets and triggered a major turning point in US international aviation policy. Bermuda 2 symbolizes the direction we are moving AWAY from. Rather, the US international policy is now based upon active competitive principles. (US CAB, 1978: 60–61) (Capitals added)

'Open Skies': A Reversal of US Aviation Policy

In 1978, the US government adopted a strategy formulated to 'open-up' international air service agreements to greater competition through a process of generalized deregulation. According to Dresner and Tretheway (1992: 172–173), most of these agreements allowed carriers 'the freedom to set capacity without governmental interference, allowed additional routes between (and beyond) two signatories, promoted competitive rather than IATA price-setting, and strictly limited governmental authority over fare-setting'. The introduction of greater pricing freedom through more liberalized bilaterals increased the potential for the diversion of traffic from protectionist markets to more liberalized countries (Pustay 1993). The US strategy of penetrating the North Atlantic market by establishing 'beachhead' agreements with key European countries (e.g. the 1978 Netherlands bilateral) led to other countries later renegotiating agreements with the US to maintain a competitive advantage (e.g. the 1996 German bilateral).

Kasper (1988: 89) noted that 'by using the "carrot" of access to large, economically attractive markets and the "stick" of diversion', the US achieved significant liberalization in some European markets. A few countries initially resisted the trend towards liberalization (e.g. France) but many countries embraced the 'open skies' approach (e.g. Austria, Belgium, Czech Republic, Denmark, Finland, Iceland, Italy, Norway, and Sweden) although most of these countries have small domestic markets. Because of the geographic disparities in market size between the US and many other nation states, it became apparent that a multilateral approach was needed and the focus of regulatory reform switched to the European Union in the 1990s.

European Liberalization

During the late 1980s, the EU initiated discussions about establishing a more competitive air transportation market to complement reform in other sectors of the economy relating to trade and tariffs. Although the traditional picture of European aviation was one of 'institutionalized cartelization and collusion' (Button 1996: 279), the privatization of previously state-run British Airways coupled with the existence of a robust and less regulated charter airline industry run by low-cost tour operators to sun-spot cities on the Mediterranean rim offered an alternative perspective.

EU liberalization was gradually phased-in through a series of three aviation packages that became effective in 1987, 1990 and 1993, respectively. By the early 1990s, the EU had successfully removed most of the regulatory constraints acting on intra-European air transport relating to fares, frequency of service, market entry and capacity constraints. Since 1997, EU airlines have even been able to operate between points within an EU country besides the country with which the airline is registered (i.e. the ninth freedom or 'stand alone' cabotage). By contrast, cabotage within the US is prohibited by law, meaning it is illegal for a foreign carrier to operate a purely domestic route within America. Although these EU reforms stimulated competition and partly explained the emergence of low-fare carriers like easyJet and Ryanair, the EU had yet to fully reconcile the conflicting goals of ensuring a competitive industry within Europe relative to the global competitive positions of EU carriers. For example, some globally oriented EU carriers viewed intra-European traffic as merely hub feed and considered the proliferation of competitors on domestic routes as an impediment to their globalization strategies. Bernard Attali (ex-President of Air France) considered EU liberalization as 'a short-sighted approach focusing only on intra-European competition', which will ultimately weaken 'the airlines of Europe in the battle against their non-European counterparts' (Graham 1992: 249).

If the EU is now a fully unified and liberalized market similar, in many ways, to the US domestic market, EU policy makers argued that external relations and the negotiation of aviation bilaterals with non-EU member states like the US should fall under the rubric of the European Commission (the executive body of the EU) and not individual member states. In 2002, the European Court of Justice in a landmark decision asserted that bilateral agreements between EU and non-EU countries were contrary to community law and compromised deregulation in the EU's single market (*Aviation Week and Space Technology*, 2002). Bilateral agreements have traditionally mandated that participating airlines be owned substantially by nationals of the home country – the so-called 'nationality clause'. However, the then European Commission Vice President Loyola de Palacio suggested that the 'unlawful nationality clauses' in bilateral accords are contrary to the spirit and goals of the 1957 Treaty of Rome that first established the European Community. Such a ruling had significant implications for countries like the Netherlands who had already negotiated an aggressively 'open skies' agreement with the US in 1992 that provided considerable freedom on routes from the US to Amsterdam and beyond. Resolving these extra-territorial issues became crucial given the fundamental role that EU–North America and EU–Asia markets play in determining the overall health of the international air transportation industry. During the late 2000s, proposals for a Transatlantic Common Aviation Area (TCAA) began to emerge as the European Commission and the US Department of Transportation contemplated the possibility of an 'open skies' accord across the North Atlantic.

The EU–US 'Open Skies' Agreement: Traffic Rights and National Security

Although developing a Common Transport Policy had been one of the major goals of the Treaty of Rome, air transportation was excluded from this EU-wide policy platform because of the relatively small size of the airline industry in 1957. In the absence of a community-wide policy on air transportation in the EU, the US approach in dealing with EU nations had been to fill the policy vacuum by developing a 'beggar-thy-neighbor' strategy by initiating liberal air service agreements with individual EU member states like the Netherlands that forced others to follow suit in order to maintain market share (Button 2009).

All this changed in 2007 when the EU and the US agreed to a TCAA after nearly four years and 11 rounds of stop and start negotiations. Although the European Commission wanted to pursue a broad based liberalization strategy that included cabotage and ownership matters, the TCAA focused largely on traffic rights. Under the final agreement, any EU airline was allowed to fly from any EU city to any US city. Conversely, any US airline can now fly into any EU airport. All airlines now have fifth freedom 'beyond rights' and there are no restrictions on capacity, flight frequencies, or tariffs. According to Doganis (2010), the TCAA represented a major breakthrough because it created a vast 'open skies' market between most of Europe and the US, and it relaxed the conventional 'nationality clause' contained in most traditional bilaterals.

That said, the US was reluctant to relax the strict ownership and control rules for US airlines in the TCAA negotiations, in part because since the passage of the Civil Aeronautics Act of 1938, Congress has required that US citizens own or control at least 75 per cent of the voting interests of US airlines. According to the US General Accounting Office (2003: 2) the ownership and control restrictions were historically put in place for four primary reasons: '(1) protection of the then fledgling US airline industry, (2) regulation of international air service through bilateral agreements, (3) concern about allowing foreign aircraft access to US airspace, and (4) military reliance on civilian airlines to supplement airlift capacity'. Both the US Department of Transportation in 1991 and the Bush Administration in 2003 proposed amendments to relax the restrictions on foreign-owned voting stock of US airlines from 25 to 49 per cent but Congress did not embrace either of these proposals. The ICAO and the IATA, along with the major US network carriers, have also supported increases in foreign investment limits, since it would likely allow US airlines greater access to global capital while also being consistent with EU and other bilateral partner foreign investment restrictions, although little of this logic has gained much traction in Congress.

Much of the contemporary logic for limiting foreign investment in US airlines rests squarely on issues of national security, the economy, and politics. The US Department of Defense (DOD) has traditionally opposed increasing foreign ownership, in part because foreign investors might discourage the continued voluntary participation of US airlines in the Civil Reserve Air Fleet (CRAF) programme. Under the CRAF programme, US airlines provide DOD with supplemental airlift capacity in emergencies. In return, US carriers are granted preferred access to US government peacetime airlift contracts worth over $2 billion per year in revenue (Bolkcom 2006; Cosmas et al. 2008). Increased foreign investment could also put jobs at risk since some jobs may be transferred to foreign workforces – a concern that deepened after 9/11 given the massive reductions in US carrier employment levels in the early 2000s. However, given the financial difficulties faced by many US carriers, additional investment may also stimulate domestic aviation by providing much needed sources of new capital. Additional concerns focused on the safety challenges of a post 9/11 era, since increased foreign investment could place additional burdens on the Federal Aviation Administration's safety protocols regarding foreign aircraft that are transferred to a US registry. That said, thousands of planes belonging to foreign investors land and take off from US airports without incident and the planes hijacked on 9/11 all belonged to US airlines.

The end result is that the EU–US 'open skies' agreement is simply a first step, a compromise, short-term agreement that effectively opened the skies over the North Atlantic regarding traffic rights but fell short of a fully open market since it failed to address the crucial role of cabotage and the flexible movement of capital. In 2010, the EU and the US did agree to expand the 2007 agreement although no consensus was reached regarding the removal of the remaining barriers to foreign ownership and control of airlines. Under the terms of the second-stage agreement, the US granted EU carriers greater access to travel by American government employees which had been previously restricted under the 'Fly America' programme where officials travelling on behalf of the US government were required to fly on US airlines. The US also agreed to explore ways that a proposed American trading system for carbon emissions could be integrated with an existing EU system although no deadlines were discussed and the current US administration appears to have put these negotiations on the back-burner.

Meanwhile, the EU has decided to push ahead with its plan to make all flights into the EU subject to the emissions-trading system (ETS) which has now been passed into law. One problematic issue is that the ETS applies to flight miles generated outside EU airspace which European regulators argue is consistent with ICAO guidelines. The US and others have argued that this infringes on air space sovereignty and breaks the terms of the Chicago Convention. However, in late 2011 the European Court of Justice's Advocate General ruled that the inclusion of international aviation in the ETS was compatible with the provisions and principles of international law. The impasse is troublesome given the substantive environmental impacts generated by air transportation and it is likely that the ICAO will have to play a more significant role in future negotiations.

All of this ignores an additional problem which is the significant gridlock faced by airport authorities on the ground given the projected trans-Atlantic growth rates as a result of the open skies agreement. Button (2009: 69) has persuasively argued that 'the transatlantic open skies agreement does little to resolve the congestion issues at airports' particularly regarding the way in which airport landing slots are allocated on either side of the Atlantic.

What About the Geopolitics of Airports?
The Political Economy of Airport Slot Allocations

While the demand for air travel has increased as markets deregulated, the capacity of airports to handle this demand has been expanding less rapidly resulting in severe congestion and delay problems in places like New York and London (Czerny et al. 2007; *The Economist* 2011; Levine 2009). According to Madas and Zografos (2010), over half of Europe's 50 largest airports have already reached or are close to reaching their saturation points, and only a handful of airports plan major developments to expand capacity. Although building additional runways and airport terminals might remedy the acute gridlock in the North Atlantic and Asian markets in the long-term, Graham (2003: 120) has argued that 'in many cases environmental, physical, or financial constraints have meant that in practice this has not been a feasible or desirable option'. The end result is that more attention has focused on developing short-term solutions with an emphasis placed on better demand management techniques including more appropriate regulatory mechanisms for allocating airport slots (Brueckner 2008; Czerny et al. 2007; Debbage 2000, 2002; Fukui 2010; Levine 2009; Madas and Zografos 2008, 2010; Sieg 2010).

Airport slots are usually defined as, in effect, permission to schedule a flight at a particular airport at a particular time, although approved slots are only required at designated capacity-constrained airports where the demand for runway and gate access exceeds the capacity of the airport. Currently, in all parts of the world except the US, the mechanism for allocating landing slots is voluntary industry self-regulation through the International Air Transport Association (IATA) – a powerful airline lobby group. IATA has identified 155 slot-constrained (or fully coordinated) airports that require formal procedures to allocate slots including 98 airports in Europe and 45 airports in the Asia-Pacific region. Many US airports are also capacity constrained but are not subject to the IATA Scheduling Committee rules (Graham 2003).

Since 1946, IATA has developed various administrative procedures for allocating scarce airport capacity. As a growing number of airports became increasingly congested over time, IATA started to host twice yearly Schedule Co-ordination Conferences that administratively allocated landing slots at the capacity-constrained airports. The slot schedules were planned in six-monthly seasons and effectively 'connected the dots' of global airline networks. Although most allocations tend to be sorted out before a conference starts, they still play a vitally important role in allowing airlines and airport slot coordinators to meet face-to-face to resolve conflicts and swap slots with other airlines. Consequently, through a process of administrative rationing, IATA has been able to essentially outline the key spatial parameters of growth for international air transportation at these twice yearly summits.

One key principle established early on at the IATA slot conferences was the basic notion of grandfather rights where an airline that held and used a slot in the previous season has the right to operate it again. Part of the logic for this approach is it provides route network stability for incumbents that may have invested significant capital in developing routes. Others argue that grandfather rights are essentially anti-competitive, serving to advantage incumbents over would-be new entrants (Dempsey 2001). For example, Deloitte Touche (2008) estimated that of the 9,562 slots available at Heathrow Airport during summer 2008, 9,462 (or 99 per cent) were claimed under grandfather rights. According to Gillen (2007: 52) 'the IATA process protects the status quo, entrenches incumbents, is anti-competitive, and is generally blocking effective entry'.

In response to this criticism, IATA introduced a 'use-it-or-lose-it' rule to minimize slot hoarding by the dominant airlines where slots not used 80 per cent of the time over a prescribed time period are relinquished and put back into a pool to be reallocated to other carriers, including new entrants. It should be noted that the 'use-it-or-lose-it' rule was temporarily suspended after 11 September 2001 since so many airlines dropped routes because of the sudden downfall in traffic, but did not want to lose their historical slots.

Within the EU, slot allocation comes under Regulation 95/93 which was introduced in 1993. Unlike the voluntary IATA system, the EU rules are legally binding and place a higher premium on transparency and impartiality. One important difference is that the European regulation mandated that the slot coordinator must be independent of all airlines at the airport. However, Regulation 95/93 also recognized the historical merit of grandfather rights that favoured incumbents, and many critics have argued the EU slot regulations did nothing more than codify the status-quo (Bass 1994; Button et al. 1998; UK Civil Aviation Authority 1998).

On the other side of the Atlantic, access to most US airports is based on a 'first-come-first-served' approach where landing slots are not subject to IATA rules, nor administered by an independent slot coordinator, but are subject only to normal air traffic control rules. Consequently, US carriers simply schedule flights to account for expected delays at the more congested airports. One historical exception to this approach is the High Density Rule (HDR) airports (i.e., Chicago O'Hare, JFK, LaGuardia, and Washington Reagan). Given the heavy traffic at all four airports, a slot quota mechanism was introduced in 1968 at each of these high density airports to limit air traffic congestion and noise. Furthermore, since 1986, the FAA has allowed domestic slots at the HDR airports to be bought and sold for money, rather than merely being swapped for other slots as is the case in the 'one-for-one' trading system established by IATA.

The US approach to slot trading is in stark contrast to EU Regulation 95/93 which allowed slots to be freely exchanged but was silent on the matter of price and ownership. However, this changed in 2008, when the European Commission announced that slots could be exchanged for monetary considerations although the level of trading varies by country. In the UK, a 1999 High Court ruling involving the alleged sale of slots at Heathrow Airport by Air UK to British Airways suggested that slots can be traded for money. Consequently, slot trading in the so-called 'grey' market has long been a recognized practice in the UK, even before the 2008 EU ruling. By contrast, Claus Ulrich, head of Germany's slot coordination body FHKD recently indicated that slot trading rarely occurs in Germany although he saw a growing demand for trading (*Airline Business*, 2007).

In the United States, although the right to buy and sell slots at the HDR airports enhanced flexibility, new entrant airlines complained that it unfairly forced them to pay for slots that incumbents had gotten free under grandfather rules (Levine 2009). Partly in response to these concerns, Congress enacted the Wendell H. Ford Aviation Investment and Reform Act for the 21st Century (AIR-21) in 2000 that terminated slot restrictions for all the HDR airports except Reagan National by 2007. However, congestion and delays increased dramatically at the HDR airports. By 2008, these delays had become so chronic that 'many peak-hour LaGuardia-Reagan National flights using jets are now scheduled for the same duration as the piston-engined propeller planes of 1953' (Levine 2009: 59). Consequently, the FAA ended up resurrecting the slot markets and placing temporary limitations on flight operations to prevent delays.

Developing more innovative slot policies that better manage scarce resources is critical given the profound ways in which airport infrastructural constraints can shape accessibility levels between origins and destinations. One approach might be to encourage secondary slot markets directly between the airlines (rather than the conventional IATA-based primary slot trading that currently exists between the airport slot coordinator and the airline) (Fukui 2010). Although the financial terms of slot transfers between airlines are not generally made public, it has been estimated that peak-hour slots at London's Heathrow Airport are worth from $48 million to $68 million per pair (Levine 2009). The Heathrow slots are so valuable that Deloitte Touche (2008) estimated that British Airways had the most valuable slot portfolio in the world, worth a staggering £2 billion compared to a market capitalization for the entire British Airways group of £2.6 billion.

By allowing market prices to determine slot allocations, it is assumed that one end result is a more efficient allocation of slots. However, relying on secondary markets has had mixed results (Fukui 2010) and poses several challenges. First, it is unclear who actually owns the slots. The FAA has explicitly ruled that slots do not represent a property right for the airlines but instead are an operating privilege subject to FAA control. However, the quasi-private property status of existing slots has been highlighted in a number of well-publicized airline transactions. For example, Continental Airlines recently paid $209 million for four slots at Heathrow (Button, 2009). A second concern is that the pre-existing slot holders were essentially given grandfathered slot rights for free, representing an unwarranted windfall gain for incumbents that places new entrants at a competitive disadvantage. Despite these challenges, Deloitte Touche (2008) have recently argued that one important first step to broader slot trading might be the introduction of a web based transparent trading system that is controlled by a joint EU/US regulator.

An alternative approach has been to introduce slot auctions (Button 2007; Cohen et al. 2009; Sentence 2003). Rather than slot-holders willingly engaging in slot exchanges through secondary trading, a slot auction would formally recirculate a certain percentage of slots each year, thus setting temporal limits on the grandfathered rights of the incumbents. In 2008, the FAA initiated a proposal to auction off 10 per cent of the slots at JFK, LaGuardia and Newark airports but these proposals were met with stiff opposition from the airlines, the Port Authority of New York and New Jersey (the airports operator), and leading politicians. Senator Charles Schumer from New York characterized the proposed auctions as insanity and argued 'auctions have never been tried and were hatched by a handful of ivory-tower types in the administration' (Cohen et al. 2009: 570). In 2009, the Obama administration dropped the plans for auctions in the New York area. Part of the problem is that a single slot is of no practical value since airlines want bundles of slots to complete a return flight for a given city-pair market. According to Button (2007: 303), 'at the minimum they want one take-off slot at the origin of the service and one landing slot at the destination'. The end result is that the first slot auction would need to be a combinatorial auction where participants bid on combinations of slots rather than single slots. A major problem with this approach is the complexity involved in such an initiative. According to Cohen et al. (2009), combinatorial auctions are rare and, even with modern computing, determining the winning bid within a realistic amount of time can be difficult. Another set of concerns revolves around international flights that are largely inflexible given the narrow time window to leave New York for Europe, and vice versa. Any disruption that affects the connecting flights, times and frequencies of international flights might make the route unprofitable. For these reasons, auctions have yet to be implemented on a broad scale at any EU or US airport.

One potential solution may germinate from the 2007 EU–US 'open skies' agreement that removed restrictions on routes rights across the North Atlantic (Button 2009; Humphreys and Morrell 2009). Previously, a series of restrictive aviation bilaterals limited route options across the Atlantic, but under the 'open skies' era any EU airline is now allowed to fly from any EU city to any US city while any US airline can now fly into any EU airport. The end result is that the JFK–Heathrow bottleneck and other congested city-pair markets may be ameliorated as alternative destinations emerge.

The Rest of the World: A Mixed Bag of Liberalization and Protectionism

For all the regulatory innovation across the North Atlantic, much of the rest of the world still clings to relatively restrictive Bermuda I-type aviation bilaterals when negotiating air service agreements. Most of these sorts of aviation markets remain constrained in terms of: 1) the number of different airlines that can enter the market; 2) the number of flights and airline seats offered; and 3) the types of airfares offered to consumers. According to Jomini et al. (2009), approximately 30 per cent of international traffic was governed by a restrictive, first-generation air service agreement in 2005. However, restrictive aviation markets are no longer the norm. The ICAO (2010) estimated that 32 per cent of all country-pairs with non-stop scheduled passenger air services and 57 per cent of the flight frequencies offered worldwide in 2009 operated through either a bilateral 'open skies' agreement or some form of liberalized regional/plurilateral arrangement (compared to just 7 per cent and 32 per cent, respectively, in 1995).

The rapid diffusion of liberalization is partly explained by the healthy increases in passenger traffic after liberalization. A 2006 study by InterVISTAS found that after liberalization, traffic growth typically averaged 12 to 35 per cent above its pre-liberalization levels. Additionally, the elevated levels of competition in liberalized markets tend to put downward pressure on airfares. According to IATA, since the passage of the EU–US 'open skies' accord in 2007, average discount economy fares across the North Atlantic have decreased by 8 per cent in comparison with America's consumer price index.

For these reasons, both bilateral and multilateral liberalization has begun to spread to other parts of the world including EU bilateral liberalization with Morocco and Egypt and moves towards full domestic market liberalization in Australia, India, Thailand, and New Zealand. Some of the most notable examples include various plurilateral regional agreements in the Asia-Pacific region and the Middle East. In 2001, the US brokered the Multilateral Agreement on the Liberalization of International Air Transport (MALIAT) with four other like-minded members of the Asia-Pacific Economic Cooperation (APEC) that included Brunei, Chile, New Zealand, and Singapore. The MALIAT was notable because it granted fifth freedom rights plus the free determination of capacity and tariffs. The overall goal was to broaden its membership but it has failed to attract many new or significant signatories. Other multilateral initiatives included the establishment of a regional 'open skies' agreement between the 10 members of the Association of South East Asian Nations (ASEAN) region. One challenge was reconciling the geopolitics generated by the significant variation in the size of the respective ASEAN member state economies. For example, Laos and Cambodia have very limited aviation markets when compared to the substantive traffic hubs in Brunei and Singapore. As a result, the timetable for reform was to be gradually phased in through 2015 with the goal of providing unrestricted access for airlines of an ASEAN member state to operate flights in the region. Perhaps one of the most embryonic initiatives is the efforts of the Gulf Cooperation Council (GCC) to liberalize air transportation in the Middle East. The Middle East has witnessed significant growth in the aviation industry in recent years and several nations in the GCC have adopted unilateral open skies agreements (including Bahrain, Kuwait, and the United Arab Emirates). Many GCC countries have small home markets and have aggressively sought out major traffic flows through their hubs by negotiating sixth freedom rights with European and Asian countries. These so-called sixth freedom carriers include Emirates Airlines which has successfully attracted a significant amount of European–Asian traffic through its Dubai hub. One major stumbling block has been the largely protectionist stance taken by Saudi

Arabia – the only GCC country with a substantive domestic market. However, all this changed in late 2011 when the Saudi Arabian General Civil Aviation Authority announced that it will be inviting tenders for foreign airline operators and investors to operate flights from Saudi airports. It remains unclear what precise direction this initiative will take, but the ongoing liberalization of one of the fastest growing aviation regions in the world is likely to transform the geopolitics of air transportation.

Conclusion

The transnational nature of air transportation means that any analysis of the geographies of commercial aviation must be inherently grounded in a fundamental understanding of the geopolitics of the global policy frameworks that shape the industry. Although international air transportation can readily transcend boundaries of language and culture, the movement of passengers and cargo by air is not perfectly fluid. Even in an era of rapid globalization, nation-state boundaries can frequently act as impediments to movement since different countries may embrace different regulatory regimes when governing their own national air space. According to Doganis (2010: 63), 'an appreciation of the regulatory environment is fundamental for an understanding both of airline economics and of the reasons why airline operating and marketing decisions sometimes appear to be irrational or even contradictory'.

One theme stressed in this chapter is that the geopolitics of air transportation defies a simple categorization of liberal versus protectionist philosophies because the regulatory regime varies so dramatically from country to country. In the EU, carriers possess a full range of traffic and ownership rights although airports lack capacity and sufficient landing slots. By contrast, the US has a sizable domestic market but is unable to attract substantive foreign capital because of onerous ownership and control regulations. Throughout the rest of the world, the liberalization of aviation markets is spotty and significant parts of Africa and Asia continue to cling to protectionist policies. As the world, and especially the North Atlantic market begins to slowly climb out of the cyclical downturn of 2008/9, one key question is whether or not this accelerates or dampens the geopolitics of liberalization.

References

Adey, P., Whitehead, M. and Williams, A. 2011. Introduction: Air-Target – Distance, Reach and the Politics of Verticality. *Theory, Culture and Society* 27(7–8): 173–187.

Airline Business. 2007. Slot Machines, 23(10): 70–74.

Aviation Week and Space Technology. 2002. EC Vice President Advocates Transatlantic Deregulation, 7(18 February): 47.

Bass, T. 1994. Infrastructure Constraints and the EC. *Journal of Air Transport Management* 1(3): 145–150.

Bolkcom, C. 2006. *Civil Reserve Air Fleet (CRAF).* Congressional Research Service (CRS) Report for Congress. Order Code RL33692, 18 October 2006.

Brueckner, J.K. 2008. Slot-Based Approaches to Airport Congestion Management. *CESifo Working Paper No. 2302.*

Budd, L. 2009. Air Craft: Producing UK Airspace, in Cwerner, S., Kesselring, S. and Urry, J. (eds) *Aeromobilities.* London: Routledge, pp. 115–134.

Butler, D.L. 2001. Technogeopolitics and the Struggle for Control of World Air Routes, 1910–1928. *Political Geography* 20: 635–658.

Butler, G.F. and Keller, M.R. 1994. International Aviation Policies: Is it Time for Change? *Transportation Quarterly* 48(4): 367–380.

Button, K. 1996. Liberalizing European Aviation: Is There an Empty Core Problem? *Journal of Transport Economics and Policy*, September, 275–291.

Button, K. 2007. Auctions – What Can We Learn From Auction Theory for Slot Allocation, in Czerny, A.I., Forsyth, P., Gillen, D. and Niemeier, H. (eds) *Airport Slots: International Experiences and Options for Reform.* London: Ashgate, pp. 291–309.

Button, K. 2009. The Impact of EU–US 'Open Skies' Agreement on Airline Market Structures and Airline Networks. *Journal of Air Transport Management* 15(2): 59–71.

Button, K., Haynes, K. and Stough, R. 1998. *Flying Into the Future: Air Transport Policy in the European Union.* Cheltenham: Edward Elgar.

Cohen, J.P., Coughlin, C.C. and Ott, L.S. 2009. Auctions as a Vehicle to Reduce Airport Delays and Achieve Value Capture. *Federal Reserve Bank of St. Louis Review,* November/December, 569–584.

Cosmas, A., Belobaba, P. and Swelbar, W. 2008. Framing the Discussion on Regulatory Liberalization: A Stakeholder Analysis of Open Skies, Ownership and Control. *MIT International Center for Air Transportation – White Paper.*

Cresswell, T. 2010. Towards a Politics of Mobility. *Environment and Planning D: Society and Space* 28: 17–31.

Czerny, A.I., Forsyth, P., Gillen, D. and Niemeier, H. 2007. *Airport Slots: International Experiences and Options for Reform.* London: Ashgate.

de Murias, R. 1989. *The Economic Regulation of International Air Transport.* London: McFarland and Company.

Debbage, K. 2000. *Air Transportation and International Tourism: The Regulatory and Infrastructural Constraints of Aviation Bilaterals and Airport Landing Slots,* in Robinson, M., Evans, N., Long, P. et al. (eds) *Management, Marketing and the Political Economy of Travel and Tourism.* Gateshead: Business Education Publishers Ltd.

Debbage, K.G. 2002. Airport Runway Slots: Limits to Growth. *Annals of Tourism Research* 29(4): 933–951.

Deloitte Touche. 2008. *Open Skies, Open for Business? Is it Time to Value Slots and Recognise Them on Balance Sheets?* London: Deloitte Touche Ltd.

Dempsey, P.S. 2001. Airport Landing Slots: Barriers to Entry and Impediments to Competition. *Air and Space Law* 26(1): 20–48.

Doganis, R. 2010. *Flying Off Course: Airline Economics and Marketing.* London: Routledge.

Dresner, M. and Tretheway, M.W. 1992. Modelling and Testing the Effects of Market Structure on Price. *Journal of Transport Economics and Policy* 26(2): 171–184.

Duval, D.T. 2008. Regulation, Competition and the Politics of Air Access Across the Pacific. *Journal of Air Transport Management* 14: 237–242.

Duval, D.T. and Macilree, J. 2011. The Political Economy of Trade in International Air Transport Services, in Mosedale, J. (ed.) *Political Economy of Tourism: A Critical Perspective.* London: Routledge, pp. 225–241.

Economist, The. 2011. Runways Required, 28 May, 72.

Fukui, H. 2010. An Empirical Analysis of Airport Slot Trading in the United States. *Transportation Research Part B* 44: 330–357.

Gillen, D. 2007. *Airport Slots: A Primer*, in Czerny, A.I., Forsyth, P., Gillen, D. and Niemeier, H. (eds) *Airport Slots: International Experiences and Options for Reform.* London: Ashgate, pp. 41–59.

Graham, A. 1992. A Conflict of Interests: The European Commission's Proposals for Competition in the Scheduled Airline Industry. *Area* 24(3): 245–252.

Graham, A. 2003. *Managing Airports: An International Perspective.* Oxford: Elsevier.

Graham, S. 2004. Vertical Geopolitics: Baghdad and After. *Antipode* 36: 12–23.

Humphreys, B. and Morrell, P. 2009. The Potential Impacts of the EU/US Open Sky Agreement: What Will Happen at Heathrow after Spring 2008. *Journal of Air Transport Management* 15(2): 72–77.

International Civil Aviation Organisation. 2010. *Overview of Trends and Developments in International Air Transport.* Montreal: ICAO.

Jomini, P., Chai, A., Achard, P. and Rupp, J. 2009. *The Changing Landscape of Air Service Agreements.* Working paper.

Kasper, D.M. 1988. *Deregulation and Globalisation: Liberalising International Trade in Air Services.* Cambridge: American Enterprise Institute.

Levine, M.E. 2009. Airport Congestion: When Theory Meets Reality. *Yale Journal on Regulation* 26(1): 37–88.

Madas, M.A. and Zografos, K.G. 2008. Airport Capacity vs. Demand: Mismatch or Mismanagement? *Transportation Research Part A* 42: 203–226.

Madas, M.A. and Zografos, K.G. 2010. Airport Slot Allocation: A Time for Change? *Transport Policy* 17: 274–285.

Pustay, M.W. 1993. Toward a Global Airline Industry: Prospects and Impediments. *Logistics and Transportation Review* 23(1): 103–128.

Sentence, A. 2003. Airport Slot Auctions: Desirable or Feasible? *Utilities Policy* 11: 53–57.

Shaw, J. and Sidaway, J.S. 2010. Making Links: On (Re)Engaging with Transport and Transport Geography. *Progress in Human Geography* 35(4): 502–520.

Sieg, G. 2010. Grandfather Rights in the Market for Airport Slots. *Transportation Research Part B* 44: 29–37.

UK Civil Aviation Authority 1998. *The Single European Aviation Market: The First Five Years.* CAP 685. London: CAA.

US Civil Aeronautics Board 1978. *CAB Annual Report to Congress.* Washington, DC: US Government Printing Office.

US General Accounting Office 2003. *Issues Relating to Foreign Investment and Control of U.S. Airlines.* Washington, DC: US Government Printing Office.

Wheatcroft, S. 1994. *Aviation and Tourism Policies: Balancing the Benefits.* London: Routledge.

Williams, A.J. 2010. A Crisis in Aerial Sovereignty? Considering the Implications of Recent Military Violations of National Airspace. *Area* 42(1): 51–59.

Williams, A.J. 2011. Reconceptualising Spaces of the Air: Performing the Multiple Spatialities of UK Military Airspaces. *Transactions of the Institute of British Geographers* 36: 253–267.

Williams, A.J. 2013. Re-Orientating Vertical Geopolitics. *Geopolitics* 18: 225–246.

Chapter 3
The Economic Geography of Air Transport

John T. Bowen, Jr

Introduction

Every day, the world's airlines operate more than 80,000 commercial flights, which together trace the economic geography of a world in motion. Some features of that geography are long-standing. Nearly 60 per cent of all flights in 2012 departed from a North American or European airport, continuing the domination of the regions in which civil aviation first emerged a century ago. The busiest metropolitan areas, ranked by total scheduled seats per week, remain the familiar triumvirate of London, New York, and Tokyo,[1] Sassen's (2001) celebrated 'global cities'. And the world's top airline (again ranked by capacity) was Delta Air Lines, perpetuating the stature of US carriers atop the rankings. In air transportation, as in other features of economic geography, there is considerable inertia.

And yet, aviation, more than any ground transport mode, is fluid and the geography of the airline industry in the early twenty-first century is as much about change as stasis. Few regions better illustrate the dynamism of air transportation than the Persian/Arabian Gulf. The region's three so-called 'super-connectors' – Emirates, Etihad, and Qatar Airways – each of which already had a presence in six continents, added dozens of new destinations in 2012 alone: from Maputo, Tbilisi, and Yangon for Qatar Airways to Buenos Aires, Seattle, and Dublin for Emirates. Yet the expansion of aviation is hardly limited to a single region. Emerging markets in Asia, Africa, and Latin America have all witnessed the rapid proliferation of new services and the growth of existing ones. The overall result has been the kinetic realignment of global aviation as traditional patterns of core and periphery are eroded.

This chapter is about the economic geography of air transportation – both the features which persist and those that are new. Later chapters in this volume examine individual regions so here the focus is on the global scale. Four features of the spatial organization of aviation will be highlighted in the sections that follow. First, the relative importance of air transportation is correlated with economic development and the result is striking inequality in air accessibility; however, the recent success of emerging markets has fostered a degree of convergence between the 'aeromobility' (Adey et al. 2007) of high-income and middle-income economies. Second, the geography of the air passenger industry has been affected by two main phenomena over the past few decades: the rise of low-cost carriers (LCCs) and the consolidation of the three main global airline alliances (Star, oneworld, and SkyTeam). Third, although about 40 per cent of air cargo is carried in the bellies of passenger aircraft (Boeing 2012), the importance of freighter aircraft has helped to separate the geographies of air cargo and air passenger flows. Finally, the economic geography of aviation is shaped by

---

1 In 2012, the total passenger capacity figures in these three metropolitan areas were: London (5 airports), 1.6 million seats per week; New York City (6 airports), 1.4 million seats per week; and Tokyo (2 airports), 1.2 million seats per week (OAG 2012).

the technical specifications of contemporary airliners, but simultaneously acts as influence upon future technologies. Given the fluidity of aviation and the durability of jetliners, it is likely that decades from now, aircraft currently on the drawing board will carry passengers and cargo over networks further transformed by the forces discussed in this chapter.

Before proceeding, a note about the methodology used in this chapter is in order. Many of the analyses that follow are based on schedules data from the Official Airline Guide (OAG), a digital compilation of schedules for almost all of the world's airlines. OAG data represent a rich resource for mapping the topography of the global economy. The data used here come from 1998 and 2012 and, it should be noted, require considerable processing (e.g. in SPSS) to yield the analyses reported below.

Aviation and Economic Development

The Boeing 787, among the newest jetliners flying at the time this chapter was written, made its maiden commercial voyage on a route linking Tokyo and Hong Kong in October 2011. That made it the first of Boeing's famed series of jetliners not to debut on a route commencing in the United States or Europe (Bowen 2010) and so the flight was a small measure of Asia's ascent as one of the world's leading economic regions. In fact, almost all Dreamliner flights in its first year of operations began or ended in Japan, home to the two launch carriers for the new jet: ANA and Japan Airlines. The third carrier to fly the 787 received less attention, but the addition of the plane to Ethiopian Airlines' growing fleet in August 2012 was symbolic, too. Ethiopian is among Africa's most ambitious carriers (*Economist* 2012). The airline industry across much of that region and other emerging markets has grown in tandem with economic development.

The relationship between economic development on the one hand and the relative size of the aviation sector on the other is demonstrated in Figure 3.1, which displays these two variables for the 15 largest economies of the world in 2012 (closed diamonds) and, for comparison, the comparable information for the same countries in 1998 (open diamonds). For both years, there is a clear pattern with greater airline capacity per capita in more developed countries. This relationship is driven by the two of the principal sources of aviation passenger demand: tourist traffic and business traffic. In the US in particular over 50 per cent of airline trips are undertaken for leisure or holiday purposes (US BTS, 2006), an emphasis also evident in air traffic between Australia and the rest of the Asia-Pacific region (O'Connor and Fuellhart, this volume), and in surveys of budget airline passengers in Ireland and Malaysia (O'Connell and Williams 2005). Inasmuch as leisure travel is strongly dependent upon disposable income, its growth with economic development is unsurprising. More complex are the myriad connections between business travel and economic development. Business air travel facilitates the spatial division of labour and is strongly associated with the so-called knowledge economy (Debbage 1999; Debbage and Delk 2001; Button and Taylor 2000). International air travel, more specifically, has been found to foster higher levels of trade and to ameliorate language differences and other border effects (Poole 2010). Through such linkages, air travel not only expands with development but also contributes to further development.

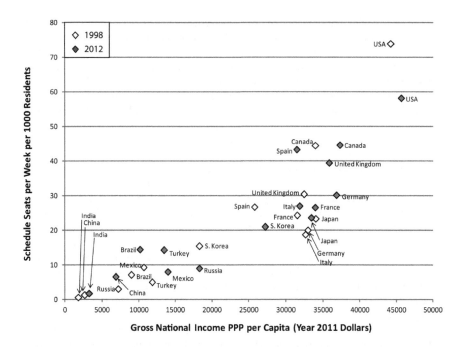

Figure 3.1   Economic development and scheduled airline seat capacity, 1998 and 2012

Note: For the 15 largest economies, economic development is measured in gross national income per capita adjusted for purchasing power parity in 2011 and 1998. The data for 1998 have been adjusted for inflation to facilitate comparison. Airline capacity for the same countries is measured in total scheduled seats per week per 1,000 residents for one week each in early 1998 and 2012.

Sources: OAG 1998 and OAG 2012; World Bank 2012.

Indeed, Figure 3.1 suggests that beyond some threshold income level, per capita airline capacity increases exponentially.[2] Today, the majority of developing countries are well below that threshold, but the speed of economic growth suggests that many will cross it in the decades ahead with daunting ramifications for the air transport sector, for those who live near airports, and for the world more generally given the growing share of greenhouse gas emissions attributable to aviation. Between the two sample years, most countries moved up and to the right in the figure. The best-known emerging markets – the famed BRICs – were among the biggest movers in the graph. Per capita seat capacity grew fivefold in China, threefold in India and Russia, and doubled in Brazil. Interestingly, several African economies – far outside the ranks of the top 15 economies shown in Figure 3.1 – staged even more impressive air traffic growth; per capita seat capacity grew by at least a factor of five in Nigeria, Burundi, Ghana, and Sierra Leone.

---

2   A similar conclusion can be drawn when data for a much larger sample of countries is graphed. See Bowen (2013).

The growth of air transportation in many (but certainly not all) developing countries has begun to change the isolation of Sub-Saharan Africa and other impoverished regions in the global airline industry. Earlier studies (Bowen 2002; Zook and Brunn 2006) highlighted that isolation, and with regard to Africa, in particular, the paucity of air services has been one element in what Naudé (2009) termed the continent's 'proximity gap' impeding economic development. For instance, the 38 African countries which lie between the Tropic of Cancer and the Tropic of Capricorn had a combined population of 748 million in 2012 but about as many seats per week combined on scheduled air services as Turkey (75 million people) alone (OAG Max data 2012; PRB 2012). Weak air accessibility means weak access to distant markets, capital, and tourists.

Of particular concern in Africa is the lack of connections among countries within the region, hampering the development of larger markets and economies of scale. Ethiopian Airlines, for instance, has grown very rapidly over the past decade, and as noted above its fleet now includes the innovative 787; but optimism about the carrier's future growth is tempered by the limited traffic feed it draws from Ethiopia's hostile neighbours (*Economist* 2012); in 2012, there were fewer than a dozen flights per day from Ethiopia (a country of 87 million people) to its six bordering countries combined (OAG 2012). A similarly emaciated regional network is found in Central Asia, which is encumbered by its own 'proximity gap'. Tajikistan, for instance, was linked by nonstop flights to just three of the other '-stans' in 2012, having no flights at all to neighbouring Uzbekistan and nearby Turkmenistan.

At the opposite end of the spectrum are the small countries that have thrived as air traffic hubs with good intermediacy (Fleming and Hayuth 1994) among major world regions or as tourist havens and have levels of air service that are off the scale in Figure 3.1, including Singapore (123 seats per 1,000 people), the United Arab Emirates (183), and the Bahamas (236). The cases of Singapore and the UAE are particularly important because their success has exerted a demonstration effect on developing countries, including China (Francis 2004), that want to exploit aviation for their own development. Both Singapore and the UAE (especially Dubai) have successfully attracted tourist flows, manufacturing investment, regional and global headquarters, and logistics and distribution centres based on their accessibility in international airline networks (Bowen 2000; Lohmann et al. 2009).

Ultimately, the flows of people, goods, money, information, and ideas through major airline hubs augment not only these cities' wealth but also their power in the global economy. A number of authors, therefore, have used airline network accessibility as a measure of stature in the world-city system (Cattan 1995; Shin and Timberlake 2000; Smith and Timberlake 2001; Matsumoto 2004; Lee 2009; Mahutga et al. 2010). The results of such studies tend to confirm the dominance of the leading business and financial centres. There are, it should be noted, significant methodological problems with the use of airline data for this purpose (Derudder and Witlox 2008), especially the lack of data showing true origin-destination flows instead of traffic by flight segment.[3] Nevertheless, aviation data remain attractive in studies of urban networks because they permit a granular analysis of the flows among cities across the world and because the traffic that comprises those flows – especially business traffic – is redolent of power.

---

3   For instance, it is usually impossible to determine the volume of traffic or capacity between, say, Sydney and London since a stop between the two cities is required. This limitation tends to inflate the apparent importance of intermediate hubs such as Singapore and Dubai and reduce that of cities caught in the shadows of such hubs (e.g. Jakarta).

Cities at the top of the global hierarchy are distinguished not only by their accessibility but also by the quality of airline services as O'Connor and Fuelhart (2012) report. Using the categories of the Globalization and World Cities (GaWC) Research Network at Loughborough University (see www.lboro.ac.u/gawc/group.html), they compared services at 41 'alpha' cities (e.g. New York, Singapore), 40 'beta' cities (e.g. Hamburg, Dubai), and 45 'gamma' cities (e.g. Calcutta, Ho Chi Minh City). Alpha cities were characterized by disproportionately abundant services by low cost carriers (LCCs) and the carrier alliances, meaning that these metro areas have the best of both worlds: the low-cost, high frequency services to short- and medium-haul destinations characteristic of LCCs and the integrated services to global business destinations prioritized by the alliances. O'Connor and Fuellhart's analyses point to the importance of putting carriers in the foreground of any analysis of air services and so it is to the world's airlines that this chapter now turns.

The Spatial Structure of Air Passenger Services

Qantas, the Australian flag carrier, has one of the global airline industry's most familiar liveries; yet its red-and-white kangaroo bedecked airplanes visit surprisingly few foreign markets. In 2012, the carrier's network extended to just 22 international destinations, down from 30 in 1998. The limited extent and recent contraction of the Qantas network is at first surprising given the carrier's position as one of the largest airline enterprises in the world (Table 3.1), particularly in an era of globalization. Yet the reach of Qantas goes well beyond the routes flown by its own jets. First, Qantas is only one of the two main airline brands in the Qantas Group; the other is Jetstar, an LCC created in 2003. By 2012, Jetstar's revenue was equal to about one-third that of the core passenger business of Qantas (Qantas 2012). Second, Qantas is a member of oneworld, one of the three principal passenger airline alliances, the primary purpose of which is to mesh individual airline networks into globe-encircling systems feeding traffic from one carrier to another. Interestingly, one of the few foreign destinations *added* to Qantas' downsized foreign network between 1998 and 2012 was Dallas-Fort Worth, a primary hub for oneworld partner American Airlines. Alliances and low-cost carriers are two of the most prominent features of the contemporary airline industry and are discussed later in this section, but first a still more important feature of the industry is examined: the hub-and-spoke network.

Network Economies: The Elaboration of Airline Hub-and-Spoke Systems

The airline industry is characterized by relatively low market concentration. In 2011, the top 15 airline entities (some of which, like Qantas Group, combine multiple carriers) had a combined global market share of 46 per cent (Table 3.1); the comparable measure in 1998 was 54 per cent (based on analysis of *Air Transport World* 1999). The decline is partly attributable to the flowering of the LCC phenomenon. Yet almost all of the largest carriers in the world remain full-service network carriers, a class of airline defined by multiple on-board service classes including premium cabins; a mixture of short, medium, and long-haul services; and strongly centralized hub-and-spoke networks.

Partly because of such networks' importance, there is a substantial body of work in geography in which graph theoretic measures are used to summarize airline network

Table 3.1   Top 15 airlines by passenger-kilometres, 2011

Rank (1998)	Airline enterprise	Alliance	Revenue passenger-kilometres (billions)	Market share (%)	Number of world's 100 most populous metropolitan areas served
1 (3)	Delta Air Lines	SkyTeam	310	6.1	44
2 (1)	United Airlines	Star Alliance	294	5.8	33
3 (8 and 13)	Air France/KLM	SkyTeam	217	4.3	55
4 (2)	American Airlines	oneworld	203	4.0	36
5 (4 and 25)	IAG Group	oneworld	169	3.3	48
6 (15)	Southwest Airlines	None	167	3.3	12
7 (48)	Emirates Airline	None	153	3.0	50
8 (9)	Lufthansa	Star Alliance	141	2.8	55
9 (35)	China Southern	SkyTeam	108	2.1	40
10 (11)	Qantas Group	oneworld	102	2.0	16
11 (16)	Cathay Pacific	oneworld	102	2.0	28
12 (10)	US Airways	Star Alliance	98	1.9	20
13 (42)	Air China	Star Alliance	93	1.8	44
14 (12)	Singapore Airlines	Star Alliance	87	1.7	38
15 (18)	Air Canada	Star Alliance	84	1.7	28
Top 15			2,327	46.0	
All airlines			5,062	100.0	

Note: The IAG Group includes British Airways and Iberia.
Source: Air Transport World 1999; Air Transport World 2012; ICAO 2012.

characteristics (Taaffe, Gauthier, and O'Kelly 1996). For example, the beta[4] and gamma[5] indices for Delta Air Lines were 2.5 and 0.015 respectively, indicating few edges (nonstop routes) in relation to the number of vertices (cities served). Further, the majority of airports in the Delta network had a degree[6] of 1, 2, or 3; these are the 'spoke' cities connected to one or more of the carrier's hubs. The hubs, of course, are distinguished by a high degree: Atlanta, 209 (out of 333 other cities served); Minneapolis-St Paul (a hub acquired through Delta's merger with Northwest), 135; Detroit (another former Northwest hub), 134; Salt Lake City, 84; and Memphis (the smallest of the old Northwest hubs), 58. As a point of comparison, the corresponding figures for Emirates, leader among the Gulf super-connectors were: beta index, 2.24; gamma index, 0.039; and highest degree node, Dubai at 100 out of 107 other cities served (Analysis of OAG 2012 data).

4   The beta index is the ratio of edges (nonstop routes) to vertices (airports) and will be low in a network such as Delta's with many airports connected by a handful of hubs.
5   The gamma index measures the ratio between the actual number of edges (nonstop routes) and the maximum number possible if every vertex were linked to every other vertex by an edge. Delta's index is that of a very sparse network.
6   The degree is the number of other vertices in a network to which a vertex is connected by a single edge each (i.e. the number of nonstop destinations).

The advantages of hub-and-spoke networks include economies of density and economies of scope. Economies of density refer to the lower per passenger or per ton cost of serving a link when traffic with multiple origins or destinations is bundled at the hub; bundling allows some combination of more frequent service (which can be advantageous in gaining market share) or service with larger aircraft (which typically have lower unit costs). Economies of scope describe the ability of a hubbing carrier to efficiently compete in many more city-pair markets than would be possible without such concentrated connections. For instance, the linkage of a single new city to Delta's Atlanta hub opens up hundreds of new one-stop city-pairs.

Economies of density and scope help to account for the long-term expansion of airline networks via mergers (e.g. Delta's merger with Western Air Lines in 1987 and Northwest Airlines in 2010), acquisitions (e.g. Delta's purchase of much of Pan Am's transatlantic network in 1991), and organic growth. In the case of Delta, these varied sources of growth have powered its expansion from an 81-city network that had little reach beyond the eastern and southern US on the eve of deregulation in 1978 to a 334-city network stretching to six continents.

For the hubs at the centre of such networks, positionality brings both privileges and perils. On the one hand, a hub enjoys inherently superior accessibility and numerous studies have documented the ensuing economic advantages (e.g. Hakfoort et al. 2001; Kasarda and Lindsay 2011). On the other hand, a hub-and-spoke network confers significant market power to a carrier in its hub(s). For instance, Delta Air Lines and its regional affiliates accounted for 77 per cent of seat capacity from Atlanta in early 2012 (OAG 2012). Such 'fortress hubs' have been associated with artificially high fares (Goetz 2002), a 'peril' that mitigates to some degree the many development benefits that hubs enjoy. Further, smaller hubs are vulnerable to the cutbacks that accompany shifts in airline strategy, especially following mergers. Northwest's former hub in Memphis, for instance, has lost many spokes since the airline's merger with Delta (Russell 2012). Delta severed Memphis' only transatlantic nonstop, a four times per week service to Amsterdam. Consolidation and capacity discipline on both sides of the Atlantic has triggered a similar breaking of so-called 'pencil routes', funnelling more traffic via major hubs such as Atlanta (Russell 2012).

The shift of services from small to large hubs has reinforced the significance of hub-and-spoke networks. While it is true that in some markets, the past decade has seen a rapid proliferation of point-to-point routes bypassing traditional hubs, the largest hubs remain reasonably secure in their dominance of global traffic flows. In 2012, 84 per cent of seat capacity was on flights that began or ended in one of the 100 busiest passenger hubs; in 1998, the comparable proportion was only marginally higher at 85 per cent (OAG 1998; OAG 2012). The world had never been as well integrated by air services as it was in 2012, but that integration was premised on connections via well-situated hubs.

Airline Alliances

Even with Delta's expansion, the carrier's network – especially outside the US – is far from pervasive. Of the 100 most populous metropolitan areas in the world, for instance, Delta served only 44 in 2012 (see last column of Table 3.1) – lacking a direct presence in such major cities as Dhaka, Melbourne, Nairobi, Jakarta, and Guangzhou. The limitations of the Delta network are partly related to incomplete liberalization, yet even where Delta as an American carrier enjoys the relevant traffic rights, there is often too little commercial traffic to warrant scheduled services. The same is true for other carriers. For instance, Uganda is among the dozens of countries with which the US has an Open Skies agreement (see US Department of State 2013), thereby opening the market between the two countries to any Ugandan or American carrier, including Delta; yet no US airline serves the country. Airline alliances, however, allow carriers to expand their presence where regulatory barriers and/or limited market size impede expansion. Several of Delta Air Lines' partners in the SkyTeam alliance, for instance, do fly to Uganda.

SkyTeam is one of the three main airline alliances, along with the Star Alliance and oneworld. In early 2012, the numbers of carriers in these three alliances were 15, 25, and 10, respectively. Each provided service to cities worldwide, including most of the world's 100 largest metropolitan areas: SkyTeam (84 of the 100); Star Alliance (95); and oneworld (69). And it is not just in the largest cities that the alliances matter. In early 2012, the three alliances combined accounted for 40 per cent of global seat capacity (OAG 2012). Across the world's major regions, the alliances' combined share ranged from 13 per cent in the Middle East and North Africa to 56 per cent in North America (Table 3.2).

The alliances emerged as an important feature of the airline industry during a time when economic globalization accelerated, making easy travel on a global scale more important – especially for high-yielding business traffic. The alliances also materialized at virtually the same time that low-cost carriers (LCCs) took off in developed markets, capturing much of the industry's leisure traffic and forcing the full service network carriers to depend more heavily on business traffic. Alliances are aimed squarely at high frequency business travellers. Alliance members synthesize their networks via integrated frequent flyer programs, code-sharing,[7] and schedule meshing – all facilitated by antitrust immunity (ATI) in some key markets (e.g. several SkyTeam carriers enjoy ATI over the transatlantic – Keiner et al. 2009).

Following tentative developments in the late 1980s (e.g. equity cross-investments and marketing agreements between KLM and Northwest Airlines and among Delta Air Lines, Singapore Airlines, and Swissair), today's trio of big alliances began to take shape in the 1990s, and have grown fairly steadily since then. For instance, Ethiopian Airlines is among the newest members of the Star Alliance. As Table 3.1 indicates, among the largest 15 airline enterprises in 2011, only Southwest Airlines (first among the LCCs, for whom alliance membership holds little appeal) and Emirates have so far failed to join an alliance.

I turn to the LCCs below, but first a note about Emirates. The rapid expansion of the super-connector's network has given it a global reach – especially in developing regions – almost unmatched by any other single airline (see last column of Table 3.1). Accordingly, Emirates does not need alliance membership in the way that more regionally circumscribed network carriers do. At the same time, concerns about unfair competition by Emirates has made it unwelcome in many quarters. For instance, Lufthansa – a founding member of the Star Alliance – has shunned the Gulf carriers (Thomas and Dunn 2012).

In late 2012, Qatar Airways agreed to become a member of oneworld, but Etihad and Emirates remain apart. Yet both carriers (and many others outside the big three alliances) have diverse partnerships with individual carriers. Emirates' most important relationship

---

7   Code-sharing refers to the practice of applying an airline's code (e.g., 'QF' for Qantas) to a flight operated by a partner airline so that in computer reservations systems, the flight appears to be part of the code-sharing carrier's network. For instance, Qantas code-shares on dozens of domestic flights in the US (e.g. QF 4429 from Dallas to Oklahoma City), especially to and from American Airlines' hubs in Dallas-Ft Worth and Chicago.

Table 3.2   Alliances' and low-cost carriers' share of scheduled seat capacity, 2012

Region	Weekly seat capacity	Share of seat capacity				
		Star Alliance*	oneworld*	SkyTeam*	Three Alliances	LCCs
South, East & Southeast Asia	22,413,853	15.1	6.8	20.2	42.0	19.1
North America	18,912,817	24.7	13.2	18.2	56.1	28.2
Europe	17,561,362	15.2	9.7	8.3	33.1	30.6
Latin America & the Caribbean	6,798,062	2.4	12.8	5.8	21.0	28.7
Southwest Asia & North Africa	3,966,452	8.4	3.3	1.4	13.1	11.6
Southwest Pacific	2,334,916	15.8	31.0	2.3	49.1	15.0
Sub-Saharan Africa	1,660,580	24.7	5.2	9.3	39.2	8.0
World	73,648,042	16.3	10.2	13.7	40.2	24.3

Note: * Includes only main member airlines, not regional affiliates (e.g. Singapore Airlines is included in the Star Alliance but not the smaller carriers in which SIA has a stake such as regional carrier Silkair).
Source: OAG 2012.

is with Qantas (Thomas and Dunn 2012). In 2012, the two carriers formed a new 10-year partnership intended to mesh their networks at Dubai. The deal was a response to the erosion of market share which Qantas and British Airways (BA), the two main carriers at either end of the Kangaroo Route, suffered at the hands of carriers based in Southeast Asia and the Middle East. The new Qantas–Emirates tie-up gave Qantas one-stop access to destinations across Europe (e.g., Sydney–Dubai–Munich via the new linkup instead of Sydney–Singapore–London–Munich in Qantas' earlier arrangement with BA) and gave Emirates traffic feed from across the Southwest Pacific. Together, the two carriers encircle the globe, reflecting the inexorable tendency of airline networks to expand. Domestically, that drive has been expressed most often via organic growth, mergers, and acquisitions; but in international markets, alliances and strategic partnerships have provided a more flexible path towards the same direction (see Chapter 13 for more information about Emirates).

Low Cost Carriers

Low cost carriers (LCCs) accounted for just under a quarter of global scheduled air passenger capacity in early 2012, a remarkable achievement for a group of carriers that barely existed in the early 1980s. This estimate is based on the combined capacity of 120 airlines identified as low-cost carriers, budget airlines, etc. in trade journal coverage of the airline industry and in the carriers' own media.[8] The great majority of low-cost carriers

---

8   I have followed the approach described in Bowen (2010, Chapter 7) but updated the list developed then to account for subsequent market entrants and exits.

are very small, a reflection of their newness. The 10 largest[9] by seat capacity (Southwest Airlines – USA, Ryanair – Ireland, easyJet – UK, Gol – Brazil, Lion Air – Indonesia, JetBlue – USA, AirTran – USA, AirAsia – Malaysia, Norwegian Air Shuttle – Norway, and Westjet – Canada) offered more seats per week in early 2012 than all the other airlines in this group combined (OAG 2012).

The largest of the LCCs and in many ways the most influential is Southwest Airlines. As is now well-known, Southwest began in the early 1970s as an intra-Texas carrier (Bowen 2010). It rapidly gained market share over the Texas Triangle linking Houston, Dallas-Ft Worth, and San Antonio, where it was free from the regulatory strictures imposed on interstate (and international) carriers. The deregulation of US air passenger services in 1978 freed Southwest to expand into other states, which it began to do in a methodical fashion. In the decades since, the 'Southwest Effect' – the reduction in fares that accompanies the carrier's entrance in a new market – has spread across most of the United States (Vowles 2001; Morrison 2001).

Key elements of Southwest's strategy have been duplicated in markets across much of the world: a light-hearted approach to (minimal) in-flight services, very high frequency services (and therefore economies of density), a predilection for lower cost secondary airports (e.g. Midway Airport in Chicago instead of O'Hare International), services with very few aircraft types (in Southwest's case, several versions of the Boeing 737), and somewhat less reliance on traditional hubbing. With regard to the latter, the beta and gamma indices for the Southwest 72-city network in 2012 were 6.6 and 0.187, respectively. These values are still far from those of a true point-to-point network[10] but do reflect the much smaller dependence on hub connections in the Southwest network versus that of a carrier like Delta.

The LCC has become the favoured model for new entrants across much of the world since the early 1990s. LCCs have taken a wide variety of forms (Gábor 2010); in other words, few are direct copies of Southwest. One way in which they differ is in the source of start-up funds. Capital for the new carriers has come from private equity sources, stock markets, and the full-service network carriers. Many of the latter have launched LCC subsidiaries, including the aforementioned case of Jetstar, a subsidiary of Qantas. Jetstar further illustrates the franchising that some successful LCCs have pursued. The Jetstar family includes affiliates based in Singapore, Vietnam, and Japan, with a Hong Kong offshoot in development at the time this chapter was written (Jetstar 2013). AirAsia and the Virgin Group are other enterprises that have employed franchising to enter new markets. This mode of market entry is especially attractive where regulatory barriers (such as national protection of flag carriers and, in the US, policies limiting foreign ownership of airlines) make other forms of entry difficult or impossible (Denton and Dennis 2000).

The long history of the LCCs in North America and Europe, the greater abundance of capital and consumer spending power in these markets, and their more extensive liberalization go far to account for the strength of the American and European budget carriers. LCCs accounted for 28 per cent and 31 per cent of seat capacity in North America and Europe, respectively (OAG 2012). Their share in Latin America and Asia (especially

---

9 In earlier analyses (Bowen 2010), Air Berlin and Virgin Australia were identified as being among the largest LCCs, but both carriers have evolved in ways that make them more like network carriers.

10 In a perfect point-to-point network, the values for Southwest would be: beta index, 71 and gamma index, 1.00.

Southeast Asia) was also impressive (Table 3.2). The corresponding figures for some individual countries are even higher. For example, in Indonesia, LCCs had a combined 64 per cent share of capacity in early 2012 (OAG 2012). Conversely, LCCs have barely gotten off the ground in mainland China where their share was a paltry 5 per cent (OAG 2012), reflecting continued protection of China's large state-owned full service network carriers (Wassener 2012).

In more developed markets, conversely, the LCCs face a dilemma. On the one hand, there are fewer untapped short-haul markets in which the budget airlines can expand, and on the other hand, full-service network carriers have slashed capacity and costs becoming more formidable competitors especially on mid- to long haul routes. In response, LCCs have sought more business traffic and have expanded into longer-haul markets (Francis et al. 2007). These are both more lucrative but also more costly markets to serve. Accordingly, in the US, the gap in revenue per available seat-mile (ASM) and the gap in cost per ASM between the LCCs and the full service network carriers are both smaller than ever before[11] (Hazel, Stalnaker and Taylor 2012).

The Spatial Structure of Air Cargo Services

While low-cost carriers and full service network carriers converge along some dimensions, the larger air passenger and air cargo businesses are diverging. As evidence of the latter proposition, consider the Dixie Jet. Several times a week, a 747 freighter flies nonstop from Huntsville International Airport in Alabama to Luxembourg. The jet sports the livery of Swiss freight forwarder Panalpina and is owned and flown by the American carrier Atlas Air. The same two companies also offer frequent freighter services between Huntsville and Houston, Mexico City, London's Stansted Airport, and Hong Kong (Banham 1995; *Journal of Commerce* 2011). Panalpina's Dixie Jet, as these services via the Huntsville hub are collectively known, has given Huntsville (metropolitan population 417,000) a level of international connectivity very few cities of its size can rival.

The Dixie Jet service exemplifies two distinctive spatial features of air cargo services. First, air cargo flows are more strongly localized than air passenger flows. Northern Alabama made sense to Panalpina decades ago because the economy of the surrounding region featured automotives, pharmaceuticals, and other sectors with a strong propensity to use air cargo based on rapid product cycles and high value-to-weight ratios (Bowen 2012). Second, air cargo networks are, to a limited degree, separate from air passenger networks. Huntsville, for instance, ranks 144th among US cities in terms of air passenger traffic but 43rd in terms of air cargo traffic (BTS 2013).

There are significant disparities between the global geography of the 30 busiest air cargo hubs and the 30 busiest air passenger hubs (Figure 3.2). Air passenger traffic, especially in economy class, is chiefly a form of consumption and rises with the growth of the middle class virtually anywhere. Air cargo traffic conversely is related to production and is dominated by specific, high value-to-weight goods – especially electronics and perishables – whose output is geographically concentrated. Low-cost airfreight has facilitated the concentration of those industries by permitting a new scale of production and distribution.

---

11 In 2011, the cost per domestic ASM for US network carriers was 13.7¢ versus 12.2¢ for LCCs. Revenue per domestic ASM for the two categories was 13.6 and 12.8, respectively (Hazel, Stalnaker and Taylor 2012).

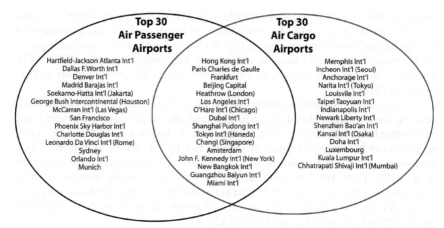

**Figure 3.2   Distribution of top 30 airports for air passenger and
air cargo traffic, 2011**

Note: While sixteen airports ranked among the top 30 for both air passenger and air cargo flows, the remaining airports shown in figure (e.g. Sydney and Anchorage) highlight the divergence between the spatial distributions of these two forms of air traffic. The positions of airports within the figure reflect their rankings. Atlanta had the highest volume of passenger traffic among airports not ranked highly in cargo flows (in fact, Atlanta's airport ranked first among all airports in passenger traffic), Memphis ranked first in cargo flows among airports not highly ranked in passenger flows, and Hong Kong had the best combined ranking (11th in passengers and 1st in cargo).

Source: ACI 2011a; ACI 2011b.

Nevertheless, the geographies of air passenger and air cargo flows are not entirely dissimilar. In fact, about 40 per cent of air cargo revenue tonne-kilometres are performed in the bellyholds of passenger aircraft (Boeing 2012). Freighters are the industry's workhorses on heavily trafficked trunk routes, but passenger jets are crucial in providing traffic feed to hubs and in supplementing freighters on capacity-constrained routes. It is unsurprising therefore that so-called combination carriers which provide both passenger and cargo services dominate the rankings of the world's leading air cargo carriers (Table 3.3).

The long-term trend has been for freighters to become increasingly important, especially on routes to, from, and within Asia (Bowen 2004). The growth of air cargo over the busiest trade corridors, such as Asia–North America, justifies more capacity than bellyholds alone can supply. To put passenger and freighter aircraft into perspective, a Boeing 747–400 passenger aircraft has a typical capacity of just over 400 passengers and about 15 tonnes of cargo; as a pure freighter, the airplane (with a strengthened main deck, a nose door, and other alterations) has a capacity of 110 tonnes of cargo. Moreover, freighters permit air cargo carriers to give cargo first priority (an important concern in an era of time-based competition), to go where the cargo is regardless of air passenger demand, and to fly at times that make most sense for cargo shippers (i.e. late at night after the production day has ended). The geographic freedom conferred by freighters also permits airlines to route traffic via uncongested, relatively lower cost hubs. For instance, the main United Parcel Service (UPS) hubs include Louisville in the United States,

Table 3.3   Top 15 airlines by freight tonne-kilometres, 2011

Rank (1998)	Airline enterprise	Airline type**	Revenue tonne-kilometres (millions)	Market share (%)	Operating fleet*** Combination aircraft	Freighters
1 (1)	FedEx	I	15,104	7.4	0	359
2 (6 & 9)	Air France/KLM	C	11,294	5.4	352	6
3 (3)	UPS Airlines	I	10,910	5.3	0	215
4 (11)	Cathay Pacific	C	9,648	4.7	99	24
5 (2)	Lufthansa	C	9,487	4.6	281	18
6 (4)	Korean Air	C	9,474	4.6	107	24
7 (39)	Emirates Airline	C	8,132	4.0	144	10
8 (5)	Singapore Airlines	C	7,174	3.5	109	11
9 (8 & 40)	IAG Group*	C	6,156	3.0	335	0
10 (12)	China Airlines	C	5,670	2.8	48	19
11 (13)	Cargolux	A	5,039	2.5	0	16
12 (14)	EVA Air (Taiwan)	C	4,883	2.4	46	9
13 (114)	Atlas Air (USA)	A	4,681	2.3	0	15
14 (34)	Air China	C	4,415	2.2	262	9
15 (33)	LAN Airlines (Chile)	C	3,612	1.8	63	4
Top 15			115,679	56.6		
All airlines			202,400	100.0		

Note: * The IAG Group includes British Airways and Iberia; ** Airline types: A = all-freight airport-to-airport carrier; C = combination carrier; I = integrator. See text for explanation; *** Where appropriate, the fleet size figures include both the main airline and the cargo subsidiary of the same parent company (e.g., Singapore Airlines and Singapore Airlines Cargo).
Source: Air Transport World 1999; Air Transport World 2012; Air Transport World 2011; Boeing 2012.

Cologne in Europe, and Shenzhen in Asia although the carrier also has a major presence at Philadelphia, Miami, and Shanghai (Bowen 2012).

As Table 3.3 indicates, the air cargo industry comprises three sorts of airlines: combination carriers such as Air France/KLM that move both passengers and freight; airport-to-airport all-freight carriers such as Panalpina's Dixie Jet partner Atlas Airlines; and the integrators, especially FedEx, UPS, and DHL. The integrators, which provide integrated high-speed air and ground services, emerged as important factors in the air cargo business beginning in the late 1970s and have since established global networks (Bowen 2012).

The factors that have propelled the integrators into household names across much of the world are similar to the forces fuelling the growth of air cargo more generally, including the turn towards time-based competition in many industries, the spatial disaggregation of product networks, and the trend towards higher value-to-weight ratios in manufactured goods. In many markets, air cargo was deregulated earlier and more aggressively than the more politically sensitive air passenger business, helping to foster dynamism and market responsiveness. By 2012, global air cargo revenue represented about 15 per cent of total air transport revenue (Boeing 2012).

The forces that have buoyed air cargo volumes remain at work, but growth has slowed considerably since about 2004. Revenue tonne-kilometres grew about 6.7 per cent per year between 1981 and 2004 but only about 2.0 per cent per year between 2004 and 2012 (Boeing 2012). The global economic slowdown and higher fuel prices are among the key reasons but the air cargo industry also faces renewed competition from surface modes. In both the US and European Union, trucking provides a cost competitive alternative for time-definite services. And in intercontinental markets, technological improvements in containerized ocean freight including improved track-and-trace capabilities have eroded the advantages of airfreight for some products. Improved supply chain visibility generally reduces the need for the urgency air cargo provides (Boeing 2012). Perhaps the newest threat to the air cargo industry is the recent modest trend towards 'onshoring' as some formerly offshore work returns to the US and Europe (*Economist* 2013). Among the main reasons some firms are turning away from offshore production are the increasingly high cost of labour in developing countries, the disadvantages of separating production and research, and – of particular relevance here – the expense in both time and money of intercontinental transportation. Air cargo carriers have provided a means of attaining speed-to-market in global production networks but at a substantial expense. Air transportation has come remarkably far in its first century, but it remains a high cost mode.

Technology and the Future Economic Geography of Air Transportation

The future competitiveness of aviation, like its past performance, will be determined to a considerable degree by advances in airframe, aircraft engine, and air traffic control technology. Consider this: between 1998 and 2010, the real price of oil rose more than 400 per cent; yet despite that increase, over the same period global air passenger-kilometres and freight tonne-kilometres grew 69 per cent and 67 per cent, respectively (ICAO 1999; ICAO 2012; Energy Information Administration 2012). The expansion of aviation (an inherently energy-intensive mode) in defiance of the upward spiral in fuel prices owes much to the emergence of developing country markets and the liberalization-engendered transformation of the airline industry discussed in this chapter. But technology has also played a role. The most celebrated commercial aircraft introduced over the past decade, including the Airbus A380 and the Boeing 787, have been marvels of efficiency. Airbus, for instance, claims that Singapore Airlines' replacement of 10 Boeing 777-300ER per week on the Singapore–Paris sector with daily A380 service yielded a 20 per cent increase in capacity and a 3 per cent fuel savings (Creedy 2009). Newer versions of the narrow-body Boeing 737 and Airbus A320 have delivered striking efficiency gains, too. In fact, much of the recent tightening of the cost gap between LCCs and full service network carriers in the US is attributable to fleet upgrading by the latter (Hazel, Stalnaker and Taylor 2012). In the future, similar advances in new aircraft models and upgraded versions of existing airplanes will be important to sustaining the growth of aviation.

What will the specifications of those new aircraft be? The future technological development of aviation lies outside the scope of this chapter but what can be said is that the economic geography of air transportation will play a key role in shaping the characteristics of future aircraft. Historically, the technological specifications of new aircraft have reflected the demands of the airline industry's most important customers. In the early decades of aviation, that meant TWA and Pan Am (Bowen 2010, Chapter 4). More recently, Asian carriers, especially Singapore Airlines, have been influential (Bowen 2007). Indeed, the size of the A380 and the exceptionally long range of the newest wide-body aircraft are specifications meant specifically to appeal to Asian markets (e.g. see Dupont and Burger 2003 on the significance of Asia to the A380). Future shifts in the geography of the global economy may give other regions added clout in shaping future aircraft specifications.

Further development in low- and especially medium-income countries has other important implications for aviation technology. To date, the aerospace industry has been strongly dominated by the United States, Western Europe, and to a lesser extent Japan (Bowen 2010, Chapter 4). Human capital resources have been one key reason. The emergence of the Chinese aircraft industry in particular has been slowed by the lack of engineers and other skilled personnel. With development, that constraint is likely to ease, which could foster more competition beyond the duopoly of Airbus and Boeing for jets with more than 120 seats. The Chinese-produced Comac C919, with a capacity of 130 to 190 seats (i.e. directly challenging the Boeing 737 and Airbus A320), is scheduled for entry into service as early as 2016 (Warwick 2012). Although orders for the C919 have so far come overwhelmingly from Chinese carriers, changes in the aircraft industry such as this will affect the broader airline industry to the degree that more rivals engender further technological advances in airframes and aircraft engines that sustain or even augment aviation's competitive position versus ground transport modes.

At the same time that shifts in economic geography affect the aircraft industry and the features of the planes it produces, the specifications of the world's jetliners will in turn help to define the architecture of the global economy. Ultra-long-haul nonstops such as the daily Qantas flight from Sydney to Dallas-Ft Worth and the nightly FedEx flight from Hong Kong to Memphis[12] are emphatic expressions of globalization and the acceleration of everyday life made possible by advances in aviation technology. And the deployment of the 'Superjumbo' Airbus A380 and the Boeing 747-8 on transcontinental and intercontinental routes have lowered unit costs through economies of scale, facilitating what Giddens referred to as 'time–space distanciation' (Cassell 1993) in everyday life.

More than is true of most modes, aviation has historically strained at the edge of the technological frontier. Yet the most significant planes of the early twenty-first century are not wide-bodies like the 787 and A380, but rather narrow-bodies. In 2012, the various versions of the narrow-body 737 and A320 accounted for 60 per cent of global seat capacity – and overwhelmingly dominate the fleets of LCCs (OAG 2012). Accordingly, airlines and the air-framers alike have attached great importance to the A320 neo (new engine option) and 737 MAX, scheduled for entry-into-service in 2015 and 2017, respectively (Jawarowski 2012). Boeing and Airbus have promised that each airplane will provide efficiency gains on the order of 15 per cent over current versions, though of course the manufacturers ferociously debate the merits of their respective champions in this tectonic battle for aviation's second century (Mecham 2012). How that debate turns out remains up in the air, but it seems reasonably safe to forecast that the A320 neo and 737 MAX will be the most popular new jetliners of the first half of the twenty-first century

The continued significance of narrow-body jets is testament to the limits of globalization (or, expressed another way, the continued importance of local and national concerns). In 2011, the average air passenger journey globally was 1,874 kilometres, only marginally higher than the same measure in 1998 (estimates derived from ICAO 1999 and

---

12 Compared to services requiring a refuelling stop (usually in Anchorage), FedEx's nonstop transpacific links gives manufacturers in Asia two additional hours of production per day to still meet the cut-off time for next-day deliveries in the US (Levitz 2010).

ICAO 2012). The small change in average journey length despite the launch of many ultra-long-haul flights over the 14 year time span reflects, in part, the massive proliferation of intra-regional routes in developing regions, especially Asia. Yet that process has barely begun in some areas including, as noted above, the paucity of routes among Ethiopia and its neighbours. Ultimately, there remain many thinly traversed patches on the map of world airline services. The aircraft that fill those gaps will neither be particularly large nor long-range, but rather medium-sized jets plying short- and medium-haul routes spun across a newly 'aeromobile' developing world.

Acknowledgements

The author thanks Andrew Goetz and Kevin O'Connor for their very helpful comments on an earlier version of the chapter and Central Washington University for funding the purchase of the data upon which the analyses in the chapter are based.

References

ACI [Airports Council International]. 2011a. Cargo Traffic 2010 Final. Available at: http://www.aci.aero/Data-Centre/Annual-Traffic-Data/Cargo/2010-final [accessed: 28 January 2013].

ACI [Airports Council International]. 2011b. Passenger Traffic 2010 Final. Available at: http://www.aci.aero/Data-Centre/Annual-Traffic-Data/Passengers/2010-final [accessed: 28 January 2013].

Adey, P., Budd, L. and Hubbard, P. 2007. Flying Lessons: Exploring the Social and Cultural Geographies of Global Air Travel. *Progress in Human Geography* 31(6): 773–91.

Air Transport World. 1999. World Airline Traffic Statistics 1998, July, 75–88.

Air Transport World. 2011. Individual Airline Fleets, July, 93–106.

Air Transport World. 2012. The World's Top 25 Airlines, July, 43.

Banham, R. 1995. Panalpina Builds Europe-to-Alabama 'Bridge'. *Journal of Commerce*, 26 June, 4.

Boeing Commercial Airplanes. 2012. *World Air Cargo Forecast 2012–2013.* Available at: http://www.boeing.com/commercial/cargo/wacf.pdf [accessed: 17 January 2013].

Bowen, J. 2000. Airline Hubs in Southeast Asia: National Economic Development and Nodal Accessibility, 1979–1997. *Journal of Transport Geography* 8(1): 25–41.

Bowen, J. 2002. Network Change, Deregulation, and Access in the Global Airline Industry. *Economic Geography* 78(4): 425–39.

Bowen, J. 2004. The Geography of Freight Aircraft Operations in the Pacific Basin. *Journal of Transport Geography* 12(1): 1–11.

Bowen, J. 2007. Global Production Networks, the Developmental State, and the Articulation of Asia Pacific Economies in the Commercial Aircraft Industry. *Asia Pacific Viewpoint* 48(3): 312–29.

Bowen, J. 2010. *The Economic Geography of Air Transportation: Space, Time, and the Freedom of the Sky.* London: Routledge.

Bowen, J. 2012. A Spatial Analysis of FedEx and UPS: Hubs, Spokes, and Network Structure. *Journal of Transport Geography* 24(3): 419–31.

Bowen, J. 2013. Continents Shifting, Clouds Gathering: The Trajectory of Global Aviation Expansion, in *Sustainable Aviation Futures*, edited by L. Budd, S. Griggs and D. Howarth. Bingley, UK: Emerald, 37–63.

BTS [Bureau of Transportation Statistics]. 2006. America on the Go: Long Distance Transportation Patterns: Mode Choice. Available at: http://www.bts.gov/publications/america_on_the_go/long_distance_travel_patterns/ [accessed: 14 April 2007].

Button, K. and Taylor, S. 2000. International Air Transportation and Economic Development. *Journal of Air Transport Management* 6: 209–22.

Cassell, P. 1993. *The Giddens Reader*. Stanford, CA: Stanford University Press.

Cattan, N. 1995. Attractivity and Internationalisation of Major European Cities: The Example of Air Traffic. *Urban Studies* 32(2): 303–12.

Creedy, S. 2009. Airbus Proclaims its A380 a Success. *The Australian*, 22 May, 31.

Debbage, K.G. 1999. Air Transportation and Urban-Economic Restructuring: Competitive Advantage in the US Carolinas. *Journal of Air Transport Management* 5: 211–21.

Debbage, K.G. and Delk, D. 2001. The Geography of Air Passenger Volume and Local Employment Patterns by US Metropolitan Core Area: 1973–1996. *Journal of Air Transport Management* 7: 159–67.

Denton, N. and Dennis, N. 2000. Airline Franchising in Europe: Benefits and Disbenefits to Airlines and Consumers. *Journal of Air Transport Management* 6(4): 179–90.

Derudder, B. and Witlox, F. 2008. Mapping World City Networks Through Airline Flows: Context, Relevance, and Problems. *Journal of Transport Geography* 16(5): 305–12.

Dupont, W.-P. and Burger, T. 2003. A380: A Solution for Airports. *Fast* 33: 7–16.

Economist, The. 2012. Ethiopian Dares to Dream. Available at: http://www.economist.com/blogs/gulliver/2012/09/ethiopian-airlines [accessed: 12 December 2012].

Economist, The. 2013. Coming Home, 19 January. Special Report: Outsourcing and Offshoring, 6.

Energy Information Administration. 2012. Domestic Crude First Purchase Price by Area. Available at: http://www.eia.gov [accessed: 2 March 2012].

Fleming, D.K. and Hayuth, Y. 1994. Spatial Characteristics of Transportation Hubs: Centrality and Intermediacy. *Journal of Transport Geography*, 2(1): 3–18.

Francis, G., Dennis, N., Ison, S. and Humphreys, I. 2007. The Transferability of the Low-Cost Model to Long-Haul Airline Operations. *Tourism Management* 28(2): 391–8.

Francis, L. 2004. Liberal Values: China's Airline Sector Leads Asia in Opening Up its Local Aviation Market to Competition – and the Reforms are Gathering Pace. *Flight International*, 26 October, 40.

Gábor, D. 2010. Low-Cost Airlines in Europe: Network Structures after the Enlargement of the European Union. *Geographica Pannonica* 14(2): 49–58.

Goetz, A.R. 2002. Deregulation, Competition, and Antitrust Implications in the US Airline Industry. *Journal of Transport Geography* 10(1): 1–19.

Hakfoort, J., Poot, T. and Rietveld, P. 2001 The Regional Economic Impact of an Airport: The Case of Amsterdam Schiphol Airport. *Regional Studies* 35(7): 595–604.

Hazel, B., Stalnaker, T. and Taylor, A. 2012. *Airline Economic Analysis February 2012*. [Online: Oliver Wyman]. Available at: http://www.oliverwyman.com/media/OW_Raymond_James_2012_FINAL.PDF [accessed: 26 January 2013].

ICAO [International Civil Aviation Organization]. 1999. Airline Financial Results Positive in 1998 Despite Flat Traffic. Press Release PIO 07/99, dated 2 June.

ICAO [International Civil Aviation Organization]. 2012. Robust Traffic Growth Expected until 2014. Press release COM 14/12, dated 5 July.

Jawarowski, R. 2012. Stage is Set. *Aviation Week & Space Technology*, 23 January, 120.

Jetstar. 2013. Jetstar Network – The Jetstar Group. [Online: Jetstar]. Available at: http://www.jetstar.com/mediacentre/facts-and-stats/jetstar-network [accessed: 27 January 2013].

Journal of Commerce. 2011. Panalpina Adds Second Hong Kong-Huntsville Flight, 12 May. Available at: http://www.joc.com/international-logistics/logistics-providers/panalpina-adds-second-hong-kong-huntsville-flight_20110512.html [accessed: 15 January 2013].

Kasarda, J.D. and Lindsay, G. 2011. *Aerotropolis: The Way We'll Live Next*. New York: Farrar, Straus and Giroux.

Keiner, R.B., Halloway, L.B. and Murphy, G.F. 2009. Airline Alliances, Antitrust Immunity, and Mergers in the United States. Crowell & Moring legal brief. Available at: http://www.crowell.com/ [accessed: 29 July 2010].

Lee, H.-S. 2009. The Networkability of Cities in the International Air Passengers Flows 1992–2004. *Journal of Transport Geography* 17(3): 166–75.

Levitz, J. 2010. FedEx Looks to 777s for an Edge. *The Wall Street Journal*, 14 July, B1.

Lohmann, G., Albers, S., Koch, B. and Pavlovich, K. 2009. From Hub to Tourist Destination – An Explorative Study of Singapore and Dubai's Aviation-Based Transformation. *Journal of Air Transport Management* 15(5): 205–11.

Mahutga, M.C., Ma, X., Smith, D.A. and Timberlake, M. 2010. Economic Globalization and the Structure of the World City System: The Case of Airline Passenger Data. *Urban Studies* 47(9): 1925–47.

Matsumoto, H. 2004. International Urban Systems and Air Passenger and Cargo Flows: Some Calculations. *Journal of Air Transport Management* 10(4): 241–9.

Mecham, M. 2012. End of the Beginning. *Aviation Week & Space Technology*, 9 July, 68.

Morrison, S.A. 2001. Actual, Adjacent, and Potential Competition: Estimating the Full Effect of Southwest Airlines. *Journal of Transport Economics and Policy* 35(2): 239–56.

Naudé, W. 2009. Geography, Transport and Africa's Proximity Gap. *Journal of Transport Geography* 17(1): 1–9.

OAG. 1998. OAG Max (CD-ROM). April.

OAG. 2012. OAG Max (CD-ROM). February.

O'Connell, J.F. and Williams, G. 2005. Passengers' Perceptions of Low Cost Airlines and Full Service Carriers: A Case Study Involving Ryanair, Aer Lingus, Air Asia, and Malaysia Airlines. *Journal of Air Transport Management* 11: 259–72.

O'Connor, K. and Fuellhart, K. 2012. Cities and Air Services: The Influence of the Airline Industry. *Journal of Transport Geography* 22(1): 46–52.

Poole, J.P. 2010. Business Travel as an Input to International Trade. UC Santa Cruz Working Paper. Available at: http://www.scu.edu/business/economics/upload/Poole.pdf [accessed: 4 June 2013].

PRB [Population Reference Bureau]. 2012. 2012 World Population Data Sheet. Available at: http://www.prb.org/pdf12/2012-population-data-sheet_eng.pdf [accessed: 4 February 2013].

Qantas. 2012. *Qantas Annual Report 2012*. Available at: http://www.qantas.com.au/info detail/about/investors/2012AnnualReport.pdf [accessed: 13 December 2012].

Russell, E. 2012. Strategic Partners. *Airline Business* 28(9): 30–33.

Sassen, S. 2001. *The Global City: New York, London, Tokyo*. Princeton, NJ: Princeton University Press.

Shin, K.H. and Timberlake, M. 2000. World Cities in Asia: Cliques, Centrality and Connectedness. *Urban Studies* 37: 2257–85.

Smith, D.A. and Timberlake, M. 2001. World City Networks and Hierarchies 1979–1999: An Empirical Analysis of Global Air Travel Links. *American Behavioral Scientist* 44: 1656–77.

Taaffe, E.J., Gauthier, H.L. and O'Kelly, M.E. 1996. *Geography of Transportation*. 2nd Edition. Upper Saddle River, NJ: Prentice Hall.

Thomas, A. and Dunn, G. 2012. World in Motion. *Airline Business*, 28(12), November: 42–4.

US Department of State. 2013. Open Skies Agreements. Available at: http://www.state.gov/e/eb/tra/ata/index.htm [accessed: 15 January 2013].

Vowles, T.M. 2001. The 'Southwest Effect' in Multi-Airport Regions. *Journal of Air Transport Management* 7(4): 251–8.

Warwick, G. 2012. Narrow Focus. *Aviation Week & Space Technology*, 24 September, 48–54.

Wassener, B. 2012. Added Routes Signal Growth for China's Sole Low-Cost Carrier. *International Herald Tribune*, 29 November, 16.

World Bank. 2012. GNI Per Capita, PPP (current international $). Available at: http://data.worldbank.org/indicator/NY.GNP.PCAP.PP.CD/countries [accessed: 15 December 2012].

Zook, M.A. and Brunn, S.D. 2006. From Podes to Antipodes: Positionalities and Global Airline Geographies. *Annals of the Association of American Geographers* 96(3): 471–90.

Smith, D.A. and Timberlake, M. 2001. World City Networks and Hierarchies 1977-1990: An Empirical Assessment of Global Air Travel Links. *American Behavioral Scientist* 44:1656-78.

Taaffe, E.J., Gauthier, H.L., and O'Kelly, M.E. 1996. *Geography of Transportation*, 2nd Edition. Upper Saddle River, NJ: Prentice Hall.

Thomas, A. and Unger, C. 2013. World in Motion: Airline Business. 28(1), November 2013.

US Department of State. 2013. Open Skies Agreements. Available at: [http://www.state.gov/e/eb/rls/othr/ata/114805.htm]. [accessed 15 January 2014].

Vowles, T.M. 2001. The Southwest Effect in Multi-Airport Regions. *Journal of Air Transport Management* 7(4): 251-8.

Waterside, G. 2012. National Export Strategy. *Work & Space*. Technology, 24 September. 19-24.

Wassener, B. 2012. Added Routes Signal Growth for China's Sole Low-Cost Carrier. *International Herald Tribune*, 28 November, 16.

World Bank. 2012. GDP Per Capita, PPP [Current International $]. Available at: [http://data.worldbank.org/indicator/NY.GDP.PCAP.PP.CD]. Washington: The World Bank. [2013].

Zook, M.A. and Brunn, S.D. 2006. From Podes to Antipodes: Positionalities and Global Airline Geographies. *Annals of the Association of American Geographers* 96(3): 471-90.

Chapter 4
Social and Cultural Geographies of Air Transport

Peter Adey and Weiqiang Lin

Introduction

In recent years there have been calls for a revisioning of existing geographical research on air travel mobilities (Adey et al. 2007; Cwerner et al. 2009; Pirie 2009). What first seemed apparent was that the aviation world had remained the subject of sophisticated econometric models and policy analysis, historical geographies of infrastructure development, local government politicking, and other well-trodden concerns such as airport protests and environmental disputes, issues which had resumed once more in the face of government deregulation of airports and a decline in the belief of the promise of flight (Corn 1983). The airport had seemed to be one of the key sites of focus for a growing body of work finding both dissatisfaction and fascination in the apparent banality of air travel and its pseudo globalized spaces.

All this attention may have reflected a particular moment in time, following particular social, economic and political changes that have enabled air transport to become so commonplace (Augé 1995), as well as the emergence of particular research agendas such as the 'new mobilities' paradigm, that would attend to the social as mobility (Urry 2002; Cresswell 2006) and, therefore, the way air travel would shape societies, culture and politics, and the role societies could play in re-shaping aviation.

What seems clear now is that the more traditional accounts of air travel did not simply reflect a staid set of interests. Rather they failed to account for air travel on its own terms, as an object or a culture in its own right, and even as a means to explore wider issues such as housing struggles and planning disputes and other social inequalities. Meanwhile it was not as if transport geographers were unable or unwilling to explore the questions of 'new mobilities'. Instead, they seemed to be preoccupied with other issues and conceptual agendas that proved to be more pressing or pragmatic to them. This had the unintended effect of emptying aeromobility somewhat of its social content and context, and, furthermore, divorcing it from a series of different theoretical interests that were being brought to the car, or 'auto-mobilities' (Featherstone 2004). Air travel, then, held an enormously productive and potential space for a different kind of academic study.

In this chapter we look at the field and explore how its development has taken off in sometimes quite unanticipated directions. We examine how what perhaps holds these studies of the social and cultural geographies of air transport together is an attention to the 'little', or to the 'small', unanticipated and unintended emotions, affects, senses, urges and nuances of life in-the-air. And it is perhaps through those 'little things' that we might attend to a series of new encounters, horizons and spatial formations of air transport and reappraise the initial concerns of the field. Before we sketch out just where these research encounters have taken us, however, we first try to account for the fact that while the airport might appear to have been one of the primary spaces where this research has touched down, research of this kind has been multi-sited and scalar. What is more, social and cultural geographies of air transport have developed far more nuanced deconstructions of any sense of separation between what goes on in the skies and life on the ground.

Airspaces: Meetings of Earth and Sky

One new thread that has emerged pertains to the fresh understandings that have been gleaned regarding the surfaces and volumes in which air travel takes place. Whereas the concept of airspace was previously taken for granted as a 'medium' for air transport, it is now beginning to be given far more serious attention as a field that has to undergo multiple rounds of cultural and political treatment before flight operations can become a reality. Budd's (2009) work on 'air-craft' is apposite in this respect, as she sketches out the complex procedures that are involved in the organization of this space. By exploring how UK airspace is demarcated, directed by air traffic controllers and navigated by pilots in highly particular ways, her analysis demonstrates the contingency of airspace on a myriad of mutually supportive and constitutive actors before it can be mobilized. It is through this contingency that we can begin to realize the difficult and often artificial separation of air and ground, even from the technical construction and demarcation of airspace.

Still on the composition of airspace, technologies have been identified as another critical component in these aerial ecosystems. They do not only make flight an achievable feat in the first place, but also have a fundamental bearing on how airspace is to be experienced and approached. Budd and Adey's (2009) interrogation of how piloting is performed as a series of simulated anticipations corroborates this argument by drawing attention to the ways in which airspace, among other facets of aviation, is increasingly 'flown' with the aid of computer software and code (Kitchin and Dodge 2011). Mediated by systems such as fly-by-wire, TCAS (Traffic Alert and Collision Avoidance System) and flight training simulators, airspace is hence encountered by pilots less as a mass of air or an atmosphere (see for instance McCormack 2008), but a network of data points and virtual realities that sense and apprehend airspace quite differently to the human body, or even the tensed but distributed surfaces and equipment of early fixed wing and dirigible flight.

Other authors show a greater interest in the capacity of airspace to be flexibly adapted. Focusing on military uses of the air, Williams (2011: 254) argues that while civil airspace is composed of 'permanent' air lanes and control sectors, military airspace is multifariously configured as different types of spaces, such that each can be 'activated and deactivated according to usage requirements'. Lin (2013a) on the other hand differs on the suggested stasis of civil air lanes, positing that they can likewise be re-organized when circumstances call for their alteration. Reflecting on regulatory responses to the 2011 Puyehue-Cordón Caulle eruption and volcanic ash incident, his work elucidates how a complete shutdown of flight operations had been averted because of the spontaneous measures taken by the authorities of Australia and New Zealand to (temporarily) rescale the jurisdiction and height profile of their airspace. We might even observe that the fluidities of airspace are being somehow clawed back in long term proposals for a Single European Sky, and not only in emergency circumstances.

To be sure, there are limits to how far such improvisations can be made. If we reflect on a prior ash incident involving the eruption of Eyjafjallajökull, we might argue that that disruptive episode, which resulted in a 10-day halt of European flights, has only exposed the technological limits of airspace, and the fragility of how it has gone about organizing its disparate infrastructure and complex systems. Adey and Anderson (2011) similarly pick up on the allergy of airspace to unexpected intruders and exigencies, but more specifically trace the root of its vulnerability to an overreliance on imperfect systems of anticipation and speculation, that had unravelled when their design limits were exceeded during the Icelandic eruption (see also Adey et al. 2011). Understood as such, airspace is scarcely immune to the risks prevalent in aeromobilities (Urry 2009), but constitutes another weak link in a chain of possible structural failures.

Yet, not all breakdowns are a result of unanticipated risks and events. Williams (2010) intimates a more deliberate and geopolitically inflected form of incursion and interruption in her consideration of the UK–US imposition of no-fly zones on Iraqi airspace. By incorporating the air as part of a state's territorial integrity, the airspace violations she surfaces not only speak to a different kind of 'disruption', but also offer a counterpoint to the flight stoppages suffered by European states in the Eyjafjallajökull incident, despite (and indeed because of) their full control of airspace. Still on geopolitical interference, Lin (2013b) more recently tracks the development of a European-initiated ecological regime for governing the 'sustainable' use of airspace. Aimed at curbing the effects of climate change through capping atmospheric carbon emissions, the scheme, for Lin, harbours a simultaneous potential to 'disrupt' the technical carrying capacity of airspace, by dint of the radiative limits artificially imposed on it.

Shifting the focus from its proneness to interruptions to its spectacular affordances, airspace can yet array another, more intimate form of politics, this time through symbolisms and pedagogies. The air figures as a theatrical backdrop for aerial spectacles, a tool of propaganda for the state, and a stage on which national performances can be enacted in other historical studies within the field. Narrating a similar story in colonial South Africa, Pirie (2009) argues that Alan Cobham's roving air 'circus' in the 1930s represents an anxious inculcation of British 'airmindedness' in the colony, in an attempt to bond South Africa closer with the rest of the Empire. In both cases, airspace is afforded a particular vista and skyward gaze, such that flying, in the form of air displays, do not so much transport as impress its ideologies upon its spectators. As a corollary, airspace is also tethered to the ground not through the airport terminal but balconies and galleries (Adey 2008), upon which the cinematic canvas of airspace unfolds.

Taken together, what these studies have shown is something that tries to go beyond prefatory descriptions of how airspace works. Instead, they have highlighted the socio-cultural import of this realm, as well as how airspace is closely imbricated with issues concerning mobilities, immobilities, socio-technical modalities, military-scapes, geopolitics and national/colonial ideologies. This host of 'serious' preoccupations partly explains why airspace is treated, in practice, as a space to be fearfully and rationally approached. As a corollary of the kinds of agenda it tends to set, it is also a domain whose occupation and control are often deemed the sole preserve of a 'deserving' few, particularly men and the wealthy (Millward 2007, 2008; DeLyser 2010). Indeed, even despite the relatively careful attention of this burgeoning 'aeromobile' literature to reconcile the existing and dominant accounts of 'life in the air' to a middle-class, male, white, western traveller, we could argue that the growth of the aeromobilities literature has not yet moved enough from this ground (although see Birtchnell and Caletrio 2013).

Given this inherent politics, perhaps airspace is just beginning to be (re)discovered as lively fodder with new stories to be told, as explored below. As long as one is willing to look past its discursive facades, it will not just be a glass one sees through darkly. Overall, we see the development of airspace as not only a techno-geopolitical category, but the performance of disparately connected subjects, discourses, materialities, mobilities and technologies that befuddle earth and sky.

New Geographies of Air Transport

Cultural-Economies

If prior studies of air transport appeared resolutely locked within transport economics and logistics of rational decision makers, recent work shows considerable nuancing through approaches more in-tuned to the cultural-economies of the airport as a complex organizational system (see Klauser 2009 on the competing imperatives around surveillance) in line with – and not separated from – a broader political-economic context of forces which undeniably express themselves in the life of the airport. Donald McNeill (2010) even comprehends the airport as a 'coagulation of spread-sheets', a conglomeration of technologies, inputs, outputs, and undeniable tensions that have expressed themselves in the hassle, passions and frustrations, that were so well catalogued in the failed opening of Heathrow's Terminal 5 in 2008. Such an approach – a 'cultural-economy' of air transport – does not simply recognize the association of airports and national pride, or progress, as historical work has shown (Adey 2010), nor does it exclude the subtler experiential geographies of air transport from the broader political-economic contexts that have shaped air travel to the detriment of the passenger's experiences. In the case of London's Heathrow, this might be regulatory changes, the state divestment of state assets, and BAA's (now Heathrow Airport Limited's) dominant market position which has since seen their monopoly broken up. In this sense, as a 'big-thing' (Jacobs 2006), the airport is understood in a far wider economic context which does not draw attention away from but takes it directly to the little things of terminal life. This might describe research much more sensitive to the actual organization, conditions and complexities of social life in the airport workforce, or indeed, design process. Or, as McNeill illustrates, a more nuanced understanding of the kind of work and employment that not only make up but that circulate the air transport system.

In this kind of vein, then, and turning to the labour of airport design, a social and cultural geography of air transport, according to Nikolaeva (2012), can be both decentred and made that much more complex, because the airport should be understood as far more than a monolithic structure – 'never simply an airport'. Neither is it simply authored by a star or omniscient architect. Instead, Nikolaeva argues that the work of 'airport design should rather be seen as a continuous series of negotiations, struggles and compromises between specific professional circles that have some common agendas to address but pursue different objectives', or, more succinctly, airport design is 'a struggle between contested visions of mobility' (2012: 544). The process is a socially contested one between different cultures of work, involving compromise, negotiation and hopefully resolution between different people and professionalized expertise, as well as one of testing and experimentation.

Such a focus is particularly helpful and leads, as we saw earlier, to particular forms of labour and work (see also Cresswell 2006) not only of those who service and are employed within the diverse industries of the airport, but how air transport mediates other forms of work and also consumption (see also Faulconbridge and Beaverstock 2008). For example, McNeill (2009) shows again how the kinds of patterns of mobility witnessed through the airport owes much to the built/organizational form of the airport hotel, and the kinds of work and leisure it supports. Air transport is certainly not as far away from the anonymous ubiquity other writers have levelled at it as we might have first thought. In this sense, the airport hotel and the routes, hubs and scheduling of the aviation industry as a system, connecting to other systems, become for Claus Lassen a corridor-like structuring 'mechanism' (McNeill 2011: 94). The structure is 'structuring' because it seduces, catering for many of the needs of particular kinds of work and leisure. Thus as we will explore later, such corridors might be understood to connect seamlessly even to one's home, bringing the hotel rooms, lounges, conference facilities, 'an exoskeleton' (McNeill 2011: 225) of sorts, closer in with ease.

However, the attention of this kind of research to the small scale, insofar as it demands our attunement to the experiences, rhythms and patterns of life on the move within the air transport system (Cwerner, Kesselring and Urry 2009), also reveals its considerable pauses, and moments of slowness. Even despite the freneticism of, for some, the incredible connectivity performed through the compulsion to proximity by meetingness that air travel can appear to stimulate, this does require huge amounts of mobility *for* very short periods of immobility. And there is a tension in this. For instance, the airport hotel is an ideal allegory for the capacity of airports to temporarily fix capital, whether through corporate take-overs and capital investment in infrastructure, often paid with considerably leveraged debt. This capital fixing comes with the temporary stoppage, lodging and pausing to complete numerous kinds of encounters. One of the most dominant is of course particular sorts of work and business. Drawing on Faludi's (1982) account, McNeill (2009) details a Venezuelan export-importer who booked a room in an airport hotel, struck a deal with an American executive and left the airport without setting foot in the city. While this might have once sounded exceptional, it is no longer such.

Surfaces

If geographies of flight have been able to account for what it was to inhabit a space other than the ground, they have also demonstrated that the aerial view was not the abstract space of suspended god's eye vision that has been proposed. Nor was the ground the blank canvas of early passenger's dreams or the transposition of the planner's imaginations from their similarly synoptic position. Social and cultural geographies of air transport have become increasingly attuned to a stranger and thicker relationship between the air and the surface of the earth as, ironically, an attention to surfaces is an oxymoronic elaboration of wholes and volumes. It is, in certain terms, an obfuscation as much as it is a revelation.

This work has been developed especially well in the cultural and historical geographies of military aviation as well as civil protection planning during World War II. In Isla Forsyth's (2013a, b) ground-breaking work on military camoufleurs, we learn of remarkable tales of invention and mimicry in the strange mangle of science, technologies, professions and practice as camouflage was inspired by nature, ecology and artistic trends, all so as to deter and distract the perspective from the sky. The view from the aeroplane was one to be imagined, embodied and simulated so that camoufleurs could find ways to mis-direct it away from valuable targets.

In James Robinson's (2012, 2013) study, attention is turned towards the relationship between the aeroplane and the civilian sphere, as civil camouflage designs sought to 'distract the attentions of the aerial bomber', away from the civilian and 'vital' infrastructure of war production and civilian life. Serving a dual role, protection from the skies meant physical shelter-by-mis-direction, as well as a boost to the collective sentiment or 'morale' of the populace following evasion from danger. It is clear that these were not simply 'elite' practices of high ranking civil service, scientists or military officers, rather, that the concealment of Britain from the aeroplane involved what Robinson (2012) has described in the terms of an 'active participation', an enrolment of the public – for example – in several newspaper debates over the changing landscape of 1940s Britain that camouflage designs were encouraging. Indeed, camouflage was one among many activities which mobilized a kind of aerial citizenship which took for granted and also promoted a measure of 'air-mindedness' in young people's enthusiasm for flight.

Taken together, these perspectives illustrate that not only was the aerial view to be confused, dazzled, and tricked or fooled, but that to conflate the aerial perspective with the eye is a mistake. What appears key for both Robinson and Forsyth was how militarized aeromobility required a series of counter-practices of concealment and camouflage that required an immersion in both grounded and aerial perspectives. Moreover, to take such cultural and historical geographies of aviation – to tell these narratives of military and civil camouflage requires a story of what Forsyth has called 'immersion in space, both aerial and earthly, through the mingling of diverse actors, human, nonhuman and technological' (Forsyth 2012: 58).

Entubulation

In contrast to airspaces which could be seen to be ruled by masculinist logic and rationality the entubulated spaces of the aircraft take on yet another form of ambivalent and varied style. While Simonsen (2010) documents how early cabins were adorned with experimental notions of modernity, speed and exhilaration at the dawn of the air age, Martin (2011) reminds us that these spaces also represent a form of 'protective cocooning' for the privileged, a capsularization that shields worthy inhabitants – not stowaways – from the 'violence of speed'. Wielding a livelier imagination, Linstead (1995) posits that the cabin can be more crassly figured as a place akin to, but yet more than, a mother's womb: paradoxically, it seeks to hide passengers from the pernicious elements outside, while hiding from view the reality of its own exterior as a phallus-shaped projectile hurtling through the air.

Framed in this context, the sheltering care provided by aerial entubulations must also be contextualized within the death-defying moves its outer skin performs. Lucy Budd's (2011) historical account of early air travellers' discomforting in-flight experiences in the 1920s and 1930s gives clue to this liminal state of being in the air, of being cradled and put in peril at once. Explicitly, her work highlights the aberrance of human occupation of the stratosphere, and exposes the leakiness and susceptibility of aircraft to the extreme weather conditions they are immersed in. While technologies of entubulation have significantly improved since then, flying continues to pose real physical challenges to travellers today, as airplanes fly higher, faster and over longer ranges, and airlines attempt to seat passengers closer together, in a bid to maximize profits (Budd et al. 2011).

The evolution of the cabin from a space of novelty and exclusivity to one of long-distance mass travel inevitably introduces new health hazards to passengers. Here, the aircraft's entubulation becomes entangled with the human body's own entubulated compositions that have been displaced from the ground. In particular, conditions such as deep-vein thrombosis, ear and sinus pains and increased cardio-respiratory risks have emerged as regular concerns in aviation medicine. Yet, passengers are tasked to surveil and take charge of their own 'wellness' and, at the same time, to become aware of their aerial medical vulnerability in an extension of the governmental logics of airports. Be it through the generic health advice airlines seek to communicate to passengers through in-flight literatures (Budd, Warren and Bell 2011), or reminders about personal vigilance against pathological conditions like SARS that incubate on-board but manifest later (Ali and Keil 2006; Aaltola 2012), air travellers are called upon to act responsibly as (communal) users of not just the cabin, but also its onward vectors back on the ground and across national borders.

Besides their wellbeing, passengers are also expected to observe in-flight safety rules dutifully, as part of a normative ethos of security permeating through the assemblage of aviation. Bissell and colleagues' (2012) reflection on Air New Zealand's *Bare Essentials* in-flight safety demonstration is instructive in this respect, unravelling how the risqué use of naked, body-painted flight-attendant models in the 2009 video represents a form of pedagogical tool for disciplining and demanding attention from captive passengers (Adey 2007). Yet, the video simultaneously blurs the seriousness of its message, introducing humorous and seductive elements that vacillate in and out of diverse registers of control and freedom. In short, their analysis underscores how aircraft cabins are ambiguously both a governmental space and an imperfectly coded regime. Betraying their airtight corrals are effervescent socialities and possibilities for departures that signal their ultimate recalcitrance to 'capturing' bodies as disciplined or biopolitically produced subjects.

On a slightly different trajectory, other scholars have emphasized the service function latent within these entubulations. Hochschild's (1983) seminal work addressing the gendered 'emotional labours' invested by flight attendants has been particularly salient as a foil against which later studies refer. While it is now widely recognized that the airline industry, through the deliberate packaging of flight attendants' emotional acts as a ware for sale, has set an example for the commercialization of human feelings, Lin's ongoing work on the 'Singapore girl' forwards another interpretation. By contextualizing the comfort-work performed by the 'girls' within the strategy fields of postcolonial Singapore, he demonstrates how emotional labour in this instance entails more than a capitalistic transaction between passenger and crew, but also the selective packaging of ambiguous notions of Oriental charm for the male, Western audience.

The perfumed atmospheres on-board are however not just maintained by the emotional work of crew members but are also facilitated by props. Flight attendants' fashion is one key ingredient that has been used to enhance on-board atmospheres, and construct a legible identity for the otherwise indistinct aircraft. While the cabin was once the domain of male stewards who wore waiter's jackets, the introduction of stewardesses in the 1930s opened the way to new fashion statements – of blouses, jaunty hats and sensible skirts (Lovegrove 2000). Not to be estranged from their wearers, these costumes were an extension of the feminine bodies of the crew and meant to be an addition to the cabin's cheeriness (Barry 2007). Later, in the 1960s, the industry even went so far as to experiment with bolder styles, including hot pants, miniskirts and flesh-revealing suits, for female flight attendants' uniforms, transforming the cabin yet again into sexualized spaces and gentlemen's clubs of the skies (Boris 2006; Whitelegg 2007).

Clearly then, if there is one thing that these analyses agree on, it is that aerial entubulations are not simply tools for carriage, but spaces for testing out new cultures and ways of being in the air. Though they seem like inert zones for waiting, these womb-like structures engender, in their deep recesses, designs, formats, and atmospheres that map onto constantly evolving aviation norms and orders. Yet, the normativities that bind them can also precipitously lose their grip, when passengers step out of line (Morgan and Nickson 2001), and flight attendants refuse their emotional scripts (Murphy 2002; Bolton and Boyd 2003). Airlines, too, can tease about formal(ized) procedures, by, for instance, sporting a growing (and continuing) cast of 'fun' characters, from the finger-wagging Deltalina (Delta Airlines) to (fully-clothed) hobbits (Air New Zealand) in their safety videos. Yet, it is precisely through such a messy and iterative process of experimentation, with things on the ground and in the sky, that aircraft cabins are given their porous character. Hidden within them are not just travellers-by-air, but fertile test beds for new cultural trends and unexpected glimpses of tomorrow.

Conclusion: Creative Aeromobilities

Finally, as we see creative forms of response and interruption to some of the over-determining narratives of politics and power that air travel has been accused of producing and reproducing, we can anticipate a further emergent area of social and cultural geographies of air transport: that is, the burgeoning geographies of air transport with artistic and creative practice. Of course, aviation has never been divorced from this kind of appreciation, even within geography. Cosgrove (1999) first considered the manipulation of experiences of linear and aerial perspectives in his essay comparing Heathrow to a Georgian country estate or park. Landscape, in his essay, is 'recovered' in scenes. A certain genre of light, land and movement is expressed in the staging of landscape to aeromobility. Take the aesthetics of the airliner coming in to land, descending out of holding pattern down to the runway, 'This changing angle of vision and the speed and trajectory of descent make for a continuous kinesis as relations among landscape elements shift' (Cosgrove 1999: 229). Clearly much of the work we have explored elucidates the discomfort, the disconcerting, the thrill or the passivity of air transport, and often uses a piece of art such as an evocative installation piece, to illustrate it or elicit some response. More critically, however, it is in that act of illustration where more recent work might depart.

The field might profit by exploring the artistic, aesthetic and creative life – or the creative process itself and its relation to the production of aeromobilities. As we have seen already, Forsyth (2013a, 2013b) and Robinson's (2013) research both encountered the deception of the aerial view within far wider movements in landscape architecture and the convergence of aesthetics, the biological sciences and emergent military practices. This new mingling of practice reversed the processes of aerial photographic interpretation in order to deceive precisely that view. What too about the life of art in an airport complex? There have been earlier explorations of airport architecture involving less a star architect of some megaproject – although therein lies the possibility to decentre the architect's authorship – to the complexities of the airport's diverse functions. There are also accounts of the smaller scale excavation of community spaces for faith, prayer, play and spectatorship within an airport's grounds. And it is that sensitivity to the playful where two such PhD projects have begun in our own institution. The first is the work of a visual artist exploring several themes first through her own art works that responds to the airport by seeking to deconstruct, examine, reimagine, and push a series of particular experiences we associate with air travel and life in transit, from time-out of joint, placelessness and simultaneity, to the ways in which new media are augmenting or re-mediating such spaces (Booker 2012). The second follows the process through which art-work is commissioned and curated within a terminal space currently being built. This project examines how an airport commissions art and displays it, and the knotty processes that involves in relation to brand image, the passenger experience and quite different ways of understanding and knowing airport spaces.

References

Aaltola, M. 2012. Contagious Insecurity: War, SARS and Global Air Mobility. *Contemporary Politics* 18(1): 53–70.

Adey, P. 2007. 'May I Have Your Attention': Airport Geographies of Spectatorship, Position, and (Im)Mobility. *Environment and Planning D: Society and Space* 25(3): 515–536.

Adey, P. 2008. Architectural Geographies of the Airport Balcony: Mobility, Sensation and the Theatre of Flight. *Geografiska Annaler: Series B, Human Geography* 90(1): 29–47.

Adey, P. 2010. *Aerial Life: Spaces, Mobilities, Affects.* London: Wiley-Blackwell.

Adey, P. and Anderson, B. 2011. Anticipation, Materiality, Event: The Icelandic Ash Cloud Disruption and the Security of Mobility. *Mobilities* 6(1): 11–20.

Adey, P., Anderson, B. and Lobo-Guerrero, L. 2011. An Ash Cloud, Airspace and Environmental Threat. *Transactions of the Institute of British Geographers* 36(3): 338–343.

Adey, P., Budd, L.C.S. and Hubbard, P. 2007. Flying Lessons: Exploring the Social and Cultural Geographies of Global Air Travel. *Progress in Human Geography* 31(6): 773–791.

Ali, S.H. and Keil, R. 2006. Global Cities and the Spread of Infectious Disease: The Case of Severe Acute Respiratory Syndrome (SARS) in Toronto, Canada. *Urban Studies* 43(3): 491–509.

Augé, M. 1995. *Non-places: Introduction to an Anthropology of Supermodernity.* Verso Books.

Barry, K.M. 2007. *Femininity in Flight: A History of Flight Attendants.* Durham, NC: Duke University Press.

Booker, C. 2012. 'Open Sky' Acrylic on Canvas. Available at: http://artandairport.word press.com/2012/10/23/open-sky-acrylic-on-canvas-clare-booker/.

Birtchnell, T. and Caletrio, J. (eds) 2013. *Elite Mobilities.* London: Routledge.

Bissell, D., Hynes, M. and Sharpe, S. 2012. Unveiling Seductions Beyond Societies of Control: Affect, Security, and Humour in Spaces of Aeromobility. *Environment and Planning D: Society and Space* 30(4): 694–710.

Bolton, S.C. and Boyd, C. 2003. Trolley Dolly or Skilled Emotion Manager? Moving on from Hochschild's Managed Heart. *Work, Employment and Society* 17(2): 289–308.

Boris, E. 2006. Desirable Dress: Rosies, Sky Girls and the Politics of Appearance. *International Labor and Working-Class History* 69: 123–142.

Budd, L. 2009. Air Craft: Producing UK Airspace, in S. Cwerner, S. Kesselring and J. Urry (eds) *Aeromobilities.* London; New York: Routledge, pp. 115–134.

Budd, L. 2011. On Being Aeromobile: Airline Passengers and the Affective Experiences of Flight. *Journal of Transport Geography* 19(5): 1010–1016.

Budd, L. and Adey, P. 2009. The Software-Simulated Airworld: Anticipatory Code and Affective Aeromobilities. *Environment and Planning A* 41(6): 1366–1385.

Budd, L., Bell, M. and Warren, A. 2011. 'Taking Care in the Air': Jet Air Travel and Passenger Health, a Study of British Overseas Airways Corporation (1940–1974). *Social History of Medicine* 25(2): 446–461.

Budd, L., Warren, A. and Bell, M. 2011. Promoting Passenger Comfort and Wellbeing in the Air: An Examination of the In-Flight Health Advice Provided by International Airlines. *Journal of Air Transport Management* 17(5): 320–322.

Corn, J.J. 1983. *The Winged Gospel: America's Romance with Aviation, 1900–1950.* New York: Oxford University Press.

Cosgrove, D.E. 1999. Airport/Landscape, in J. Corner (ed.) *Recovering Landscape: Essays in Contemporary Landscape Architecture.* New York: Princeton Architectural Press, pp. 221–232.

Cresswell, T. 2006. *On the Move: Mobility in the Modern West.* New York: Routledge.

Cwerner, S., Kesselring, S. and Urry, J. (eds) 2009. *Aeromobilities.* London: Routledge.

DeLyser, D. 2010. Flying: Feminism and Mobilities – Crusading for Aviation, in T. Cresswell and P. Merriman (eds) *Geographies of Mobilities: Practices, Spaces, Subjects.* Burlington, VT: Ashgate, pp. 83–96.

Faludi, S. 1982. Airport Hotels Shedding Stopover Image. *New York Times*, 14 June 1982.

Faulconbridge, J. and Beaverstock, J.V. 2008. Geographies of International Business Travel in the Professional Service Economy, in Hislop D. (ed.) *Mobility and Technology in the Workplace.* London: Routledge, pp. 87–102.

Featherstone, M. 2004. Automobilities: An Introduction. *Theory, Culture & Society* 21(4–5): 1–24.

Forsyth, I. 2013a. Subversive Patterning: The Surficial Qualities of Camouflage. *Environment and Planning A* 45(5): 1037–1052.

Forsyth, I. 2013b. Designs on the Desert: Camouflage, Deception and the Militarization of Space. *Cultural Geographies* (forthcoming).

Hochschild, A.R. 1983. *The Managed Heart: Commercialization of Human Feeling.* Berkeley: University of California Press.

Jacobs, J.M. 2006. A Geography of Big Things. *Cultural Geographies* 13(1): 1–27.

Kitchin, R. and Dodge, M. 2011. *Code/Space: Software and Everyday Life.* Cambridge, MA: MIT Press.

Klauser, F. 2009. Interacting Forms of Expertise in Security Governance: The Example of CCTV Surveillance at Geneva International Airport. *The British Journal of Sociology* 60(2): 279–297.

Lin, W. 2013a. Flying Through Ash Clouds: Improvising Aeromobilities in Singapore and Australasia. *Mobilities* 1: 1–18.

Lin, W. 2013b. A Geopolitics of (Im)Mobility? *Political Geography* 34: A1–A3.

Linstead, S. 1995. Averting the Gaze: Gender and Power on the Perfumed Picket Line. *Gender, Work and Organization* 2(4): 192–206.

Lovegrove, K. 2000. *Airline: Identity, Design and Culture.* London: Lawrence King Publishing.

Martin, C. 2011. Desperate Passage: Violent Mobilities and the Politics of Discomfort. *Journal of Transport Geography* 19(5): 1046–1052.

McCormack, D.P. 2008. Engineering Affective Atmospheres on the Moving Geographies of the 1897 Andrée Expedition. *Cultural Geographies* 15(4): 413–430.

McNeill, D. 2009. The Airport Hotel as Business Space. *Geografiska Annaler: Series B, Human Geography* 91(3): 219–228.

McNeill, D. 2010. 'Behind the Heathrow Hassle': A Political Cultural Economy of the Privatized Airport. *Environment and Planning A* 42: 2859–2873.

Millward, L. 2007. *Women in British Imperial Airspace: 1922–1937.* Montreal: McGill-Queen's University Press.

Millward, L. 2008. The Embodied Aerial Subject: Gendered Mobility in British Inter-War Air Tours. *Journal of Transport History* 29(1): 5–22.

Morgan, M. and Nickson, D. 2001. Uncivil Aviation: A Review of the Air Rage Phenomenon. *International Journal of Tourism Research* 3(6): 443–457.

Murphy, A.G. 2002. Organization Politics of Place and Space: The Perpetual Liminoid Performance of Commercial Flight. *Text and Performance Quarterly* 22(4): 297–316.

Nikolaeva, A. 2012. Designing Public Space for Mobility: Contestation, Negotiation and Experiment at Amsterdam Airport Schiphol. *Tijdschrift voor economische en sociale geografie* 103(5): 542–554.

Pirie, G. 2009. British Air Shows in South Africa, 1932/33: 'Airmindedness', Ambition and Anxiety. *Kronos: Southern African Histories* 35(1): 48–70.

Robinson, J. 2012. Invisible Targets, Strengthened Morale: Static Camouflage as a 'Weapon of the Weak'. *Space and Polity* 16(3): 351–368.

Robinson, J. 2013. 'Darkened Surfaces': Camouflage and the Nocturnal Observation of Britain, 1941–1945. *Environment and Planning A* 45(5): 1053–1069.

Simonsen, D.G. 2010. Transitrum: Flykabiner og supermodernitetens ikke-steder. *Scandia* 74(2): 103–126.

Urry, J. 2002. *Sociology Beyond Societies: Mobilities for the Twenty-First Century.* London: Routledge.

Urry, J. 2009. Aeromobilities and the Global, in S. Cwerner, S. Kesselring and J. Urry (eds) *Aeromobilities.* London/New York: Routledge, pp. 26–38.

Whitelegg, D. 2007. *Working the Skies: The Fast-Paced, Disorienting World of the Flight Attendant.* New York: New York University Press.

Williams, A.J. 2010. A Crisis of Aerial Sovereignty? Considering the Implications of Recent Military Violations of National Airspace. *Area* 42(1): 51–59.

Williams, A. 2011. Reconceptualising Spaces of the Air: Performing the Multiple Spatialities of UK Military Airspaces. *Transactions of the Institute of British Geographers* 36(2): 253–267.

Chapter 5
Environmental Externalities of Air Transport

Tim Ryley

Introduction

Global aviation has developed rapidly over the last 100 years, transforming commercial air travel from a luxury item for the few to an activity undertaken by nearly 3 billion passengers a year. Even when demand has been affected in the short-term through events such as the 1991 Gulf War, the September 2001 terrorist attacks, and the SARS epidemic, there has been an underlying longer-term growth in air travel. However, accompanying this growth have been increasing concerns surrounding the environmental externalities of air transport. In the broader context of sustainable development, although aviation may be considered by some to be economically and socially sustainable, it is generally considered to be environmentally unsustainable owing to its reliance on carbon intensive fossil fuels.

Environmental externalities in this context refer to the costs associated with aviation. This chapter discusses these costs using a geographical framework, from global phenomena such as climate change to more local aspects such as the issue of noise disturbance around airports. The discussion incorporates measures that may reduce the externalities of air transport and the wider implications such interventions may have for the air transport industry.

Environmental Externalities of Air Transport at the Global Scale

To date, much of the environmental debate surrounding aviation has focused on its contribution to anthropogenic global climate change. There has always been a globally changing climate, but in recent times it has been possible to link increased levels of key greenhouse gas emissions, which perturb the global climate, to human activity. The Intergovernmental Panel on Climate Change Fourth Assessment Report (IPCC 2007) states that it is very likely human activities are causing an unprecedented increase in average temperature for many regions of the world, and that the probable temperature rise by the end of the twenty-first century will be between 1.8°C and 4°C, coupled with an increasing level of unpredictable and extreme weather patterns. While there is a general consensus among scientists that climate change is happening, questions remain over the scale of the process. Much of this uncertainty relates to the difficulty with the prediction elements of climate models that result from the chaotic and dynamic nature of weather systems.

The transport sector is a major contributor to greenhouse gases and atmospheric pollution. Transport currently accounts for 22 per cent of global carbon dioxide emissions (International Energy Agency 2012), most of which originate in industrial countries. This proportion is set to increase owing to the relative expense and difficulty of 'decarbonising' the sector and achieving emissions reductions when compared against other sectors such as industrial and domestic use coupled with anticipated growing demand for transport, particularly air transport.

The growing proportion of carbon dioxide emissions from aviation (which currently stands at around 3 per cent of emissions from all sectors) means that the sector will take an increasingly significant proportion of any future carbon budget (Anderson et al. 2007; Bows-Larkin and Anderson 2013). Yet while much of the focus until recently has been on carbon, other non-carbon emissions from aircraft and aviation sources affect the global climate. These pollutants include nitrous oxides, water vapour (which, under certain atmospheric conditions creates condensation trails (contrails) that block or reflect solar energy) and the highly potent greenhouse gas methane (Bows et al. 2008; Carleton and Travis 2013). The effects of these pollution species are less well understood and more difficult to account for than carbon dioxide as the quantity with which they are emitted varies according to flight phase, engine thrust setting, engine temperatures and atmospheric conditions.

The difficulty of quantifying, managing and mitigating aviation's environmental impacts is exemplified at an international level by the debates and challenges facing the Kyoto Protocol and the European Union's Emissions Trading System (see Anger-Kraavi and Köhler 2013, for a detailed discussion) and at a national level by the United Kingdom's Climate Change Act (United Kingdom Parliament 2008). The Climate Change Act states that the UK will reduce carbon dioxide emissions by 80 per cent by 2050 from 1990 levels, with an interim target of a reduction of at least 34 per cent by 2020. Achieving these targets is particularly challenging for aviation given the forecast increases in air travel demand. Indeed, despite a dip in demand due to the 2008/09 economic recession, air travel in the UK has increased over the last 10 years with 219 million terminal passengers at United Kingdom airports in 2011 compared with 167 million in 1999 (Civil Aviation Authority 2012).

The Stern Review (Stern et al. 2006), commissioned by the UK government to examine the implications of climate change, calls for the aviation industry and air passengers to cover the external costs of air travel. The review identified the growing contribution of air travel to greenhouse gas emissions, and supported the use of market forces to help aid regulation. In addition to concerns about increased air travel, the Stern Review recognises that there is no prospect of significant sustainable fuel source breakthroughs in the aviation sector, certainly in the short-term to mid-term time horizon.

At a European level, the primary aviation-related mitigation policy measure has been the EU Emission Trading System, introduced in 2005. It was intended that the aviation industry would be included in the scheme from 2012. This became a contentious issue in the air transport industry, with some airlines and countries questioning the suitability and fairness of the scheme (see Anger-Kraavi and Köhler 2013).

Green taxes are one way of restraining demand (and emissions) that can also encourage an uptake of cleaner technology. Discussion concerning national aviation taxes applied across a range of countries (see Keen and Strand 2007) recognises that there is competition between nations regarding domestic airlines, airports and associated aspects such as the tourism industry that can all influence tax levels. Air Passenger Duty is a United Kingdom aviation tax case study. Introduced in 1994, Air Passenger Duty is the only tax levied on United Kingdom air travel and is charged at a flat rate fee which varies by end destination per aircraft. Air Passenger Duty levels have been tweaked in recent years to make them more consistent with the level of emissions per passenger. However, it is not clear how much of the money raised by Air Passenger Duty is used by the United Kingdom Government towards mitigating the environmental externalities from air transport. When the general public were asked to express their views on aviation tax in response to the recent rise in Air

Passenger Duty, it was found that people generally preferred an independently managed and accountable fund (Ryley et al. 2010).

Much on-going research concerns technological improvements, and in particular exploring the feasibility of alternative fuels such as biofuel. These alternatives are mid-term to long-term developments given the timescale required to make such fuels operational. Other technological improvements can be achieved through improving the airframe and engine design. IATA (2009) claims that the following technological improvements could reduce emissions per aircraft: retrofit (7–13 per cent reduction), production updates (7–18 per cent reduction), new aircraft design before 2020 (25–50 per cent reduction), and new aircraft design after 2020 (25–50 per cent reduction)

Some airlines, including Flybe and easyJet of the UK, have undertaken environmental marketing, particularly around increased load factors that reduce emission levels per passenger and newer, more efficient aircraft. It is the newer aircraft that passengers perceive as the most effective way of reducing the environmental impact of air travel, and many passengers can differentiate between airlines based on environmental image (Mayer et al. 2012). However, a change in behaviour is limited. There have been very low uptake levels for voluntary air travel carbon offsetting schemes, whether directly from airlines or third-party sources. In such schemes, the equivalent amount of carbon dioxide is prevented or removed elsewhere say through planting trees or alternative energy generation.

There are broader tensions at play between the environmental concerns and the wider economic and social elements, further complicated by the range of air transport stakeholders. As awareness of the scope and scale of climate change increases, there are some commentators (e.g. Bows et al. 2008) calling for stronger action in response to 'dangerous' levels of climate change. In relation to climate change and transport, given the timing of the recent economic downturn and the arguable delay in action towards reducing environmental externalities in transport it is easy to take a pessimistic tone. There is the hope that climate change impacts have been overestimated, that transport policy makers will suddenly change tack on climate change issues, and that there will be further unexpected behavioural and technological changes relating to transport (Chapman and Ryley 2012).

Given the projected increase in air travel demand and associated impacts, one response is to reduce air travel, although individuals are reluctant to reduce this due to the social benefits offered to them. Evidence can be gleaned from an environmental segmentation study by the Department of the Environment, Food and Rural Affairs (2008), based on a large-scale survey. A range of actions to reduce the carbon footprint of individuals were tested. As well as personal transport, the 12 actions tested covered improvements to household efficiency, reductions in the impact of food consumption, and reductions in the emissions from travel. The three personal transport actions were to use more efficient vehicles, to use private cars less for short trips, and to avoid unnecessary short-haul flights. The three transport behaviours were the three actions with the highest levels of actual behaviour and the highest level of carbon emissions impact. Of these three behaviours, unnecessary flights had the highest carbon emissions impact, which puts the air transport environmental externalities into perspective against other sectors.

Davison and Ryley (2010) show that proportionally few people show a willingness to change their air travel behaviour; only a small segment of the population are trying to fly less for environmental reasons. Barr et al. (2010) demonstrate that even the most committed environmentalists who behave sustainably in some areas of their life, such as with recycling, are unwilling to cut back on their low-cost air travel. This behavioural tendency extends as well to professional geographers and other academics who regularly attend international conferences which in most cases require significant air travel (Nevins 2013).

Bowen (2010) looks ahead to the future and states that following an initial century of unconstrained growth in air travel, the twenty-first century will witness a series of constraints upon air transport, not only relating to environmental issues but also other challenges such as oil scarcity and terrorism threats. There are a series of tough choices ahead to deal with the range of environmental externalities from air transport. As noted by Budd and Ryley (2012), some individuals may have to reduce or stop flying as a result of increased taxes and legislation implemented in response to environmental externalities. It would be preferable to have managed growth that benefits all, rather than just the affluent minority (Daley 2010).

Environmental Externalities of Air Transport at the Local Scale

Local air transport environmental externalities cover a broad range of aspects. They include the development of airports and associated infrastructure; noise pollution, water pollution from surface run-off; local air quality pollutants such as carbon monoxide and nitrogen oxides; solid waste from scrapped aircraft and waste oil and tyres; groundwater contamination; and biodiversity management. Some of these environmental impacts relate to the life cycle aspects of air transport, from the construction of aircraft and airports right through to the disposal of scrapped airframes and associated components.

Noise can be a major local environmental issue for residents living close to airports. They have to contend with not only the noise of aircraft taking off and landing but also the associated airport operations, such as access by surface transport. Noise can be a major issue for airports and many have made commitments to compensate local residents through community funds and/or finance home insulation schemes to reduce the impact of aircraft noise (Davison et al. 2010).

Although much of the aviation-related effort has fallen on reducing aircraft emissions, airports have been under increasing pressure to quantify and assess their role in reducing environmental externalities. The nature of airport planning engenders different environmental issues and challenges depending on the national context. For instance, German airport development tends to be influenced by strong environmental lobbying and a lengthy planning process (Caves and Gosling 1999). A further important context for airport development is the function. For example, many countries in southern Europe are dependent on air transport for tourism and the economic and social benefits provided by incoming holidaymakers.

The role of airport expansion in London and the south-east of England is a contentious issue that stems partly from the lack of available land for airport development, as well as the scale of the capital investment involved. Proposed options include the development of a third runway at Heathrow Airport and building on reclaimed land in the Thames Estuary, although the latter is likely to have significant environmental impacts in terms of affecting local wildlife habitats. Given the airport noise impacts and strong NIMBY (Not In My Back Yard) sentiment within local areas surrounding current and potential airport sites, the political stakes are high. It is difficult to balance shorter-term business arguments against the longer-term environmental impacts.

Regulation, in the form of an Environmental Impact Assessment, is compulsory for most major airport developments (Ison et al. 2002). At Hong Kong, a range of environmental measures were implemented to minimise construction noise, monitor dust, introduce compensatory conservation measures, and special handling facilities for hazardous material and chemical waste. This was all underpinned by strong links between the government developing the airport and the surrounding community. The large-scale nature of the project meant that aside from building the airport, there was also the levelling of two islands, land reclamation, and the development of a new town, a harbour crossing, a tunnel, a 34 km airport railway and a 30 km expressway (Ison et al. 2002).

For airport decision-makers, in terms of day-to-day operations, there are a range of mitigation measures that can be undertaken to reduce emissions. These include building-related energy improvements and recycling efforts in the airport buildings, and more efficient operations within an airport. Airports could attempt to become carbon neutral, either eliminating emissions from ground operations or offsetting them elsewhere. Returning to local noise impacts, a range of mitigation measures can be implemented including targets for airports to reduce noise levels, flight bans for certain hours (typically night-time), improvements in aircraft technology and financial compensation to nearby residents.

Another issue for airports relates to passenger surface access, with the issues of reducing access by private vehicles either as double (drop-off/pick-up, taxi) or single (car/park) trips to and from the airport. Some surface access trips could easily be transferred to public transport options such as bus and rail. Many passengers travel long distances to access airports. An air travel survey of passengers in the East Midlands regions of the UK (Ryley and Davison 2008) showed that whilst more had naturally used the nearby airports (East Midlands Airport 88 per cent, Birmingham International Airport 79 per cent), many passengers had also accessed the London-based airports (Heathrow 67 per cent, Gatwick 63 per cent, Luton 58 per cent, Stansted 44 per cent), which are all over 100 km away. There are also environmental externalities from associated journeys to and from airports, including employees and associated airport organisations such as aircraft food suppliers, hotels, car hire, freight companies and security organisations. As such, the airport itself is not in control of all operations with a range of stakeholders with vested interests, such as public transport operators and third party tenants, requiring negotiation and compromise in relation to environmental issues.

Discussion and Conclusion

This chapter has presented environmental externalities from aviation with a geographical focus. Although there are many environmental externalities, it is arguably climate change that is of the greatest concern. Mitigation responses are varied and it is difficult to achieve a major reduction in air transport environmental externalities in the short-term. Technological improvements represent marginal gains over a long-term timescale whereas behavioural change appears to be limited. For short-haul air transport trips there is often the possibility of a surface transport alternative. However, a difficulty remains that there are strong economic and social benefits from long-haul air transport journeys for which there are no substitutes.

Following calls for the external costs of flying to be absorbed by the air transport industry and consumers, economic instruments incorporating aviation have been introduced at the national and continental scale such as Air Passenger Duty and the EU Emissions Trading System. Such measures need to be adapted to ensure they are appropriate and fair responses to environmental externalities. At the local level of an airport system, small scale environmental gains can be achieved by improving surface access journeys to-and-from airports, energy within terminal buildings, the efficiency of operations and aircraft technologies, but arguably a larger scale response is required.

Given the international nature of air transport, environmental mitigation measures increasingly could be global, say an international version of the EU Emissions Trading Scheme, but it is difficult when other nations are attempting to scupper the current scheme at a lower spatial scale. International agreement on measures tends to be difficult with strong differences in opinion between countries. Any fuel-related tax developments are also limited by the Chicago Convention agreement. The geographical difficulty of linkages between the international and national spheres is highlighted by the challenge of attributing air transport emissions back to their source, and any subsequent allocation generates arguments of fairness and equity.

The geographies of air transport come into play at the lower level spatial scales, as highlighted in this chapter. The location of surrounding communities can affect the level of noise impacts from an airport. A tension appears when such local externalities mix with global environmental concerns. For instance, when determining aircraft take-off paths there is the trade-off between minimising global carbon emissions whilst reducing the local impacts from aircraft noise. It is very difficult to determine which of the externalities should take precedence.

The location of airports in sub-national regions within countries can become a pressing environmental issue, as shown by the case of airport expansion in London and the southeast of England. As with many of the issues concerning the global level environmental externalities, it is in the political system at the national level that the challenges are particularly prevalent, in this case the decision where to locate a new airport or expand an existing airport. It can be concluded, therefore, that although environmental externalities have impacts across the spatial levels, the difficulties are particularly evident in the political and economic elements of the macro-scale, where nations and regional blocs of countries co-operate and compete.

References

Anderson, K., Bows, A. and Footitt, A. 2007. *Aviation in a Low Carbon EU.* A research report by the Tyndall Centre, University of Manchester for Friends of the Earth. Available at: http://www.foe.co.uk/resource/reports/aviation_tyndall_07_main.pdf [accessed: 10 September 2013].

Anger-Kraavi, A. and Köhler, J. 2013. Aviation and the EU Emissions Trading System, in Budd, L., Griggs, S. and Howarth, D. (eds) *Sustainable Aviation Futures.* Bingley: Emerald, pp. 109–130.

Barr, S., Shaw, G., Coles, T. and Prillwitz, J. 2010. 'A Holiday is a Holiday': Practicing Sustainability, Home and Away. *Journal of Transport Geography* 18: 474–481.

Bowen, J. 2010. *The Economic Geography of Air Transportation. Space, Time, and the Freedom of the Sky.* Abingdon: Routledge.

Bows, A., Anderson, K. and Upham, P. 2008. *Aviation and Climate Change: Lessons for European Policy.* London: Routledge.

Bows-Larkin, A. and Anderson, K. 2013. Carbon Budgets for Aviation or Gamble with Our Future? in Budd, L., Griggs, S. and Howarth, D. (eds) *Sustainable Aviation Futures.* Bingley: Emerald, pp. 65–84.

Budd, L. and Ryley, T. 2012. An International Dimension: Aviation, in Ryley, T.J and Chapman, L. (eds) *Transport and Climate Change*. Bingley: Emerald.

Carleton, A.M. and Travis, D.J. 2013. Aviation-Contrail Impacts on Climate and Climate Change: A Ready-to-Wear Research Mantle for Geographers. *The Professional Geographer* 65(3): 421–432.

Caves, R.E. and Gosling, G.D. 1999. *Strategic Airport Planning*. Oxford: Pergamon.

Chapman, L. and Ryley, T. 2012. Chapter 14: Conclusions, in Ryley, T.J and Chapman, L. (eds) *Transport and Climate Change*. Bingley: Emerald.

Civil Aviation Authority. 2012. *UK Airport Statistics 2011*. Available at: http://www.caa. co.uk/default.aspx?catid=80&pagetype=88&sglid=3&fld=2011Annual [accessed: 10 September 2013].

Daley, B. 2010. *Air Transport and the Environment*. Farnham: Ashgate.

Davison, L. and Ryley, T. 2010. Tourism Destination Preferences of Low-Cost Airline Users in the East Midlands. *Journal of Transport Geography* 18(3): 458–465.

Davison, L., Ryley, T. and Snelgrove, M. 2010. Regional Airports in a Competitive Market: A Case Study of Cardiff International Airport. *Journal of Airport Management* 4(2): 178–194.

Department for Environment, Food and Rural Affairs (DEFRA). 2008. *A Framework for Environmental Behaviours: A Report*. Department for Environment, Food and Rural Affairs, United Kingdom.

International Air Transport Association (IATA). 2009. *A Global Approach to Reducing Aviation Emissions*. IATA, Montreal. Available at: http://www.iata.org/SiteCollection Documents/Documents/Global_Approach_Reducing_Emissions_251109web.pdf [accessed: 10 September 2013].

Intergovernmental Panel on Climate Change (IPCC). 2007. *Climate Change 2007, IPCC 4th Assessment Synthesis Report*. Available at: http://www.ipcc.ch/publications_and_ data/publications_ipcc_fourth_assessment_report_synthesis_report.htm [accessed: 10 September 2013].

International Energy Agency (IEA). 2012. CO_2 *Emissions from Fuel Combustion*. Available at: http://www.iea.org/co2highlights/co2highlights.pdf [accessed: 10 September 2013].

Ison, S., Peake, S. and Wall, S. 2002. *Environmental Issues and Policies*. Pearson Education.

Keen, M. and Strand, J. 2007. Indirect Taxes on International Aviation. *Fiscal Studies* 28(1): 1–41.

Mayer, R., Ryley, T. and Gillingwater, D. 2012. Passenger Perceptions of the 'Green Image' Associated with Airlines. *Journal of Transport Geography* 22: 179–186.

Nevins, J. 2013. Academic Jet-Setting in a Time of Climate Destabilization: Ecological Privilege and Professional Geographic Travel. *The Professional Geographer* DOI: 10.1080/00330124.2013.784954.

Ryley, T. and Davison, L. 2008. UK Air Travel Preferences: Evidence from an East Midlands Household Survey. *Journal of Air Transport Management* 14(1): 43–46.

Ryley, T., Davison, L., Bristow, A. and Pridmore, A. 2010. Public Engagement on Aviation Taxes in the United Kingdom. *International Journal of Sustainable Transportation* 4(2): 112–118.

Stern, N., Peters, S., Bakhshi, V. et al. 2006. *Stern Review on the Economics of Climate Change*. HM Treasury. Available at: http://webarchive.nationalarchives.gov.uk/+/http:/ www.hm-treasury.gov.uk/sternreview_index.htm [accessed: 10 September 2013].

United Kingdom Parliament. 2008. *Climate Change Act*. London: HMSO. Available at: http://www.legislation.gov.uk/ukpga/2008/27/contents/enacted [accessed: 10 September 2013].

Chapter 6
The Role of Airports in Air Transport

Anne Graham and Stephen Ison

Introduction

The airport sector has experienced significant change over the last few decades, and has recently been subject to a harsh economic environment as a result of factors outside of its control. The aim of this chapter is to detail the patterns of airport traffic, both passengers and cargo, the complex nature of airports and their role, as they bring together the activities of the airfield, terminal, handling services and the ground transport facilities. All of this has taken place against a backdrop of commercialisation and privatisation, and as such this chapter considers the changes which have taken place in this regard. In addition, the issue of balancing aeronautical and non-aeronautical revenues is examined along with ground access and the pressure resulting from surface access traffic growth. Finally, the whole area of airports, the environment and economic development is considered.

Patterns of Airport Traffic

According to Airports Council International (ACI), world airports handled 5.4 billion passengers, 93 million cargo tonnes and 77 million aircraft movements in 2011 (ACI 2012a). Reflecting overall trends within the air transport industry, airport traffic has grown substantially in the last few decades, albeit with periodic fluctuations due to economic recessions or other external factors, such as the Gulf War in 1991. There has been however a much more volatile environment during the last decade as a result of natural disasters, socio-political upheaval and other shock events such as 9/11, SARS, swine flu, the Eyjafjallajökull ash cloud, the Japanese earthquake and Arab Spring uprisings. In addition, the recent global credit crunch and deep economic recession have had a major impact on traffic in 2008 and 2009, with economic factors and high fuel prices continuing to create considerable uncertainty, particularly within Europe due to the Eurozone debt crisis. Overall passenger numbers grew by 5.3 per cent in 2011 with preliminary figures showing a smaller increase in 2012 of 3.9 per cent. Meanwhile cargo traffic remained stagnant between 2010 and 2012, mostly as a result of low business and consumer confidence in many of the largest international economies (ACI 2013).

As a consequence traffic patterns are unclear over the short-term, but in the long-term it is predicted that passenger numbers will increase by 4.1 per cent per annum, with the volume more than doubling to exceed 12 billion by 2031. Cargo operations are expected to grow at the faster rate of 4.5 per cent and reach around 225 million tonnes by 2031 (ACI 2012b). As a result, providing additional capacity to meet demand (if this is desired), particularly in regions where there are significant funding shortages or environmental pressures, will continue to be a key and on-going challenge for many airports.

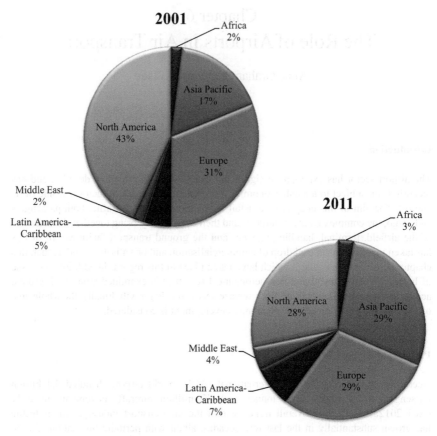

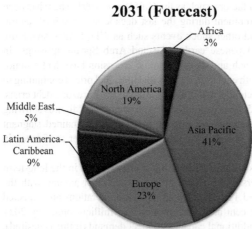

Figure 6.1   Passenger traffic by world region
Source: Derived from ACI 2012a.

For many years the airport industry has been dominated by North America and Europe. However a combination of strong economic development in a number of Asian countries and slower economic growth, combined with more mature demand in more advanced economies, has resulted in the Asia-Pacific passenger market share now representing 29 per cent of the total world market (virtually the same share as Europe and North America) compared with 17 per cent in 2001. Traffic levels in other regions remains relatively low, even though they have increased quite substantially. Of the seven billion additional passenger numbers being forecast for 2030, around three quarters will be at airports within emerging/developing economies rather than in advanced markets. Many of these passengers will use airports in Asia-Pacific and as a result these airports are predicted to be handling four out of every 10 passengers by 2031 (Figure 6.1).

Passenger figures at individual airports reflect the importance of the North American, European and Asia-Pacific regions. In 2011 out of the 20 largest global airports, six were US airports, eight were Asia-Pacific and five were European (Table 6.1). For a number of years Atlanta has been the largest global airport but there are indications that Beijing airport, in spite of a slow-down of economic activity in China, may be close to this position in 2012. It was only ranked eighth in 2006 (with around 56 million passengers) and 20th in 2004 (with 35 million passengers) and before that outside the top 20, with just 22 million passengers in 2000. Other Asian airports that have moved into the top 20 include Guangzhou, Shanghai and Jakarta, whilst a number of US airports, such as Houston, Phoenix, Newark, Detroit and Minneapolis have dropped out. The only airport not from these three major regions is Dubai which has experienced rapid growth in recent years – rising from 27th position in 2007 with around 34 million passengers to its current 13th position with 51 million passengers. This airport has benefitted from the ambitious expansion plans of Emirates Airlines combined with the advantage of its strategic location which is relatively close to a large share of the world's total population, and in particular is very suitable as serving as a transcontinental hub between Europe and East/South Asia. In terms of international passengers, Heathrow has held the top position for many years, with London being the dominant node in the global air transport network.

With regards to cargo tonnes, Europe has occupied third position in recent times with around 20 per cent of the market share. In 2001 North America had a share of 43 per cent compared with 27 per cent for Asia-Pacific but by 2011 the relative importance of these regions was reversed with this latter region now handling 37 per cent of all traffic. Not all the major cargo airports coincide with the major passenger airports. Hong Kong is the largest airport followed by Memphis which is the base of Federal Express. Louisville, the base for UPS, is also an important cargo airport as is Anchorage which has a relatively small passenger volume. Again Dubai airport is the only airport in the top 20 outside of these three world regions, being located seventh in the world rankings.

Another key indicator of airport size is aircraft movements. Here North America remains dominant since the average size of aircraft is smaller due to competitive pressures, shorter sectors and the dependence on domestic traffic, especially due to a lack of rail as a competitive long-distance mode. Within the top 20 airports, 14 are North American. By contrast the larger than average aircraft size in the Asia-Pacific regions means that none of the busiest airports are located here, with the exception of Beijing. In the future, the long-term growth in aircraft movements is likely to be less than with passengers – as it has been in the past – due to a higher proportion of larger aircraft (such as the A380) being used and airlines flying with higher load factors.

Table 6.1   The world's top 20 airports 2011

	Passengers (millions)		Cargo (000s tonnes)		Movements (000s)
Atlanta	92389	Hong Kong	3977	Atlanta	923
Beijing	78675	Memphis	3916	Chicago O'Hare	879
London Heathrow	69433	Shanghai	3085	Los Angeles	703
Chicago O'Hare	66701	Anchorage	2543	Dallas FW	647
Tokyo Haneda	62584	Incheon	2539	Denver	628
Los Angeles	61862	Paris CDG	2300	Charlotte	540
Paris CDG	60970	Dubai	2270	Beijing	533
Dallas/FW	57803	Frankfurt	2215	Las Vegas	531
Frankfurt	56436	Louisville	2188	Houston	517
Hong Kong	53328	Tokyo Narita	1945	Paris CDG	514
Denver	52849	Singapore	1899	Frankfurt	487
Jakarta	51178	Miami	1842	London LHR	481
Dubai	50978	Los Angeles	1682	Phoenix	462
Amsterdam	49755	Beijing	1640	Philadelphia	448
Madrid	49644	Taipei	1627	Detroit	443
Bangkok	47911	London LHR	1569	Amsterdam	437
New York JFK	47684	Amsterdam	1550	Minneapolis	437
Singapore	46544	New York JFK	1349	Madrid	429
Guangzhou	45040	Bangkok	1322	Toronto	428
Shanghai	41448	Chicago	1312	New York JFK	411

Source: ACI 2012a.

The Role of the Airport Operator

Airports combine a wide range of services and facilities in order to fulfil their complex role. This includes the activities in the airfield, the terminal and the handling services that provide the link for passengers, their baggage and cargo between these two areas. Outside of the terminal there will also be the facilitation of ground transport. All these activities can be provided either by the airport operator or by a third party, with the way in which these activities are offered, and whether there are competing services, having a major impact on price and the quality of service. Competing services are most common in the commercial area, which tend to be outsourced due to a lack of expertise on the part of the airport operator, limited bulk buying power and insufficient supply infrastructure to effectively provide them. Ground handling can also be provided by the airport operator, airlines or specialist ground handling companies. However this is a more controversial issue as in some parts of the world it was, or maybe still is, common practice for the national airline or airport operator to have a monopoly or near monopoly in providing these activities. As a result of this in Europe, the European Union introduced the Ground Handling Directive in 1996 to stimulate more competition, but arguably there is still scope for improvements to be made to efficiency levels and the quality of service offered (Airport Research Centre 2009; Steer Davies Gleave 2010). Another contentious issue is security where costs have risen in recent years as a result of more stringent controls. Sometimes security is the responsibility of the airport operators as typically is the case at many European airports where security represents 35 per cent of operating costs and 40 per cent of manpower (ACI-Europe 2010a), whereas elsewhere security provision may be viewed as being more of the Government's responsibility, as in the United States where the Federal government plays a much greater role. This creates an uneven playing field for the world's airlines.

The extreme case of outsourcing occurs when total terminals are leased to airlines, as at certain US airports such as New York JFK and a few major Australian airports. Potentially greater use of competing terminals could allow for varying quality standards and facilities to be offered, although operational efficiency and economies of scale could be lost as a consequence. As competitive forces within the aviation sector continue to grow, arguably this could be considered as the logical direction for the airport industry to follow. However practical examples to date are difficult to find, with the most likely case, a second competing terminal at Dublin airport, failing to materialise.

To a certain extent, similar arguments can be extended to consider whether airports should be operated as individual entities, or as a group or system. Throughout the world, there are many examples of the latter situation. This may make sense for strategic, co-ordinated planning and in order to benefit from shared costs and expertise, but it also raises issues relating to cross-subsidisation of airport charges and whether competition is restricted. The most significant case here is undoubtedly the former UK BAA (now Heathrow Airport Holdings) company which used to own four airports in the South East (including London Heathrow, Gatwick and Stansted) and three in Scotland. After 20 years of fierce debate concerning the advantages and disadvantages of this group ownership, the UK's competition authority finally concluded in 2009 that such group ownership did inhibit competition and ordered BAA to sell Gatwick, Stansted and Edinburgh or Glasgow (Competition Commission 2009). This was achieved by 2013.

Irrespective of who actually provides the various airport activities, traditionally an airport has offered a fairly common set of services and facilities with very little segmentation taking place. The focus has been very much a 'one-size-fits-all' airport. However airline deregulation has led to the development of more diverse airline models, and at the same time stronger competitive forces have emerged between airports (Forsyth et al. 2010). Indeed many airports are now competing for regional and national traffic, whilst there are some that are even competing at an international level, such as the European airports Frankfurt and London Heathrow and the Asian airports of Singapore, Seoul Incheon and Hong Kong. As a result the airport operator is now paying far greater attention to differentiating its services and facilities to meet the requirements and expectations of diverse airline operators.

Some airports, such as Frankfurt or Paris Charles de Gaulle, have focused on the needs of members of global alliances. Alliance members want to be able to share and achieve cost economies and brand benefits from operating joint facilities, such as check-in and lounges, and, where possible, have adjacent stand parking. This is difficult to achieve for airports that were designed and built before these alliances existed. Many airports serving alliances, and others such as Dubai, strive to compete as a hub for transfer traffic and work hard on improving the quality of connections. Copenhagen airport's 'World Class Transfer Hub' initiative of 2010 is a good example of this. A few airports, such as Frankfurt or Doha have provided (with their airline partners) dedicated terminals for their premium passengers. At the other extreme, airports have provided specialist facilities for low cost carriers (LCCs). These airlines require quick turnarounds, and as such do not like using airbridges or airport buses and generally do not require airline lounges and transfer passenger or baggage facilities. Some airport operators have gone as far as to open new or refurbished low cost

Table 6.2   Examples of low-cost facilities

Airport	Date of opening	Type of terminal
Tampere-Pirkkala	2003	Refurbished cargo terminal
Warsaw	2004	Converted supermarket
Budapest	2005	Refurbished old terminal
Amsterdam	2005	New piers off existing terminal
Marseille	2006	Refurbished cargo terminal
Kuala Lumpur	2006	New terminal
Singapore	2006	New terminal
Bremen	2007	Refurbished warehouse
JFK	2008	New terminal incorporating old TWA terminal
Lyon	2008	Refurbished cargo terminal
Copenhagen	2010	New pier off existing terminal
Bordeaux	2010	New terminal

Note: Not all these facilities are still open.
Source: Compiled by the authors from various sources.

terminals or gate facilities with simpler designs and lower service standards which typically have lower passenger charges associated with them (Table 6.2).

Whilst such segmentation may be viewed as a natural reaction to the evolving airline industry, it does raise important issues. International Civil Aviation Organisation (ICAO) and EC regulations relating to airport charges permit differentiation as long as the charges are cost related and transparent. However many non-LCC airlines remain fearful that this may result in them subsidising LCC operations through such charging practices. As a result and particularly in Europe, this has led to a number of legal challenges and is one of the key reasons why the planned LCC facilities at Brussels airport never opened. So in spite of the principle of differential pricing being firmly rooted in airline strategies, it has yet to be fully accepted within the airport sector.

Management of Airport Infrastructure

Commercialisation and Privatisation

In addition to airline deregulation and liberalisation, which have been a major driving force in transforming the operating environment of airlines, there have been simultaneous changes within the airport sector, as its role has shifted from that of public utility to that of a dynamic, commercially oriented business. This commercial paradigm has meant that there is far greater consideration of the non-aeronautical aspects of an airport and also more focus on marketing activities to entice potential customers. By taking this commercialisation trend to its limits, airport privatisation has occurred. In a global study of 459 airports in 2007, ICAO found that 24 per cent of airports were either partially or fully under private ownership (ICAO 2008). Within Europe in 2008, 13 per cent of airports were owned by public-private shareholders and nine were fully privatised – with nearly half of all European passengers travelling through these partial or fully privatised airports (ACI-Europe 2010b).

Meanwhile in emerging/developing markets, or low/middle income countries as defined by the World Bank, 49 countries were involved with private participation with their airports, which represented more than US$34 billion investment commitment between 1990–2011 (World Bank 2013).

The first airport privatisation occurred in the United Kingdom in 1987 with the 100 per cent share flotation of the state run organisation BAA. However most airport privatisations have taken place in the last 20 years. The first wave came in the mid to late 1990s. This was known as the 'gold-rush' period, because of numerous opportunities and high prices paid, but it almost came to a total halt in the early 2000s as a result of the industry crisis caused by 9/11 and other external factors. However around 2004 privatisation was back on the agenda for a number of governments world-wide, albeit with much more cautious investors than in the past, but then again this was subsequently slowed down by the onset of the credit crunch and economic recession.

The extent of government influence on the sector following privatisation, for example whether ownership as well as management is handed over to the private sector, or whether there is partial as opposed to full privatisation, is always controversial. Many governments favour retaining at least some control, because of the strategic role that airports play as national or regional assets, or as crucial nodes in the formulation of integrated transport planning policies. Hence different airport privatisation and public–private partnership (PPP) models have evolved. These include share flotation, trade sales when some, or all, of the airport is sold to trade partners, concessions which typically last for 20–30 years and ownership is retained by the government – with a special type of concession option being the so-called build-operate-transfer (BOT) model when a substantial new investor is needed. Overall only a minority of privatisations have involved total ownership being handed over to the private sector. Moreover concessions and BOT type models have been particularly popular in emerging markets where there is a clear desire to retain ownership, but at the same time a strong need for major airport expansion and modernisation. Table 6.3 shows that airport privatisation has been a global trend, with the exception of North America where local public ownership remains the norm in the United States (apart from a very limited pilot privatisation programme) and with a 'not-for-profit' governance model in Canada.

Two of the most important drivers of privatisation have been the potential efficiency gains and the need for new investment. Whilst privatisation has undoubtedly brought new or expanded facilities at many airports, the evidence relating to efficiency gains is somewhat mixed and inconclusive (Graham 2011). Moreover in more recent years any ideological justifications related to private versus public control have tended to be downplayed, or become non-existent, with most focus being on the need for extra funding, and perhaps additionally the desire to acquire management and operational expertise. However the current difficult economic climate has added an extra dimension to this. From a negative viewpoint, investment funds may be difficult to obtain, as was the case with the failed privatisation of Chicago Midway in 2009. On the other hand, privatisation can be seen as a way to raise funds to support sovereign debts as was the situation with the recent sale of the airport company ANA in Portugal and the aborted privatisation of Madrid and Barcelona airports. Poor financial performance during these hard times has also led to an increase in secondary sales and in the extreme case Frankfurt Hahn airport has actually been brought back into public control as has Cardiff airport in Wales. Meanwhile in various emerging economies, higher traffic forecasts have meant that privatisation is still seen primarily as a route to pursue modernisation and expansion objectives, as was witnessed in Brazil in 2012.

Table 6.3   Examples of partial and full airport privatisations

Share flotation	Trade sale	Concession	BOT
Austria: Vienna	Australia: Brisbane, Melbourne, Sydney, Perth and 15 other major airports	Argentinean Airport System	Canada: Toronto Terminal 3
China: BCIA, Hainan Meilan	Belgium: Brussels, Charleroi, Liege	Bolivia: La Paz, Santa Cruz, Cochabamba	Albania: Tirana
Denmark: Copenhagen	China: Xi'an	Brazil: São Paulo Guarulhos, Sao Paulo	Bulgaria: Varna and Burgas
France: AdP	Germany: Dusseldorf, Hanover, Hamburg, Luebeck	Viracopos Campinas, Brasilia	Cyprus: Larnaca and Paphos
Germany: Fraport	Hungary: Budapest	Columbia: Barranquilla, Caratagena, Cali	Georgia: Tbilisi and Batumi
Italy: Rome, Florence, Venice, Pisa	Italy: Naples, Rome, Turin	Costa Rica: San Jose	Greece: Athens
Malaysia: Malaysia Airports	Malta	Croatia: Zagreb	India: Hyderabad, Bengaluru
New Zealand: Auckland	New Zealand: Wellington	Dominican Republic: 6 airports including Santo Domingo	Jordan: Amman
Slovenia: Ljubljana	Slovakia: Kosice	Jamaica: Montega Bay	Philippines: Manila international terminal
Switzerland: Zürich	South Africa: ACSA	Kosovo: Pristina	Saudi Arabia: Medinah
Thailand: AOT	Sweden: Skavsta	India: Delhi, Mumbai	Tunisia: Monastir and Enfidha
UK : BAA	US: Sanford Orlando, Stewart International	Maldives: Male	Turkey: Ankara, Izmir
	UK: Birmingham, Bristol, Manchester and 12 others	Mexico: South East Group, Pacific Group, North Central Group	UK: Birmingham Eurohub
		Peru: Lima and 12 regional airports	US: New York JFK international arrivals terminal
		Portugal: ANA	
		Russia: St Petersburg	
		Turkey: Antalya, Gazipasa	
		UK: Luton	
		Uruguay: Montevideo	

Note: The table only shows the first sale that was made. Further sales may have been made.
Source: Compiled by the authors from various sources.

In short, the climate for privatisation in the future, and the exact model favoured, will remain largely influenced, after political factors, by general economic conditions coupled with the prospects for future traffic growth.

One of the most visible consequences of privatisation has been the emergence of international airport companies. These include the traditional operators at airports such as Frankfurt, Zurich and Singapore, and newer airport companies or subsidiaries, such as Hochtief Airports, Vinci Airports and TAV Airports. Without privatisation, this internationalisation of the airport industry could not have happened. However, in spite of these developments, the level of concentration with the airport industry remains relatively low compared with other service sectors, and indeed with airlines. Moreover some operators, for example the former BAA and Copenhagen airport, have reversed their previous international policies to focus on core national assets. Arguably this lack of concentration and absence of a convincing appetite for international expansion may be due to the fact that although international operations can potentially grow profits, spread risks and provide the opportunity to benefit from shared knowledge, expertise and financial resources, the gains may not always be that significant. Moreover the scope for increasing revenues from common products, shared marketing and brand benefits, as is common with other sectors, is very much more limited.

Aeronautical and Non-Aeronautical Areas

The commercial airport paradigm that has replaced the traditional public sector model has changed the balance between aeronautical and non-aeronautical revenues, with a greater reliance on the non-aeronautical areas. Indeed globally in 2011 non-aeronautical revenues accounted for nearly half (47 per cent) of all airport revenues (ACI 2012c). One way to consider modern airports is to see them as so-called two sided businesses or markets which offer services to both passengers and airlines (Gillen 2011). These businesses provide platforms for two distinct customers who both gain from being networked through the platform. The positive interdependence means that airport operators will be incentivised to compete for airline traffic and passengers as these will influence both their aeronautical and non-aeronautical revenue. If passengers stay away, this will affect the airlines that might then have to leave the airport. If airlines reduce or withdraw their services, this will reduce passenger numbers and consequently the non-aeronautical sales.

With this in mind, airport operators have been under increasing pressure in the more deregulated and competitive aviation environment, combined with the difficult economic times, to offer an attractive airport charges package to their airline users. Traditionally airports and airlines have not entered into any formal relationship, with the exception of the United States where there are legally binding long-term use and lease agreements. However the more commercial aviation industry now offers greater opportunities to develop stronger relationships. Already a few examples exist, such as Copenhagen airport and the major airports in Australia, which have voluntarily agreed the levels of charges directly with their airline customers over a time period of up to five years. This is as a result of their governments adopting a light handed approach to airport regulation. As the competitive forces grow, there is a convincing argument for more governments to adopt this type of regulatory approach rather than a more heavy handed control, such as a price cap, which exists at a number of airports such as Heathrow, Dublin or Paris (Copenhagen Economics 2012). Another parallel development has been the negotiation of long-term (5–20 years) bilateral agreements or contracts between LCCs and airports, particularly within Europe, where airlines agree on certain growth commitments in return for financial incentives offered by the airport operators. This has been driven primarily by the increased buying power of LCCs which has resulted in more business risk for the airports. Such contracts can be seen as a way in which airports can potentially introduce more stability into this increasingly unstable situation and hence again may represent a viable option for more widespread use in the future, particularly with this type of traffic (Starkie 2012).

With such pressures on aeronautical charges, the incentives to develop additional non-aeronautical revenues remain as strong as ever. However gone are the days when airports could easily achieve this merely by adding more commercial space or extending the range of basic facilities (Graham 2009). Increasing competitive pressures from internet shopping coupled with security restrictions, especially related to limits on liquids carried on-board, and less consumer disposable income has meant that airport operators have had to work much harder to grow these revenues. They are having to be more inventive to increase the passenger's spend, particularly by diversifying their offers, adopting general retail outlet or shopping mall practices to increase loyalty, such as discount schemes, and taking advantage of technology developments in areas such as the internet, mobile apps, social media and near field communication technology.

Within this new balance of aeronautical and non-aeronautical revenues, a third dimension of growing concern to airport operators is that of the passenger satisfaction or experience. Whilst a high satisfaction rate is unlikely to have a large influence over the passenger's airport choice (which will be largely driven by location and airline factors), it may well have an effect on their willingness to use commercial facilities. Thus the trade-off between lower airport costs that will filter through to lower charges, maximising commercial revenues and satisfying customers, is a constant challenge faced by many airport operators. The low cost terminal is a good example here where the more limited commercial facilities and lack of a shopping mall atmosphere, brought about by the desire to reduce the costs for the airlines, may actually inhibit passengers from spending. This helps explain why both Amsterdam and Copenhagen offer low cost facilities after the passengers have experienced the full commercial offer at the airport and why Singapore and Kuala Lumpur airport are now developing new LCC terminals with a wider range of commercial offerings.

Airport Ground Access

An important issue related to airport infrastructure is ground access. The private vehicle dominates ground access travel and this has created significant difficulties for airports in terms of increased traffic congestion and vehicle emissions (Humphreys and Ison 2005). The approach to this problem has changed over time with 'predict-and-provide' (where the demand for use of the network is forecast and provision made for that use in terms of key infrastructure) giving way to a more 'demand management' oriented approach. This approach emphasises the importance and value of utilising existing infrastructure more efficiently rather than constantly accommodating demand through infrastructure construction. In order to bring about a shift to more sustainable modes of ground transport there has been an increase in interest in policy options such as the provision of information on alternatives to the private car and encouraging car sharing for employees. These measures are often referred to as 'soft' or 'smarter choice' policy options, and are distinct from the so called 'hard' alternatives such as road pricing (Cairns et al. 2008). This is reflected in the case of the UK where the Department for Transport (2012) published a *Draft Aviation*

Policy Framework (DfT 2012) which seeks a sustainable approach to UK aviation by making more efficient use of existing airport capacity and states that 'proposals for airport development must be accompanied by clear ground access proposals which demonstrate how the airport will ensure easy and reliable access for passengers, increase the use of public transport by passengers to access the airport, and minimise congestion and other local impacts' (DfT 2012: 83). As such, they state that improving ground access to airports means that 'high quality, efficient and reliable road and rail access to airports contributes greatly to the experience of passengers, freight operators and people working at the airport. Greater use of low carbon modes to access airports also has the potential to reduce CO_2 emissions, as well as leading to less congestion and improved air quality' (DfT 2012: 31). In addition, rail access is seen to offer 'efficient and environmentally-friendly connections to airport, particularly for larger airports where passenger numbers are sufficient to justify fast and frequent services' (DfT 2012: 32).

Ground Access Users

The users of ground access essentially fall into three categories, namely, passengers, employees and visitors (Ashford et al. 2013). The relative split between these categories varies considerably between airports and depends on such factors as the airport's location and size, the time of day, week and year, and the kind of service the airport provides, for example, being mainly passenger or cargo focused (Humphreys et al. 2005; Ashford et al. 2013). Users possess different characteristics and therefore it is important that ground access strategies take them into account. The characteristics are summarised in Table 6.4.

Passengers can be split into business and leisure users who possess different ground access characteristics. Passengers in the main represent the majority of ground access journeys and the issue of congestion is likely to be more problematic when there is a large share of passengers being dropped-off and picked-up. For example, Heathrow Airport estimates that 70 per cent of CO_2 emissions generated from ground access traffic are from drop-off/pick-up (BAA 2009). Passengers, particularly leisure users, generally favour the use of the private car since it is seen as being more comfortable, flexible, reliable (in a situation where the journey time is critical), and relatively easy for transporting heavy luggage (Kazda and Caves 2008; Humphreys and Ison 2005). For these reasons the taxi is also perceived as a favourable mode (de Neufville and Odoni 2003). The fact that the majority of leisure passengers will be carrying luggage is seen as a main reason deterring public transport use (Coogan et al. 2008). In addition, leisure passengers are likely to be travelling from home and thus have access to a car for their journey whereas visitors to a region will most probably not have access to a private car (Coogan et al. 2008).

Each airport will have *employees* accessing and egressing on a daily basis. A full time employee may make in the region of 500 trips to and from the airport per year (Humphreys and Ison 2005) and they can account for one-third of airport journeys, although this can be much higher if the airport hosts the headquarters of a large aviation company (Humphreys and Ison 2005; Graham 2013). Employees are frequent car users not least since public transport is often unsuitable for their requirements. Given the 24-hour/7-days a week nature of airports, employees often need to travel at times and from geographical localities poorly served by public transport (Humphreys and Ison 2005). Airport employees invariably work shift patterns and this can exacerbate the problem of traffic congestion at various times of the day (Humphreys et al. 2005). While all this is the case, airport operators are in the main keen to limit the supply of employee parking, given that passenger spaces generate 7–10

Table 6.4   Airport user characteristics

Type of user	Ground access characteristics
Passenger:	
Business	• Relatively frequent number of flights taken. • Time critical. • Likely to be travelling with less luggage than the leisure airport user. • More inclined to use high speed rail to and from the airport, if such facilities exist.
Leisure	• Relatively infrequent number of flights taken. • Cost critical. • Predominantly private car and taxi used to access airport because of perceived convenience, flexibility, comfort, reliability and need to transport luggage. • There is a tendency to be anxious, tired and stressed because of the unfamiliar surroundings, language, presence of luggage and time critical nature of the journey.
Employee	• Daily journeys. • High private car usage because of the specific origin and destination on the airport site, working hours outside the main public transport times of operation, subsidised or in fact free car parking, reliability critical, flexibility and comfort. • Shift patterns result in peaks in employee traffic throughout the day. • Destination dispersed across the airport site.
Visitor	• 'Kiss-and-Fly' passengers dropped off and/or collected by private car from the airport by 'meeters-and-greeters' mainly for convenience. • Creates four access/egress journeys as opposed to two normally. This can involve the use of extensive kerb and circulation space. • Could outnumber passengers in some cases. • Visitors to airports catering/retail facilities.

Source: Adapted from Budd et al. 2011.

times more annual revenue than the same space dedicated for employee use (Humphreys and Ison 2005). For these reasons airport operators are keen to encourage employee mode shift to more sustainable options such as public transport, cycling and walking and car sharing, although this can be difficult given that the majority of employees are not directly employed by the airport operator. In this regard, it is estimated that 90 per cent of airport staff are employed by third party tenant companies. *Visitors* to an airport include those accompanying departing passengers (kiss-and-fly) and arriving passengers (meeters-greeters) and airports with a larger share of passengers travelling for leisure reasons will be subject to proportionally higher numbers of this type of visitor.

Ground Access Strategy

Table 6.5 identifies the various strategic options available to airport managers when addressing the issue of ground access, with the focus on more sustainable modes. The policy options comprise both market and non-market based measures; some short and

Table 6.5   Ground access policy measures

	Private vehicle transport	Public transport	Other
Market-based instruments	• Parking charges • Road user charging • Levy on workplace parking	• Concessionary fares • Through ticketing	
Command and control instruments	• Accessible park and ride • Parking restraint • Physical restraint on traffic • Car sharing	• Improved rail investment • Accessible light rail and bus-based rapid transit schemes • Enhanced local bus provision • Reallocation of road space to public transport, such as dedicated bus lanes • Improved marketing and wider availability of real-time information about public transport travel • Taxi sharing schemes • Improvements to the quality and security of the waiting environment	• Travel plan development • Greater priority to cycling • Greater priority to walking

Source: Adapted from Humphreys and Ison 2003.

others longer term. Short-term strategies for addressing ground access issues relate to a range of operational measures or physical improvements. The management of passenger car parking, for example, can be addressed via the price mechanism and the allocation between the various forms of parking space, be it for pick-up and drop-off, short-stay or long-stay parking or rental car parking. In order to address the issue of congestion at drop-off/pick-up areas a number of airports, such as London Luton in the UK, have introduced charges. In terms of employee ground access, airports have tended to rely on 'softer' incentive-focused measures to encourage the use of more sustainable modes. These incentives have included development of staff travel plans and car-sharing schemes. Airport operators are faced with a dilemma when it comes to car parking. While there are clear economic reasons for attracting the private vehicle since car parking revenues form a major component of an airport business, there are the environmental objectives mentioned earlier. There is also the pressure of balancing the competing demand for passenger and employee spaces. Car parking is also important in terms of an airport's competitive advantage or indeed disadvantage. As for *longer term* strategies they have typically involved the physical improvements to existing, or construction of, new infrastructure. Given the high volume and growth of traffic experienced at larger airports, the maintenance of road infrastructure is important. In addition, the provision of dedicated high occupancy vehicle (HOV) lanes or bus priority lanes can aid the situation. These are already common in the US but are increasingly being considered in a UK context. Rail provision is also receiving attention, since it allows for high passenger numbers and can also form part of a public transport hub, with critical mass a prerequisite for supporting regular services.

Overall, it is important to state that at least from a UK perspective, the commercialisation and privatisation of airport infrastructure and transport services has made the coordination of ground access planning difficult, since operation for the benefit of shareholders has been central (Ison et al. 2011).

Airports, the Environment and Economic Development

Environmental Impacts of Airports

From a broader perspective, ground access initiatives are just one of a whole range of policies that airport operators and other stakeholders have adopted to address airport environmental impacts and achieve higher standards of sustainability. Apart from the global effects on climate change due to aircraft emissions, there are also more localised impacts related to noise; air pollution; water pollution and use; waste and energy management; and the need to protect wildlife, heritage, and the landscape (see chapters 5 and 8, this volume). As a result many airports differentiate their charges by noise levels, and an increasing number do this for emissions as well (e.g. London Heathrow, Frankfurt, Zurich and Stockholm Arlanda). Many airports are also subject to night time or noise bans or restrictions, often government imposed, such as at Amsterdam, Frankfurt, Brussels, Madrid, Washington National and Wellington. These policies can have a significant impacts on the operations of certain types of airlines, especially cargo carriers. A notable case is DHL which shifted its European cargo base from Brussels airport to Leipzig because of night time noise limitations at Brussels airport.

Airport operators use land-use planning and management measures as well as noise and emission abatement policies to reduce the local air and noise pollution, in addition to using a range of measures to reduce carbon emissions (Girvin 2009; Berry et al. 2008). Indeed, a few airport operators such as Swedavia in Sweden are now carbon neutral and a growing number of airports also belong to ACI-Europe's Airport Carbon Accreditation programme that was launched in 2009 and was subsequently extended to ACI-Asia-Pacific members in 2011.

However as environmental pressures grow, it has become progressively more difficult to significantly expand airport operations or build new airports. The level of concern varies from country to country, but is particularly high in a number of European countries and the US, where frequent examples exist of local communities fiercely opposing airport expansion. As a result, many airports in these areas remain congested and unable to grow. This compares with other parts in the world, such as Asia and the Middle East, where environmental capacity (as opposed to physical capacity), which is set by consideration of the impacts of an airport's operation upon the local environment and the lives of residents of local communities, has played a much lesser role.

Economic Impacts of Airports

Airports can also have a significant economic impact on the surrounding local area. First, there are direct (or primary) impacts and indirect and induced (or secondary) impacts (associated with income, employment, capital investment and tax revenues) which are caused as the result of the airport being a generator of economic activity. Second, there are impacts which occur due to the presence of the airport which include wider spin-off, magnetic or catalytic benefits (or tertiary impacts) such as inward investment or the development of tourism. Therefore airports can potentially not only have a role to play by being a significant economic activity in their own right but also by supporting other sectors of the economy.

The direct effects are those associated with the operation of the airport with activities of the airport operators itself, the airlines, the concessionaire, the handling agents and other agencies. This direct effect will vary according to factors such as the volume and nature of passenger and cargo traffic, the role of the airport and the amount of commercial development. Globally the Air Transport Action Group (ATAG) (2012) estimated that in 2010 of the 8.4 million jobs directly generated by the air transport industry, 0.5 million were employed by airport operators, in airport management, maintenance and security and also there were 4.9 million other jobs on-site at airports, for example associated with government border agencies, restaurants, retail outlets and hotels. Airlines or handling agents (including flight and maintenance crew and check-in staff) accounted for a further 2.2 million employees. There is a rule of thumb estimate that for every million passengers, there will be 900–1,000 direct jobs at an airport. Globally at ACI airports this estimate appears fairly close with a figure of 1,100 (ACI 2008). Over the years this has been decreasing and is likely to fall further as the industry becomes more efficient and productive, partly through the use of technology, for instance with passengers' processes such as check-in and boarding.

The indirect impact is related to the chain of suppliers of goods and services to the direct activities, which includes utilities and fuel suppliers, food and retail good suppliers and construction and cleaning companies, whilst the induced impact is due to the effect that these direct and indirect activities have on local employee personal spending in areas such as housing, transport, food and retail. In the US, it is estimated that for every 1,000 direct jobs there were another 2,400 induced and indirect jobs (CDM Smith 2012). Such impacts need to be related to the size of the economy under consideration since as it increases so does the likelihood of goods and services required by airport-related companies being supplied within the area, rather than being imported from outside. Within Europe, York Aviation (2004) found that 1,000 direct jobs supported 2,100 jobs nationally, 1,100 jobs regionally or 500 jobs sub-regionally.

Whilst these direct, indirect and induced impacts can be significant for airports, they are not the same as the net benefits, as is sometimes wrongly implied in economic impact studies. For example, not all employment opportunities can be viewed in a positive light if there is already near or full employment in the vicinity of the airport. Clearly the costs associated with airport operations also need to be considered. These will be internal costs (e.g. construction and operation costs) and external costs, especially related to environmental problems such as noise and air pollution. Indeed in spite of the new dynamics within the airport industry, there are still a significant number of examples of expensive, large and over-designed airports being built to satisfy the desires of politicians, or to gain civic or regional status, which within an economic context will result in negative net benefits by nature of the fact that the costs will significantly exceed the resultant benefits.

The Links between Airports and Economic Development

The catalytic impacts of airports can contribute to the economic development of the surrounding area (Green 2007; Percoco 2010). In terms of business development, airports can arguably play an important role in influencing company location decisions because of the accessibility benefits they bring for both people and goods. Thus an airport can enhance the competitiveness of the surrounding economy and contribute to swift and convenient exports and imports ranging from the export of fresh and perishable fruit from less developed economies or the import of essential components for IT and pharmaceuticals products.

The existence of an 'airport city' within the surrounding area of a number of airports may also be an additional factor which companies will take into account when choosing their location. These exist when an airport expands beyond the boundaries of the traditional business in the terminal and diversifies by developing facilities such as office complexes, business parks and free trade zones; distribution and logistics centres; sport, cultural and entertainment amenities, shopping centres; and medical services (Kasarda 2009). In some cases airport cities have continued to develop outwards with the boundaries between the airport and its surrounding urban area becoming increasingly blurred. As a consequence, a new urban form, known as an aerotropolis has emerged. Airport cities and aerotropoli can now be found in most parts of the world. They are particularly prevalent in Asia and the Middle East where there tend to be newer airports surrounded by a large amount of open land. Notable examples are Hong Kong's 'SkyCity', Incheon's 'Air City' and Kuala Lumpur's 'Gateway Park'; and there are many others currently under development, such as Beijing's 'World City' and 'Dubai World Central'. More typical, however, are dispersed office, commercial, and industrial facilities near airports that have led to more sprawling suburban development and the planning challenges that accompany it.

Meanwhile, regions without an airport, or those who have not reached the critical mass needed to provide an adequate range of services, may find themselves economically disadvantaged. However it is problematic to formally determine the causality between airport activities and wider economic development in that is it building or expanding an airport that has encouraged economic development, or is it a developing economy that is responsible for the increase in demand for air services and airports in the region? (Button et al. 2010). Moreover a company's location decision will be influenced by a wide range of factors (such as the labour market, relative costs, availability of land, trade and the taxation policy) and it is extremely difficult to isolate and quantify the influence solely due to the presence of an airport.

Airports may also play a role by enabling both business and leisure tourists to visit the surrounding region. This may be particularly relevant to tourism markets associated with city breaks, conferences, long-haul travel and package holidays which are dependent on air services. There are many examples, especially for island economies, where the provision of suitable airport infrastructure and subsequent air services has allowed for the tourism potential of the destination to be realised. LCCs with their airport partners, particularly in Europe, have been identified as transforming some relatively unknown regions into new international destinations (ELFAA 2004). However as with business development, the causality between air transport and tourism development is problematic in that, for example, do new air services and airports encourage new tourism infrastructure (e.g. new hotels) or does expanded tourism infrastructure present an opportunity for airlines to develop air services out of the airport?

Once again impacts should not be confused with net benefits to regional economies in general. For example the availability of nearby air services at a local airport may increase the use of imported goods and services at the expense of local products, or encourage residents to holiday abroad rather than take more local visits. Moreover increased industrial and economic activity around an airport may drain the city centre of resources, or merely shift output and employment from another region. There are also 'perpetuity' effects where a construction of an airport, may change the structure of the economy, for example from fishing or agriculture to tourism (Button et al. 2010). However limited evidence related to these 'net of shift' or perpetuity effects exists, with a rare exception being Forsyth (2006) who found that in Australia airport development can bring benefits to regions but not necessarily net benefits to the whole country.

Policies to Encourage Economic Development

Even though the exact link between airports and economic development with any shift effects cannot be easily determined, in recent years there has been an increase in policies which aim to encourage the economic development thought to be associated with airport development. This may be as broad as supporting airport city developments by setting up an enterprise zone which may offer relief from business tax, a fast track planning process or some other benefits. There may also be much more targeted policies such as providing incentives for airlines to operate out of certain airports. Such incentives may have purely commercial objectives to grow the business at the airport and raising profits, but if the airport is under public ownership there may be broader goals related to increasing the connectivity of the airport and thus encouraging economic development. However such public fund incentives offered to airlines can be controversial as arguably they can be considered as state aid or subsidies which can distort competition and trade.

Within Europe, there was a significant development at Brussels South Charleroi airport (which is owned by the regional government) around a decade ago (Barbot 2006). In 2001 Ryanair established it as its first continental base by entering into an agreement with the airport operator which resulted in a net payment of over €3 million to Ryanair. As a result this agreement was challenged in the European courts as being illegal state aid to Ryanair and the airline was ordered to repay some of this financial support – although Ryanair successfully won an appeal against this decision in 2008. In the meantime, partly as a result of the original decision and also because of EC investigations into incentives offered by other public airports to airlines, the EC issued guidelines on the financing of regional airports and state-aid that can be offered. This stipulates that the aid must be strictly linked to and must not exceed the extra start-up costs, should generally be limited to three years and decrease during its duration. Since the issuance of the guidelines around 20 additional cases have been considered but this remains an uncertain area until new guidelines, which are currently under review in part because of Ryanair's successful appeal, are established.

Incentives may also be offered by national or local government or agencies (STRAIR 2005). This is in addition to government support for public service obligation (PSO) routes in Europe, or Essential Air Service (EAS) routes in the United States which are aimed at providing basic air connectivity rather than encouraging further growth. For example, Malina et al. (2011) found that at as many as 17 Spanish airports, agreements had been made between airlines and regional governments in which the airline is offered certain payments in return for increased traffic. Elsewhere, in Malta, the government offered an incentive scheme, in collaboration with Malta airport, to encourage new carriers to the country as part of its goal in growing and diversifying its tourism industry (Graham and Dennis 2010). Early evidence showed that new services had indeed developed but little diversification had taken place as more collaboration with other tourism sectors would be needed. The UK route development fund (RDF) was another interesting example of a public fund provided by regional development agencies funds to support new services that were deemed beneficial to the region's overall economic development by encouraging better business links or inbound tourism in areas. Whilst the specific impacts have been mixed and a significant proportion of the routes have not survived, Smyth et al. (2012) concluded in relation to Scotland which had the largest number of RDF routes, that the overall impact had been positive on the Scottish economy. Meanwhile in the United States, the situation is somewhat different as direct help from publicly owned airports to encourage general economic development is not possible since FAA regulations only allow airport revenues to be used to enhance airline services, although other public bodies are allowed to support new services through so-called 'co-op. marketing funds', and risk sharing mechanisms such as revenue guarantees and community ticket trusts or travel banks (Weatherill 2006). However the overall evidence related to the net impacts of such support here, as in other parts of the world, is relatively scarce.

Conclusions

The trend in airport traffic, be it passenger or cargo, has been one of substantial growth in recent times and as such it could be argued that expansion in airport capacity will be required in order to meet the demand, with resultant environmental implications. While the airport industry has been dominated by North America and Europe this is changing with expansion in various Asian countries. For example, in mid-2012 the Civil Aviation Administration of China announced that over 80 new airports would be built between 2011 and 2015, in addition to the expansion of over 100 existing airports, the aim being to create a national network of airports covering almost 90 per cent of China's population by 2020 (Yongqiang 2012).

Over time, airports have displayed a more competitive edge. A number have worked hard to sell themselves as a major hub for transfer traffic or as a specialist low cost carrier airport. Privatisation has been driven by a need for extra funding and the desire to obtain management and operational expertise. As part of this dynamic, non-aeronautical aspects of an airport's make up have come to the fore with a focus on marketing aimed at attracting new customers. Moreover airports have paid more attention to offering attractive airport charging packages to the airline users. The growth in passenger numbers however has created problems for airports in terms of ground access resulting from both traffic congestion and vehicle emissions. A demand management approach has become more prevalent focusing on the efficient use of existing infrastructure, encouraging sustainable modes. Short term strategies involving the management of car parks, the development of staff travel plans and car sharing schemes has been developed. In the long term selective construction and new infrastructure have been seen as important, as too the possibility of rail provision. While traffic creates a negative impact around airports through congestion and emissions associated with aircraft operations and ground access, there are also significant positive economic impacts to the surrounding area. These are problematic to measure, but can be defined as primary, secondary and tertiary impacts associated with income, employment, business investment and tourism development. Ultimately this can all lead to what can be referred to as an airport city, or even a new urban form called an aerotropolis.

References

ACI (2008) ACI Airport Economics Survey 2007. Montreal: ACI.
ACI (2012a) ACI releases its 2011 World Airport Traffic Report, press release 27 August. Available at: http://www.aci.aero/News/Releases/Most-Recent/2012/08/27/ACI-Relea ses-its-2011-World-Airport-Traffic-Report-Airport-Passenger-Traffic-Remains-Strong -as-Cargo-Traffic-Weakens (accessed: 30 January 2013).
ACI (2012b) ACI releases its Global Traffic Forecast 2012–2013, press release 25 October. Available at: http://www.aci.aero/News/Releases/Most-Recent/2012/10/25/ACI-Relea ses-its-Global-Traffic-Forecast-20122031-Global-Passenger-Traffic-will-Top-12- Billion-by-2031 (accessed: 30 January 2013).
ACI (2012c) In the Money. *Airport World* 17(6): 24–25.
ACI (2013) Passenger Traffic Grows by 4% in 2012 as Growth in Air Freight Remains Flat, press release 7 February. Available at: http://www.aci.aero/News/Releases/Most- Recent/2013/02/07/Passenger-Traffic-Grows-by-4-in-2012-as-Growth-in-Air-Freight- Remains-Flat (accessed: 9 February 2013).
ACI-Europe (2010a) *An Outlook for Europe's Airports.* Brussels: ACI-Europe.
ACI-Europe (2010b) *The Ownership of Europe's Airports.* Brussels: ACI-Europe.
Airport Research Center (2009) Study on the Impact of Directive 96/67/EC on Ground Handling Services 1996–2007. Aachen: Airport Research Center.
Ashford, N., Stanton, M., Moore, C. et al. (2013) *Airport Operations: 3rd Edition.* London/ New York: McGraw-Hill.
ATAG (2012) *Aviation: Benefits Beyond Borders.* Geneva: ATAG.
BAA (2009) News release: Financial Results for the Year up to 31 December 2008. Available at: http://www.baa.com/assets/B2CPortal/Static%20Files/BAA-FY-2008resu lts.pdf (accessed: 24 February 2013).
Barbot, C. (2006) Low-Cost Airlines, Secondary Airports, and State Aid: An Economic Assessment of the Ryanair–Charleroi Airport Agreement. *Journal of Air Transport Management* 12(4): 197–203.
Berry, F., Gillhespy, S. and Rogers, J. (2008) *ACRP Synthesis Report 10: Airport Sustainability Practices.* Washington, DC: Transportation Research.
Budd, T., Ison, S.G. and Ryley, T. (2011) Airport Ground Access: Issues and Policies. *Journal of Airport Management* 6(1): 80–97.
Button, K., Doh, S. and Yuan, J. (2010) The Role of Small Airports in Economic Development. *Journal of Airport Management* 4(2): 125–136.
Cairns, S., Sloman, L., Newson, C. et al. (2008) Smarter Choices: Assessing the Potential to Achieve Traffic Reduction Using 'Soft Measures'. *Transport Reviews* 28(5): 593–618.
CDM Smith (2012) *The Economic Impact of Commercial Airports in 2010.* Cincinnati: CDM Smith.
Coogan, M., MarketSense Consulting and Jacobs Consultancy (2008) Ground Access to Major Airports by Public Transportation, ACRP (Airport Cooperative Research Programme) Report 4, Transportation Research Board of the National Academies. Washington, DC.
Competition Commission (2009) *BAA Airports Market Investigation.* London: Competition Commission.
Copenhagen Economics (2012) *Airport Competition in Europe.* Copenhagen: Copenhagen Economics.

de Neufville, R. and Odoni, A. (2003) *Airport Systems: Planning, Design and Management.* London; New York: McGraw Hill.

Department for Transport (2012) Draft Aviation Policy Framework. Available at: https://www.gov.uk/government/uploads/system/uploads/attachment_data/file/2739/draft-aviation-policy-framework.pdf (accessed: 24 February 2013).

ELFAA (2004) *Liberalisation of European Air Transport: The Benefits of Low Fares Airlines to Consumers, Airports, Regions and the Environment.* Brussels: ELFAA.

Forsyth, P. (2006) Estimating the Costs and Benefits of Regional Airport Subsidies, a Computable General Equilibrium Approach. German Aviation Research Society Amsterdam Workshop, June–July. Available at: http://www.garsonline.de/Downloads/060629/Forsyth%20-%20Paper%20-%20Regional%20Airport%20Subsidies.pdf (accessed: 30 January 2013).

Forsyth, P., Gillen, D., Mueller, J. and Niemeier, H.-M. (eds) (2010) *Airport Competition.* Farnham: Ashgate.

Gillen, D. (2011) The Evolution of Airport Ownership and Governance. *Journal of Air Transport Management* 17(1): 3–13.

Girvin, R (2009) Aircraft Noise-Abatement and Mitigation Strategies. *Journal of Air Transport Management* 15(1): 14–22.

Graham, A. (2009) How Important are Commercial Revenues to Today's Airports? *Journal of Air Transport Management* 15(3): 106–111.

Graham, A. (2011) The Objectives and Outcomes of Airport Privatisation. *Research in Transportation Business and Management* 1(1): 3–14.

Graham, A. (2013) *Managing Airports: An International Perspective: 4th Edition.* Abingdon: Routledge.

Graham, A. and Dennis, N. (2010) The Impact of Low Cost Airline Operations to Malta. *Journal of Air Transport Management* 16(3): 127–136.

Green, J.K. (2007) Airports and Economic Development. *Real Estate Economics* 35(1): 91–112.

Humphreys, I.M. and Ison, S.G. (2003) Ground Access Strategies: Lessons from UK Airports, proceedings of the 82nd meeting of the Transportation Research Board. Washington, DC, USA, Paper No. 03–2220: 1–23.

Humphreys, I.M, and Ison, S.G, (2005) Changing Airport Employee Travel Behaviour: The Role of Airport Surface Access Strategies. *Transport Policy* 12(1): 1–9.

Humphreys, I.M., Ison, S.G., Francis, G. and Aldridge, K. (2005) UK Airport Surface Access Targets. *Journal of Air Transport Management* 11(2): 117–124.

ICAO (2008) *Ownership, Organization and Regulatory Practices of Airports and Air Navigation Services Providers 2007.* Montreal: ICAO.

Ison, S.G., Francis, G., Humphreys, I.M. and Page, R. (2011) UK Regional Airport Commercialisation and Privatisation: A Longitudinal Study. *Journal of Transport Geography* 19(6), November, 1341–1349.

Kasarda, J. (2009) Airport Cities. *Urban Land* 68(4): 56–60.

Kazda, A. and Caves, R.E. (2008) *Airport Design and Operation: 2nd Edition.* Bradford: Emerald.

Malina, R., Albers, S. and Kroll, N. (2011) Airport Incentive Programs: A European Perspective, Working Paper 107, Department of Business Policy and Logistics. Cologne: University of Cologne.

Percoco, M. (2010) Airport Activity and Local Development: Evidence from Italy. *Urban Studies* 47(11): 2427–2443.

Smyth, A., Christodoulou, G., Dennis, N. et al. (2012) Is Air Transport a Necessity for Social Inclusion and Economic Development? *Journal of Air Transport Management* 22: 53–59.

Steer Davies Gleave (2010) Possible Revision of Directive 96/67/EC on Access to the Ground Handling Market at Community Airports. London: SDG.

Starkie, D. (2012). European Airports and Airlines: Evolving Relationships and the Regulatory Implications. *Journal of Air Transport Management* 21: 40–49.

STRAIR (2005) Air Service Development for Regional Development Agencies. Brussels: STRAIR.

Weatherill, J. (2006) North American Airline Incentives: Best Practices and Emerging Trends. *Journal of Airport Management* 1(1): 25–37.

World Bank (2013) Private Participation in Infrastructure Database. Available at: http:// ppi.worldbank.org/explore/ppi_exploreSubSector.aspx?SubSectorID=5 (accessed: 5 February 2013).

Yongqiang, Y. (2012) China Airport Boom: Will There Be a Bust. *Time Magazine*, 2 November 2012. Available at: http://world.time.com/2012/11/02/china-airport-boom-will-there-be-a-bust/.

York Aviation (2004) *The Economic and Social Impact of Airports in Europe*. Macclesfield: York Aviation.

Chapter 7
Global Cities and Air Transport

Ben Derudder and Frank Witlox

The growth in the volume of air travel has permitted the inauguration of express services which, with the availability of large long-range equipment, will encourage direct and nonstop services between the major metropolitan centers. For the future [...] carriers will be offering two types of services: the conventional services between all important cities and direct nonstop express services wherever the traffic volumes justify.

Barnes 1946: 437

Introduction

Historically, the economic expansion of cities has been interrelated with the development of transport infrastructures connecting them (for an overview, see Derudder and Witlox 2013). As perceptively predicted in 1946 by Barnes, a time in which air transport was a negligible means of transportation compared to shipping and rail, this longstanding connection has also been very visible in the on-going expansion of air transport networks. Strong and diverse connectivity through air transport links has become a vital component of the economies of major cities, as it provides fast personal access for business, social, or recreational purposes, as well as fast physical access to resources and markets.

Indeed, even in a world where information is increasingly conveyed through information technology, crucial information is still exchanged by direct face-to-face communication (e.g. Faulconbridge 2010). In the face of contemporary globalization, this has encouraged agglomeration in 'global cities' or 'world cities' (Hall 1966, 1984), which because of their historically strong concentrations of information-gathering and informational-exchanging activities have come to assume key positions as nodes for national and international movement, especially by air travel.

The relationship between air travel and global city-formation is symbiotic. On the one hand, the myriad business connections between global cities logically create an enormous demand for air transport. For instance, the integration of the world's major financial markets, organized from global cities, helps explain the many direct flights between London, Hong Kong, New York, Tokyo, Paris and Singapore: these connections enable the circulation of information and knowledge through embodied flows commonly known as 'business travel' (Beaverstock et al. 2009). On the other hand, air transport in and by itself is sometimes perceived as a lever towards attaining global city status. For instance, Hong Kong's carrier Cathay Pacific boasts the tag line 'Hong Kong: Asia's world city' as part of a broader boosterist policy in which connectivity in airline networks is mobilized to assert the city's 'place' in the universe of global cities.

As a consequence, today's major cities harbour major airports (e.g. London and New York boast several big airports), just as interactions between these major cities are reflected in major air transport linkages (e.g. London and New York are connected by numerous direct flights). In this chapter, we will tease out the complex dimensions of this seemingly commonsensical relation from the perspective of the shifting geographies of global airline networks.

Over the past few decades, air transport networks have developed and internationalized very unevenly in space and time. Various waves of liberalization in the air transport sector, technological developments, the overall internationalization of economic activity, increasing purchasing power and booming levels of tourism, changing policy frameworks, and a constant downward pressure on operating costs have collectively led to a sharp rise in air transport connections in general and international air transport connections in particular. However, because a range of very complex and overlapping geographies characterizes each of these developments, there has been marked variation in the seemingly straightforward relation between urban-economic development and air transport connectivity.

A good example would be some of the recent developments in the Gulf region. As of October 2012, Dubai International Airport has become the tenth busiest airport in the world by passenger traffic, and the sixth busiest airport in the world by cargo traffic (http://www.aci.aero, accessed 18 October 2012). Meanwhile, Dubai's flag carrier Emirates now operates more than 2,500 flights per week to 122 cities in 74 countries across 6 continents (www.emirates.com, accessed 18 October 2012). Two further developments make these figures even more striking.

First, although Dubai is the most conspicuous example, the real story is that this approach is being replicated across the Gulf region. In practice, this always involves government strategies of vigorous investments in airport infrastructure as well as the development of a significant 'flag carrier'. This carrier thereby adopts a business model aimed at (1) connecting the focus city with key 'global cities' as well as (2) facilitating 'hub strategies' (i.e. serving as a switching point for traffic between, say, cities in Australia and Europe). In recent years, the Gulf region has thus seen the reproduction of Dubai's boosterist approach to air transport expansion. Abu Dhabi with Abu Dhabi International Airport/Etihad Airways and Qatar with Doha International Airport/Qatar Airways, for instance, have become major players in their own right (see Figure 7.1a).

Second, one of the most compelling features of Gulf cities' rise in air transport networks is the pace at which these developments unfold. Dubai, for instance, has acquired its present stature in about two decades. But perhaps even more astonishing are the suggestions that this is just the beginning. Dubai International Airport's present upgrade to accommodate 75 million passengers per year is only temporary, as operations will at some point move to the newly built Al Maktoum International Airport, which has an anticipated annual capacity of 160 million passengers. And again, Dubai's continued expansion serves as a benchmark for other cities in the region: Doha and Qatar are equally eyeing further expansion, while Bahrain and Oman are looking into similar developments centred on Manama/Gulf Air and Muscat/Oman Air (see Figure 7.1b).

The important point here is that although the Gulf region's air transport developments broadly reflect the broader economic rise of its chief cities in the global economy, it is equally clear that something more intricate is going on. Against this backdrop, the objective of this chapter is to provide a more detailed overview of the present-day links between developments in the world's major cities and their connectivity in global air transport networks. We will thereby loosely adopt the perspective of the literature on the emergence of 'global cities', in which major cities are conceptualized as nodes undergirding the

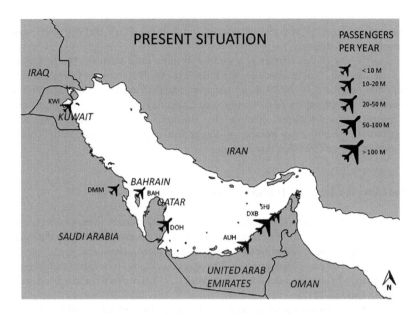

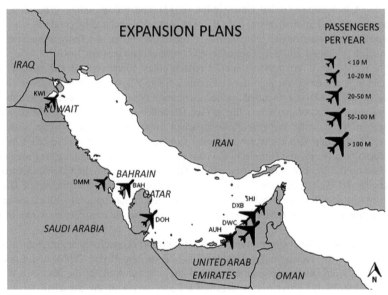

Figure 7.1   Existing and planned airport infrastructure in the Gulf Region

Note: Figure 7.1a (top) and 7.1b (bottom). Existing and planned airport infrastructure capacity in the Gulf Region (Data source: Centre for Asia Pacific Aviation, 2010; inspiration drawn from Bowen and Cidell 2011; key: AUH = Abu Dhabi International Airport, BAH = Bahrain International Airport, DMM = Sharjah International Airport, DOH = Doha International Airport, DWC = Dubai World Central Al Maktoum International Airport, DXB = Dubai International Airport, KWI = Kuwait International Airport, SHJ = Sharjah International Airport).

interdependent skein of material, financial, and cultural flows that together sustain
contemporary globalization (Knox and Taylor 1995).[1]

The remainder of this chapter is organized in three main sections. The first section
provides broad empirical evidence for the links between the (economic) development of
global cities and the geographies of air transport connectivity. The second section takes
a closer look at the complex causality in the contemporary relation between global urban
development and air transport connectivity. The third section discusses some major
'exceptions' by identifying a number of forces that may either significantly boost or
downgrade a city's air transport connectivity.

Global Cities in Global Air Transport Networks

Our starting point is an empirical examination of how a city's stature in the global economy
is reflected in its connectivity in air transport networks. To this end, we compare the relative
position of 65 major cities according to two indicators of global urban prominence with their
position in global air passenger networks. The selection of cities is based on their presence
in a recent study by management consultancy firm A.T. Kearny (www.foreignpolicy.com,
accessed 18 October 2012).

Table 7.1 provides various rankings of the 65 cities. The first set of rankings is drawn
from the A.T. Kearney Global Cities Index (2012), and reflects cities' gross domestic
product (GDP) and 'globalization' (GLOB). The latter is calculated by combining a city's
score on 25 metrics across five 'globalization dimensions' (business activity, human capital,
information exchange, cultural experience, and 'political engagement').

The second set of rankings in Table 7.1 reflects cities' connectivity in airline networks.
The rankings are based on data derived from a Sabre Airport Data Intelligence (ADI)
database. Sabre's ADI is a so-called 'global distribution system', which contains worldwide
booking information on passenger flights (see Derudder and Witlox 2005). The database
contains information for the year 2009 on actual routes flown by passengers. Data for
cities with multiple airports were combined to obtain measures for cities as a whole
(e.g. combining Narita and Haneda in the case of Tokyo). The two rankings featured here
are based on the number of origin/destination (OD) passengers and the volume of transfer
passengers (HUB), respectively. In addition, we include a ranking of demographic size of
the cities to assess if, and to what degree, this would distort our appraisal of the association
between urban-economic development and connectivity in air transport networks at the
global scale.

Although both global city-formation and air transport connectivity are often measured
on more elaborate indicators (e.g. Taylor 2004; Zook and Brunn 2006), and working
with rankings obviously implies that some of the original detail in the data is lost, the
data in Table 7.1 do provide a straightforward assessment of the association between
global city-formation and air transport connectivity without the need for complicated
mathematical transformations.

---

1   In our discussion, we will mainly focus on the geographies of air passenger transport.
O'Connor (2010) has shown that the geographies of freight have a more complex association with
global city-formation. For instance, in terms of airfreight, in 2010 cities such as Memphis, Louisville
and Anchorage featured in the top 10 of most-connected airports, which suggests a looser link with the
wider urban economy (see, however, Button and Yuan 2013).

Table 7.1 Relative position of global cities in air transport networks; cities are ranked according to their average position across all indicators

Rank	City	Rank on global city indicators		POP*	Rank on air transport connectivity	
		GLOB*	GDP*		OD**	HUB**
1	Tokyo	3	1	1	3	8
2	New York	1	2	6	2	9
3	London	2	5	28	1	4
4	Paris	4	6	20	4	5
5	Chicago	6	4	25	9	2
6	Los Angeles	7	3	12	7	14
7	Hong Kong	5	14	31	10	11
8	Shanghai	21	21	7	5	24
9	Beijing	15	33	13	6	18
10	Sao Paulo	35	9	3	28	17
11	Singapore	8	23	38	20	13
12	Seoul	10	19	22	11	23
13	Washington	13	10	42	8	12
14	Madrid	17	22	34	19	16
15	Moscow	25	13	19	23	36
16	Toronto	14	20	36	31	25
17	Sydney	9	24	43	27	26
18	San Francisco	12	16	46	13	27
19	Atlanta	40	15	39	14	1
20	Frankfurt	20	20	64	22	3
21	Mexico City	30	8	5	51	40
22	Mumbai	46	25	4	32	33
23	Boston	19	11	41	16	47
24	Munich	33	18	35	35	15
25	New Delhi	45	32	2	24	37
26	Dubai	27	49	56	25	6
27	Buenos Aires	22	12	11	57	54
28	Houston	38	17	40	34	10
29	Bangkok	36	42	32	18	19
30	Istanbul	41	30	21	41	21
31	Rome	28	37	49	17	22
32	Milan	42	39	52	15	48
33	Amsterdam	29	60	63	29	7
34	Brussels	11	48	54	39	38
35	Guangzhou	57	38	27	12	29
36	Taipei	39	26	53	30	31
37	Barcelona	26	31	37	26	61
38	Vienna	18	40	55	45	28
39	Rio de Janeiro	49	27	14	43	35

Rank	City	Rank on global city indicators		POP*	Rank on air transport connectivity	
		GLOB*	GDP*		OD**	HUB**
40	Manila	51	34	15	40	52
41	Miami	33	54	58	21	42
42	Zurich	24	58	61	46	20
43	Osaka	47	7	16	58	51
44	Jakarta	53	47	24	42	49
45	Shenzhen	62	28	26	33	39
46	Cairo	43	36	17	52	50
47	Berlin	16	46	48	36	56
48	Montreal	31	35	44	54	44
49	Kuala Lumpur	48	65	57	38	30
50	Johannesburg	52	43	45	50	32
51	Dublin	44	55	62	37	46
52	Stockholm	23	52	59	44	57
53	Bogota	54	45	29	59	43
54	Copenhagen	37	59	60	47	34
55	Karachi	60	50	10	62	53
56	Kolkata	63	44	8	61	64
57	Chongqing	65	57	23	49	41
58	Bangalore	58	53	30	56	55
59	Tel Aviv	50	40	50	53	65
60	Dhaka	64	50	9	63	62
61	Ho Chi Minh City	61	56	33	55	59
62	Lagos	59	63	18	60	60
63	Geneva	32	61	65	48	58
64	Nairobi	56	64	47	65	45
65	Caracas	55	62	51	64	63

Source: * www.foreignpolicy.com; ** own calculations based on Sabre data.

An inspection of Table 7.1 reveals that there are indeed some broad parallels between the different indicators. For instance, Tokyo as one of the world's largest, economically leading, and most globalized cities is also one of the most connected cities in air passenger networks. At the other end of the scale, Caracas is relatively small in demographic and economic terms and not very globalized, and combines this with modest air transport connectivity.

In addition to these broad parallels, there are also notable outliers. Dubai and Amsterdam, for instance, boast exceptionally strong air transport connectivity compared to their population size.[2] This gap is less important when looking at their GDP, and even

2 Note, however, that these comparisons are being complicated by diverging definitions of metropolitan areas. Schiphol Airport, for instance, is of course not just the 'Amsterdam Airport' but rather the airport for a much larger urban area that includes major cities such as Rotterdam, Utrecht and The Hague.

Table 7.2   Rank correlations between urban development and
**   air transport indicators as listed in Table 7.1**

	O/D	HUB
GLOB	.708*	.616*
GDP	.612*	.537*
POP	.076	-.005

Note: * Statistically significant at the 1 per cent level.

smaller still when looking at their level of globalization. The obverse pattern can be observed for cities such as Kolkata and Karachi.

To assess the strength of the associations in a more accurate and systematic way, we calculated rank-correlation coefficients for the different combinations (see Table 7.2). The main patterns emerging here are that:

- unlike at the national scale (see, for instance, Debbage and Delk 2001), there is no significant correlation between population size and air transport connectivity indicators (see Van De Vijver et al. 2014); at the scale of the global economy, a city's size does not allow us to predict its connectivity in air transport networks (or the other way round);
- in contrast, both a city's level of globalization and the absolute size of its economy are moderately strongly correlated with its connectivity in air transport networks, with globalization exhibiting the stronger parallels;
- the correlations for globalization and economic size are somewhat stronger with origin/destination traffic than with transfer traffic: some cities have come to play a specific role in airline networks as switching points for traffic, and this role is somewhat less linked with a city's level of globalization and economic development.

In sum, there are indeed broad parallels between cities' position in the global economy on the one hand and global geographies of air transport networks on the other hand. Importantly, population size does not mediate these parallels. In addition, as these parallels are far-from-perfect, there seem to be intervening processes at work.

Overall, this suggests that the seemingly straightforward link between global city-formation and air transport connectivity should serve as the starting point for more interesting and pertinent questions. For instance, exactly how does sizable air transport connectivity facilitate a city's globalization and economic development? Or looking at it from the opposite angle: exactly how does a city's sizable globalization and economic development facilitate its air transport connectivity? And how can we understand exceptions such as Amsterdam, Dubai and Karachi? The remainder of this chapter explores these questions in more detail.

Parallels

A Schematic Model

Correlation coefficients do not allow inferring causality (Neal, 2011; Button and Yuan, 2013). However, it is clear that the relationships between development and airline connectivity are 'circular and cumulative' (O'Connor and Scott 1992: 251); a city's globalization and economic development are creators of demand for air transport, just as air transport facilitates a city's globalization and economic development. Figure 7.2, adapted from Ishutkina and Hansman (2009), describes how air transport connectivity is related to the metropolitan economy.

First, a city's air transportation system is shaped by its infrastructural capability (e.g. constraints because airports operate at near-maximum capacity, as in London Heathrow) and regulatory framework (e.g. take-off and landing constraints at Brussels Airport at night time). Second, the degree to which the potential capabilities of a city's air transportation system are used, depends on the supply of, and demand for air transport: airlines provide supply through pricing and scheduling of flights, and this is in turn based on actual or anticipated revenues and profitability derived from demand for particular routes. Third, at the macro-economic level, a city's air transportation system impacts the metropolitan economy in two ways: directly by providing employment (and subsequent multiplier effects), and – perhaps even more importantly – indirectly by enabling effects such as providing access to markets, people, capital, ideas and knowledge, attractions, labour supply and skills, etc. The structure of the metropolitan economy, in turn, generates specific levels of demand for air travel. Put differently: levels of demand are not determined just by size of the metropolitan economy, but also by the relative business and leisure attractiveness of that economy. Debbage and Delk (2001), for instance, have shown that the relative size of the advanced services sector in US cities tends to create extra demand, while Lang and Nicholas (2012) have related Las Vegas' sizable air transport connectivity to the city's function as an entertainment centre involving many short-term visits.

Example: New York City's Connectivity

To show how this formal model operates in practice, we briefly reiterate the discussion based on observations regarding the linkages between New York City's air transport system and its metropolitan economy.

First, New York City is a multi-airport system, with its chief nodes John F. Kennedy International Airport, LaGuardia Airport, and Newark Liberty International Airport. Collectively, these airports can and do handle more than 100 million passengers per year. However, there is a broad agreement that new capacity is urgently needed as the airports operate at near-maximum capacity.

Second, the capabilities of New York City's air transportation system largely reflect market dynamics of matching supply and demand. The demand for connections to/from New York City is strong and diverse enough to warrant strong and diverse supply of connectivity by different airlines (and therefore competition). The latter has been facilitated by the deregulation of the airline industry within the United States in the late 1970s, as well as progressive deregulation of air transport connections to and from the United States (Goetz and Vowles 2009). However, given that New York City's airports operate at near-capacity, it is – at least in relative terms – not that commonly used by carriers to connect

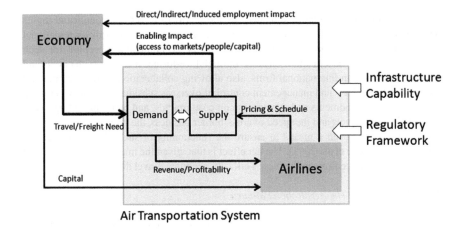

Figure 7.2   Circular and cumulative relationships between urban-economic development and airline connectivity

Source: Adapted from Ishutkina and Hansman 2009.

passengers; if cities were to be ranked based on the relative proportion of hub passengers in total traffic, it would not make the global top 25 (Derudder et al. 2007).

Third, New York City's air transportation system impacts the metropolitan economy, and is in turn impacted by it. According to 2004 estimates prepared by the Port Authority, New York City's airports involved 137,880 jobs, which collectively accounted for more than 7 billion US$ in wages. However, it also enables job creation and earnings. For instance, data collected through the US Department of Commerce Office of Travel and Tourism Industries (OTTI) International Survey of International Air Travellers has shown the strong preference foreigners have for visiting New York City: the city ranks as the first or second destination of choice for most international travellers to the United States. In 2010, the city welcomed almost 50 million visitors, including 9.7 million international travellers. The economic significance of the tourism sector, empowered by the well-connected air transport system, is indeed enormous: total visitor spending was more than US$30 billion in 2010, with international visitors contributing a disproportionate amount of that total during their stay. There is no question that travel and tourism are now critical industries for New York City: total visitor spending in New York City (domestic and international) has doubled since 2001, and tripled over the past 20 years.

Meanwhile, the structure of the New York City's economy generates high levels of demand for international air travel. As we have seen, tourism is a main element of the city's attraction, but there is also the nature of the Manhattan service economy. In her analysis of the rise of 'global cities', Sassen (2001) emphasizes that New York City is home to many globalized service firms in finance, consultancy, law, and advertising. Firms such as Ernst & Young, HSBC Bank, and Accenture have created worldwide office networks covering major cities in most or all world regions, and New York City commonly has offices with important functions and expertise within these networks. The way in which this sector operates leads to enormous levels of demand compared to cities with a very different economic structure. Bel and Fageda (2008) have empirically shown that headquarters of knowledge-intensive sectors are much more influenced by the supply of direct intercontinental flights than are those of non-knowledge-intensive sectors. The reason for this is that international business travel is an important labour process in the accumulation of capital for such firms, facilitating the enactment of business through face-to-face meetings with clients and subcontractors and, in international firms, also allowing collaboration between employees in cross-border projects and management control of overseas subsidiaries). Partly acting as a substitute for secondments and expatriation on cost grounds, and partly providing a new means to increase levels and the speed of cross-border business, the growth in international business travel has been a means to ensure the functioning of such globalized services firms (Faulconbridge et al., 2009). The net effect is that, given the importance of high-level offices of such service firms in the New York City economy, travel demand is boosted.

Policy Implications: The Aerotropolis Mantra

Unsurprisingly, the observation that the metropolitan economy in general and specific segments of the metropolitan economy in particular can benefit from the supply of good air transport activity has been picked up in urban policy. For instance, observations such as Bel and Fageda's (2008: 489) that 'a 10 per cent increase in the supply of intercontinental flights involves around a 4 per cent increase in the number of headquarters of large firms located in the corresponding urban area' (see also Brueckner 2003; Neal 2010) have led to considerations about how urban economies can 'benefit' from the supply of air transport activity.

Perhaps the starkest expression of this line of thinking is Kasarda's well-known 'Aerotropolis' concept. The basic idea underlying the Aerotropolis concept is that airports have become, and therefore need to be recognized as, the main drivers of business location and urban development in the twenty-first century (see Kasarda and Lindsay 2011). It advances a form of urban development that places airports in the centre, with cities growing around them, connecting workers, suppliers, executives, and goods to the global marketplace. As Kasarda puts it:

> (As) more aviation-oriented businesses are being drawn to airport cities and along transportation corridors radiating from them, a new urban form is emerging – the Aerotropolis – stretching up to 20 miles (30 kilometers) outward from some airports. Analogous in shape to the traditional metropolis made up of a central city and its rings of commuter-heavy suburbs, the Aerotropolis consists of an airport city and outlying corridors and clusters of aviation-linked businesses and associated residential development. (http://www.aerotropolis.com/airportCities/about-the-aerotropolis, accessed 13 March 2013)

Although not directly based on Kasarda's writings, recent policy thinking about the development of Amsterdam Schiphol Airport provides a good example of this vantage point. Rather than envisaging the airport as a mere supplier of connectivity to match demand, it is more broadly framed and marketed as (part of) 'the Dutch mainport', i.e. an air transport-enabled gateway between urban centres in the Netherlands and the rest of the world. The aviation network offered at Schiphol is thereby recognized as a key asset for the metropolitan economy, and the strategic vision of Schiphol is aimed at the integral development of aviation and non-aviation activities (see www.schiphol.nl). This includes offices for corporate headquarter and high-end services near the airport, between the airport and Amsterdam (the so-called Zuidas), as well as numerous airport express trains to major regional business and residential concentrations. Although Kasarda's writings have been criticized from various quarters (for an overview, see Charles et al. 2007), policy frameworks revolving around 'using' airport connectivity as leverage for 'urban development' have become widespread.

Exceptions

The discussion in the previous section has made the empirical parallels between global city-formation and air transport connectivity clearer: the sheer size of global cities' economies leads to sizable demand in connectivity; the relative travel-intensity of important parts of global cities' economies (e.g. international tourism and global headquarters of financial and producer services firms) further enlarges this demand; and well-developed airport infrastructure tends to attract further global city functions.

This brings us to the need to discuss major outliers, i.e. cities that are much stronger or much weaker connected than expected based on the size or structure of their metropolitan economies. Following Bowen (2002), we argue that the key drivers of the shifting geographies of air transport networks – beyond changing geographies of metropolitan demand – are the role of the state and changes in aircraft technology. In this section, we discuss some major developments in this regard.

The Intersection of Geography, Technological Advances, and Geographies of Demand

A first twist to the straightforward relation between urban development and air transport connectivity is the complex interplay between location, aircraft technology, and changing geographies of demand. A good example is O'Connor's (1995) model of how certain cities have risen and declined in airline networks as aircraft technology developed (Figure 7.3). When applied to the case of Southeast Asia, the first phase in this model occurred during the 1930s, when basic linear services were established. Since the flying range of aircraft was limited, intermediate stops had to be made. For instance, a flight across the Pacific required stops at Hawaii, Wake, Midway, Guam and the Philippines (just as a flight across the Atlantic implied stops at Gander and Shannon). As the technical capabilities of aircraft improved substantially, there started to be a 'by-passing' effect in a second phase: throughout much of the 1940s and 1950s, routes between major destinations still had a linear structure, but some stops simply disappeared. Throughout the 1960s and 1970s, a third phase emerged as aircraft technology started to permit long distance routes, which supported the development of a network structure that better reflected the size and function of markets as predicted by Barnes (1946), while airports such as Wake/Midway on the transpacific route (and Shannon/Gander on the transatlantic route) lost the bulk of their traffic. As a consequence, the airports of large cities started to see the development of 'feeder services', with smaller urban markets connecting to them, to subsequently connect to the wider network. This resulted in the hesitant emergence of what is commonly termed a hub-and-spoke organization, with feeding services to major cities that are strongly inter-connected. From the early 1980s, the adoption of large-capacity airliners such as Boeing 747s, combined with the increased demand for connectivity across the globe, implied that such hub-and-spoke forms of organization have become a key feature of contemporary air travel.

Why does this matter? To a certain extent, some hubs in the hub-and-spoke organization of airline networks are simply major cities, because these have sizable demands for

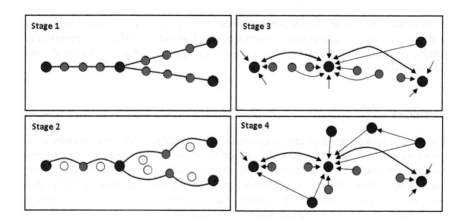

**Figure 7.3   Evolution of airline networks in Southeast Asia following
technological advances**

Source: O'Connor 1995; adapted from http://people.hofstra.edu/geotrans/eng/ch3en/conc3en/stages
devairnet.html.

diversity connectivity anyway (see New York City's position as hub in Table 7.1). However, some of the 'hubs' are cities that have a 'favourable' (i.e. intermediate, see Fleming and Hayuth, 1994) geographical location viz. the demand for connections. For instance, in the case of Southeast Asia, one particular market has shaped the overall geographical outcome: the so-called 'Kangaroo Route' (Figure 7.4). The term 'Kangaroo Route' traditionally refers to air routes flown by Qantas between Australia and the United Kingdom via the Eastern Hemisphere. However, although the term is formally trademarked by Qantas, it stands more broadly for the major international market of air traffic between Australia and Europe. Customarily, these connections require a stopover, which in turn facilitates hubbing to allow smooth connections between all major Australian cities on the one hand and all major European cities on the other hand.

Cities such as Singapore owe their sizable hub connectivities for a large part to their intermediate en route location in the historical development of the Kangaroo Route. The continued relevance of the Kangaroo Route is shown by the fact that other airlines/cities try to attract passengers making this connection; China Southern now markets this route as the 'Canton Route' (via Guangzhou), just as Emirates is increasingly capturing air passenger flows between cities in Australia and Europe through the 'Falcon Route' and a strategic partnership with Qantas (via Dubai).

The recent rise of a city such as Dubai is, however, not simply confined to the success of the 'Falcon Route'. It can be noted that there is no major agglomeration on the globe that is further than 8,000 miles away from Dubai, implying that each major city is within Dubai's reach (8,000 miles implies a 17-hour flight, which has up until now been the longest commercial service, i.e. Singapore Airlines abandoned Newark–Singapore route). As a result, Dubai is one of the few cities that is truly at the crossroads of the current global economy as any two major cities on earth can be connected with no additional stops (e.g. *The Economist* 2010a). Although this was, of course, also the case in the not-so-distant past, increasing levels of demand for global connections between erstwhile poorly

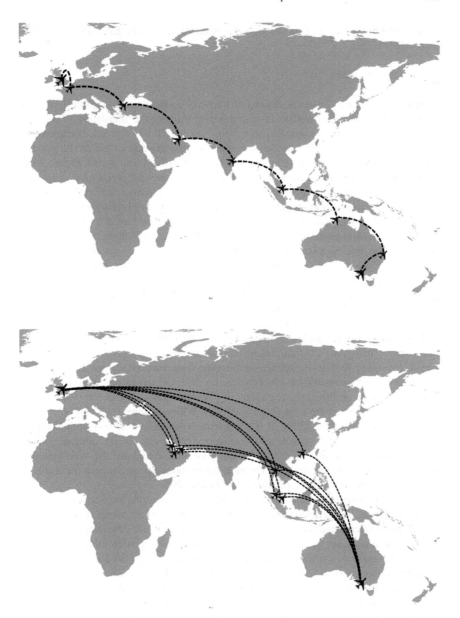

Figure 7.4   The 'Kangaroo Route' in the face of technological evolutions
                    (the Melbourne–London example), initial stage and present stage

connected regions such as South Asia, Latin America and Africa have opened up new major opportunities.

Uneven Liberalization

A second important force in the shaping of inter-city connections through air passenger flows is the very uneven liberalization of air transport markets; the 'translation' of potential or existing demand into air transport connections between cities is in practice hampered by all sorts of explicit and implicit market distortions. A good example of this can be found in the evolution of the air transport connections between Kuala Lumpur and Singapore. Until recently, these connections were heavily regulated. This somewhat paradoxical situation – both countries (especially Singapore) have long been at the forefront of liberalizing access to their airport(s) – obviously reflects the complicated and troubled relations between both countries. As a consequence, despite a high degree of economic and social inter-dependence, regulatory barriers impeded commercial air travel on the Kuala Lumpur–Singapore route. This regulation was organized through a somewhat curious truce: not only was there a bilateral agreement limiting the number of flights between both cities, but above all there was a monopolistic air shuttle agreement between competitors Malaysian Airline System (MAS) and Singapore Airlines (SIA) on this route, resulting in average fares in the mid-2000s of around 400US$ for a 45-minute flight on what would otherwise have been a route characterized by strong competition (and therefore low average fares).

Paralleling improved Malaysia/Singapore relations, and with a wider regional ASEAN agreement to deregulate air transport markets in the making, low-cost carrier AirAsia started clamouring for fair competition on the route. As a consequence, the Transportation Ministries of both countries sat down (before the ASEAN agreements required them to do so) and agreed on lifting the regulation of passenger flights in late 2007. The results were spectacular to say the least (see Figure 7.5). Where in June 2007 only 42 weekly flights were organized, the lifting of this restriction resulted in a more-than-doubling of the number of flights (107 by June 2009), organized by a more diverse range of carriers. Over and above the changed level of connectivity on offer, there have also been a number of (inter-related) qualitative changes. The most conspicuous change has been the degree of penetration of low-cost carriers, offering prices below 100$.

The Kuala Lumpur–Singapore connection is of course a specific and very extreme case. But the important lesson here is that the urban geographies of air transport networks can be boosted by liberalizing access, or hindered by the lack of such liberalization. This can clearly be seen when contrasting the positions of Karachi and Dubai in Table 7.1.[3]

The regulation of commercial air travel in Pakistan is organized through its Civil Aviation Authority (CAA, www.caapakistan.com.pk). The overall guiding principle underlying Pakistan's 'National Aviation Policy' is that commercial air transport should not be liberalized, but rather carried out 'by an optimum number of airlines to encourage competition without dissipating the market'. This potential 'dissipation', it would seem, primarily means protecting Pakistan's 'flag carrier' Pakistan International Airlines (PIA). For instance, the emergence of a true competitor to PIA is complicated by the fact that the '(o)peration by private carriers on the international routes should be linked with their continued operation on domestic routes for at least one year and meeting all mandatory

---

3   There are also more implicit barriers, such as (1) continued state involvement in carriers and airports, and (2) path dependency in access to airports.

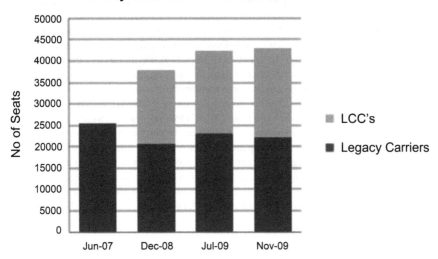

Figure 7.5   Number of weekly seats on Kuala Lumpur–Singapore route: From regulation to deregulation

Source: Ng 2009.

conditions of domestic operations to justify acquisition of international routes'. These 'mandatory' conditions refer, amongst other things, to a number of routes to be flown. Furthermore, '(t)o contain predatory pricing and unfair competition, both internationally and domestically [...] a system of filling of tariffs and compliance thereof' is put in place. International connectivity is limited to a set of bilateral agreements (e.g. with the UK), which are only pursued if it is clear that 'the commercial interests of Pakistan are not compromised'. The overall consequence of this continued protection of PIA through a sustained tight regulation of the market is that supply of connections to/from Karachi is effectively stifled.

The development of Dubai's connectivity, in contrast, is boosted as aviation has come to take centre stage in the development strategy of what is essentially an autocratically run 'quasi city-state' (Sidaway 2008). Dubai's connectivity growth has materialized through the expansion of Dubai's flag carrier (Emirates) and its airport infrastructure (Dubai International Airport, and the recently opened Al Maktoum International Airport with a design capacity of 120 million passengers and 12 million tons of cargo per year). Both Emirates and the airports are owned by the Government of Dubai through its commercial investment arms. The latter guarantees flag carrier Emirates and airport operators a very favourable political environment to say the least.

First and foremost, the overall responsibility of Sheik Ahmed Bin Saeed Al-Maktoum for all aviation-related activities in Dubai and the lack of (the possibility of) a 'NIMBY-culture' with respect to airport expansion or new airport projects ensure that the airline does not face infrastructure bottlenecks (which increasingly stifle the growth prospects of airports elsewhere). Secondly, Emirates profits from the very low charges at its home airport. While landing fees are by and large identical to those at major European airports, no airline flying into Dubai has to pay any additional charges (such as noise charges etc.). This is because the airport infrastructure and all related services are provided by Dubai's government and fully financed from the state budget. It is a hotly debated issue whether this particular fee regime is a form of indirect subsidy to Emirates. Judged against the European Union's state aid rules, this would probably not be the case since Dubai operates a very liberal 'open skies' policy and all airlines are subject to the same non-discriminatory treatment.

Thirdly, Emirates – like all other companies doing business in Dubai or, for that matter, in most Gulf states – benefits from Dubai's low tax regime, which only subjects subsidiaries of foreign banks and energy companies to corporate tax. Obviously, this is a huge advantage as long as the company remains profitable. The 'Dubai approach' has frequently been challenged and questioned in the world of air transport economics, not least by its competitors. But for the sake of our argument, the point is simply that its policy framework is infinitely more conducive to the development of air transport connections than in the case of Karachi, hence the differences in Table 7.1.

Political Geographies

In the previous paragraphs, we have argued that Dubai's remarkable air transport connectivity is facilitated by (1) its strategic location in the face of shifting economic geographies of air transport demand, as well as (2) its government's very proactive liberalization policies. The latter point also shows that there are multiple routes to, and reasons behind adopting 'open skies': while today the airline markets in the United States and Dubai (and other Gulf city-states) are characterized by deregulated markets, the way in which this has been implemented is quite different. In the United States, the air transport market was deregulated through the 'Airline Deregulation Act', which is a 1978 United States federal law intended to remove government control over fares, routes and market entry of new airlines from commercial aviation. Regulation was phased out, eventually allowing passengers to be exposed to market forces in the airline industry. The underlying rationale of this United States deregulation is clear, as it parallels a broad move from the late 1970s onwards towards minimizing government involvement in the economy: air transport was but one of the many sectors in which state regulation gave way to market forces. The situation in the Gulf, however, is quite different, as the deregulation of air transport access is not much a reflection of a desire to 'free' the economy of state involvement, but in contrast a state-led development project involving quite intricate visions of why air transport connectivity 'matters' (Derudder et al. 2013).

In the Gulf region, power struggles are directly related to the region's political and territorial fragmentation. After the gradual retreat by the British from the region over the period 1961–71, regional political elites coming from various clan backgrounds either pursued the path of full sovereignty (e.g. Bahrain and Qatar), or chose a form of cooperation with a substantial degree of autonomy (e.g. Abu Dhabi and Dubai in the formation of the United Arab Emirates (UAE)). In each of these cases, the boom of the oil economy spurred rapid growth of the dominant urban centre, leading to a de facto political-geographical constellation of (quasi) city-states (Sidaway 2008). Why is this relevant when making the comparison with the United States?

First, power struggles among autocratic elites in the Gulf region leads to rationalizing massive 'infrastructure' development. Today's economic diversification policies away from oil dependence are characterized by huge infrastructure investments, with air transport

Figure 7.6   Different rationales for the 'Dubai model' in a single Emirates advertisement – objective and constructed centrality in the global economy

infrastructure as the most conspicuous example (Bowen and Cidell 2011). Dubai has been the main example here, since its limited oil resources forced its elites into other strategies from the very inception of their quasi-sovereignty. Under the 'visionary' guidance of the autocratic Al-Makhtoum family, Dubai thus engaged in a broad-scale city-marketing strategy copied from other 'successful' entrepreneurial city-states such as Singapore. The Dubai model essentially envisioned the attraction of capital flows through a strategy of rapid and massive infrastructural developments, the implementation of a business-friendly regulatory framework, and intense place-marketing targeted at international luxury tourism (see, for instance, the other dimension of the Emirates advertisement in Figure 7.6). Invariably, this implied introducing state-of-the-art infrastructures as 'phallic' symbols for international prominence, essential to realize a self-fulfilling prophecy that goes well beyond Kasarda's Aerotropolis discourse (Derudder et al. 2013). In air transport terms, these strategies are marshalled through both a 'national' airport and a flag carrier as unmistakable symbols of the city-state's vision on territorial sovereignty. Dubai's 'successful' strategy has thereupon been mimicked by other (quasi) city-states in the region, whereby the rationale of being competitive amongst peers further normalizes speculative infrastructure developments at the level of individual city-states. Rather than a hallmark example of free market liberalism as in the United States, then, the liberalization of air transport market is part of a strategy to capitalize on boosterist infrastructure development which is, in turn, contingent on the region's political-geographical constellation.

Second, it can be argued that the instant construction of airline connectivity is expected to facilitate a wider self-fulfilling prophecy in which Gulf cities are to become part of the 'universe' of global cities (Acuto 2010). Rather than the desire to pursue the alleged virtues of free markets as in the United States, aggressive air transport investments in the Gulf can be interpreted as a strategy to define and influence the discursive space about the role and position of individual cities in a global, urban-centred economy (cf. Engelen and Glasmacher 2013). Such an entrepreneurial strategy is, of course, not a Gulf invention per se. It draws on a long tradition of strong quasi city-states that use infrastructural investments to become both an entrepôt and a destination for globalized capital. In the case of Hong Kong's flag carrier Cathay Pacific, for instance, the tagline 'Asia's world city' is used to define and construct the role of the city-state in the global economy. Another well-known example is that of Singapore, where the combination of huge investments in (air)port infrastructure and a free-market doctrine jump-started the economy through the attraction of globalized capital flows (Olds and Yeung 2004). Yet, what seems particular about the Gulf model is the normalization of massive infrastructure investments through self-orientalizing discourses that project global geo-economic shifts (i.e. 'the rise of the East') onto the role that particular cities are bound to play in such a re-Oriented world. For instance, the most powerful contemporary mantra is that Gulf cities are deemed the designated hubs for connecting East and West, and this through recycling and reviving earlier spatial representations such as a 'New Silk Road' (see also *The Economist* 2010b). Importantly, these images also resonate with the popularization of Gulf cities by investment banking communities and financial media as profitable emerging markets aka 'global cities' in and by themselves. It is therefore no surprise that Dubai's position in the global geographies is better reflected by its 'globalization' than by its economic (let alone its demographic) size.

Conclusions

Given the seemingly clear-cut association between urban-economic development and connectivity in air transport networks, it is no surprise that urban systems have been examined through the lens of the geographies of air transport networks. For instance, in what has become a classic paper in urban-economic geography, Taaffe (1962) held that it was possible to study the urban system in the United States by analysing the air transport connections between its major cities. In recent years, this line of thinking has led to the consideration of the global city-system based on the positions held by cities in global airline networks (see Keeling 1995; Smith and Timberlake 2001; Matsumoto 2004; Zook and Brunn 2006; Grubesic and Matisziw 2012). In this chapter, we have explored the underlying rationale for such analyses: we have shown that the parallels between global city-formation and air transport do indeed broadly hold; explored the dynamics and policy implications of these parallels in more detail; and examined the processes underlying some major exceptions.

To conclude this chapter, we want to emphasize that the patterns and processes we have described here are not set in stone. Following O'Connor (1995) and Bowen (2002), we have argued that shifting geographies of demand, liberalization of air transport, and technological developments have reshaped the geographies of air transport connectivity over the past few decades. This implies that ongoing and future changes may once again reshape these geographies. Two examples of such changes make this clear.

First, the future of what may be termed 'very long-haul air travel' may impact the fate of today's hubs. Take, for instance, the ever-recurring rumours that Australian carrier Qantas wants to start direct flights between Sydney and London (as well as other bold long-haul routes to, for instance, New York). Before this is possible, however, further technological improvements need to be made to existing aircraft models, but there seems to be a consensus that this will be feasible sooner rather than later. Indeed, Boeing and Airbus are currently exploring improvements to the A380 and the B777/B787 with the Sydney–New York and Sydney–London connections in the back of their mind. In a recent interview with Australian Business Traveller, Airbus executive vice president Tom Williams said that these super-long flights were 'the holy grail we're always chasing'. However, apart from the technological feasibility of such routes, there remain serious questions regarding their economic viability because of the strain on passengers and the significantly worse fuel efficiency. For instance, for a long time Singapore Airlines operated the longest non-stop route in the world between Singapore and Newark (a 15,345 km journey using the shortest great circle distance, the Sydney–London great circle distance is 17,016 km) but decided to pull out of this market as the route was not economic. The jury is still out on such 'very long-haul air travel', but the crucial point here is that such developments would affect the fate of the likes of Singapore, Dubai, or Hong Kong.

Second, and related to the first example, there is some uncertainty as regards the future organization model of global air travel. This can clearly be seen in the opposing visions of the future of air travel as visible in the development of Airbus' A380s and Boeing's B787s. The A380 is built around the assumption that airlines will continue to fly smaller planes on shorter routes (spokes) into a few large airports (hubs), and then onward to the next hub on giant airplanes to capitalize on economies of scale as in the fourth stage of O'Connor's (1995) model. The B787, in turn, represents a fundamentally different vision that does not take the current hub-and-spoke model as a given. The assumption here is that traveller preferences will be defined by the desire for high-frequency direct flights, so that carriers will seek to capitalize on economies of scope, adding a fifth stage to O'Connor's (1995) model. Again, the jury is still out on the future model (some sort of combination of both models seems probable, however), but if the hub-and-spoke model becomes less dominant then air transport networks will probably align more closely with the demand for connections between metropolitan areas.

References

Acuto, M. (2010) High-rise Dubai Urban Entrepreneurialism and the Technology of Symbolic Power. *Cities* 27(4): 272–284.

Barnes, I.R. (1946) The Economic Role of Air Transportation. *Law and Contemporary Problems* 11: 431–445.

Beaverstock, J., Derudder, B., Faulconbridge, J. and Witlox, F. (eds) (2009) *International Business Travel and the Global Economy*. London: Ashgate.

Bel, G. and Fageda, X. (2008) Getting There Fast: Globalization, Intercontinental Flights and Location of Headquarters. *Journal of Economic Geography* 8(4): 471–495.

Bowen, J. (2002) Network Change, Deregulation, and Access in the Global Airline Industry. *Economic Geography* 78(4): 425–439.

Bowen, J.T. and Cidell, J.L. (2011) Mega-Airports: The Political, Economic, and Environmental Implications of the World's expanding Air Transportation Gateways, in S.D. Brunn (ed.) *Engineering Earth: The Impacts of Mega-engineering Projects*. Dordrecht/Heidelberg/London/New York: Springer, pp. 867–888.

Brueckner, J.K. (2003) Airline Traffic and Economic Development. *Urban Studies* 40: 1455–1469.

Button, K. and Yuan, J. (2013) Airfreight Transport and Economic Development: An Examination of Causality. *Urban Studies* 50(2): 329–340.

Charles, M.B., Barnes, P., Ryan, N. and Clayton, J. (2007) Airport Futures: Towards a Critique of the Aerotropolis Model. *Futures* 39(9): 1009–1028.

Debbage, K.G. and Delk, D. (2001) The Geography of Air Passenger Volume and Local Employment Patterns by US Metropolitan Core Area: 1973–1996. *Journal of Air Transport Management* 7: 159–167.

Derudder, B. and Witlox, F. (2005) An Appraisal of the Use of Airline Data in Assessing the World City Network: A Research Note on Data. *Urban Studies* 42: 2371–2388.

Derudder, B. and Witlox, F. (eds) (2013) Global Cities: Infrastructures, in Peter J. Taylor (ed.) *Major Works: Global Cities, Volume III*. London: Routledge.

Derudder, B., Devriendt, L. and Witlox, F. (2007) Flying Where You Don't Want To Go: Empirical Analysis of Hubs in the Global Airline Network. *Tijdschrift voor Economische en Sociale Geografie* 98: 307–324.

Derudder, B., Bassens, D. and Witlox, F. (2013) Political-Geographical Interpretations of Massive Air Transport Developments in Gulf Cities. *Political Geography* 36: A4–A7.

Economist, The (2010a) Super-Duper-Connectors from the Gulf. Available at: http://www.economist.com/node/16274353 [accessed: 19 October 2012].

Economist, The (2010b) Rulers of the New Silk Road. Available at: http://www.economist.com/node/16271573 [accessed: 19 October 2012].

Engelen, E. and Glasmacher, A. (2013) Multiple Financial Modernities. International Financial Centres, Urban Boosters and the Internet as the Site of Negotiations. *Regional Studies* 47(6), 850–867.

Faulconbridge, J.R. (2010) Global Architects: Learning and Innovation through Communities and Constellations of Practice. *Environment and Planning A* 42: 2842–2858.

Faulconbridge, J.R., Beaverstock, J.V., Derudder, B. and Witlox, F. (2009) Corporate Ecologies of Business Travel in Professional Service Firms: Working Towards a Research Agenda. *European Urban and Regional Studies* 16: 295–308.

Fleming, D.K. and Hayut, Y. (1994) Spatial Characteristics of Transportation Hubs: Centrality and Intermediacy. *Journal of Transport Geography* 2(1): 3–18.

Goetz, A.R. and Vowles, T.M. (2009) The Good, the Bad, and the Ugly: 30 Years of US Airline Deregulation. *Journal of Transport Geography* 17(4): 251–263.

Grubesic, T.H. and Matisziw, T.C. (2012) World Cities and Airline Networks, in B. Derudder et al. (eds) *The International Handbook of Globalization and Global Cities*. Cheltenham, UK; Northampton, MA: Edward Elgar.

Hall, P. (1966) *The World Cities*. London: Weidenfeld and Nicolson.

Hall, P. (1984) *The World Cities*. London: Weidenfeld and Nicolson (Third Edition).

Ishutkina, M. and Hansman, R.J. (2009) *Analysis of the Interaction between Air Transportation and Economic Activity: A Worldwide Perspective*. Working paper. Available at: http://hdl.handle.net/1721.1/44957.

Kasarda, J. and Lindsay, G. (2011) *Aerotropolis: The Way We'll Live Next*. Farrar, Straus and Giroux: New York.

Kearney, A.T. (2012) *2012 Global Cities Index and Emerging Cities Outlook*. Available at: www.atkearney.com/documents/10192/dfedfc4c-8a62-4162-90e5-2a3f14f0da3a.

Keeling, D.J. (1995) Transport and the World City Paradigm, in P.L. Knox and P.J. Taylor (eds) *World Cities in a World-System*. Cambridge: Cambridge University Press, pp. 115–131.

Knox, P. and Taylor, P.J. (eds) (1995) *World Cities in a World-System*. Cambridge: Cambridge University Press.

Lang, R.E. and Nicholas, C. 2012. Las Vegas: More Than a One-Dimensional World City, in Derudder, B., Hoyler, M., Taylor, P.J. and Witlox, F. (eds) *International Handbook of Globalization and World Cities*. New York: Edward Elgar, pp. 497–506.

Matsumoto, H. (2004) International Urban Systems and Air Passenger and Cargo Flows: Some Calculations. *Journal of Air Transport Management* 10(4): 239–247.

Neal, Z. (2010) Refining the Air Traffic Approach: An Analysis of the US City Network. *Urban Studies* 47: 2195–2215.

Neal, Z. (2011) The Causal Relationship between Employment and Business Networks in U.S. Cities. *Journal of Urban Affairs* 33(2): 167–184.

Ng, J. (2009) *The Impact on Airports in Southeast Asia: What Deregulation Means*. Working paper. Available at: http://ardent.mit.edu.

O'Connor, K. (1995) Airport Development in Southeast Asia. *Journal of Transport Geography* 3(4): 269–279.

O'Connor, K. (2010) Global City Regions and the Location of Logistics Activity. *Journal of Transport Geography* 18(3): 354–362.

O'Connor, K. and Scott, A. (1992) Airline Services and Metropolitan Areas in the Asia-Pacific Region, 1970–1990. *Review of Urban and Regional Development Studies* 4(2): 240–253.

Olds, K. and Yeung, H.W.C. (2004) Pathways to Global City Formation: A View from the Developmental City-State of Singapore. *Review of International Political Economy* 11(3): 489–521.

Sassen, S. (2001) *The Global City*. Princeton, NJ: Princeton University Press.

Sidaway, J.D. (2008) Globalising the Geohistory of City/State Relations: On 'Problematizing City/State Relations: Towards A Geohistorical Understanding of Contemporary Globalization' by Peter Taylor. *Transactions of the Institute of British Geographers* 33(1): 149–151.

Smith, D.A. and Timberlake, M.F. (2001) World City Networks and Hierarchies, 1977–1997: An Empirical Analysis of Global Air Travel Links. *American Behavioral Scientist* 44: 1656–1678.

Taaffe, E.J. (1962) The Urban Hierarchy: An Air Passenger Definition. *Economic Geography* 38: 1–14.

Taylor, P.J. (2004) *World City Network: A Global Urban Analysis*. London: Routledge.

Van De Vijver, E., Derudder, B., Bassens, D. and Witlox, F. (2014) Filling Some Black Holes: Modeling the Connection between Urbanization, Infrastructure, and Global Service Intensity in 112 Metropolitan Regions across the World. *The Professional Geographer* 66(1): 82–90.

Zook, M.A. and Brunn, S.D. (2006) From Podes to Antipodes: Positionalities in Global Airline Geographies. *Annals of the Association of American Geographers* 96: 471–90.

Chapter 8
The Sustainability of Air Transport

Christopher Paling, Paul Hooper and Callum Thomas

Introduction

During the latter half of the twentieth century, the telecommunications, shipping and air transport sectors facilitated the development of a global economy and an increasingly multi-cultural society. Despite international conflicts, outbreaks of disease and economic downturns, civil aviation has demonstrated exponential growth for the past 50 years, driven by a wide variety of factors including growing affluence and the development of the World Wide Web and most recently by the rapid emergence of the BRICS[1] economies. The benefits of being linked to the rest of the world by a network of air routes are significant, as aviation promotes trade, inward investment, travel for leisure and education, tourism and much more. However, observers are questioning whether this aviation-based development is sustainable because of the industry's environmental impacts (Rothengatter 2010; Thomas et al. 2010).

The social and economic impacts associated with global mobility have been very significant indeed (ATAG 2012a; Brathen and Halpern 2012). Some airports have been shown to be the largest catalysts for economic activity in the city/regions they serve and some economies have become highly dependent upon air transport (ATAG 2008). This is evidenced by the significant reliance of many Mediterranean countries and geographically remote islands upon aviation based tourism (Daley et al. 2008) or economies in Sub-Saharan Africa dependent upon the export of 'out of season' food and flowers to Europe (MacGregor and Vorley 2006).

The adverse environmental and social consequences of meeting demand (primarily aircraft noise disturbance and poor air quality around airports, and growing fuel consumption and climate change emissions) are, however, significant. Some of these impacts are already constraining airport growth, and others, such as fossil fuel use and climate change emissions could push up the cost of air travel, and in the longer term threaten the growth of the entire industry. The global air transport industry therefore provides a useful example of how the concept of sustainable development can be applied to a single sector of the economy.

Transport is essential for the carriage of people and goods and facilitates the operation and competitiveness of an economy (Eddington 2006). Civil air transport plays a particular role in the transport system providing for the high-speed transport of people and high value goods over long distances (IATA 2011). The innate tension that exists between the need for governments to facilitate economic growth (in order to secure the associated economic, social and political benefits) by supporting mobility and the need to take effective action to prevent environmental degradation is at the heart of the sustainability debate.

Over the coming decades, it is likely that environmental and social issues will put increasing pressure upon the growth of the transport industry and significantly change the

---

1   BRICS countries are Brazil, Russia, India, China and South Africa.

way we travel. If it is not possible to achieve further reductions in the environmental impact of air transport then governments may be forced to turn to greater regulation. However, it is evident that the balance between the drive for development and environmental protection will vary from one region of the world to another and this presents a particular challenge for air transport as it is regulated at a global level and subject to numerous bilateral agreements between nation states. This will be demonstrated later in this chapter in terms of the responses of the International Civil Aviation Organization (ICAO[2]) to the challenges posed by aircraft noise and carbon emissions. This chapter considers different perspectives of sustainability as they apply to the aviation industry and how the environmental impacts arising from air transport will influence its growth.

The Growth of Air Travel

The air transport industry is little over a century old but since the Wright brothers undertook their first historic flight in 1903, the industry has changed the course of human history. During the first half of the twentieth century, a global network of air routes started to emerge providing communication links (primarily for mail) across large countries, continents and empires. The number of passengers carried and the frequency of flights was however still very low.

　　The two world wars acted as significant catalysts for the industry, speeding up its technological development (such as the jet engine) and improving aviation infrastructure. At the end of World War II, many military pilots were recruited in to civil aviation and the industry started to grow quickly, fuelling both trade and the fledgling international tourism industry. Throughout the 1950s and 1960s air travel was still expensive and regarded as glamorous, luxurious and the mode of transport for the rich and famous. In 1965, a return flight between London and Los Angeles cost the equivalent of £5,755 (at today's prices) in comparison to nearer £750 today. It was because of this dramatic reduction in the cost of flying, coupled with growing levels of wealth in the industrial world, that the idea of a 'foreign holiday' became an achievable goal for an increasing number of people. This accelerated following the entry into service of the Boeing B747 and other wide-bodied jets in the mid-1970s and two decades later the development and growth of the low-cost airline phenomenon. These changes widened access to air transport to low-income and previously excluded groups, enabling more people in developed economies to share the opportunities available to mainstream society. In doing so, however, it also created a new market that saw demand driven as much through pricing, as through promotion of the product offered by air transport.

　　The growth and development of the air transport industry has mirrored the development and spread of industrialization. For this reason, the most mature air transport markets are found in North America, Europe, parts of South America, Japan, Australia and New Zealand, where exponential growth in air transport has occurred over the past 60–70 years (Amaeshi and Crane 2006; Graham and Shaw 2008) and growth rates of 3.5–5.5 per cent per annum are forecast (Kaszewski and Sheate 2004; Owen et al. 2010).

　　The recent rapid development of the BRICS economies and Asia-Pacific region has been accompanied by air transport growth rates of over 10 per cent per annum (Kaszewski

---

2　The United Nations global regulatory body for civil air transport (www.icao.org).

and Sheate 2004: Owen et al. 2010). For example, the twelfth Five-Year Plan for economic development across the People's Republic of China will see 82 new airports built by 2015, increasing China's airport capacity by nearly 50 per cent (*The Guardian* 2013). This redistribution of air transport across the globe has resulted in the emergence of new global airport 'hubs' such as the Gulf states,[3] which are now becoming increasingly reliant upon air transport.

Over the next 50 years, aviation could potentially play a very significant role in supporting the creation of a truly global 'community' and in particular the social and economic development of the poorest parts of the world (Africa, Central Asia and parts of South America) where ground transport infrastructure is extremely poorly developed and where distances between major centres of population and economic activity can be very significant. But, this will take place within the context of tightening environmental and social pressures that could significantly impact upon the long-term growth of the industry.

The ability of the industry to respond to those environmental challenges, through technological and operational improvement, the use of 'sustainable' biofuels and the development of new business models will determine its sustainability and therefore the role that air transport will play in the low carbon economy beyond 2050.

The Role of Aviation in Society (a UK Perspective)

The air transport industry has come to play a very significant role in the development of the UK socio-economy because of the UK's geographical location, because the country was a pioneer in aerospace development, because of its role as a global political and commercial power, and because of the expectations of its population. The United Kingdom is an island state, set on the geographical periphery of the European continent in which most of its trading partners reside. For this reason alone, aviation plays a more important role in the transport system than it does in, for example, Germany where high-speed rail has far greater potential for medium and longer distance routes.

Air transport supports regional economic growth and competitiveness by providing high-speed accessibility over long distances for business travel and for the carriage of high value goods (DETR 2000). A number of studies have been undertaken in the UK to quantify the link between transport and development (e.g. SACTRA 1999). In addition to academic studies relating specifically to aviation, a series of reports into the economic benefits associated with the continuing growth of the UK air transport industry have been commissioned by government and the industry (OEF 1999, 2002, 2006). Finally, significant bodies of evidence on wealth generation and job creation have been presented to public inquiries associated with major airport developments in recent years such as Manchester Airport's second runway and Heathrow Terminal 5. Although some of the assumptions or detailed figures in a number of these reports have been subject to question (e.g. IPPR 2001) it is clear that the air transport industry makes a major contribution to the UK economy (DfT 2012).

Air transport plays a particular role in supporting inbound tourism to the UK, which was worth £15.1 billion in 2011 (DfT 2013). It supports the post-industrial knowledge

---

3   For example, Dubai International Airport as a hub for the airline Emirates and Abu Dhabi International Airport as a hub for Etihad Airways, both in the United Arab Emirates.

economy, finance, research and development, and higher education. Many researchers now take it for granted that they are able to meet with colleagues from around the world to exchange ideas (Hoyer and Noess 2001), a factor that will have contributed to increasing the rate of innovation and academic progress. Universities are now increasingly enrolling international students from around the world both as undergraduates and as researchers. A total of 302,680 students from non-EU countries were enrolled at UK universities in 2011/12 (HESA 2013). This brings direct and substantial economic benefits but also subsequent trade and business links.

The value of UK aviation cannot be measured just in terms of job and wealth creation alone. It plays a much wider role in society enabling access and thereby facilitating the full participation of the UK in the global society and economy. It has in addition changed, or influenced, the lives of a very significant proportion of the UK population in a variety of different ways. In 2001, approximately 50 per cent of the UK population made at least one journey by air (DfT 2002). However, despite the growth in low-cost airlines, the lowest income social classes in the UK remain excluded from foreign holidays due to a combination of lack of internet access (for booking), credit card ownership and sufficient disposable income (IPPR 2001).

There is a considerable body of literature that addresses the wish to travel as opposed to the need to travel (e.g. Shaw and Thomas 2006; Gössling et al. 2009). The experience of travel is inherently attractive and many would argue that the excitement of air travel, to a greater degree perhaps than other modes of transport is attractive in its own right (Urry 2002). More than this, air transport has, through the development of the international tourism sector, provided global access for UK consumers enabling travel for leisure and personal fulfilment.

Global aviation has contributed to far greater mobility for employment, a factor that significantly influences economic migration patterns. This has resulted in a major change in the diversity of UK society with all the benefits this brings in terms of a multi-cultural society and understanding. A consequence has been a growing demand for air travel to maintain social and family networks, to meet religious or family commitments and to enable expatriate communities to enjoy a 'taste of home'.

The airfreight sector has further increased consumer choice by supporting global internet commerce through the transport of high-value and time-sensitive goods and access to 'out of season' food and flowers. The viability of this market is being impacted by rising air transport costs and the differential between labour and resource costs in different parts of the world and concerns over the climate costs of such practices (Neiberger 2009). Air transport enables residents of remote and island communities (such as the Scottish Isles) to enjoy greater participation in the wider society, be that for access to employment, education, the arts, and health services (Grieco 2002; Graham 2002).

The economic and social benefits of a growing air transport industry (as summarized in Table 8.1) are therefore both varied and significant. In addition, air travel remains a significant aspiration for UK residents. For this reason, there is a significant will to safeguard the industry's operation and its opportunity for future growth and such policies are at the forefront of many government agendas (e.g. DfT 2012).

The magnitude of the social and economic benefits that arise from the continuing growth and development of the air transport industry are mirrored by the associated environmental and social costs (Tunstall Pedoe et al. 1996; Morrell et al. 1997; Upham et al. 2003) and these are now starting to constrain its growth as is discussed below.

**Table 8.1   The social and economic impacts associated with
the air transport industry**

Economic benefits

Global Transport Network	• Facilitates global trade with an estimated economic impact of 8 per cent of global GDP; • National and regional integration into the global economy (access to import and export markets); • High-speed and global access to resources and opportunities for development; • Preferable mode for long distance movement of high-value, low-bulk goods; • Facilitates the exchange of knowledge and technology.
Employment	• Direct (those employed by the industry); • Indirect (those employed in the industry's supply chain); • Induced (spending by employees of the aviation industry and its supply chain); • Catalytic (employment from wider economic activity drawn to an area because of air transport accessibility).
Leisure and tourism markets	• An estimated 40 per cent of tourists now travel by air, significant employment creation.
Support of multi-national alliances	• For example, the European Union.

Social benefits

Personal fulfilment	• The experience of air travel embodies significant appeal; • Increased leisure and tourism opportunity and access to long-haul destinations.
Cultural development	• Supports the maintenance of increasingly dispersed social and family networks; • Creation of a multicultural society; • Supports international sporting events, such as the Olympics.
Social inclusion and development	• May be only transportation network or point of access in remote areas and islands; • Possibility to improve living standards and contribute to alleviating poverty through integration to the global economy.
Humanitarian aid	• Facilitates fast delivery of humanitarian aid on a global scale.
Travel for education, research and exchange of ideas	• Potentially contributes to increasing the rate of innovation and academic progress; • Establishes new networks, relationships, business and trade links; • Creates opportunity to study aboard.

Source: Adapted from Grayling 2001; Graham and Shaw 2008; Thomas et al. 2010; ATAG 2012a.

Environmental Impacts at Airports

The ability of an airport to grow in response to demand and so support city/region development is dependent upon its operational capacity and its potential for future growth. Historically this was related to the capacity of its infrastructure (its terminals, runways, aprons, taxiways and surface access facilities) and the availability of land in the surrounding area for further infrastructure development. Increasingly, however, environmental issues establish the operational limits of an airport. Almost 15 years ago, the European Commission expressed the view that environmental issues had the potential to constrain aviation growth (Coleman, 1999). This has given rise to the concept of 'environmental capacity constraints at airports' (Eurocontrol 2003).

Upham (2001a) addresses the theoretical aspects of environmental capacity in relation to aviation in some detail. But, at a functional and operational level, such issues limit growth when noise disturbance, local air quality or carbon emissions approach or exceed regulatory limits or the tolerance of local residents. But they can also arise from the need to ensure sufficient resources (energy and water) to meet peak operational demand. This is becoming increasingly difficult in all parts of the world, due to competition from other sectors of the economy and households with growing demands, and because of the changing climate.

The changing climate has the potential to impact upon airport operational capacity in a variety of ways (ACRP 2012; DEFRA 2012). The incidence of disruption, delays and diversions is likely to increase because of more extreme weather events, such as high winds or heavy downpours that overwhelm the drainage system leading to apron flooding. Prolonged periods of extreme summer heat have resulted in taxiways and apron areas melting at some airports and are leading to others to plan to extend their runways. Finally, in the longer term sea-level rise and increased storminess will be a threat to many airports across the globe. The UK Met Office identified 34 airports in Europe alone that would be affected by projected sea-level rises (Eurocontrol 2010).

Airport operators need to develop an environmental risk assessment methodology to enable them to assess ultimate runway, apron and terminal infrastructure, which can be realistically anticipated for a particular site, and the surface access infrastructure likely to be needed to serve it in order to meet anticipated demand and to address environmental constraints. They need to invest sufficient resources in environmental management and mitigation if they are to ensure future capacity. They need to work with their service partners (especially airlines) and where necessary enforce controls to ensure corporate environmental targets are met and that the total environmental impact of their airports is kept to a commercially sustainable minimum. Airlines wishing to develop operations at a particular airport should also take a proactive approach to encouraging the development of environmental best practice in order to secure their own future.

For airports, the challenge is to maximize their environmental capacity and potential for growth by minimizing their adverse environmental and social impacts, by maximizing self-sufficiency in terms of low carbon energy and water supplies and by maximizing the socio-economic benefits that accrue to the regions they serve. By targeting such benefits towards communities most adversely affected by airport operations it may be possible to reduce opposition to, or increase tolerance of the irreducible disturbance caused by their operations.

Global Impacts of Air Transport

At a global level, the longer term growth of air transport is threatened by the implications of aircraft emissions for climate change (IPCC 1999). In recent years, a number of influential reports (e.g. Stern 2006) have confirmed the magnitude of the threat posed by climate change to society and economies across the world. It is now accepted by the great majority of scientists (IPCC 2007), by governments (UNFCCC 2012) and by the air transport industry (ATAG 2012b) that the climate is changing as a result of human activities and that urgent and widespread action is required to reduce carbon dioxide emissions if the worst effects of climate change are to be avoided. This has resulted in global, international and national carbon reduction objectives. The Kyoto Protocol required developed countries to make reductions in six greenhouse gases (UNFCCC 1998), and many countries have individually made carbon reduction commitments, such as the UK with a target of an 80 per cent reduction by 2050 based on 1990 levels (HM Government 2008).

Three elements of policy are seen as being required for an effective response to the climate change challenge, all of which could potentially severely impact on aviation (Stern 2006):

- The internalization of the carbon costs of products and services, through taxation, emissions trading or regulation;
- Technology policy, to drive the development and deployment at scale of low-carbon and high-efficiency products;
- Action to remove barriers to energy efficiency, and to secure the engagement of individuals.

Civil aviation is responsible for 2–3 per cent of global anthropogenic CO_2 emissions (IPCC 1999). Given the fact that, globally, air transport demand is increasing faster than technological and operational improvement, the Inter-Governmental Panel on Climate Change (IPCC 1999) forecast that by 2050 aviation's share of human induced CO_2 could rise to 5 per cent. Other aircraft engine emissions (oxides of nitrogen (NO_x) and methane (CH_4)), contrail and cirrus cloud formation (Carleton and Travis 2013; Lee et al. 2009) also have an impact when released at high altitudes on the earth's climate. Sausen et al., 2005 suggest that aviation's contribution to climate change could be about twice that of its CO_2 emissions alone.

Considerable funds have been invested by governments and industry that have in the past delivered technological improvements and helped in part to compensate for growth and the increasing cost of oil. Further improvements to airframe and engine technologies[4] will be more hard won and significantly more expensive to achieve. Meanwhile faster fleet modernization can also mitigate the growth in air travel, although this has significant implications for airline economics. Further, given the anticipated rate of growth of the industry, increasing 'eco-efficiency' alone will not be sufficient to fully compensate for growth. All industries will need to develop radically new ways of delivering services, including 'step changes' in technology. For aviation this is likely to require the development of alternative means of propulsion, but even IATA[5] acknowledges that 'carbon free flight' is decades away and is likely to significantly impact upon the cost of flying, particularly given the fact that with entirely new types of fuel, new fuel supply and maintenance infrastructure will be required at airports throughout the world (IATA, 2011).

As well as airports, airlines, aircraft manufacturers, aircraft engine manufacturers and air navigation service providers must address the environmental impacts of their business operations and products/services. An aircraft manufacturer can address the environmental impacts of an aircraft's entire life cycle (adapted from Airbus 2013):

---

4 For example, the EU ACARE (www.europa.eu) programme aims to deliver a 50 per cent fuel efficiency improvement and an 80 per cent reduction in NO_x by 2020 relative to 2000 whilst simultaneously reducing noise.

5 The International Air Transport Association representing the world airlines.

- Investing in research to design cleaner aircraft;
- Managing their supply chain;
- Managing the manufacturing process;
- Optimizing aircraft operations and maintenance; and
- Inventing new best practices for dissembling and recycling end-of-life aircraft.

Biofuels provide an alternative to fossil fuel derived kerosene, which can be used in conventional aircraft engines. However, major aircraft manufacturers (e.g. Airbus and Boeing) and airlines, whilst recognizing the important role that these alternatives could play in the short to medium term, also acknowledge the logistical challenges presented by the significant quantities of fuel that would need to be produced and are investigating the sustainability implications of their production, refinement and distribution. The industry has stated that all aviation biofuels must be 'sustainable' (ATAG 2009), most likely meeting the requirements of the Roundtable on Sustainable Biofuels (RSB)[6] standard (Airbus 2013). Alternative fuels, such as that produced through the Fischer-Tropsch process, also have potential but considerably more research is required to enable their production and use on a commercial scale.

Improvements to air traffic management have the potential to contribute a 10 per cent reduction in aviation climate change emissions. A collaborative approach is required involving airlines, air navigation service providers and others. At a European level, such improvements are being promoted through SESAR[7] and in the US, by the FAA funded NextGen[8] programme. Meanwhile the ASIRE programme in the Asia-Pacific region involves airlines and ATM providers carrying out expeditious ground movements and flights, tailored to local weather conditions, and the type and weight of the aircraft being used.

Carbon offsetting is a mechanism for compensating for greenhouse gas emissions generated by a particular activity by paying for equivalent emissions savings or reductions to be made elsewhere in the economy. A growing voluntary carbon offset market is emerging for passengers and companies using air transport, but this approach is problematic because it does not in itself support the move towards low carbon air travel and these funds support CO_2 reductions in other sectors of the economy, instead of providing the significant resources needed to deliver step changes in airframe, engine and fuel production technologies (Hooper et al. 2008).

The Future Availability of Aviation Fuel

'Peak oil', the date at which the maximum rate of oil extraction is reached, has been projected for many years (Hubbert 1956), although there have been successive claims that additional reserves remain yet to be discovered or exploited (Longwell 2002). The International Energy Agency describes an optimistic outlook for future oil supplies, largely based on hydraulic fracturing (IEA 2012). However, the rapid industrialization and rise in consumption by developing economies, particularly the BRICS economies,

6   Further information is available at: http://rsb.org/.
7   Single European Sky ATM Research (SESAR) programme, further information available at: www.eurocontrol.int/content/sesar-and-research.
8   US Federal Aviation Administration's NextGen programme, further information available at: www.faa.gov/nextgen/.

has significantly increased the demand for oil (IEA 2012). Further, it is emerging that the extraction and refinement of some untapped oil reserves (particularly deep sea and oil shale reserves) will prove to be extremely costly in both economic and environmental terms (Longwell 2002). There is concern that global reserves of accessible fossil fuels will become a diminishing resource at the same time as demand for aviation fuel continues to grow (Schlumberger 2010; World Bank 2012). Concerns about long term fuel (in)security are driving the development of alternative aviation fuels that are derived from biological feedstocks such as algae and jatropha (see Gegg 2014). The latest generation of these fuels are now certified for commercial use and while concerns about costs and the production scales remain, a number of major airlines including Air New Zealand, Virgin Atlantic, KLM and United have performed trial flights using fuels derived from different feedstocks in varying blends and reported no significant effect on aircraft performance (see Gegg et al. 2015).

Sustainable Development and the Air Transport Industry

The concept of sustainable development recognizes the interdependency and integration of environmental, social and economic concerns. The term was popularized by the Brundtland Commission (WCED 1987) as '*development which meets the needs of the present without compromising the ability of future generations to meet their own needs*'. It acknowledges there are limits to growth, or environmental consequences of growth, that resources (such as fossil fuels) are limited, and that there is a need to maintain important environmental functions (such as the climate system) for present and future generations (Ekins and Simon 1999). While this is a very general aspiration, that all can aspire to, there is difficulty in determining exactly what this means for an individual industry or industrial process. The term has also been subject to very different interpretations by different sectorial groups with radically different perspectives of what a sustainable society would look like (Upham et al. 2003; Forsyth 2011).

If, as some suggest, sustainable development requires that environmental criteria be established as the principal limits to economic activity, then future growth will be limited by the rate of technological development. From this perspective, a sustainable society would be one in which resources are used more slowly than the earth can produce them, that wastes are produced more slowly than the Earth can 'absorb' them and that human needs are met world-wide (derived from Natrass and Altomare 1999). Given the anticipated rate of aerospace technological development, the current growth of the air transport industry is unsustainable, in respect of both climate change emissions and oil consumption. It is for this reason that groups argue that air transport is not commensurate with a low carbon economy (IPPR 2001; T&E/CAN-Europe 2006). This suggests that either alternative ways need to be found for delivering the services currently provided by the air transport industry or that the economy should be restructured and social expectations managed to reduce the reliance on or demand for air travel.

The aviation industry is focused upon highlighting the social and economic benefits of air transport and minimizing its adverse environmental impacts (Upham 2001b; ATAG 2008; ATAG 2012b). The sustainability challenge for airlines is that some critical environmental impacts, primarily noise, engine emissions and fuel consumption, are forecast to grow for the short to medium term at least, with the sector remaining a legacy user of carbon fuels and emitter of CO_2.

Governments, while acknowledging the concept of environmental limits to growth (as evidenced by global efforts to prevent dangerous climate change and promote the move towards a low carbon economy), seek also to maximize opportunities for economic development and social progress through the development of the air transport industry. In the context of sustainable development, policy-makers have to consider (DETR 2000; EC 2011; DfT 2013):

- The way in which air transport supports different sectors of national and regional economies (for example tourism);
- Whether those services can be delivered by other, more environmentally benign modes of transport (such as high-speed trains) or through other media (such as ICTs, the internet and videoconferencing);
- The popularity of air travel with the general public;
- The fact that currently air transport demand is increasing across the globe and national states are dependent upon their integration within the global economy; and
- Whether air transport is too important economically and socially, that other sectors of the economy can achieve the necessary savings (in CO_2 emission or consumption of carbon fuels) to allow aviation to grow (Brokking et al. 1997; CCC 2009).

Sustainable Development, Global Regulation and Regional Interests

One particular challenge in respect of the sustainable development of the air transport industry is the fact that it is a global industry that is subject to international governance. Global bodies that have an interest in the issue of aviation and climate change are the UN Framework Convention on Climate Change (UNFCCC) and within the UNFCCC, the Inter-Governmental Panel on Climate Change (IPCC). International aviation climate change emissions were excluded from the mandatory obligations and national reduction targets of the Kyoto Protocol (UNFCCC 1998). But, under Article 2.2, ICAO was given the mandate to 'pursue limitation and reduction' of international aviation emissions.

In respect of its two major environmental impacts, the disturbance caused by aircraft noise and climate change, international policy is developed by the Committee for Aviation Environmental Protection (CAEP) of ICAO. As a UN body, ICAO has to take account of the views of its individual member states when developing new policy and regulation. In this regard, its ability to develop responses to these issues is dependent upon:

- National interests relating to aviation and national economic growth rates (e.g. the BRICS economies);
- Reliance of nation states on aviation (e.g. the USA, Australia);
- National airline interests (all); and
- National oil interests (e.g. the Gulf States and Russia).

ICAO promotes technological improvement to reduce emissions of local air quality pollutants and noise from aircraft through its certification process that sets performance requirements for future types of aircraft. At present it has no regulatory or target-setting role on greenhouse gasses (GHG) beyond a commitment to 'limit or reduce' emissions from this sector. ICAO has issued guidance to countries on how to develop state action plans to reduce aviation's climate change emissions (ICAO 2011). And, CAEP is currently working on a CO_2 standard for new aircraft engines (ICAO 2011).

The European Union's reservation over 'mutual agreements' at the 36th Assembly of ICAO, September 2007 sent strong signals of dissatisfaction because of its view that ICAO's perspective to simply 'limit or reduce' the growth in aviation greenhouse gas emissions was not robust enough. As a result, the EU brought forward proposals for the inclusion of air transport into its emissions trading system from 2012.

The European Union's Emissions Trading System (ETS) sets a cap on aviation emissions from flights within European airspace, with further growth only permitted through the purchase of CO_2 credits from other sectors or fleet modernization. However, this action is being opposed by a number of airlines, trade bodies and a number of major countries within ICAO (e.g. US, India, China and Russia). As a result, at the time of writing, the EU has suspended the ETS for flights departing the European Union – 'stopping the clock' – for one year while negotiations take place within ICAO for an appropriate, global alternative.

The issue of aircraft noise disturbance is equally challenging in respect of securing a global solution. Countries, and the airports within them, differ significantly in terms of traffic levels, number of people exposed to noise, need for air transport growth and levels of opposition to noise in local communities.

The challenge for ICAO in resolving the above tensions is considerable. This leads to significant delays in the time taken to agree and implement new certification standards and any phase out requirements. Given the on-going and strong growth of the industry and improvements in aircraft technology, such delays negate the value of the regulatory improvements. The need to develop regulation that meets such different national interests can lead to the adoption of the 'lowest common denominator' whereas what is actually needed is a system that promotes rapid and continual improvement and the adoption of 'best practice', in keeping with the principles underlying sustainable development.

Conclusion

Over the past 50 years the air transport industry has grown exponentially and globally, both driving, and being driven by, the development of the global economy and global society. Over this time, environmental issues have increasingly impacted upon the development of the industry as rapid growth has outstripped technological and operational improvements, a situation that is forecast to continue for the foreseeable future.

There are, however a wide variety of very logical reasons why the global air transport industry, while able to deliver technological and operational improvements to compensate for growth, finds it very difficult to do so rapidly enough. These include the fact that:

- While quite dramatic aero-engine and airframe improvements were achieved during the 1960s and 1970s, these are getting increasingly difficult and costly to deliver.
- With no technological step change on the horizon, global aviation is likely to be a legacy user of fossil fuels and producer of greenhouse gas emissions.
- While aircraft can be made quieter, they will always produce noise.
- Trade-offs between reducing noise, nitrogen dioxide emissions, and carbon dioxide emissions exist for many technological and operational interventions, whereby it can be necessary to prioritize some improvements over others.

- Certification of new technologies and procedures are complex and take a long time, in part because of the safety implications.
- The international nature of the industry which must take account of the sovereignty of individual nation states and their economic and political circumstances.
- The high cost of airport infrastructure and new aircraft makes it economically difficult for operators (particularly in developing countries) to modernize their aircraft and infrastructure rapidly enough.
- The industry is highly competitive and price-driven.
- Services offered by the air transport industry are very attractive, such that demand can remain resilient even during economic downturns.
- Demand and growth are so strong reflecting the emergence of a truly global society.

There is an urgent need to address the issues surrounding the sustainability of air travel head on. It appears unlikely that long-term growth and carbon emissions will be offset by technological and operational improvements. Aviation biofuels have the potential to reduce the industry's reliance upon fossil fuels but the challenge here is the availability of feedstocks and their sustainable production. This may explain why many aviation actors highlight the role of market-based measures (emissions trading schemes, carbon offsets) to drive down 'net' emissions from the industry to levels compatible with national and international emission reduction targets. In this context, it is clear that regulators in many parts of the industrialized world (initially), while unwilling to impose additional burdens on the air transport industry or constrain its growth, may be unable to avoid such action in the future unless it can prove that it is changing the way in which it operates and is not simply running 'business as usual'.

Industry and government responses to the environmental challenges posed by air transport will have significant financial implications for the cost of flying, and this could over the coming decades adversely impact upon demand. In addition, in the absence of a technological step change, the continuing reliance on carbon fuels could bring into question the economics of the industry and the role it is able to play in supporting socio-economic development in a low carbon economy post 2050. This would have implications for the future development of the global economy and society.

References

Amaeshi, K.M. and Crane, A. (2006) Stakeholder engagement: A mechanism for sustainable aviation. *Corporate Social Responsibility and Environmental Management* 13(5): 245–260.

ACRP (2012) *Airport Climate Adaptation and Resilience. A Synthesis of Airport Practice.* Airport Cooperative Research Programme, Transportation Research Board of the National Academies, Washington. Available at: www.trb.org/Main/Blurbs/167238.aspx [accessed: 8 July 2013].

Airbus (2013) *Sustainable Aviation Environmental Innovations.* Available at: www.airbus. com/innovation/eco-efficiency/ [accessed: 3 July 2013].

ATAG (2008) *The Economic and Social Benefits of Air Transport.* Air Transport Action Group, Geneva. Available at: www.atag.org/our-publications/archived-publications. html [accessed: 3 July 2013].

ATAG (2009) *Beginner's Guide to Aviation Biofuels*. Air Transport Action Group, Geneva. Available at: www.atag.org/our-publications/latest.html [accessed: 3 July 2013].

ATAG (2012a) *Aviation – Benefits Beyond Borders*. Air Transport Action Group, Geneva. Available at: www.atag.org/our-publications/latest.html [accessed: 3 July 2013].

ATAG (2012b) *A Sustainable Flightpath Towards Reducing Emissions*, Air Transport Action Group, Geneva, Switzerland. Available at: www.atag.org/our-publications/latest.html [accessed: 3 July 2013].

Brathen, S. and Halpern, N. (2012) Air Transport Service Provision and Management Strategies to Improve the Economic Benefits for Remote Regions. *Research in Transportation Business and Management* 4: 3–12.

Brokking, P., Emmelin, L., Engström, M-G. et al. (1997) An Environmentally Sustainable Transport System in Sweden – A Scenario Study. KFB-Rapport 1997: 3, KFB – Swedish Transport and Communications Research Board, Stockholm.

Carleton, A.M. and Travis, D.J. 2013. Aviation-contrail Impacts on Climate and Climate Change: A Ready-to-Wear Research Mantle for Geographers. *The Professional Geographer* 65(3): 421–432.

CCC (2009) *Meeting the UK Aviation Target – Options for Reducing Emissions to 2050, Executive Summary*. Committee on Climate Change, London. Available at: www.the ccc.org.uk/publication/meeting-the-uk-aviation-target-options-for-reducing-emiss ions-to-2050/ [accessed: 13 July 2013].

Coleman, R.J. (1999) Environmentally sustainable capacity. *Proceedings of the ECAC/EU Dialogue with the European Air Transport Industry: Airport Capacity – Challenges for the Future*. Salzburg 15–16 April, 118–125. European Civil Aviation Conference, Neuilly sur Seine Cedex, France. Available at: www.ecac-ceac.org.

Daley, B., Dimitriou, D. and Thomas, C. (2008) The Environmental Sustainability of Aviation and Tourism, in Graham, A. and Papatheodorou, A. (eds) *Aviation and Tourism*. Aldershot: Ashgate, pp. 239–253.

DEFRA (2012) *Adapting to Climate Change: Helping Key Sectors to Adapt to Climate Change. Government Report for the Adaptation Reporting Power*. Department for Environment, Food and Rural Affairs, London: 9–21. Available at: www.gov.uk/ government/publications/adapting-to-climate-change-helping-key-sectors-to-adapt-to-climate-change [accessed: 13 July 2013].

DETR (2000) *The Future of Aviation. The Government's Consultation Document on Air Transport Policy*. Department of Environment, Transport and the Regions, The Stationery Office, London.

DfT (2002) *The Future Development of Air Transport in the United Kingdom: Scotland, Summary Consultation Document*. Department for Transport, The Stationery Office, London.

DfT (2012) *Developing a Sustainable Framework for UK Aviation: Scoping Document*. Department for Transport, London. Available at: www.gov.uk/government/consul tations/sustainable-framework-for-uk-aviation-consultation [accessed: 11 July 2013].

DfT (2013) *Aviation Policy Framework*. Department for Transport, London. Available at: www.gov.uk/government/publications/aviation-policy-framework [accessed: 11 July 2013].

Eddington, R. (2006) *The Eddington Transport Study. Main Report: Transport's Role in Sustaining the UK's Productivity and Competiveness. Volume 1 – Understanding the Relationship: How Transport Can Contribute to Economic Success*. Department for Transport, London. Available at: http://web.archive.org/web/20080324002356/

http://www.dft.gov.uk/about/strategy/transportstrategy/eddingtonstudy/ [accessed: 8 August 2013].

Ekins, P. and Simon, S. (1999) The Sustainability Gap: A Practical Indicator of Sustainability in the Framework of the National Accounts. *International Journal of Sustainable Development* 2(1): 32–58.

Eurocontrol (2003) *The Concept of Airport Environmental Capacity: A Study for Eurocontrol*. Eurocontrol, Brussels. Summary available at: http://www.cate.mmu.ac.uk/projects/the-concept-of-environmental-capacity-for-airports/ [accessed: 13 July 2013].

Eurocontrol (2010) *'Challenges of Growth' Environmental Update Study: Climate Adaptation Case Studies*. Eurocontrol, Brussels. Available at: www.eurocontrol.int/articles/challenges-growth [accessed: 13 July 2013].

EC (2011) *Roadmap to a Single European Transport Area – Towards a Competitive and Resource Efficient Transport System: White Paper*. European Commission, Brussels. Available at: http://ec.europa.eu/transport/themes/strategies/2011_white_paper_en.htm [accessed: 13 July 2013].

Forsyth, P. (2011) Environmental and Financial Sustainability of Air Transport: Are They Incompatible? *Journal of Air Transport Management* 17: 27–32.

Gegg, P.K. (2014) *Factors Affecting the Emergence, Development and Uptake of Aviation Biofuels*. Unpublished PhD thesis, Loughborough University.

Gegg, P.K., Ison, S. and Budd, L.C.S (2015) Stakeholder Views of the Factors Affecting the Commercialisation of Aviation Biofuels in Europe. *International Journal of Sustainable Transportation* (forthcoming).

Gössling, S., Ceron J., Dubois, G. and Hall, M.C. (2009) Hypermobile Travellers, in Gössling, S. and Upham, P. (eds) *Climate Change and Aviation*. London: Earthscan.

Graham, B. (2002) 'The Role of Air Transport in a Regional Economy', paper presented at ESRC Mobile Network seminar, *The Social Impacts of the UK Air Transport Industry*, Imperial College, London, 24 July 2002.

Graham, B. and Shaw, J. (2008) Low-cost Airlines in Europe: Reconciling Liberalization and Sustainability. *Geoforum* 39(3): 1439–1451.

Grayling, T. and Bishop, S. (2001) *Sustainable Aviation 2030*. London: IPPR, 8.

Grieco, M. (2002) 'The Scottish Aviation Gateway – Problems, Prospects and Policy Possibilities', paper presented at ESRC Mobile Network seminar, *The Social Impacts of the UK Air Transport Industry*, Imperial College, London, 24 July 2002.

Guardian, The (2013) *Why China Doesn't Need More Airports*. Available at: www.guardian.co.uk/environment/2013/apr/03/china-air-transport [accessed: 11 July 2013].

HESA (2013) *Non-UK Domicile Students*. Higher Education Statistics Agency. Available at: www.hesa.ac.uk/index.php?option=com_content&task=view&id=2663&Itemid=161 [accessed: 11 July 2013].

HM Government (2008) *Climate Change Act 2008*. The Stationery Office, London. Available at: www.legislation.gov.uk/ukpga/2008/27/contents [accessed: 11 July 2013].

Hooper, P., Daley, B., Preston, H. and Thomas, C. (2008) *An Assessment of the Potential of Carbon Offset Schemes to Mitigate the Climate Change Implications of Future Growth of UK Aviation*. Centre for Air Transport and the Environment, Manchester.

Hoyer, K. and Noess, P. (2001) Conference Tourism: A Problem for the Environment, as Well as for Research? *Journal of Sustainable Tourism* 9(6): 451–470.

Hubbert, M.K. (1956) *Nuclear Energy and the Fossil Fuels*. American Petroleum Institute, Spring Meeting of the Southern District, San Antonio, Texas, 7–9 March 1956.

IATA (2011) *Vision 2050*. International Air Transport Association, Montreal. Available at: www.iata.org/pressroom/facts_figures/Pages/vision-2050.aspx [accessed: 11 July 2013].

ICAO (2011) *Guidance Material for the Development of States Action Plans: Towards the Achievement of ICAO's Global Climate Change Goals*. International Civil Aviation Organization, Montreal. Available at: www.icao.int/environmental-protection/Pages/action-plan.aspx [accessed: 11 July 2013].

IEA (2012) *World Energy Outlook*. International Energy Agency, Paris. Available at: http://www.worldenergyoutlook.org/ [accessed: 8 August 2013].

IPCC (1999) *Aviation and the Global Atmosphere*. A special report of the Intergovernmental Panel on Climate Change (Geneva) Working Groups I and III, Penner, J.E., Lister, D.H., Griggs, D.J. et al. (eds). Cambridge/New York: Cambridge University Press. Available at: www.grida.no/climate/ipcc/aviation/ [accessed: 2 July 2013].

IPCC (2007) *Contribution of Working Group I to the Fourth Assessment Report of the Intergovernmental Panel on Climate Change, 2007*. Solomon, S., Qin, D., Manning, M. et al. (eds). Cambridge/New York: Cambridge University Press.

IPPR (2001) *Sustainable Aviation 2030*. Institute for Public Policy Research, London. Available at: www.ippr.org.uk/uploadedFiles/projects/s_a_2030_discuss.pdf [accessed: 11 July 2013].

Kaszewski, A.L. and Sheate, W.R. (2004) Enhancing the Sustainability of Airport Developments. *Sustainable Development* 12(4): 183–199.

Lee, D., Fahey, D., Forster, P. et al. (2009) Aviation and Global Climate Change in the 21st Century. *Atmospheric Environment* 35: 3520–3537.

Longwell, H.J. (2002) The Future of the Oil and Gas Industry: Past Approaches, New Challenges. *World Energy* 5(3): 100–104.

MacGregor, J. and Vorley, B. (2006) *Fair Miles? The Concept of 'Food Miles' Through a Sustainable Development Lens*. The International Institute for Environment and Development, London. Available at: http://pubs.iied.org/11064IIED.html [accessed: 1 July 2013].

Morrell, S., Taylor, R. and Lyle, D. (1997) A Review of Health Effects of Aircraft Noise. *Australian and New Zealand Journal of Public Health* 21(2): 221–236.

Natrass, B. and Altomare, M. (1999) *The Natural Step for Business: Wealth, Ecology and the Evolutionary Corporation*. New Society Publishers, Gabriola Island, Canada.

Neirberger, C. (2009) Air Freight: Trends and Issues, in Gössling, S. and Upham, P. (eds) *Climate Change and Aviation*. London: Earthscan.

OEF (1999) *The Contribution of the Aviation Industry to the UK Economy, Final Report*. Oxford Economic Forecasting, Oxford.

OEF (2002) *The Economic Contribution of the Aviation Industry to the UK: Part 2 – Assessment of Regional Impact*. Oxford Economic Forecasting, Oxford.

OEF (2006) *The Economic Contribution of the Aviation Industry in the UK*. Oxford Economic Forecasting, Oxford.

Owen, B., Lee, D.S., and Lim, L. (2010) Flying into the Future: Aviation Emissions Scenarios to 2050. *Environmental Science and Technology* 44(7): 2255–2260.

Rothengatter, W. (2010) Climate Change and the Contribution of Transport: Basic Facts and the Role of Aviation. *Transportation Research Part D* 15: 5–13.

SACTRA (1999) *Transport and the Economy*. Mackay, E. (ed.) Advisory Committee on Trunk Road Assessment, UK.

Sausen, R., Isaksen, I., Grewe, V. et al. (2005) Aviation Radiative Forcing in 2000: An Update on IPCC (1999). *Meteorologische Zeitschrift* 14(4): 555–561.

Schlumberger, C.E. (2010) Are Alternative Fuels an Alternative? *Annals of Air and Space Law* XXXV(I): 119–152.

Shaw, S. and Thomas, C. (2006) Discussion Note: Social and Cultural Dimensions of Air Travel Demand: Hyper-mobility in the UK? *Journal of Sustainable Tourism* 14(2): 209–215.

Stern, N. (2006) *The Economics of Climate Change: The Stern Review*. Cambridge: Cambridge University Press.

Thomas, C., Hooper, P. and Raper, D. (2010) Air Transport in an Environmentally Constrained World. *Journal of Airport Management* 5(1): 4–6.

T&E/CAN-Europe (2006) *Clearing the Air: The Myth and Reality of Aviation and Climate Change*. Available at: www.transportenvironment.org/publications/clearing-air-myth-and-reality-aviation-and-climate-change [accessed: 12 August 2013].

Tunstall Pedoe N., Raper D.W. and Holden J.M. (1996) *Environmental Management at Airports: Liabilities and Social Responsibilities*. London: Thomas Telford.

Upham, P. (2001a) Environmental Capacity of Aviation: Theoretical Issues and Basic Research Directions. *Journal of Environmental Planning and Management* 44(5).

Upham, P. (2001b) A Comparison of Sustainability Theory with UK and European Airports Policy and Practice. *Journal of Environmental Management* 63.

Upham, P. (2003) Introduction: Perspectives on Sustainability and Aviation, in Upham, P., Maughan, J., Raper, D. and Thomas, C. (eds) *Towards Sustainable Aviation*. London: Earthscan.

UNFCCC (1998) *Kyoto Protocol to the United Nations Framework Convention on Climate Change*. United Nations, Bonn. Available at: http://unfccc.int/key_documents/kyoto_protocol/items/6445.php [accessed: 11 July 2013].

UNFCCC (2012) *The Doha Climate Gateway, COP18/CMP8*. United Nations, Bonn. Available at: http://unfccc.int/key_steps/doha_climate_gateway/items/7389.php [accessed: 10 July 2013].

Urry, J. (2002) 'Small Worlds and Large Distances', paper presented at ESRC Mobile Network seminar, *The Social Impacts of the UK Air Transport Industry*, Imperial College London, 24 July 2002.

WCED (1987) *Our Common Future*. World Commission on Environment and Development. Oxford: University Press.

World Bank (2012) *Air Transport and Energy Efficiency*. Available at: www.worldbank.org/WBSITE/EXTERNAL/TOPICS/EXTTRANSPORT/0,contentMDK:20457460~menuPK:337136~pagePK:210058~piPK:210062~theSitePK:337116,00.html [accessed: 11 July 2013].

PART II
Regional Approaches

PART II
Regional Approaches

Chapter 9
Geographies of Air Transport in North America

Sean Tierney

Introduction

At more than $425 billion in direct economic impacts and employing more than 5.6 million people, the value of the global airline industry is larger than some countries in the G20. In many respects, aviation is a tangible World Wide Web. Whether it is for business expansion, tourism, or cargo movements, the air transport system lubricates our physical connections in much the same way our information neurons are fused by the Internet. Small cities and remote locations can thrive if they are connected to the aviation system, just as diminished air service can result in economic decline (Nolan et al. 2005). But the air transport system is geographically uneven. In terms of the global employment and GDP contributions, nearly half of the system benefits are found in North America (Oxford Economics 2011). Some of the spoils have been enjoyed in Canada, which will be examined briefly toward the end of the chapter, but the focus will be on the US aviation market, where dynamic market forces continue to rearrange the landscape.

It is fitting that the US airline industry contributes so significantly to the modern global economy given that the US has claimed so many of the important air transport milestones. From Kitty Hawk to radar, the introduction of commercial jet powered aircraft, and the rise of low-cost carriers, the US has been home to important periods of technological and corporate innovation in aviation. The US airline industry has also had to deal with many incredible, often crippling challenges. During times when the political economy was in disarray, as it was during World War II or the first Gulf War, the airline industry suffered, but emerged in a strong position. During other shocks, like the OPEC oil embargo or the 2001 terrorist attacks, the radically shuffled corporate landscape left the airlines permanently altered.

In the last 35 years, the industry has two distinct periods for analysis: pre- and post-9/11. The two decades after deregulation witnessed the adoption of the hub and spoke, several waves of upstart carrier challenges, consolidation, and the rise of low-cost carriers. Airline industry geography took on a national flavour where hub operating decisions were made against the backdrop of demographic and economic shifts in the United States; older and rustbelt hubs were closed (LaGuardia, St Louis, and Pittsburgh)[1] in favour of better opportunities in the sunbelt (Charlotte and Phoenix). But the air transport system was also responding to the decisions of the low cost carriers who were nipping at the heels of legacy carriers and giving rise to metropolitan edge airports like Chicago-Midway or Baltimore-Washington.

The events of 9/11 mark the beginning of a second era, characterized by intra-regional shifts as larger carriers slough off shorter flights onto their regional partners in order to

---

1   Though these airports, especially LaGuardia, remain major origin-destination centres.

focus on more profitable long-haul routes. Low cost carriers have emerged as formidable market participants and have even muscled their way into major metropolitan markets to become the dominant carrier type in large markets like Denver[2] or Las Vegas. Consolidation has also continued. A pending deal merging US Air and American Airlines would mark the eighth major airline coupling in the post-9/11 era, and would put control of more than 70 per cent of enplanements in the hands of just four carriers – American, Delta, Southwest and United. Airports are influencing the marketplace as multiple airports in metropolitan areas are fighting to lure traffic, with the largest airports now reasserting themselves over secondary airports – reversing their fortunes from the prior two decades. Industry structure and service networks have shifted so much that a return to the pre-9/11 world is unlikely, with the current industry structure, marked most obviously by oligopoly, likely to define aviation and the geography of air transportation for decades.

The First Century

Pre-Deregulation

The airline industry began in earnest at the end of World War I and involved transporting mail, not people. Market forces were introduced in 1925 with the passage of the Kelly Act, where mail contracts were awarded to private carriers, but over the next two decades, mail service carriers morphed into passenger airlines as a result of new technology, scandal, enhanced oversight, and better safety. After the 1938 Civil Aeronautics Act, 'trunk-carriers' were required by the Civil Aeronautics Board (CAB) to possess 'certificates of public convenience and necessity' to engage in commercial aviation.[3] But this designation was accompanied by heavy regulations, as the CAB retained control over a wide range of industry levers, including market entry and exit, airfares, routes, mail delivery rates (subsidies), oversight of mergers, and was even involved in resolving labour disputes.

For the three decades following World War II, the CAB remained active and the airline industry grew. In 1940, the total revenues from passengers eclipsed mail revenue and by 1957, more people travelled by airplane than train. But flying was expensive. A series of rate increases in the 1970s sharpened the public's scorn of what British charter airline owner Sir Freddy Laker called 'Panamania'. In Laker's view, Panamania signified the CAB stance of ensuring that US-based Pan Am[4] profited more than promoting consumer benefits and cheaper fares (Breyer, 2003). It became clear that the CAB was suffering from regulatory capture in protecting existing carriers. Meanwhile, despite charging less money to fly along some of the same routes as the regulated interstate carriers, the profitable performance of intrastate carriers operating outside the purview of the CAB, including PSA (California) and Southwest (Texas), was drawing increased attention (Levine 1965;

---

2 Southwest and Frontier combined have a larger market share than United in Denver.

3 Trunk carriers were the large passenger airlines, some of which still fly today. Because their genesis predates regulation, trunk carriers are sometimes referred to as 'legacy' or 'network' carriers. The term 'legacy' exists because much of their cost structure predates deregulation, most importantly, their pension liabilities.

4 Pan American Airlines (Pan Am) was a US legacy carrier that, along with Trans World Airlines (TWA), pioneered many of the earliest international routes and was a US 'flag' carrier for international service before deregulation.

Keeler 1972; Douglas and Miller 1974). And so, in 1978 airline deregulation was signed into law freeing the carriers to compete on fares, schedules, and service.

Deregulation

The push to remove the regulatory apparatus from the airlines did not occur in a vacuum. It was predicated upon three very important assumptions: the industry was not characterized by scale economies, there were low barriers to entry, and that markets were contestable (Goetz 2002). It turned out that all these theoretical assumptions were illusionary; large carriers routinely flexed their muscles to suffocate upstart carriers and consolidate market share. The shortfalls of deregulation's theoretical underpinnings notwithstanding, the airlines have been free to set prices and routes ever since 1978, and the two most prominent industry responses to deregulation have endured – namely the incorporation of hub networks and the rise of low-cost carriers.

Hub and Spoke

For a variety of cost and service related reasons, the hub-and-spoke network was adopted by all the trunk carriers (henceforth referred to as full service carriers) immediately following deregulation; and in 2012, all the remaining full service carriers (FSC) have retained several hubs. In some respects, the hub and spoke system has served the aviation system well. For passengers, although there are fewer direct flights from non-hub airports, the hub system enables FSC to serve more markets at lower fares, resulting in a substantial reduction in the real cost of flying. By making ticket prices more affordable, passenger demand has soared – in the 33 years from 1978–2011 passenger levels have tripled to more than 725 million while total departures have doubled. For the airlines, hubs generate economies of size, which are the benefits enjoyed by the airlines that possess the advantages of broad network coverage, gate controls, and landing slots. Hubs enable higher load factors (via connections) but a hub's success is also a function of the local business climate, where airlines need a thriving local economy with plenty of price-inelastic business travellers that are willing to pay a premium for direct flights (Button and Lall 1999; Debbage and Delk 2001).

Hub networks are not without problems, most specifically in the form of fixed costs that are difficult to shed during periods of economic retrenchment. Among these fixed costs are things like long-term gate leases, staffed up ground crews and equipment to synchronize the passenger and airplane surge that happens several times per day, and the opportunity cost of idle aircraft that have to wait for passenger connections. And while industry consolidation has helped the airlines achieve scale economies, they have been more likely to turn that size into insolvency rather than profits as the costs of operating and maintaining multiple hubs especially during economic downturns have provided limited financial wiggle room for the airlines as they attempt to retain market share in an increasingly competitive fare environment.

Hubs have generated passenger disbenefits as well. For passengers living in hub cities, the lack of competition has meant higher fares (Borenstein 1989; US GAO 1993; Goetz 2002). Smaller communities have also suffered from higher fares as (infrequent) service is usually provided by one carrier to their concentrated hub, which is the hallmark of the short-haul, limited competition route where FSC can extract the highest prices (US

GAO 2006a). Even in somewhat larger markets, particularly those lacking low cost carriers, FSC can charge higher fares. Passengers in these markets (not necessarily hubs) are in what Goetz (2002) identified as pockets of pain, where incumbent carriers earn excessive profits. Specifically, these areas were found in the upper Midwest, Appalachia, and along the Gulf Coast.[5]

While there was a rapid adoption of hubs following deregulation, in effect giving FSC regional dominance, the subsequent industry consolidation has intensified this level of control. Where carriers have fortified their dominance in a handful of hubs, mergers enable larger firms to further clear the field of competition paving the way for fare premiums. In these instances, standard hubs become 'fortress hubs' where one airline controls more than 70 per cent of enplanements, resulting in near monopoly rents. When competitors attempt to enter the market and challenge these inflated fares, incumbent carriers fight hard to protect their market share; in some cases, the incumbent carriers have been accused of fighting dirty, engaging in predatory pricing behaviour to drive out the competition (US DOT, 2001). But prosecuting illegal predatory practices is very difficult, similar to insider trading cases where non-public information is communicated over a drink at happy hour; distinguishing between aggressively competitive pricing and scheduling adjustments and a rapacious response can be an elusive exercise.

Over the last 40 years, industry consolidation has occurred against the backdrop of regional shifts in economic vitality (Rustbelt to Sunbelt), forcing FSC to make hub retention choices (O'Kelly 1986; Button 2002). Several major hubs have been abandoned including American leaving St Louis or US Air leaving Pittsburgh. But FSC are not just reacting to exogenous shocks or industry consolidation, the expanding reach of low-cost carriers proves that an alternate network topology can be successful, forcing the airlines to deal with a different threat.

Low Cost Carriers

According to the Transportation Research Board (1999), 'probably the most significant development in the US Airline Industry during the past decade has been the continued expansion of Southwest Airlines and the resurgence of low-fare entry generally'. The point-to-point system preferred by several low-cost carriers (LCC) offers efficiencies and lower expenses compared to a hub network model. Though offering fewer markets, the linear service model has been a highly disruptive force.

The differentiating aspects of the Southwest (SWA) business model include its homogeneous fleet of Boeing 737s, which limit inventory and hone its mechanics know-how. By combining a high volume, short-haul strategy, SWA gets the industry's highest airplane utilization (Gillen and Lall 2004). Furthermore, in a point-to-point system, SWA avoids hub banking, giving them an estimated 20 per cent operating cost advantage against the legacy carriers (Leonhardt and Markels 2002). Their use of secondary airports to bypass expensive and congested airports has contributed to 33 straight years of profitability. Additionally, as exemplified by early advertising campaigns touting its low fares, which

---

5   As low-cost carriers in general, and Southwest Airlines in particular, continue expanding into new markets, it is likely that fare premiums will erode as they have done in the corners of the country where low cost carriers have a proven track record, principally in the southwest and the Pacific Coast markets.

declared that when you fly SWA, you can 'fly for peanuts', its 'no-frills' cost controls are apparent with its in-cabin service where there have never been any meals, just peanuts.

While it is true that the success of SWA as a pre-deregulation intrastate carrier served as one of the hymns of the deregulatory chorus, its emergence as a dominant force in the airline industry was not a foregone conclusion. In fact, the real history of LCCs is littered in failure. Between 1978 and 1990, 58 new carriers (almost all LCC) established services and only one (America West) survived (Button 2002). In the early 1980s, the first wave of LCC was offered as proof of deregulation's success, as 'no-frill' airlines made up the bulk of new carriers including PEOPLExpress, Republic, Midway, America West, Muse Air, and New York Air. The swift erosion in FSC market share was unmistakable; dropping to under 80 per cent of total enplanements by 1985, from 88 per cent in 1978. But using sophisticated yield management techniques, the FSCs challenged the upstarts with cheap fares on selective routes under-cutting the LCC, which eventually languished and the industry returned to high levels of market concentration (Borenstein 1989; Goetz and Sutton 1997; Goetz and Vowles 2009).

While the laissez-faire choir was temporarily silenced, a crescendo ensued when a new round of LCCs got off the ground in the 1990s, as FSC were hampered with recession and rising oil prices resulting from the first Gulf War. This wave included Valujet, Air Tran, Frontier, Kiwi, Spirit, Vanguard, and Western Pacific, but these LCC fared only slightly better as FSC fended off the competition. By pummelling the latest round of upstart carriers, there was little market appetite for new airlines, resulting in virtually unchallenged FSC hegemony. This industry make-up proved serendipitous, as FSC were showered with unprecedented profits resulting from the spectacular economic growth of the late 1990s.

Though many new carriers sprung up during these two initial periods, only a few of them were able to survive. From the first round, America West endured until it merged with US Air in 2005, while the second round produced Frontier Airlines and Spirit, both of which continue operations.[6] A third era of LCC began in the new century producing JetBlue and Virgin America, but the LCC stalwart remains SWA. From its pre-deregulatory roots as a Texas intrastate carrier, SWA has shrewdly and successfully challenged the large carriers in markets and along routes where new entrants emerged. Its continued success has been the source of substantial inquiry.

It was initially estimated that entry into a market by a new carrier (of any stripe) would drive down prices by 9 per cent, but that prices would soon rise again (Joskow et al. 1990). It was later shown that the impact of SWA entering a market would more permanently reduce fares (Vowles 2000; Goetz 2002). SWA was capable of driving down prices and spurring demand for air travel not only at the airport it entered, but at all airports in a multiple-airport region, a phenomenon known as the 'Southwest Effect' (Vowles 2001). Ultimately many customers were willing to bypass their closest airport to patronize SWA (Tierney and Kuby 2008; Fuellhart 2003). This phenomenon of passengers choosing a smaller airport on the urban periphery signalled a reversing of the traffic shadow[7] (Brueckner 2003). The

---

6   AirTran also started during the second wave (1994) and merged with ValuJet in 1997 but was purchased by Southwest in 2010. Southwest has bought several other competitors including Muse (1986), Morris (1994), and some assets of ATA Airlines (2008).

7   The traffic shadow says that smaller metropolitan airports will generate lower levels of traffic if they were located close to a larger more centrally located urban airport. By luring more passengers to these secondary airports, SWA was reversing the traffic shadow.

advantages of incumbency have made it difficult for upstart carriers to challenge FSC (Levine 1987), but the number of passengers in hub markets, even fortress hubs, that are suffering from higher fares is declining in direct correlation with the expansion plans of LCC (Borenstein and Rose 2007).

The success of the LCC business strategy proved too tempting for some of the legacy carriers, as they launched slimmed down versions of themselves, most notably Ted (by United) and Song (by Delta), neither of which had any staying power. The failures of these two LCC subsidiaries was not surprising, because they were using the same labour and equipment as their parent companies, so neither 'airline within an airline' could shed the higher cost structures, preventing them from functioning as true LCC equivalents. And these legacy cost structures that weigh down the largest network carriers nearly sunk the entire US aviation system in the aftermath of September 11.

The Post 9/11 Landscape

In the years leading up to the terrorist attacks, the bankruptcy landscape was quiet; TWA's dissolution in 1992 was the last FSC unable to pay its bills. The airlines rode the coattails of a strong economy when the macro fundamentals aligned to produce a healthy stretch of sustained profits. From the spike following the Iraqi invasion of Kuwait, oil prices receded for most of the decade. With a strong economy buoyed by the Internet/information technology boom and increasing global opportunities, business travellers were abundant and able to pay business-class fares, while rising wages and stock market highs supported a growing demand from leisure passengers. The years from 1995–2000 were especially good, with industry net profits exceeding $2 billion each year and totalling just over $23 billion for the six-year period. Load factors jumped to unprecedented levels during the decade, climbing from 62.4 per cent in 1990 all the way up to 72.4 per cent by 2000 (ATA 2012). Even into 2001, despite a contracting economy, the total number of enplaned passengers in the first eight months eclipsed the first eight months of 2000.

Industry success enabled the airlines to raise employee headcount (25 per cent increase), boost fleet size (15 per cent increase), and expand their level of service (12 per cent increase in departures). Unfortunately, the balance sheet strengths masked the more delicate posture reflected by the income statements. With high fixed costs, the seemingly bountiful half-decade of the late 1990s never translated into abundant net-profit margins, which peaked in 1997 at only 4.7 per cent. By 2000, they had fallen to 1.7 per cent. And with the attacks in 2001, expansion had become a handicap resulting in a collective net-loss of $8.3 billion.

Airline Finances

In the weeks following the attacks, the federal government authorized the Air Transportation Stabilization Board to distribute emergency loans which served as a lifeline for the airlines that had to ground their airplanes for days (or more). This financial assistance, as well as new lines of credit, enabled some of the airlines to survive the steep drop in demand as passenger levels fell for the first time in a decade. LCC also experienced declining enplanements and passenger yields, but erosion among the LCC was less severe compared with the FSC (US GAO, 2005). Shortly after 9/11, the wars in Afghanistan and Iraq, heightened security restrictions, an economic recession, and the SARS outbreak depressed demand and forced airlines to further reduce capacity. But this did little to shed costs. The financial pressure of debt and pension obligations did not dissipate and the cash burn became overwhelming. Net losses rose and by 2005 the industry had lost $57 billion, more than double the total profits that had been accumulated during the prosperous run at the end of the prior decade.

In the five years after 9/11, there were 22 bankruptcies (US GAO 2005), including most FSC.[8] The first was US Air in 2002; as the major airline at Washington Reagan National airport which remained closed longer than any other airport, US Air was disproportionately impacted. Later that year, United Airlines followed suit. In 2004, US Air entered bankruptcy again, followed by Northwest and Delta in 2005. There are many reasons for the legacy carrier financial distress, but two specific operational aspects are worth noting. First, the airlines have rarely had any sustained pricing power. While this is true for both FSC and LCC, the operational burden is heavier on FSC with their higher fixed costs. With democratized ticket prices, airlines must match the lowest fare along a route or risk losing market share, resulting in destructive, or ruinous, competition (Dempsey 1995).

The second explanation for the legacy carrier's frail financial conditions relates to their employees' 'defined benefit' retirement obligations[9] (US GAO 2005). Because of ruinous competition, legacy carriers have been unable to raise fares sufficiently to fully fund their pension obligations. But current and future retirees are counting on this money, so pushing off these payments does not negate their existence, it just adds to the level of debt on the company's balance sheets. And it is under the rising tides of debt that many of the legacy carriers sank. But in bankruptcy reorganization, many of the carriers have been able to transfer these pension obligations onto the Federal Pension Benefit Guarantee Corporation (PBGC). In fact, in the years since 9/11 nearly all of the carriers offloaded a share of their pension program onto the PBGC while in Chapter 11, which has been an essential lever for restructuring their business and exiting bankruptcy (Goetz and Vowles 2009). This may ensure airline solvency, but it does little to build trust with its employees.

Employee retirement arrangements have had a lot to do with the financial strength of the various airlines over the years, and that is clear when examining the breakdown of industry profits by carrier segment (Figure 9.1). With minimal retirement obligations and lower fixed costs, LCC have been profitable more regularly. FSC carriers, on the other hand, have been prone to wild swings in profitability, a trend that has gyrated wildly over the last half decade.

In the years when both airline segments earn a profit (or loss), the FSC post outsized profits (or losses), which makes some sense given that they are larger in nearly every metric. More intriguing is that of the 24 years, LCC were profitable in 17 years while the FSC were profitable in only 12. Similarly, there are several years when the LCC are profitable while the FSC lose money, but never the reverse. Most importantly, it is not simply the profitability (or losses) that matter, but the size of those profits (or losses) that signal longer-term financial strength. The surviving LCCs are riding a cost structure that (for the moment) has inoculated them against really harsh economic conditions, and this immunization continues to elude their FSC competitors.

---

8 Two airlines (Continental and American) avoided bankruptcy in this period but Continental had previously entered bankruptcy in 1983 and 1990. In 2011, American Airlines filed for bankruptcy for the first time in its history, making it the last of the major airlines to seek Chapter 11 protection.

9 Defined benefit plans have their roots in regulation, when the pension costs were simply lumped into cost calculations presented to the CAB when requesting a fare increase.

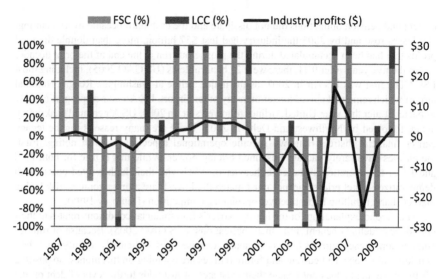

Figure 9.1   Total industry profits, and percentage of total profits (losses) attributable to FSC vs. LCC, 1987–2010 $ (billions)

Note: Southwest Airlines is the only LCC for the years 1987–1989. America West and ATA are included starting in 1990, with more LCC incorporated later in the decade.

Consolidation

Seeking a way to smooth out extreme financial swings, airline consolidation offers the familiar benefits of scale economies, corporate synergies and the elimination of some competition. Since 2001, the industry has witnessed the disappearance of several long-standing airline brands, including TWA (acquired by American), America West (merged with US Air), Continental (absorbed by United), Northwest (absorbed by Delta), and, having received preliminary approval in February 2013, the latest deal will see US Air absorbed by American (Mouawad 2013). The LCC also got in on the act with Frontier and Midwest merging in 2009[10] and Southwest buying AirTran in 2010. The difference between this round of consolidation and early rounds is that the top four carriers now control more of the aviation market than ever before (Figure 9.2).

The oligopolistic aspects of the airline industry are now more entrenched than they were toward the end of the regulatory era. In both 1977 and 1978, the top four airlines controlled just over half of all the passenger revenue miles while the top 10 airlines had just under 90 per cent of the market. Following deregulation, a wave of new entrants flooded the market and was able to capture some of the market share. By 1985, the top four had less than 45 per cent of the market and the top 10 fell below 80 per cent for the first and only time since deregulation. Throughout the 1990s, FSC re-established their dominance

---

10   This merger was orchestrated by the parent company, Republic Airways, with the new Frontier Airlines operating as a subsidiary. In 2012, Republic announced that Frontier would be spun off as an independent airline.

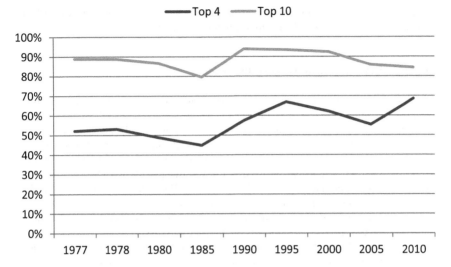

Figure 9.2   Market share of the top-4 and top-10 US airlines in select years, 1977–2010

capturing their largest share of RPM. By 2010,[11] the grip among the top 10 had eased a bit, but among the top four airlines (United, Delta, American, and Southwest), market control had swelled to nearly 70 per cent, an all-time high. Now that the US Department of Justice has approved the American – US Air deal as of November 2013, the continued crowding out of the competition will surge to even greater heights so that by 2013 the top four airlines may control as much as 76 per cent of the market, an unprecedented amount.

This latest round of consolidation has provided some breathing space for the FSC to reposition their networks and restore their balance sheets. The airlines have also tinkered with their revenue model, adopting a LCC-inspired 'à-la-carte' pricing style as opposed to an all-inclusive approach. This new revenue menu relies less on airfares and more on fees from things like checked baggage, meals, priority boarding, and extra legroom. As a result, industry wide revenues from airfares have fallen from 84 per cent of total revenue in 2000 to just 71 per cent in 2010. And in 2010, with the exception of a small loss at Virgin America, all the airlines were somewhat profitable again; a trend that has continued, in aggregate, through 2012.

This improved cost structure bodes well for the overall health of the three remaining FSC, but their capacity to leverage this strength is still viewed sceptically by Wall Street, where the airlines are persistently out of favour. At the end of 2012, despite posting several consecutive years of profits from a diverse revenue stream, the market capitalization of the largest US commercial airline was $9.3 billion for Southwest, while the combined market capitalization of the 10 largest airlines[12] was $32.8 billion, less than the valuation of online travel company Priceline.com. The financial community remains nervous that the next

---

11   Reflects United/Continental as one company, with the merger closing in October 2010.

12   As of 1 December 2012: Southwest, Delta, United, Alaska, US Air, JetBlue, Spirit, Skywest, Hawaiian, and Republic.

round of ruinous competition or a renewed spike in oil prices is imminent which helps explains why attracting capital remains a continuing struggle.

Airports – Reversing the Reverse Traffic Shadow

Passengers' willingness to drive longer distances to patronize medium- and small-hub airports gave birth to the reverse traffic shadow theory, suggesting that the smaller airports were capable of stealing traffic from their larger and geographically advantaged large-hub counterparts (Brueckner 2003). And for a while, enplanement and departure growth rates at secondary airports outpaced larger hub airports. In the wake of the post 9/11 restructuring, with LCC flying out of peripheral airports, they had a pricing (and cost) advantage over FSC which were located primarily at urban airports. But by 2008, the traditional traffic shadow reappeared, as major urban airports were capturing a majority of the passengers (Figure 9.3 and 9.4). This reversal however was not because FSC were flexing their muscles, but rather because of the changing business models for both carrier types.

To illustrate, first look at the three airports in the San Francisco metropolitan area, which in 2000 had a total of 240,039 departures, with San Francisco International Airport (SFO) capturing 53 per cent, San Jose (SJC) 26 per cent, and Oakland (OAK) with 21 per cent. FSC were responsible for nearly all of the departures at SFO, while OAK and SJC had more of a blend. By 2004, the share of total metropolitan-wide departures at SFO fell below 50 per cent, putting the reverse traffic shadow on full display as the other two airports were capturing more flights (and passengers). The rise at both airports was due primarily to increased traffic from LCC, although regional carrier activity is also evident. By 2008 however the momentum at the secondary airports stalled as total departures declined, while SFO experienced an increase in overall departures, a trend that gained strength by 2012.

Similar patterns can be seen in the Boston Metropolitan region, where through 2004 the reverse traffic shadow was observable, with the larger centrally located Boston (BOS) Logan airport losing traffic to Manchester (MHT) and Providence (PVD) on the periphery. But by 2012, Boston had nearly 79 per cent of the metropolitan departures eclipsing the total regional market share it had in 2000. After ramping up departures at MHT and PVD through 2008, LCC had cut total departures 42 per cent and 32 per cent respectively, by 2012.

Two important trends emerge in 2008 which accelerated in 2012. First, FSC are downsizing their operations at the secondary airports. In the case of OAK, FSC have only a few flights while at MHT, FSC average only a handful of departures each day. It is not just at the secondary airports where the total number of FSC departures has fallen, it is actually more dramatic at the larger urban SFO and BOS airports, where the total domestic departures by FSC from 2000 – 2012 was down 49 per cent and 36 per cent respectively. In part, this is a result of rising code-sharing agreements with regional carriers (next section). But the other important trend of the last half decade is that LCC have moved aggressively into both SFO and BOS, driving the growth of the primary airports.

Airports – The Changing Landscape at Large Hubs

LCCs have been ramping up service at large urban airports in contrast to previous years. In the examples above, both SFO and BOS were airports that SWA shunned during its

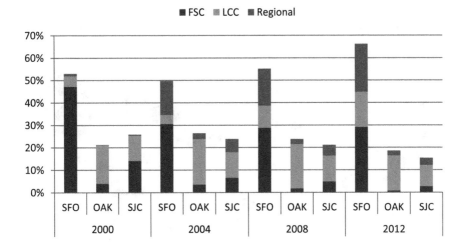

Figure 9.3   Domestic departure share by carrier type at three San Francisco metropolitan area airports, 2000–2012

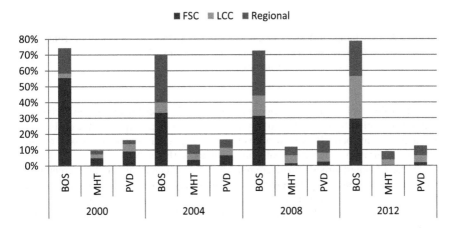

Figure 9.4   Domestic departure share by carrier type at three Boston metropolitan airports, 2000–2012

ascendancy. Whereas in 2000, LCC accounted for only 11,000 departures (8.8 per cent of the total) at SFO, by 2012, LCC had 39,146 departures (23.7 per cent of the total). Similarly in BOS, where LCC added 21,000 additional flights, an 80 per cent increase occurred in just the last four years. In other classic multi-airport regions like Ft Lauderdale (competing with West Palm Beach), Orlando (competing with Sanford), and Los Angeles (competing with several airports including: Burbank, Long Beach, Ontario, and Orange County), the larger airports are re-assuming their dominant role, albeit with LCC, rather than FSC. Even in

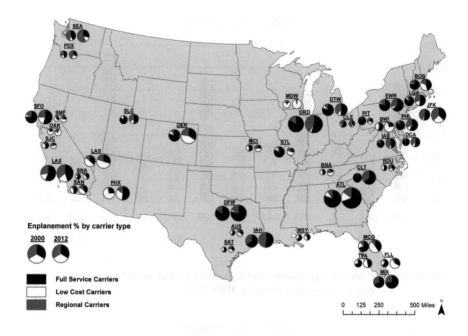

**Figure 9.5   Change in FSC, LCC, and Regional airline enplanement percentage
                  for largest US airports between 2000 and 2012**

Note: Circle size reflects total enplanements for each year.

less classically ideal multi-airport regions like Denver (70 miles from Colorado Springs) or
Charlotte (90 miles from Greensboro), traffic grows at the large airports while declining at
the smaller counterparts. But the advance of LCC at large urban airports is not only playing
out in multi-airport regions, it is a national phenomenon (Figure 9.5).

Of the 42 largest airports (there are roughly 500 commercial airports) representing 80
per cent of enplanements by domestic airlines, the steady advance of LCC is clear; despite
the combined total enplaned passenger levels at all 42 airports remaining virtually
unchanged, LCC enplaned 128 million passengers in 2012, a 49 per cent increase over
the 86 million in 2000. Meanwhile, FSC enplanements dropped from 333 million to 225
million, a 34 per cent decline. At 29 of the 42 airports, there was a 10 per cent drop by FSC
and corresponding 10 per cent rise in LCC enplanements. At more than half of the largest
airports (22 of the 42), the swing was more than 25 per cent representing a major shift in
the profile of air carrier service.

There were only four airports where the total domestic passenger enplanements by FSC
grew during this time period. At Miami, Charlotte, and JFK, the increase was minimal (less
than 5 per cent), while in Phoenix, the growth in FSC enplanements was due to former
American West traffic (a LCC) that became part of US Air (a FSC). In all other markets,
FSC traffic declined, and in some instances, this decline is being mirrored by LCC. Total
enplanement erosion, as has occurred in Pittsburgh, Detroit, Salt Lake City, Nashville,
Kansas City, and Raleigh/Durham, among others, is very worrisome for these cities as the
air carrier networks congeal around larger nodes.

For the most part though, LCC traffic grew at most airports, especially at large hubs like Denver (LCC enplanements increased 470 per cent), JFK (420 per cent), Chicago (280 per cent), and Atlanta (65 per cent). LCC domestic enplanements are now higher than FSC at some large (mostly sunbelt) hubs (Denver, Baltimore, Las Vegas, Chicago Midway, Tampa, San Diego, Orlando, Ft Lauderdale), demonstrating the strength of the SWA business model, which got its start at airports with good weather and excess capacity. But what these airports have in terms of a dominant LCC presence, they lack in terms of international connections.

In part, FSCs have been on the defensive in meeting the challenge from LCCs. In other ways however, FSC have been making a conscious choice about their operations to streamline costs and build up the most profitable market segments. These domestic enplanement trends have forced FSC to hone their attention on their hubs and cater to hub passengers. There are several features that still make a hub financially valuable and the domestic connecting traffic is only part of the equation; FSC are pivoting toward foreign markets in an effort to serve higher margin international travellers. The decline in FSC domestic enplanements at the largest airports would be far worse if not for their reorientation towards international markets (Figure 9.6).

Despite the drop in total FSC enplanements over the last decade, total international enplanements continue to grow – from 27 million to 31 million. Among the top 10 airports for international departures in 2012, all of which are international gateways for United, Delta, or American, only New York-JFK (-2 per cent) and Chicago-O'Hare (-12 per cent) experienced a decrease, while Miami, Atlanta, Newark, Houston, DFW, San Francisco, Philadelphia, and Washington-Reagan had increases. International enplanements are down in some places where it is expected (Cleveland, Pittsburgh, and Detroit) where the business climate has deteriorated and hubs were closed, but there has also been an unexpected (and unexplained) decline in a few other places (Boston and Los Angeles).

In fact, the consolidation trend among the largest carriers is best viewed through the lens of enhancing network benefits, in particular with an eye towards strengthening the connections with their international gateways. As a component of an overall network, the FSC want to retain domestic market share at these airports (to serve their feeder function), which is why the fall in domestic enplanements at these 10 airports is more mild when compared with the sharper loss of service to the LCC at most of the airports with less international traffic. For every airport that experienced an increase in international enplanements, the FSC share of the domestic market fell by less than 40 per cent in every instance. Whereas by comparison, the airports where FSC have cut back their international service, they have less incentive to retain feeder routes, which is why domestic enplanements are also down sharply.

This can be illustrated by the recent merger decision between US Air and American. US Air lacked a substantial international presence, but had an extensive and geographically diverse set of domestic hubs including Phoenix (AZ), Charlotte (NC), and Philadelphia (PA). American had well established international gateways at Miami (FL), Los Angeles (CA), and JFK (NY). Its two other hubs, in Chicago (IL) and Dallas (TX), are primarily domestic hubs, but also serve a lot of international traffic. So to enhance its international offerings, the new airline will funnel regional traffic through Phoenix or Charlotte and then on to international gateways along the coasts. In many ways, this is how the smaller, yet financially stronger US Airways first proposed the deal and why American was so receptive; American has suffered from a lack of strong domestic hubs, and it was its quest to build out/or retain domestic hubs (in St Louis, San Jose, and Nashville) that led to its eventual

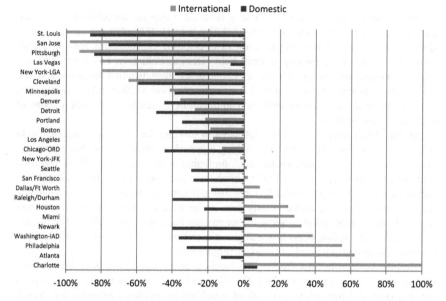

Figure 9.6   Percent change in domestic and international enplaned passengers by FSC at top US airports 2000 and 2012

Note: a) Of the 42 largest airports (representing 80 per cent of domestic carrier enplanements), only the airports with at least 50,000 international enplaned passengers in either 2000 or 2012 are displayed; b) Three airports (Phoenix, Ft Lauderdale, and Salt Lake City) are excluded from this list as they had very few international enplanements in 2000, making their increase (in percentage terms) unsuitable for this scale; c) The international increase in Charlotte was actually 199 per cent, but was condensed for this chart.

bankruptcy filing. The domestic US Air hubs will funnel traffic to its international gateways as the new American Airlines repositions itself for the decades to come.

Partnerships and Alliances

Regional Carrier Partnerships

Hubs are changing in another very important way, particularly as they relate to short-haul traffic. Service to smaller markets was an essential goal during regulation, when it was assumed that carriers would eliminate service to less profitable small markets in a free market system.[13] But FSC have incorporated hub hinterland service into their systems, a network development process that has set in motion a slow and steady transformation of the regional carriers. The number of regional airlines peaked at 247 in 1980 but has been falling ever since. By 1995, there were half as many regional carriers and by 2010 it was

---

13   This fear of small market abandonment is why Congress continues to fund the 'essential air service programme'.

half as much again. How? FSC understood that regional passengers flying into the hub were probably making a connection to a longer distance flight. With their lower cost structure, primarily as a result of cheaper labour, regional airlines make ideal partners for FSC[14] for this shorter-haul traffic (Forbes and Lederman 2007). Those commuter carriers that secured contracts with a FSC flourished, while the remaining regional airlines perished.

By outsourcing feeder route service, FSC could deploy their now-liberated aircraft to more profitable routes (or as has been the case, retire the older aircraft altogether). Over time, the nature and role of the regional carriers has changed. The 60 regional carriers in 2010 had more than 160 million passengers, 10 times as many as they did in 1980, while the average flight length has quadrupled to 476 miles. These longer flights have been made possible by replacing turboprop aircraft with regional jets. Preferred by the passengers, regional jets are faster, quieter and more comfortable. From the industry's perspective, with an average of 55 seats (compared with 16-seat turbo-props), these larger airplanes allow regional route map expansion at minimal risk to the larger airlines.

Regional partners are increasingly important to supply feeder traffic, especially at large hubs. As evidence, 63 per cent of the total departures at Chicago O'Hare in 2011 were accounted for by regional carriers. A similar reliance is observed at other major hub airports including, Detroit (66 per cent), Denver (44 per cent), Charlotte (60 per cent), and Minneapolis (52 per cent), as well as smaller or non-hub airports like New York LaGuardia (52 per cent), Cleveland (75 per cent), Milwaukee (57 per cent) and Portland (44 per cent). With these sufficiently sized aircraft, network densities are amplified as regional airlines and their FSC partners can fly previously unprofitable or underserved routes. These trends demonstrate how FSC are willing to slough off not just the short flights, but increasingly the medium length flights as well (RAA 2012).

FSCs have turned over short- and medium-haul service of the domestic market to regional partners in order to pivot to their international markets. Where in 2000, international departures accounted for 7.6 per cent, 17.1 per cent and 5.5 per cent of all departures at United, American, and Delta respectively, in 2012, international departures were 15.8 per cent, 21.3 per cent, and 13.6 per cent respectively. But FSC have to make important decisions about hub service levels that balance the total foreign destinations with profitability of serving those markets. And it is in this realm where international alliances have played a vital role in helping expand market opportunities.

International Alliances

In the absence of bi-lateral agreements with foreign countries, airlines enter into code-sharing arrangements. The agreements enable carriers to circumvent international restrictions that limit service in particular countries, but it also provides the airlines with distinct service and financial benefits; which include more destinations, higher load factors, and less expensive gate and equipment access in foreign countries. For years, airlines have built code-sharing arrangements with foreign carriers that make more destinations available to their customers and similar to the regional partner arrangements, international alliances allow for the seamless booking of travel and coordinated services such as baggage

---

14   Partnerships primarily take three forms: a) full ownership by legacy carriers; b) partial ownership by legacy carrier; or c) independent regionals with separate marketing alliance. The trend has been for regional carriers to operate independently thereby diversifying their exposure/reliance upon any one airline and enabling them to perform the feeder functions for multiple network carriers.

handling. Passenger loyalty is enhanced by increasing the number of potential international destinations, thus making their frequent flyer programs more attractive.

In the 1990s, the three largest domestic airlines (United, Delta, and American) joined forces with other large airlines to create three separate international alliances (Star, SkyTeam, and oneworld respectively). A total of 15 airlines from different continents formed the nucleus of the various alliances. By 2005, smaller airlines enhanced the service offerings for member airlines and total membership doubled. With 60 airlines in one of the three clubs, membership has doubled again in 2012. The Star alliance, with 28 members is the largest of the three. Since they are almost exclusively domestic carriers in competition with FSC, no US-based LCC has joined one of the major international alliances.

Canada

Although far smaller, the Canadian aviation system shares a few features with the US aviation market, most notably that it was deregulated (in 1987) and a few years later most of its airports were turned over to local administrative bodies. Otherwise, Canada's geography and densely clustered population distribution make its aviation market distinct. Air Canada is the only FSC, which at the end of 2012 was the 21st largest airline in the world (roughly 25 per cent the size of United Airlines, the world's largest). Unlike FSCs in the US, Air Canada claims the four busiest airports as hubs (Toronto, Vancouver, Montreal, and Calgary).[15] Canadian Airlines,[16] the penultimate FSC, was acquired by Air Canada in 2000, so for the entire post 9/11 period, the Canadian aviation market has had only one FSC.

Ever since it emerged from bankruptcy in 2004, the financial performance of Air Canada has been turbulent. Despite load factors near (or above) 80 per cent and a stable employee and fleet size, the company lost money each year from 2008–2011, before turning a small profit in 2012. Legacy costs (similar to the kinds that hamper FSCs in the US) as well as the great recession bear some of the blame, but in Canada, as in other parts of the world, the rise of a LCC, WestJet, has proven to be a highly disruptive force.

WestJet was started in 1996, and as LCCs go, some aspects of its story are familiar. It has a homogenous fleet, a lower cost-structure (non-union employees), and a point-to-point network. In other respects, its narrative deviates from the traditional LCC model; it uses major (as opposed to secondary) airports, and in an effort to capture some of the international market, WestJet has code-sharing arrangements with some of the largest airlines in the world including, among others, JAL, American Airlines, and British Airways.[17] Its rapid ascension has crowded out virtually all other LCCs in Canada as it challenges Air Canada's supremacy. In 2000, Air Canada accounted for 77 per cent of the market with WestJet's slice at just seven per cent. By the end of the decade, with WestJet controlling 35 per cent compared with 46 per cent for Air Canada, Canadian aviation has morphed into a duopoly (Transport Canada, 2012). It remains to be seen if the expansion plans recently announced

15 According to Transport Canada (2013), these airports have been the top four as measured by enplanements every year since 2000, representing 2/3 of all Canadian airport enplanement activity.

16 Pacific Western Airlines purchased Canadian Pacific Airlines in 1987 thus starting Canadian Airlines.

17 WestJet is not a formal member of any alliance. Air Canada is a founding member of the 'Star' Alliance.

by Toronto-based Porter Airlines,[18] the second largest LCC, will shake up the marketplace (Marowits 2013).

Airfares in Canada are generally higher than the US and that has created another problem for the Canadian aviation system: cross-border leakage. For a variety of factors, an estimated 5 million Canadians (of the 78 million passengers in 2012) drive to the US to catch flights (Gill 2012). By losing these passengers, network economies become more difficult to achieve particularly at the two largest airports (Toronto and Vancouver), where US alternatives (Buffalo and Seattle, respectively) offer good connectivity options. Travellers are motivated to take advantage of what was calculated as a 30 per cent cost advantage for US air carriers over their Canadian competitors. Some blame a lack of competition, but other policy choices are clear; for example, Canadian fuel taxes are three-times higher than in the US (Giuame 2006). In the absence of airport or tax restructuring, Air Canada is trying to make up for these leaked passengers (as well as take back market share from WestJet) by targeting business travellers in US cities that lack direct connections with international destinations, and offering up a Canada stop-over strategy with special hotel discounts (Air Canada 2013).

The Future

In the 30 years since deregulation, airlines have been free to compete on fares, frequency, and in-flight amenities. It was thought the free market would punish the losers and enable the winners to thrive. But since deregulation, there have been too many losers, with a correspondingly inadequate number of winners. Rising costs and inconsistent profits, operating in parallel with a new global competitive environment, will further restructure the industry. In some sense, it has already begun.

As part of this effort to reduce costs, FSC have undertaken an impressive fleet transformation. By retiring older planes, they have shifted to a more fuel efficient fleet. Initially this was a result of a drop in demand, but more recently, the airlines have had to deal with persistently high oil prices. In 1998, jet fuel accounted for only 10 per cent of operating expenses but by 2008, with oil trading four times the price from a decade ago, jet fuel represented more than one-third of their costs. But the fleet transformation has not been a 1:1 swap – older planes were retired far faster than they were replaced; the fleet size for the 10 largest airlines had dropped from more than 4,000 in the late 1990s to under 3,500 airplanes by 2010. While enplanements nudged up slightly, total number of departed seats dropped by 15.2 per cent, resulting in domestic load factors eclipsing 80 per cent for the first time in industry history (ATA 2012).

In 2008, the US entered into an Open Skies agreement with the EU that will allow US-based carriers to operate intra-EU. In part, the recent consolidation has been done increasingly with an eye towards expanding into foreign markets (Morrison and Winston 2000). Domestic carriers network reconfiguration is not just about adding more international routes, there is an expectation that they will soon have access to the 'beyond' markets. It is possible that additional arrangements with other countries or regions will further liberalize the aviation landscape and give US based carriers access to even more countries.

---

18 Similar to the business model of Southwest Airlines, Porter flies out of Billy Bishop Airport in Toronto (rather than the larger Pearson International Airport).

Further policy levers could also boost the competitive landscape prospects of the domestic airline industry. While it has been argued that the US has a free market, the government still plays a strong role. The US government could remove the limits on foreign ownership positions in US carriers, thus offering new avenues to raise capital; a move the US (towards the end of the Bush Administration) said it might entertain (Schomberg 2008). It could also enable foreign firms to start a domestic airline. Finally, eliminating the cabotage restriction would invite a host of foreign airlines to compete for domestic business, but such an agreement would only pass if US based carriers were given similar access to local traffic in other countries.

Much could also be done on the airport side, especially with privatization, which has brought benefits to airports around the world (Oum et al. 2008). Privatizing airport ownership might incentivize the expansion of gate and runway capacity, which has been shown to serve incumbent carriers but constrain competition (Cilberto and Williams 2010). Furthermore, airports could vary their landing fees by raising rates during peak periods (and discounting them at off hours) rather than the current weight-based, 'fair and reasonable' approach that has done little to mitigate congestion. Such a move would cut down on delays, congestion, missed connections, and cancellations, and financially benefit the airlines and passengers, as inefficient airport operations have cost billions of dollars (Ball et al. 2010). To better organize terminal and airspace, auctioning off the most coveted take-off and landing slots could more equitably allocate the aviation system cost onto those passengers who value their time more, and give discounted options to the flying public that are less time sensitive.

One of the most popular yet expensive reforms would be to roll out NextGen, which substitutes the current ground-based radar aircraft tracking system with a more precise satellite based system, that would optimize traffic flow, relieve congestion, and open up new airspace. Deploying NextGen would make better use of aprons and manoeuvring areas at airports, but it would also reduce costs as fewer FAA controllers would be required to supervise and direct air traffic flows. The resulting lower taxes paid by travellers on every ticket will reduce the cost of a ticket (taxes collected by the airlines for each flight segment make up a majority of the FAA budget, which is responsible for managing the air traffic control system).

There is also a need to more equitably account for the increase in private airplanes (Budd and Graham 2009). The major carriers have been petitioning the government to change the way that the airlines pay for the FAA. According to the airlines, these fees are levied in part to pay for the maintenance of the general aviation airports, which are used by smaller private planes, not commercial airlines. Increasingly though, corporate executives and the wealthier segment of the flying public, in search of increased 'aeromobility', have opted out of commercial aviation. Flying on private aircraft that do not pay these fees enables them to free-ride the runways and airspace that require federal maintenance dollars (Urry 2007).

While these ideas advance the position that airline industry stabilization is best achieved with further deregulation, others believe that certain elements of the industry should be reregulated (US GAO 2006b; Tretheway and Waters 1998). The current system is heavily reliant on the government as evidence by the PBGC role during bankruptcies or bailouts during times of macro-economic shocks. Aviation is a public good and like the financial system (twice) or the auto industry before it, the government has shown it will not permit failure. These industries have implicit (some would say explicit) government guarantees, which means they should be subject to more, not less, oversight.

Outside the policy arena, the internal make-up of the individual airlines is shaking up the industry. To continue strengthening their competitive position, and better mitigate external shocks, Delta has taken the extraordinary step of purchasing an oil refinery. In the absence of hedging, fuel represents about a third of the operating costs for an airline. But when the oil markets are rattled and prices quickly climb, the airlines lose control of their most important cost structure. Delta's oil refinery purchase was an unconventional attempt to smooth out the fluctuations in the oil markets. The industry is still monitoring the effects of this purchase, but according to its CEO, Delta paid 20–30 per cent less than their competitors for fuel in Q1 2012 (Anderson 2012).

For Southwest, the one airline with an unblemished profit record, its business model may have run its course. For one, SWA now serves many of the airports it once avoided, like Boston, Washington DC, San Francisco, or New York City. SWA now serves all of these more convenient, yet more expensive and congested airports.[19] Second, in 2011, they placed an order for an extended range Boeing 737, signalling the need for longer range aircraft, and potentially non-737 airplanes that could handle longer distances (presumably to international markets). SWA already served some international destinations as a result of its AirTran acquisition, but in late 2012, they initiated service to Puerto Rico, giving them their first organic exposure to markets outside the continental United States.

Despite increased consolidation, the immediate future could still be rocky. Airlines will have to make hub maintenance or abandonment decisions. It is worth noting that the airlines will most likely make the choice in accordance with delivering shareholder value, but the local political pressure is sure to intercede. When an airline abandons a hub, the city suffers from depressed aviation service and heightened levels of local unemployment (Ivy et al. 1995). An airport that experiences a decreased enplanement level also experiences depressed concessions, which are a vital component of the operating budgets at (especially the larger) airports. And in the case of the city of Pittsburgh, which helped finance airport expansion for US Airways, excessive public debt levels become difficult to carry in the wake of decreased passenger traffic (Grant 2009).

On the flip side, there is evidence that once a hub carrier abandons a city, LCCs move in to fill the void, resulting in cheaper airfares as was the case when US Air left Pittsburgh (McCartney 2005) or when American closed its hub in Nashville (US GAO 2005). Still, the overall level of connections and flight frequency remain deflated when compared with a fully functioning hub airport. When a city loses a hub, the disruption for the airport and the local economy is noteworthy for further research.

If the US develops high-speed rail services in the Northeast Corridor, California, and other higher-density megacity corridors, the need for short-haul air service may be reduced. The airport and airspace capacity in these corridors could then be utilized more effectively for medium- and long-haul flights. Connecting airports directly with high-speed rail could create complementary intermodal linkages that would allow airlines to specialize their services and relieve some airport and airspace capacity pressure in congested corridors.

---

19   That is not to say they don't still prefer the secondary airports, as SWA has worked hard to overturn the Wright Amendment and retain its Dallas, TX operations at Love Field, and even petitioning the city of Seattle to use Boeing Field rather than SeaTac.

Conclusion

The combination of high fixed costs, intense competition, and vulnerability to exogenous forces has led to persistently weak financial outcomes that make the airline industry prone to failure. But this poor industry performance has been unevenly distributed. As younger airlines, the LCC business model is less complex and leaner. FSC have more revenues and larger networks, but also operate expensive hubs. They also carry the financial baggage of servicing their legacy; namely the cost structure of their labour, equipment, and pension obligations that accrued during the era when fares were controlled by the CAB and could be covered with rate hike requests. In the post-deregulatory environment, it is competition and the market clearing price that determines fares, not a government agency tasked with ensuring continued industry solvency.

In some respects, the airline deregulation act of 1978 was a monumental moment. It opened the gates for any airline to complete, but this competition has continued to trip up the airlines as most have really not found their footing. As we take stock of the deregulatory movement though, the long arc of competition does appear to point towards oligopoly, where its level of market concentration exceeds what was observed before deregulation; where in 2012, three FSC, United, Delta, and American, in combination with Southwest are poised to control the largest share of passenger enplanements in the history of the industry.

A new round of upstart competition could emerge at any moment, but the economy and the financial markets remain skittish, making a sustained challenge unlikely. As a result, this concentrated market structure may be one that society will have to tolerate. While the fear of exploitation by monopoly carriers is valid, the continued success of the LCC suggests that in many markets (particularly the larger markets), the pricing power of the megacarriers could still be held in check. Even in a duopoly, competition can be fierce and consumer welfare ensured. After all, prices are based on the level of competition along a route, not the cost to fly the route. In fact the real jeopardy of having so few participants is not higher prices as a result of further monopoly concentration, but steadily increasing fares as a result of collusion. In either scenario though, it is likely that prices are set to rise.

But is this really bad news? The nexus of low fares and negative profits is unsustainable. A poorly functioning airline industry would put at risk many aspects of the modern market system and threaten the health of our long-term economic prospects. In 2010, US airlines generated $174 billion in revenues, making up more than 1 per cent of domestic GDP. In addition to direct economic contributions, the aviation sector contributes sizeable benefits in terms of direct taxes (corporate and income), passenger related fees, and the aircraft manufacturing supply chain. According to Oxford Economics (2011), the sum total contribution of air transportation to the US economy in 2010 was $669 billion (4.9 per cent of the US economy) and 9.3 million jobs.[20] This new airline landscape is one that could enable more consistent profitability, and help reverse the fortunes of an industry with such a lousy profit making track record.

---

20   In measuring the economic benefits, this report included the following contributions in its calculations: direct employment, supply chain employment, indirect (multiplier benefits), and tourism.

References

Air Canada. 2013. *Air Canada Stopover*. Online at: http://www.aircanada.com/en/travel info/traveller/stopover/ (accessed 22 November 2013).

ATA (Air Transport Association). 2012. *Economic Reports of the Airline Industry*. Online at: http://www.airlines.org/Economics/ReviewOutlook/Pages/AnnualEconomicreports oftheUSAirlineIndustry.aspx (accessed 15 November 2010).

Anderson, R. 2012. *Future of the Aviation Industry*. Speech at the US Chamber of Commerce, April 12. Washington, DC.

Ball, M., Barnhart, C., Dresner, M. et al. 2010. *Total Delay Impact Study: A Comprehensive Assessment of the Costs and Benefits of Flight Delay in the United States*. NEXTOR report, October.

Borenstein, S. 1989. Hubs and High Fares: Dominance and Market Power in the US Airline Industry. *Rand Journal of Economics* 20(3): 344–365.

Borenstein, S. and Rose, N.L. 2007. How Airline Markets Work ... Or Do They? *Economic Regulation and Its Reform: What Have We Learned?* Rose, N.L. (ed.). Chicago, Illinois: University of Chicago Press.

Breyer, S. 2003. Up for Debate: Deregulation. *Commanding Heights: The Battle for the World Economy*, companion material, transcript of interview with Stephen Breyer. New York: Simon and Schuster. Online at: http://www.pbs.org/wgbh/commandingheights/ shared/minitextlo/ufd_deregulation_full.html (accessed 17 November 2012).

Brueckner, K. 2003. Airline Traffic and Urban Economic Development. *Urban Studies* 40(4): 1455–1469.

Budd, L. and Graham, B. 2009. Unintended Trajectories: Liberalization and the Geographies of Private Business Flight. *Journal of Transport Geography* 17(4): 285–292.

Button, K. and Lall, S. 1999. The Economics of Being a Hub City. *Research in Transportation Economics* 5: 75–105.

Button, K. 1989. The Deregulation of the US Interstate Aviation: An Assessment of Causes and Consequences. *Transport Reviews* 9(1): 99–118.

Button, K 2002. Debunking Some Common Myths about Airport Hubs. *Journal of Air Transport Management* 8(2002): 177–188.

Cilberto, F. and Williams, J.W. 2010. Limited Access to Airport Facilities and Market Power in the Airline Industry. *Journal of Law and Economics* 53(8): 467–495.

Debbage, K.G. and Delk, D. 2001. The Geography of Air Passenger Volume and Local Employment Patterns by US Metropolitan Core Area: 1973–1996. *Journal of Air Transport Management* 7(2001): 159–167.

Dempsey, P. 1995. Dysfunctional Economics and the Airline Industry, in D. Jenkins and C.P. Ray (eds) *Handbook of Airline Economics*. Aviation Week Group. McGraw-Hill, pp. 185–200.

Douglas, G.W. and Miller, J.C. 1974. *Economic Regulation of Domestic Air Transport: Theory and Policy*. Washington, DC: The Brookings Institution.

Forbes, S.J. and Lederman, M. 2007. The Role of Regional Airlines in the US Airline Industry, in D. Lee (ed.) *Advances in Airline Economics*. Cambridge: Elsevier, pp. 193–208.

Fuellhart, K. 2003. Inter-metropolitan Airport Substitution by Consumers in an Asymmetrical Airfare Environment: Harrisburg, Philadelphia and Baltimore. *Journal of Transport Geography* 11(2003): 285–296.

Gill, V. 2012. *Driven Away: Why More Canadians are Choosing Cross Border Airports.* The Conference Board of Canada.

Gillen, D. and Lall, A. 2004. Competitive Advantage of Low-Cost Carriers: Some Implications for Airports. *Journal of Air Transport Management* 10(2004): 41–50.

Giuame, S. 2006. How to Make the Canadian Airline Industry More Competitive. *Tax Policy Series.* Montreal Economic Institute.

Goetz, A.R. 2002. Deregulation, Competition, and Antitrust Implications in the US Airline Industry. *Journal of Transport Geography* 10(1): 1–19.

Goetz, A.R. and Sutton, C.J. 1997. The Geography of Deregulation in the U.S. Domestic Airline Industry. *Annals of the Association of American Geographers* 87(2): 238–263.

Goetz, A.R. and Vowles, T.M. 2009. The Good, the Bad, and the Ugly; 30 Years of US Airline Deregulation. *Journal of Transport Geography* 17(4): 251–263.

Grant, A. 2009. Pittsburgh Could Foreshadow Future of Cleveland Hopkins International Airport. *The Plain Dealer,* 22 November.

Ivy, R.L., Fik, T.J. and Malecki, E.J. 1995. Changes in Air Service Connectivity and Employment. *Environment and Planning A* 27: 165–179.

Joskow, A.S., Werden, G.J. and Johnson, R.L. 1990. *Entry, Exit, and Performance in Airline Markets.* US Department of Justice Discussion Paper. EAG, 90–100.

Keeler, T.E. 1972. Airline Regulation and Market Performance. *Bell Journal of Economics and Management Science* 3(2): 399–424.

Levine, M.E. 1965. Is Regulation Necessary? California Air Transportation and National Regulatory Policy. *Yale Law Journal* 74: 1416–1447.

Levine,. M.E. 1987. Airline Competition in Deregulated Markets: Theory, Firm Strategy and Public Policy. *Yale Journal on Regulation* 4(2): 393–494.

Leonhardt, D. and Markels, A. 2002. The Days of Coasting are Gone. *New York Times,* 8 December.

Marowits, R. 2013. Porter Airlines Set to Unveil Expansion that Could Heat Up Canadian Competition. *Canadian Business,* 9 April.

McCartney, S. 2005. Why Travelers Benefit When an Airline Hub Closes. *Wall Street Journal,* D1, 1 November.

Morrison, S. and Winston, C. 2000. The Remaining Role of Government Policy in the Deregulated Airline Industry, in Peltzman, S. and Winston, C. (eds) *Deregulation of Network Industries: What's Next?* Washington, DC: Brookings, pp. 1–40.

Mouawad, J. 2013. American and US Air May Announce Merger this Week. *New York Times,* 11 February.

Nolan, J., Ritchie, P. and Rowcroft, J. 2005. Small Market Air Service and Regional Policy. *Journal of Transport Economics and Policy* 39(3): 363–378.

O'Kelly, M.E. 1986. The Location of Interacting Hub Facilities. *Transportation Science* 20: 92–106.

Oum, T.H., Yan, J. and Yu, C. 2008. Ownership Forms Matter for Airport Efficiency: A Stochastic Frontier Investigation of Worldwide Airports. *Journal of Urban Economics* 64(9): 422–435.

Oxford Economics. 2011. Economic Benefits from Air Transport in the US. Online at: http://www.benefitsofaviation.aero/Documents/Benefits-of-Aviation-US-2011.pdf (accessed 14 December 2012).

RAA.org. 2012. Regional Airline Association Annual Report, p. 13. Online at: http://www.raa.org/Media/Publications/tabid/205/Default.aspx (accessed 29 November 2012).

Schomberg, W. 2008. U.S. Surprises EU with Global Airline Ownership Plan. Reuters. Online at: http://www.reuters.com/article/politicsNews/idUSBRU00650520080513?pa geNumber=1&virtualBrandChannel=0 (May 13) (accessed 29 November 2012).

Tierney, S. and Kuby, M. 2008. Airline and Airport Choice by Passengers in Multi-Airport Regions: The Effect of Southwest Airlines. *Professional Geographer* 60(1): 15–32.

Transport Canada. 2013. Online at: http://www.tc.gc.ca/eng/policy/anre-menu-3044.htm (accessed 12 October 2013).

Transportation Research Board, National Research Council. 1999. *Entry and Competition in the US Airline Industry: Issues and Opportunities*. Washington, DC: National Academy Press.

Tretheway, M.W. and Waters, W.G. 1998. Reregulation of the Airline Industry: Could Price Cap Regulation Play a Role? *Journal of Air Transport Management* 4(1998): 47–53.

US DOT (Department of Transportation). 2001. Enforcement Policy Regarding Unfair Exclusionary Conduct in the Air Transportation Industry (Docket OST-98-3713): Findings and Conclusions on the Economic, Policy, and Legal Issues. Issued by the Department of Transportation, 17 January.

Urry, J. 2007. *Mobilities*. Cambridge: Polity Press.

US GAO (Government Accountability Office). 1993. Airline Competition: Higher Fares and Less Competition Continue at Concentrated Airports. Report GAO/RCED-93-171. Washington, DC.

US GAO (Government Accountability Office). 2005. Commercial Aviation: Bankruptcy and Pension Problems are Symptoms Underlying Structural Issues. GAO-05-945. Washington, DC.

US GAO (Government Accountability Office). 2006a. Commercial Aviation: Programs and Options for the Federal Approach to Providing and Improving Air Service to Small Communities. GAO-06-398T. Washington, DC.

US GAO (Government Accountability Office). 2006b. Airline Deregulation: Reregulating the Airline Industry Would Likely Reverse Consumer Benefits and Not Save Airline Pensions. GAO-06-630. Washington, DC.

Vowles, T.M. 2000. The Effect of Low Fare Air Carriers on Airfares in the US. *Journal of Transport Geography* 8(2000): 121–128.

Vowles, T.M. 2001. The 'Southwest Effect' in Multi-Airport Regions. *Journal of Air Transport Management* 7(2001): 251–258.

Chapter 10
Geographies of European Air Transport

Frédéric Dobruszkes

Introduction

The geography of airline flows, both the supply and the demand, results from three main drivers: 1) the geography of prior accumulations (of capital, business activities, administrative functions, immigrants and tourist facilities) and of interactions (e.g. headquarters vs. their subsidiaries, tourists vs. tourist spaces and immigrants vs. their home country) that fundamentally shape the need for mobility (see Derudder and Witlox, this volume); 2) airline strategies that tend to reply to these needs or to induce them; and 3) both national and international regulations that define the environment in which the airlines can (or cannot) expand. Within this basic framework, Europe has witnessed some major changes. Firstly, the formation and expansion of the European Union (EU) created a free market now involving 28 members, mostly extended to the European Economic Area (EEA)[1] and Switzerland. This policy notably led to firms' concentrations and relocations, more intra-EU international trade, and more medium- and long-distance travel. Europe was also the scene of major geopolitical changes with the disintegration of the communist bloc, the subsequent turn of many East Central European countries to Western Europe, notably through joining the EU, and the breakup of the former USSR, Czechoslovakia and Yugoslavia. Finally, a large part of the European airline market was almost totally liberalised, giving to the airlines a key position in drawing up networks.

This chapter investigates the main patterns of the current geography of air transport in Europe and its changes in the last two decades. Europe is considered here to be the region from the Atlantic to the Urals, although more attention will be paid to the EU liberalised airline market. Turkey is considered here as part of the Middle East region rather than as part of Europe.

From Conditional Bilateralism to Automatic Freedom: EU Liberalisation

The traditional geopolitics of bilateral air transport agreement is well known (see Debbage, this volume). The story of EU air transport liberalisation has already been addressed many times (Graham 1995; O'Reilly and Stone Sweet 1998; Kassim and Stevens 2010), and will therefore only be summarised here.

Liberalising European aviation might have been the result of a multilateral agreement between European countries. As no consensus could be found, only EU regulation could lead to the relinquishment of national sovereignty (Naveau 1996). During the 1970s and the 1980s, initiatives taken by the Commission of the European Communities – later renamed European Commission (EC) – and requests from some members of the European

---

1   Thus integrating Iceland, Liechtenstein and Norway in the EU Internal Market.

Parliament failed in this regard. Actually, the 1957 Treaty of Rome, which established the European Economic Community, allows uncertainty to persist on the inclusion of both air and maritime transport into the EU free market. The affirmative answer was indirectly given twice, in 1974 and 1986, by the European Court of Justice. The decision to liberalise was finally made in the aftermath of the 1986 Single European Act (SEA). The SEA in particular aimed at establishing a single market within the European Community by the end of 1992. A policy agenda to reach this goal was set, including the liberalisation of EU aviation. Before the so-called 'co-decision procedure' involving both the council and the European Parliament (implemented by the 1992 Maastricht and subsequent treaties, but still excluding some strategic fields), directives had been adopted by the sole Council of the European Communities, i.e. the relevant member states' ministers. Second, within the co-decision scheme, many decisions could be taken according to a qualified majority. This would soon make it easier to change aviation regulations. The decision to liberalise EU air transport was thus made by the sole council without real democratic control. [2]

The council adopted three successive packages (1987, 1990 and 1992) that progressively liberalised almost all of the EU aviation market. The third and main package was the most radical one. Largely valid from 1 January 1993 (though with various transitional schemes, including full cabotage from 1 April 1997 at the latest), it includes several regulations[3] notably setting:

- Community status: member states can only register airlines that are owned and effectively controlled, for the most part, by EU nationals or public bodies, and which satisfy some technical and financial criteria. These airlines are recognised as EU airlines.
- Free access to the whole EU market for EU airlines: this means that *getting traffic rights becomes EU-wide and automatic instead of bilateral and conditional*.
- Fares freedom with some potential safeguards for excessively high or low fares.

Of course, state aid is restricted, but there are various exceptions including public service obligations (see below), social purposes (for example, discount fares for remote island citizens), potential support to in-trouble airlines to restructure themselves and start-up aid to airlines departing from regional airports (see EC 2005). In sum, the EU followed the US example (see Vowles and Tierney in this volume) but on a multilateral basis involving 12 countries in the first stage. Subsequent new member states were of course included in the European liberalised sky. Non-EU EEA countries (i.e. Norway, Iceland and Liechtenstein, although the latter has no airport) also joined. Switzerland followed but excluded its domestic flights.

In the current context, then, nothing prevents, say, German investors from setting up a British airline to operate flights between France and Poland or within Italy. Today, this may appear commonplace, but such a situation would have been unimaginable two decades ago.

---

2   At that time, the European Parliament, along with other bodies, was only consulted for opinion.
3   Regulations 2407/92 to 2411/92, later replaced with Regulation 1008/2008 'on common rules for the operation of air services in the Community'. All can be found at http://eur-lex.europa.eu.

The Production of Air Services: Airlines as Key Players

Within the European liberalised sky, the new rules of the game have made airlines the key network designers. On the one hand, liberalisation gives them the opportunity to enter the market in both existing and niche routes. On the other hand, it involves rolling out a viable network and thus also contains the seeds for abandoning routes and bankruptcies.

The so-called flag carrying airlines have usually been privatised, although their respective states have sometimes kept significant shares (Kassim and Stevens 2010: 218). For example, the French state still holds 15.9 per cent of Air France-KLM.[4] However, they now 'play' in a market economy and have seen diverging trajectories. Most flag airlines (e.g. Air France, Alitalia, Iberia, Lufthansa and SAS) have adopted the hub-and-spoke strategy (Burghwout and de Wit 2005; Derudder et al. 2007) focused on one or two hubs corresponding usually to the largest cities or regional economies. It was typically an easy process, because their networks were often already concentrated. The main improvements were thus optimised transfers thanks to better timetables and extended networks through code-share or other agreements between airlines. The decision to operate a second hub can result from political considerations (especially in large countries with national unity concerns, like Italy and Spain), from a two-head national urban system (Italy) or from saturation at the main airport (Frankfurt in Germany). The second hub can be either more domestic- or Europe-oriented (e.g. Lyon vs. Paris) or global (e.g. formerly Milan vs. Rome). However, following economic difficulties, the trend seems to be going back to a single-hub network. For example, Iberia is progressively removing services from Barcelona (Suau-Sanchez and Burghouwt 2012) and Alitalia is abandoning its Milanese hub (Beria et al. 2011). Some excessive and/or too-rapid expansion of hubbing operations led to bankruptcies, as Sabena and Swissair showed in 2001, and led to decreases in air connectivity for cities such as Brussels, Basle and Zurich (Allé 2004; Dobruszkes 2008a). Despite new freedoms in the air, flag carriers surprisingly continue to operate flights mainly serving their home country. Actually, they may also penetrate other markets, but less visibly, by buying shares in other airlines (for example, Lufthansa bought Swiss Air Lines to penetrate the Swiss market). In other words, airlines' names do not necessarily fit with their respective capital structures.

Regional airlines have witnessed various trajectories. The dynamics of mergers (e.g. Air Vendée and Airlec formed Regional Airlines in 1992, before subsequent mergers), bankruptcies (e.g. Germany-based Aero Lloyd), significant expansions (e.g. BMI before it was bought by and integrated into British Airways) or conversion into a low-cost carrier (LCC) (e.g. Ryanair) led to a wide range of network changes that cannot be comprehensively analysed here. The low-cost revolution is arguably the most spectacular change in the European airline market, especially within the liberalised one (see below). Ryanair, formerly a failing, regional Irish airline, has become the main intra-European airline in terms of volume of seats supplied, while easyJet is ranked third (Dobruszkes 2013). Finally, charter airlines have suffered from LCC competition in the short- and medium-haul market (Francis et al. 2007; Williams 2001 and 2011). They have adopted various strategies to survive, such as moving to long-haul markets where they had to face competition from the LCCs; turning into a regular airline (e.g. Dusseldorf-based LTU), potentially a low-cost one (e.g. Monarch Airlines) or a hybrid one (e.g. Air Berlin); and selling seat-only products (e.g. Thomas Cook Airlines).

---

4 According to the Air France-KLM Registration Document 2012.

Entrepreneurial Airports

For a long time, airports were simply considered by policymakers and airlines as capital intensive facilities, necessarily state-owned and mostly managed by technicians supplying the capacity required for airlines operating the flights allowed by the bilateral agreements. Of course, some airports and public authorities have been working for a long time to secure both the expansion of the flag airline at the global level and international connectivity. Amsterdam Schiphol is a notable example (see Dierickx and Bouwens 1997), but many smaller or regional airports were actually rather lethargic. Things have changed for three main reasons.

First, air transport liberalisation has offered airlines the freedom to enter and exit the routes as they want, along with the possibility to set up new airlines and higher risks of bankruptcy. As in the US (de Neufville and Barber 1991), this has created uncertainties in (and potential volatility of) traffic at airports. Power has thus moved to the airlines; as airports are spatially locked and capital intensive, their business has become risky (Starkie 2012). Second, various airports – including Brussels, Copenhagen, Glasgow, all London ones and Rome – were partially or fully privatised and now follow profit-led strategies (Vogel 2006; Ison et al. 2011). This involves expanding traffic and other activities (car parks, shops, properties, etc.) and obtaining from public authorities sufficient guarantees on their business environment. For example, the sales agreement privatising 70 per cent of Brussels Airport (then 75 per cent) is confidential, suggesting that the Belgian federal government offered some guarantees to the buyer (Germani 2007). Finally, traditional spatial planning has largely moved to entrepreneurial approaches to regional development. As shown by Harvey (1989), 'managerial practices […] which primarily focussed on the local provision of services, facilities and benefits to urban populations' during the welfare state era have been replaced with 'urban entrepreneurialism' that aims to 'foster and encourage local development and employment growth'. This should be seen as a consequence of macro-economic changes and the advent of the post-fordist accumulation regime and its new modes of regulation. Many urban or regional public authorities now compete with each other, even within the same country or within the same administrative region, to keep or to attract firms, tourists or wealthy retired people. They notably invest in facilities and services that make them supposedly more attractive. Aviation expansion is often seen as an opportunity to create direct jobs (especially in the case of an airline's base, which involves more technical activities) and to make the area serviced appealing.

For all of these reasons, many airports, regardless of their public or private ownership, have moved from technical-oriented to business-oriented management. For example, some managers analyse routes that might be viable from their airport before canvassing relevant airlines. Various airlines select places they would serve according to the offers made by the airports and leave (or threaten to leave) if terms change or if they cannot get even more out of it. For instance, it seems that obtaining incentives is Ryanair's core strategy (Graham and Shaw 2008). Journalists have suggested that incentives might have comprised 70 per cent of its 2002–2003 profit.[5] The case of Ryanair at Brussels South Charleroi Airport (BSCA) provides further evidence of the relationship between Ryanair and entrepreneurial airports and regions. The airline started operations from the then-unknown airport in 1997. Then, negotiations for opening its first mainland base led to agreements with both the Walloon region and the airport in 2000. In 2001, newspapers suggested the airline had obtained

5 *La Tribune*, 4 February 2004.

various incentives; in 2002, a complaint against these incentives was lodged with the EC.[6] As guardian of the EU Treaty, the EC is in charge of investigating alleged state aid and deciding whether it is compatible with the EU legislation. According to the EC, Ryanair received exclusive advantages without any publicity. These benefits included one-time aid related to the launch of the new business (e.g. training costs) and permanent incentives related to both flights and passengers (e.g. discounted landing tax and ground handling tax, planes parking, marketing contributions paid by both Ryanair and the airport for each passenger in order to finance advertising and discounted fares; for the full details, see EC 2004). For the 2001 to 2003 period, these incentives corresponded to €23 million (De Beys 2004).

As most airports remain unprofitable, incentives offered to the airlines are paid by their public owners, usually in the name of jobs and long-distance accessibility. In the Ryanair/Charleroi case, the European Commission estimated that a private investor would not have taken a similar risk (EC 2004). In other words, public money is transferred from taxpayers to some airlines through the airports with the hope of social benefit. To be fair, one should nevertheless note that many incumbent flag airlines once cost a lot of money to their respective states, and airport incentive programmes are not restricted to the LCCs (see Malina et al. 2012).

Many European regional airports are apparent success stories. Charleroi Airport welcomed 6.5 million passengers in 2012, up from 0.2 million in 1998 (the first year of Ryanair's operations). However, public money invested in the airports may also be unsuccessful or the victim of changes in airlines' network strategies. One example is the Clermont-Ferrand airport fortunes and misfortunes. In the 1990s, Regional Airlines, a French airline built in 1992 from two smaller ones, linked more and more European and second-tier cities through a hub established at Clermont-Ferrand, a small city of about 261,000 inhabitants in Massif Central (Thompson 2002). Traffic grew from 268,530 passengers in 1990 to 940,000 in 2000, most of them transferring. Local authorities invested in a longer runway and in a new Regional Airlines-dedicated terminal with three satellites able to welcome 18 planes. The latter opened in 2000; in the same year, Air France bought Regional Airlines. The brand name was saved, but Air France now imposes its own network strategy. The most notable change was moving the hub from Clermont-Ferrand to Lyon, where Air France already had its secondary hub. Of course, setting up a hub in Clermont-Ferrand was surprising. The airport arguably has a central position, but the local demand is weak compared with Lyon, a city with four times the population. In one sense, the airline network geography has become more in line with geo-economic factors. However, this left Clermont-Ferrand as an orphan and wasted a lot of public resources.

The Big Bang: More Services, More Routes, More Passengers

The aviation and non-aviation dynamics highlighted in the previous sections led to a dramatic expansion of air services within and from Europe (Burghouwt 2007; Dobruszkes 2008a; Ramos-Pérez and Sánchez-Hernández 2013). The following analyses mostly rely on OAG databases that comprehensively describe regular air services (trends in charter flights are thus excluded). Multiple airports serving the same city have been merged, but do not include

---

6   The complaint came from Brussels National Airport, arguably afraid of competition from Charleroi.

Table 10.1   Changes in the volume of European air services

	January 1991		January 2012		Annual trend
	Millions of seats				
European open sky, of which	30.57	100%	63.63	100%	5%
Domestic	14.62	48%	19.27	30%	2%
European international	12.36	40%	33.58	53%	8%
Outside Europe	3.60	12%	10.78	17%	10%
Rest of Europe, of which	2.70	100%	6.27	100%	6%
Domestic	2.21	82%	2.72	43%	1%
European international	0.40	15%	2.42	39%	24%
Outside Europe	0.09	3%	1.13	18%	55%
Whole Europe, of which	33.28	100%	69.91	100%	5%
Domestic	16.83	51%	22.00	31%	1%
European international	12.76	38%	36.00	51%	9%
Outside Europe	3.69	11%	11.91	17%	11%

the remote airports used by the low-cost airlines. Data always correspond to the month of January. Because of space constraints, the diachronic analysis mainly compares 2012 with 1991, thus hiding intermediate trends.

Table 10.1 shows how the volumes supplied have changed, distinguishing the liberalised European space and the rest of Europe.[7] First, it is very clear that the liberalised space provides almost all of the supply, namely 92 per cent of all services and 98 per cent of intercontinental ones. In absolute terms, the supply has increased by 5 per cent per year; thus, it has more than doubled over two decades. It is striking that the domestic markets, which used to be more regulated, have nearly stagnated. This may be explained by the progressive expansion of High Speed Rail (HSR) services, which are mostly domestic, and by the increasing importance of EU economic integration. Also surprisingly, the intercontinental business, which is less liberalised than the intra-European one, has also seen rapid increases. Finally, international services within Europe have increased to such an extent that they now represent the largest share. In contrast, the 1991 market was still dominated by domestic services. The internationalisation of air services should be interpreted as a consequence and a cause of globalisation and the 'europeanisation' of economy, tourism, education, etc.

This increase of air services concerns both pre-existing markets, thus involving more competition, as well as new routes. Indeed, network dynamics are notable as well, as Figure 10.1 shows within the European liberalised space.[8] The number of routes has multiplied by 1.8 within two decades, from 1,812 in 1991 to 3,264 in 2012. The new routes

---

7   Analysing time series is unfortunately beyond the scope of this chapter, but it should be kept in mind that the increase is not linear, especially during times of global crisis (Dobruszkes and Van Hamme 2011).

8   One should keep in mind that part of the changes may come from charter airlines moving to regular flights or to flights whose period of operation has changed.

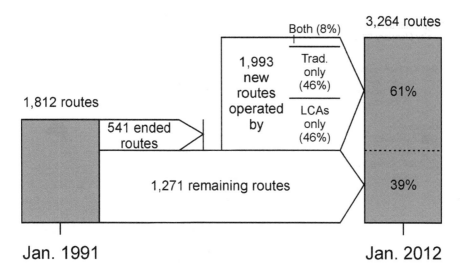

Figure 10.1   Airline route dynamics within the European liberalised space
Source: OAG Computations, F. Dobruszkes.

are much more numerous than the now-defunct ones and represent 61 per cent of the current network. Europe has thus experienced a dramatic diversification of its airline network, offering many new opportunities of direct flights and tending to open up various cities or regions. However, according to the number of seats, the new routes represent only 23 per cent of the current services. This means that the spatial diversification was only possible through many low-density routes, namely routes operating with low frequencies and/or smaller aircraft. It also means that the incumbent network always dominates the current supply. Figure 10.1 also shows that the low-cost and the traditional airlines have launched routes in separate markets, since only 8 per cent of the new routes are operated by both low-cost and traditional airlines. Going more in depth into these dynamics reveals interesting patterns; for example, cities from East Central Europe are now mainly linked to Western cities instead of Moscow (Ivy 1995; Dobruszkes 2005).

Finally, the trend in terms of passengers is also growing. Within the EU27, passenger-km grew from 346 billion in 1995 to 524 in 2010, which is +3.2 per cent per year.[9] While EU27 air and rail traffic (including shorter journeys) were similar in 1995, the former was 30 per cent larger than the latter in 2010. In 2009, high-speed rail passenger-km represented only 20 per cent of airline ones.

Current Spatial Patterns

Figure 10.2 shows the spatial pattern of air services at the city level. The market is very concentrated, with only 16 of 578 cities served by 50 per cent of the seats or 34 cities by

---

9   Source: Eurostat.

**Regular air services
by city (January 2012)**

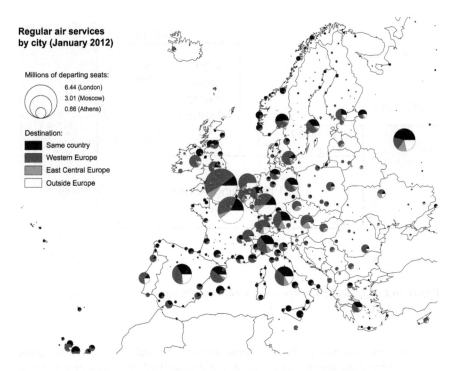

Millions of departing seats:

6.44 (London)
3.01 (Moscow)
0.66 (Athens)

Destination:

■ Same country
▨ Western Europe
▩ East Central Europe
□ Outside Europe

Figure 10.2   The geography of regular air services at the city level in 2012
Source: OAG Computations, F. Dobruszkes with Philcarto.

two-thirds. The map shows a main gap between Western Europe and East Central Europe, i.e. the former Communist states.

The main factors explaining this geography are urban size (GDP or population), economic decision-power, tourism and distance to the nearest main air passenger transport market (Dobruszkes et al. 2011). Urban size is the main factor if one considers all regular services, while economic decision-power is the main one when only international services are considered (ibid.). It is thus not surprising that the map largely reflects the European and national urban hierarchies. For example, London, Paris and Moscow dominate the UK, France and Russia, respectively, while there are more balanced patterns in two-headed countries like Italy and polycentric ones like Germany. Yet strategies led by airports, airlines (low-cost niches or hubbing) and public authorities as well as competition from HSR explain deviations from this trend. For example, Amsterdam is 'over-serviced' because of the global hubbing ambition of KLM and the Dutch government (Burghouwt and Dobruszkes 2014); 'Brussels South' Charleroi is 'over-serviced' as a Ryanair base that serves a larger region rather than the close city.

Domestic services remain important in all large countries (e.g. Russia, Sweden or Italy) and/or countries with remote islands (like Spain) or challenging topography which limits surface transport (e.g. in Norway). The map also shows that most international services go to Western Europe, even from East Central Europe. This should be seen as the logical consequence of the breakup of the former Communist bloc, the strategic realignment of

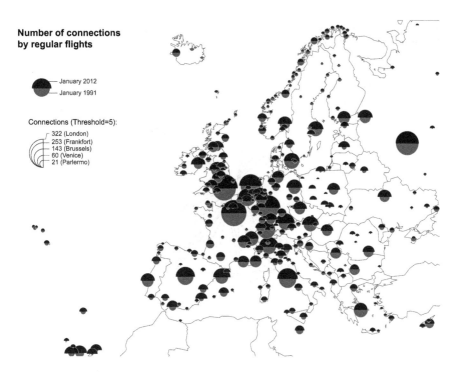

**Number of connections
by regular flights**

January 2012
January 1991

Connections (Threshold=5):
322 (London)
253 (Frankfort)
143 (Brussels)
60 (Venice)
21 (Parlermo)

Figure 10.3   The change in the number of regular air connections at the city level
Source: OAG Computations, F. Dobruszkes with Philcarto.

Aeroflot and the emergence of new sovereign states that have developed close ties with Western Europe for business, public affairs, and migration. The launch of easyJet flights between London Gatwick and Moscow in March 2013 (easyJet 2013) was indicative of the thawing of geopolitical relations between East and West Europe. Interestingly, however, the ambition of a reunified Berlin to act as a main gateway to East Central Europe seems like a failure: London, Frankfurt, Munich and Vienna are better linked to this emerging region. Berlin mostly gained new links to West European leisure destinations (Alberts et al., 2009).

Looking at the intercontinental services shows an even more concentrated pattern, with only four cities (London, Paris, Frankfurt and Moscow) served by half of the seats or 30 cities by 90 per cent of them. Furthermore, a part of intercontinental services actually goes to the surrounding areas. Looking at which cities have a direct connection with the two non-European global/world cities as suggested by Sassen (2001), we can see that only 35 cities are connected to New York, 12 of which also have a link with Tokyo. In France, for example, Paris has more than 100 flights a week to New York, but passengers from the other main cities must connect, except for a weekly flight from Nice, the main airport of the French Riviera. The longer the flight, the more connecting passengers needed to fill planes (Francis et al. 2007; Hanlon 2007). Thus, mainly large hubs are served by intercontinental services. Among them, there are market specialisations (Burghouwt and de Wit 2005; Dennis 2005) that help to understand how code shares, alliances, mergers and fusions between airlines are designed. For example, Madrid hosts good connections to Latin America, while London is

**The main regular air services
by city-pair (January 2012)**

——— Top 20% (60 routes)

----- Top 35% (154 routes)

Figure 10.4   The geography of regular air services at the route level in 2012
Source: OAG Computations, F. Dobruszkes with Philcarto.

well linked with North America and the Asia-Pacific region, so that BA and Iberia appear to be natural partners. In Scandinavia, Finnair has exploited Helsinki's advantageous location relative to the great circle routes over Russia and repositioned its hub as a gateway between Europe and the Far East while SAS has concentrated the majority of its intercontinental services at Copenhagen.

With reference to the number of connections at the city level, Figure 10.3 shows significant changes. First, London has become the most-connected city Europe-wide (even worldwide), now overtaking Paris, which lost several domestic connections (notably following HSR developments) while London gained international ones. Notwithstanding small cities abandoned by airlines or by public authorities (if air service used to be granted as a public service), most cities have experienced a wider range of connections. Not visible on the map, most of the new routes are international European. In particular, many secondary cities, for example, in Spain, are now connected to dozens of other cities, up from 10 or less two decades ago. This trend can also be seen in East Central Europe (especially in Poland), where only the capitals used to have significant air services. The LCCs here play a fundamental role, along with the flag carriers for some hub cities. The dynamics also result from the remaining charter airlines moving to the regular business (for example, Air Berlin, LTU, Monarch, etc.) and thus appearing in the databases used.

Moving to the route level (Figure 10.4), Europe as a whole is served by 3,878 regular routes. Again, the market is spatially very concentrated with 22 routes corresponding to 10 per cent of the seats and 325 routes to 50 per cent. Again, domestic markets should not be neglected, as they correspond to several top-ranked routes in terms of seats (Madrid–Barcelona, Rome–Milan, London–Edinburgh, Paris–Toulouse, etc.). The main routes link the main cities to each other or with tourist and/or insular areas (including the Canaries, the Balearics and Sicily). Symptomatically, most high-density routes from Moscow now go to Western cities rather than to its former area of influence.

The Low-Cost Revolution

Started in the US in the 1970s by Pacific Southwest Airlines followed by Southwest Airlines, the low-cost (or low-fare) business launched in Europe in the 1990s. Irish private airline Ryanair's CEO Michael O'Leary visited Southwest in 1991 and then copied its model in 1995 (Creaton 2005). The same year, easyJet started its own operations from scratch. The recipe is well known: intensive use of airplanes and labour, higher seat density, no free frills, point-to-point network (no transfers), homogenised fleet, direct sales through the Internet, various extras for a fee (for example, for luggage, more leg space, better located seat, etc.), sometimes large orders of airplanes at lower costs, very attractive loss-leader prices, and, at least within the Ryanair's strategy, state aid and rather unbalanced relations[10] with local authorities and airports (Barbot 2006; Dobruszkes 2006; Hunter 2006; Vasigh et al. 2013). Some LCCs, including Ryanair, also make extensive use of secondary airports, which are less congested (thus allowing faster turnarounds) and offer lower costs (Graham 2013).

LCCs have expanded Europe-wide and target virtually all kinds of passengers, including business ones (Huse and Evangelho 2007). They have become common for many national or international students[11] and young globetrotters (Shaw and Thomas 2006). Berster et al. (2012) estimate that the European LCCs carried 240 million passengers in 2010, corresponding to a 35 per cent market share. According to the IATA, Ryanair was the sixth largest world airline in 2011 according to the number of international passenger-km flown, although operating mainly at the intra-European scale.[12]

On the supply side, LCCs now represent 31 per cent of the regular seats within the European liberalised airspace (Dobruszkes 2013). They are also responsible for 70 per cent of the 1995 to 2012 increase in the number of intra-European flights or seats and 64 per cent of the numbers of seat-km. Their geography can be summarised as follows. LCC services are nearly contained within the European liberalised sky, plus some services between the EU and Morocco (see Dobruszkes and Mondou 2013) as well as the EU and Egypt, Israel and Russia following recent open-skies agreements. Within Europe, the LCC geography remains largely Western-oriented, despite some expansion to East Central Europe, and mainly serves larger cities as well as both urban and seaside tourist destinations. While LCCs are usually introduced as mainly serving secondary airports, one should make the distinction between regional airports (like Hahn in Germany, Carcassonne in France and Krakow in Poland) and the metropolitan areas' secondary airports (like Stansted and Luton

10 Ryanair has threatened to leave airports if its business context is changed and has carried out this threat.
11 According to the European Commission, 213,266 students received an Erasmus European mobility grant for studies or placement during the 2009–2010 academic year.
12 The top five airlines are all global FSCs.

in London or Rome Ciampino). Some of the former are advertised as serving a large city despite the distance (for example, 124 km by road between so-called Frankfurt-Hahn Airport and Frankfurt city). Regardless, low-cost services at regional airports are actually secondary, and the LCCs serve large cities through their secondary, dedicated airports but also more and more through their traditional ones. Several large airports including Madrid Barajas, Milan Malpensa or Paris CDG have indeed accommodated infrastructures and management for low-cost services (de Neufville 2006; Hanaoka and Saraswati 2011; Tchouamou Njoya and Niemeier 2011). They have either built low-cost, basic terminals or reused old terminals left by traditional airlines moving to new ones. European LCCs are also more and more present in domestic markets, including trunk routes. For example, they supply 37 per cent of the domestic seats in the UK, 35 per cent in Italy and 34 per cent in Norway.

At the route level, LCC geography is above all characterised by short-haul flights, with 79 per cent of the 2012 low-cost seats supplied on flights shorter than 1500 km. It is often believed that the LCC mainly operate niche routes (i.e. route without any competitors), but the reality is more balanced. In 2012, the niche routes represented 61 per cent of all LCC routes but only 35 per cent of the LCC seats. In other words, LCC niche routes are low-density ones on which they rarely compete with other LCCs. Conversely, 35 per cent of the LCC routes but 59 per cent of the LCC seats are supplied in frontal competition with traditional airlines. Actually, the LCC network strategy follows two main directions: launching lower-density, niche routes (Ryanair's typical approach) versus head-to-head competition with incumbent airlines on the main routes (easyJet's main strategy). The LCCs were responsible for more than a half of the 1,777 new European routes opened between 1995 and 2012 although the volatility rate is high (42 per cent of the routes once operated have disappeared). The LCCs are thus a main engine of European air network diversification. In addition, some of the largest LCCs (Ryanair, easyJet, Wizz Air) are the few EU airlines extensively using the freedoms offered by the EU liberalisation, namely, supplying plenty of flights not serving their home country. In contrast with flag carriers penetrating foreign markets by taking shares in respective airlines, the LCCs *directly* serve them under their own brand name. In this perspective, only the LCCs (although not all of them) have set up true EU-wide brands. It is not surprising that an enthusiastic journalist once remarked,

> For in recent years, Stelios Haji-Ioannou [who started easyJet] and Michael O'Leary, the two pioneers of Europe's LCCs, have done more to integrate Europe than any numbers of diplomats and ministers. They have helped to create a new generation for whom travelling to another European country is no longer exotic or expensive, but utterly commonplace.[13]

Has Liberalisation Increased Competition?

There is often confusion between liberalisation and competition. Of course, liberalisation *allows* competition, just as competition is usually a pretext to promote liberalisation. Actually, liberalisation may generate two opposite trends (Borenstein 1992): on the one

---

13   *The Economist*, 27 January 2005. Of course, the journalist forgot that the LCCs would have not have expanded if the ministers and diplomats had not decided to liberalise the European airline market.

hand, free access to the market may indeed involve more airlines providing air services and competing with incumbent airlines either on the same routes ('direct competition') or through new routes that can divert those passengers who freely choose their destination, namely tourists selecting destinations according to the supply ('indirect competition'). On the other hand, competition may lead to bankruptcies and mergers and thus to less competition at both the global or route levels. As for direct competition, between 1991 and 2005, the average level of competition decreased on international routes (because plenty of new routes operated by a single airline were opened) but strongly increased on domestic routes (which used to be even more protected from competition). If one only considers the incumbent routes, then direct competition has remained stable on average (Dobruszkes 2009). Many reasons explain the fact that a high level of competition has not become the rule, including limited market size, slot availability at congested airports, anti-competitive strategies pursued by the airlines, competition through taking shares in other airlines rather than through direct market penetration.

Beyond the Free Market: The Public Service Obligations

Although the intra-European market is mainly liberalised, the EU legislation still allows public service obligations (PSOs) to be imposed by Member States on certain routes. Member States

> may impose a public service obligation in respect of scheduled air services between an
> airport in the Community and an airport serving a peripheral or development region in its
> territory or on a thin route to any airport on its territory any such route being considered
> vital for the economic and social development of the region which the airport serves
> [...] to ensure on that route the minimum provision of scheduled air services satisfying
> fixed standards of continuity, regularity, pricing or minimum capacity, which air carriers
> would not assume if they were solely considering their commercial interest.[14]

If no carrier has commenced or is about to commence operating service on a PSO route, then the member state can limit access to this route to only one Community airline and can pay a financial compensation.[15] In January 2012, the PSO routes with limited access only represent 4 per cent of the intra-European Open Sky city-pair flown, 2.9 per cent of the flights, 1.2 per cent of the seats and 0.5 per cent of the seat-km.[16] Although one should also take into account the various incentive schemes offered to both low-cost and conventional airlines (Graham and Shaw 2008; Smyth et al. 2012), the EU has thus clearly succeeded in turning most of the EU aviation to the free market. Since there is no EU policy concerned with selecting the PSO routes, their geography is a patchwork closely linked to national, regional, or local strategies, while there are only few international ones (Dobruszkes 2007). In 2012, most PSOs can be found in Norway, France, Portugal, Greece, Italy and the United Kingdom, where they serve remote, peripheral or landlocked areas (though these notions

---

14   Article 16, Regulation 1008/2008.

15   For more details on the PSO scheme, see Regulation 1008/2008, op. cit.

16   Author's computations based on the EU list of PSOs and additional searches through the EU Official Journal. PSOs without limited access to the market account for less than one additional per cent.

are subject to debate), including islands. Only one PSO involves East Central Europe, where state intervention is really a long time ago.

Less Visible: Air Freight

The air cargo industry is a mix of integrated airlines (the 'big four', FedEx, UPS, DHL and TNT) and non-integrated airlines (that is, carriers offering airline-only scheduled services). The global, spatial trend is the latter servicing major gateway airports and the former establishing hubs at 'smaller' airports where they can enjoy lower costs and easier scheduling (Boquet 2009; Gardiner and Ison 2008). Table 10.2 tends to confirm this framework for Europe, but Paris CDG succeeded in attracting a FedEx global hub for Europe. The table also suggests that both types of cargo airlines are important in terms of traffic. Clearly, the main passenger airports are also main freight airports, because the main non-integrated airlines are large. The main exceptions are Madrid and Moscow (not freight leaders) and Luxembourg (a freight leader despite the small and non-industrial national economy). Excluding Leipzig, the main cargo airports are all in Western Europe. This is relevant with the fact that air transport is used for rather high-value products, mature markets and high-technology industries. This by nature favours the European economic core.

Integrated airlines' hubs generate night flights. Organising late collects for next-day morning deliveries on a continental scale implies late evening flights, night sorting within the hub and late night take-offs. At Liège (Belgium), for example, TNT services arrive mostly between 11 pm and 2 am and leave between 3 am and 6 am as do most of the DHL freight flights at East Midlands (UK), the country's second biggest cargo airport after London Heathrow. This often generates conflicts with populations living around the airports (see Budd, 2009, for a discussion of East Midlands) and sometimes large protests. The geopolitics of air noise related disputes may be a mix of embedded administrative, social and even ethnic patterns. The Brussels case of DHL's European hub before its move to Leipzig in 2008 is a perfect example. This federal airport is located in a Brussels' suburb but in the Flanders Region, as Brussels Region has a limited extension. Night flights used to fly over mostly wealthy suburbs, whose inhabitants are well endowed with social, political and economic resources. As a result, part of the night flights were redirected to the poorer city centre in 2003 amidst indifference (Dobruszkes 2008b). Ironically, the same rich suburbs accommodate both the high-skilled and senior managers involved in the globalisation on which the DHL business is based and the activists fighting against air noise. Airport-related noise in the Brussels region also shows that with no political solution and within the framework of consensual negotiations aiming to balance ecological, social and economic imperative, 'the task of managing social divisions fell to the judicial system which, of course, was equally unable to succeed', while DHL finally holds the key power position (Oosterlynck and Swyngedouw 2010). After a long conflict with activists, the federal state finally refused to allow significantly more night flights. As a result, DHL decided to move its hub from Brussels to Leipzig (Eastern Germany). Leipzig may seem away from the European economic core, but it is close to the many Western industries in East Central Europe. In addition, it is useful to point out that integrators not only carry urgent letters but also manage global logistic supply chains.

Table 10.2   Leading European cargo airports

Rank	City/airport	Country	2010 tons (millions)	Integrated airline's hub	Non-integrated airline's hub
1	Paris CDG	France	2.399	FedEx	Air France
2	Frankfurt	Germany	2.275		Lufthansa
3	London LHR	UK	1.551		British Airways
4	Amsterdam	The Netherlands	1.538		KLM
5	Luxembourg	Luxembourg	0.705		Cargolux
NA	Leipzig	Germany	0.663	DHL	
NA	Cologne	Germany	0.656	UPS (FedEx)	
NA	Liège	Belgium	0.639	TNT	
NA	Madrid	Spain	0.373		Iberia
NA	Moscow DME	Russia	0.161		AirBridgeCargo Airl.

Source: Airports Council International and individual airports.

Conclusion: Uncertain Futures

European aviation has experienced dramatic changes during the last two decades, leading to more services, the boom of LCCs and the bankruptcies of some large airlines. Although many cities are better interconnected than before and many travellers enjoy cheaper prices, the dynamics involve more environmental impacts (both local and global) and a decline in working conditions (EC 2007; Beria 2010; Gittel and Bamber 2010). As expected in a free market economy, labour management methods used by the LCCs are progressively adopted by conventional airlines.

The dynamics have obviously not ended yet. For example, the LCCs are still expanding; recent open-sky agreements (between the EU and the US, Morocco, etc.) involve new changes, and recurrent financial difficulties and the economic crisis force conventional airlines like Alitalia to contract their networks; meanwhile Russia is experiencing fast air services expansion.

The future is certainly uncertain. Within Europe, congested airports already restrain operations (permanently or not) at various airports including London Heathrow, London Gatwick, Frankfurt, Dusseldorf, Madrid, Milan Linate and Vienna (see EC 2011). On the one hand, congestion may limit inter-airline competition (the so-called 'fortress-hub' concept; see Zhang 1996). It also raises the issue of international competition between cities within the world-system. Evidence can be found, for example, within the current debate on London's airports future (see Banister 2012). On the other hand, some argue that airport congestion has the merit to prevent aviation expansion and related environmental impacts.

The regulation of aviation's environmental impacts is another cause of uncertainty. Until now, the EU has been rather schizophrenic. While it welcomes the launch of many new routes and the drop in fares inducing more air travel, as many EU official documents show, it also appears worried by environmental challenges. Since 2012, the EU has included both internal and external aviation in the EU emissions trading scheme (ETS). Of course, it is difficult to predict the impacts of such a scheme, notably because they would rely on several factors including non-aviation ones. Thus, it is not surprising that researchers have mixed views and may reach divergent conclusions (see Vespermann and Wald 2011; Wan and

Zhang 2011; Scheelhaase et al. 2012). In the meantime, international protests led the EU to temporarily suspend in April 2013 the EU ETS to all flights entering or leaving the EU ETS space 'to provide negotiation time for the ICAO General Assembly in autumn 2013'where a global solution would be discussed.[17]

From the EU airlines' perspective, a significant threat arguably comes from non-European global airlines and their new global hubs. Today, they expand in the Middle East (O'Connell 2011). Tomorrow, they may come from the largest emerging economies. They already compete with incumbent airlines in the intercontinental markets, which are the most profitable ones. Emirates Airlines is now the top airline based on the number of international passenger-km flown.[18] Such airlines notably connecting America and Asia may escape potential environmental regulations that would be (re)set by the EU, making the comparative advantage with EU airlines even larger. The expansion of non-European global airlines also raises the issue of whether all European intercontinental hubs could survive. London, Paris, Frankfurt, Madrid, Amsterdam, Zurich, Rome, Munich, Lisbon and some others – is this tenable in an increasingly global, liberalised market? In addition, one should not overlook EU policies also impacting third countries, as the EC has taken significant power in (re)negotiating air transport agreements with non-EU countries: it obtained some exclusive competences in negotiating with third countries; it seeks to make it possible for any EU airline to operate routes between a EU Member State and third country which signed such an agreement; and it progressively sets up a so-called European Common Aviation Area with its neighbouring countries (Western Balkan countries, Morocco, Georgia, etc.) keeping in mind a global space including 58 countries and 1 billion inhabitants.[19] Thus, it is time to link introspective research on European aviation and transport policies with the non-European dimension.

Acknowledgement

I would like to thank Aline Spriet for her lawyer's critical eye. Any remaining errors are my sole responsibility.

References

Alberts H., Bowen J. and Cidell J. (2009), Missed Opportunities: The Restructuring of Berlin's Airport System and the City's Position in International Airline Networks. *Regional Studies* 43(5): 739–758.

Allé, M. (2004), Sabena, la faillite évitable? Élaboration d'un business plan, Bruxelles, Éditions de l'Université de Bruxelles: 197.

Banister, D. (2012), *Airport Capacity: Too Little, Too Late?* Transport eBriefing, Eversheds, available at http://www.lexology.com/library/detail.aspx?g=f8630e10-fbad-4d95-b955-325db2539606 (accessed 10 January 2013).

---

17   Source: European Commission's website (accessed 15 May 2013).
18   Source: IATA.
19   Source: European Commission's website (accessed 15 May 2013).

Barbot, C. (2006), Low-Cost Airlines, Secondary Airports, and State Aid: An Economic Assessment of the Ryanair–Charleroi Airport Agreement. *Journal of Air Transport Management* 12(4): 197–203.

Beria, P., Niemeier, H.-M. and Fröhlich, K. (2011), Alitalia – The Failure of a National Carrier. *Journal of Air Transport Management* 17(4): 215–220.

Berster, P., Gelhausen, M. and Wilken, D. (2012), 'Demand and Supply Development Patterns of Low Cost Carriers in Africa, America, Europe, Australia and Asia', paper presented at the *16th ATRS World Conference*, Tainan, Taiwan.

Boquet, Y. (2009), Les hubs de fret aérien express. *BAGF* 2009–4: 472–484.

Borenstein, S. (1992), The Evolution of the U.S. Airline Competition. *The Journal of Economic Perspectives* 6(2): 45–73.

Budd, L.C.S. (2009), Air Craft Producing UK Airspace, in Cwerner, S., Kesselring, S. and Urry, J. (eds) *Aeromobilities*. Abingdon: Routledge,pp. 115–134.

Burghouwt, G. (2007), *Airline Network Development in Europe and its Implications for Airport Planning*. Aldershot: Ashgate.

Burghouwt, G. and de Wit, J. (2005), Temporal Configurations of European Airline Networks. *Journal of Air Transport Management* 11(3): 185–198.

Burghouwt, G. and Dobruszkes, F. (2014), The (Mis)Fortunes of Exceeding a Small Local Air Market: Comparing Amsterdam and Brussels. *Tijdschrift voor Economische en Sociale Geografie* (forthcoming).

Creaton, S. (2005), *Ryanair: How a Small Irish Airline Conquered Europe*. London: Aurum.

De Beys, J. (2004), La décision de la Commission européenne du 12 février 2004 sur les aides d'État accordées à Ryanair. *Courrier Hebdomadaire du CRISP* 1852, 1–36.

de Neufville, R. (2006), 'Accommodating Low-Cost Airlines at Main Airports', paper presented at the *Transportation Research Board*.

de Neufville, R. and Barber, J. (1991), Deregulation Induced Volatility of Airport Traffic. *Transportation Planning and Technology* 16(2): 117–128.

Dennis, N. (2005), Industry Consolidation and Future Airline Network Structures in Europe. *Journal of Air Transport Management* 11(3): 175–183.

Derudder, B., Devriendt, L. and Witlox, F. 2007. Flying Where You Don't Want to Go: An Empirical Analysis of Hubs in the Global Airline Network. *Tijdschrift voor Economische en Sociale Geografie* 98(3): 307–324.

Dierickx, M. and Bouwens, M. (1997), *Building Castles of the Air. Schiphol Amsterdam and the Development of Airport Infrastructure in Europe, 1916–1996*. The Hague: SDU Publishers.

Dobruszkes, F. (2005), La recomposition de l'offre aérienne en ex-Yougoslavie, in Sanguin, A.-L., Cattaruzza, A. and Chaveneau-Le Brun, E. (dir.) *L'ex-Yougoslavie dix ans après Dayton – De nouveaux États entre déchirements communautaires et intégration européenne*. Paris: L'Harmattan, 263: 164–175.

Dobruszkes, F. (2006), An Analysis of European Low-Cost Airlines and their Networks. *Journal of Transport Geography* 14(4): 249–264.

Dobruszkes, F. (2007), Air Transport Public Service Obligations in Face of Liberalisation of the European Sky. *European Union Review* 12(1–2): 105–125.

Dobruszkes, F. (2008a), *Libéralisation et desserte des territories. Le cas du transport aérien européen*. Peter Lang, coll. Action publique, pp. 285.

Dobruszkes, F. (2008b), Éléments pour une géographie sociale de la contestation des nuisances aériennes à Bruxelles. *Espace, populations, sociétés* 2008-1: 145–157. Available at: http://eps.revues.org/index2459.html.

Dobruszkes, F. (2009), Does Liberalisation of Air Transport Imply Increasing Competition? Lessons from the European case. *Transport Policy* 16(1): 29–39.

Dobruszkes, F. (2013), The Geography of European Low-Cost Airline Networks: A Contemporary Analysis. *Journal of Transport Geography* 28: 75–88.

Dobruszkes, F., Lennert, M. and Van Hamme, G. (2011), An Analysis of the Determinants of Air Traffic Volume for European Metropolitan Areas. *Journal of Transport Geography* 19(4): 755–762.

Dobruszkes, F. and Mondou, V. (2013), Aviation Liberalization as a Means to Promote International Tourism: The EU–Morocco Case. *Journal of Air Transport Management* 29: 23–34.

Dobruszkes, F. and Van Hamme, G. (2011), The Impact of the Current Economic Crisis on the Geography of Air Traffic Volumes: An Empirical Analysis. *Journal of Transport Geography* 19(6): 1387–1398.

easyJet (2013) *easyJet Launches Flights between London and Moscow*. Available at: www.coroporate.easyJet.com/media/latest-news/news-year-2013/18-03-2013a-en.aspx?sc_lang=en.

EC/European Commission (2004), Commission decision of 12 February 2004 concerning advantages granted by the Walloon Region and Brussels South Charleroi Airport to the airline Ryanair in connection with its establishment at Charleroi. *Official Journal of the European Union* L 137: 1–62. Available at: http://eur-lex.europa.eu.

EC/European Commission (2005), Community guidelines on financing of airports and start-up aid to airlines departing from regional airports. *Official Journal of the European Union* C 132: 1–14. Available at: http://eur-lex.europa.eu.

EC/European Commission (2007), *Social Developments in the EU Air Transport Sector. A Study of Developments in Employment, Wages and Working Conditions in the Period 1997–2007*. Final report prepared by ECORYS Nederland BV for European Commission, DG Energy and Transport. Available at: http://ec.europa.eu/transport/modes/air/studies/internal_market_en.htm (accessed 21 May 2013).

EC/European Commission (2011), *Impact Assessment of Revisions to Regulation 95/93*. Final report prepared by Steer Davies Gleave. Available at: http://ec.europa.eu/transport/modes/air/airports/slots_en.htm (accessed 10 January 2013).

Francis, G., Dennis, N., Ison, S. and Humphreys, I. (2007), The Transferability of the Low-Cost Model to Long-Haul Airline Operations. *Tourism Management* 28(2): 391–398.

Gardiner, J. and Ison, S. (2008), The Geography of Non-Integrated Cargo Airlines: An International Study, *Journal of Transport Geography* 16(1): 55–62.

Germani, D. (2007), Zaventem: retour sur une privatisation. *Politique* 48.

Gittel, J.H. and Bamber, G. (2010), High- and Low-Road Strategies for Competing On Costs and Their Implications for Employment Relations: International Studies in the Airline Industry. *The International Journal of Human Resource Management* 21(2): 165–179.

Graham, A. (2013), Understanding the Low Cost Carrier and Airport Relationship: A Critical Analysis of the Salient Issues. *Tourism Management* 36: 66–76.

Graham, B. (1995), *Geography and Air Transport*. Chichester: Wiley.

Graham, B. and Shaw, J. (2008), Low-Cost Airlines in Europe: Reconciling Liberalization and Sustainability. *Geoforum* 39(3): 1439–1451.

Hanaoka, S. and Saraswati, B. (2011), Low Cost Airport Terminal Locations and Configurations. *Journal of Air Transport Management* 17(5): 314–319.

Hanlon, J.P. (2007), *Global Airlines: Competition in a Transnational Industry*. Oxford: Butterworth-Heinemann.

Harvey, D. (1989), From Managerialism to Entrepreneurialism: The Transformation in Urban Governance in Late Capitalism. *Geografiska Annaler, Series B, Human Geography* 71(1): 3–17.

Huse, C. and Evangelho, F. (2007), Investigating Business Traveller Heterogeneity: Low-Cost vs Full-Service Airline Users? *Transportation Research Part E* 43(3): 259–268.

Hunter, L. (2006), Low Cost Airlines: Business Model and Employment Relations. *European Management Journal* 24(5): 315–321.

Ison, S., Francis, G., Humpheys, I. and Page, R. (2011), UK Regional Airport Commercialisation and Privatisation: 25 Years On. *Journal of Transport Geography* 19(6): 1341–1349.

Ivy, R. (1995), The Restructuring of Air Transport Linkages in the New Europe. *Professional Geographer* 47(3): 280–288.

Kassim, H. and Stevens, H. (2010), *Air Transport and the European Union. Europeanization and its Limits*. London: Palgrave Macmillan.

Malina, R., Albers, S. and Kroll, N. (2012), Airport Incentive Programmes: A European Perspective. *Transport Reviews* 32(4): 435–453.

Naveau, J. (1996), *Liberté de l'air, la grande illusion? Évolution et révolution du droit des transports aériens*. Brussels: Bruylant.

O'Connell, J. (2011), The Rise of the Arabian Gulf Carriers: An Insight into the Business Model of Emirates Airline. *Journal of Air Transport Management* 17(6): 339–346.

O'Reilly, D. and Stone Sweet, A. (1998), The Liberalization and Reregulation of Air Transport. *Journal of European Public Policy* 5(3): 447–466.

Oosterlynck, S. and Swyngedouw, E. (2010), Noise Reduction: The Postpolitical Quandary of Night Flights at Brussels Airport. *Environment and Planning A* 42(7): 1577–1594.

Ramos-Pérez, D. and Sánchez-Hernández, J.L. (2013), European World Cities and the Spatial Polarisation of Air Transport Liberalisation Benefits. *Tijdschrift voor economische en sociale geografie* 105(1): 1–29.

Sassen, S. (2001), *The Global City: New York, London, Tokyo*. 2nd Edition, Princeton: Princeton University Press.

Scheelhaase, J., Schaefer, M., Grimme, W. and Maertens, S. (2012), Cost impacts of the Inclusion of Air Transport into the European Emissions Trading Scheme in the Time Period 2012–2020. *European Journal of Transport and Infrastructure Research* 12(4): 332–348.

Shaw, S. and Thomas, C. (2006), Social and Cultural Dimensions of Air Travel Demand: Hyper-Mobility in the UK? *Journal of Sustainable Tourism* 14(2): 209–215.

Smyth, A., Christodoulou, G., Dennis, D., Al-Azzawi, M. and Campbell, J. (2012), Is Air Transport a Necessity for Social Inclusion and Economic Development? *Journal of Air Transport Management* 22: 53–59.

Suau-Sanchez, P. and Burghouwt, G. (2012), Connectivity Levels and the Competitive Position of Spanish Airports and Iberia's Network Rationalization Strategy, 2001–2007. *Journal of Air Transport Management* 18(1): 47–53.

Starkie, D. (2012), European Airports and Airlines: Evolving Relationships and the Regulatory Implications. *Journal of Air Transport Management* 21: 40–49.

Tchouamou Njoya, E. and Niemeier, H.-M. (2011), Do Dedicated Low-Cost Passenger Terminals Create Competitive Advantages For Airports? *Research in Transportation Business & Management* 1(1): 55–61.

Thompson, I. (2002), Air Transport Liberalisation and the Development of Third Level Airports in France. *Journal of Transport Geography* 10(4): 273–285.

Vasigh, B., Fleming, K. and Tacker, T. (2013), *Introduction to Air Transport Economics: From Theory to Applications*. 2nd Edition. Farnham: Ashgate.

Vespermann, J. and Wald, A. (2011), Much Ado about Nothing? – An Analysis of Economic Impacts and Ecologic Effects of the EU-Emission Trading Scheme in the Aviation Industry. *Transportation Research Part A: Policy and Practice* 45(10): 1066–1076.

Vogel, H.-A. (2006), Airport Privatisation: Ownership Structure and Financial Performance of European Commercial Airports, *Competition and Regulation in Network Industries* 2006(2): 139–162.

Wan, Y. and Zhang, A. (2011), Effects of Emission Trading Schemes, in Macário, R. and Van de Voorde, E. (eds) *Critical Issues in Air Transport Economics and Business*. London: Routledge, pp. 285–318.

Williams, G. (2001), Will Europe's Charter Carriers be Replaced by 'No-Frills' Scheduled Airlines? *Journal of Air Transport Management* 7(5): 277–286.

Williams, G. (2011), The Future of Charter Operations, in O'Connell, J. and Williams, G. (eds) *Air Transport in the 21st Century: Key Strategic Developments*. Farnham: Ashgate, pp. 85–102.

Zhang, A. (1996), An Analysis of Fortress Hubs in Airline Networks. *Journal of Transport Economics and Policy* 30(3): 293–307.

Chapter 11
Air Transport Geographies of the Asia-Pacific

Kevin O'Connor and Kurt Fuellhart

The geography of air transport in the Asia-Pacific region is shaped by interactions over time and space between the economic development, political systems and the underlying physical character of the region. Stretching east from Pakistan to New Zealand and a scatter of small island nations, and south from Japan to Australia, this region includes 35 states.[1] These vary substantially in geographic size, population and political economy, as well as on measures of economic growth and development. In addition some states have deregulated many aspects of their air industry, while others retain a conviction that government has a significant role in the planning and management of what they see as a key sector of their national economy. Taken together these aspects have created a very complex air transport geography. Airlines based in the region accounted for more than a quarter of all the passengers carried by the world's airlines in 2010, almost double their share in 1970. The significance of that outcome is underscored by the observation that the '647 million in the intra-Asia-Pacific travel in 2009 had eclipsed the number of travelers in North America as the world's largest aviation market' (IATA 2010).

The challenge is to identify the geography of the movement of these people. Initial interpretations have relied upon the understanding of the way global linkages, articulated through global cities, shape a region's air transport network (Smith and Timberlake 2001; Zook and Brunn 2006). However, Grubesic et al. (2008), while working in the same global city research context, provide a new insight on the region. The maps of flights per week and seats per week in their research show very substantial air transport activity within the Asia-Pacific region itself. The patterns in those maps are confirmed by recent analysis by Bowen (2013) who found in 2012 there were 17.2 million seats on domestic routes in the Asia-Pacific region, 5.9 million on international routes within the region (i.e. intra-regional routes), and 1.7 million on interregional global routes. That insight indicates that an understanding of intra-Asia-Pacific travel flows will provide a rich insight into the current shape and likely future of the region's transport geography and is the focus of the research in this chapter.

Intra-Asia-Pacific Air Transport

There is considerable research that shows the importance of the intra-Asia-Pacific element in the region's manufacturing trade and FDI flows (Athukorala and Hill 2010). The foundation

---

1   The countries/economies in the Asia-Pacific region are: Australia, Bangladesh, Bhutan, Brunei, Cambodia, China, Fiji, French Polynesia, Hong Kong, India, Indonesia, Japan, Kiribati, Korea DPR (North Korea), Korea Republic (South Korea), Laos, Macau, Malaysia, Maldives, Marshall Islands, Mongolia, Myanmar, Nepal, New Zealand, Pakistan, Papua New Guinea, Philippines, Samoa, Singapore, Solomon Islands, Sri Lanka, Thailand, Tonga, Tuvalu, Vietnam, and Vanuatu.

for this importance was laid in the linkage and connections created initially as Japanese and Korean firms invested in production facilities in South East Asia (Edgington and Hayter 2000). These connections stimulated trade and FDI flows, as well as the movement of key personnel. These links today have origins or destinations in most countries of the region, with a recent focus upon China (Yueh 2009) Given that much of the economic activity in the region is based in its major cities, these intra-Asian linkages are likely to be reflected in inter-city air traffic.

Analysis of the tourist industry also shows the importance of intra–regional connections. This was detected by Forsyth and Dwyer (1996: 14) who found that 'between 1970 and 1990, intra-Asian travel rose from 17 per cent to 43 per cent of all visits to Southeast Asia and from 38 per cent to 53 per cent in Northeast Asia. This was largely due to increased travel from Japan to destinations within the region but the trend is likely to continue as higher proportions of the populations of such countries as China, S. Korea, Indonesia, Malaysia and Thailand begin to travel'.

Recent tourism research provides case studies that confirm those observations (Winter et al. 2009; Cochrane 2008). These case studies also show that a number of tourist destinations (e.g. Bali, Phuket, and Macau, along with cities like Singapore and Hong Kong) draw visitors from all parts of the region.

Travel to visit friends and relations has been identified as an important part of air travel between Australia and the Asia-Pacific region by O'Connor and Fuellhart (2013) and that is likely to be the case between other countries. Research on this topic has suggested chain migration flows are relevant (Boyd 1989) and these have been significant in the region. One set of flows is associated with the Chinese diaspora, recently re-invigorated by migration out of a modernising China (Ma and Cartier 2003). Earlier migration of Indian residents to what was then Malaya may still have some resonance in current family connections, and in recent years, close connections have been created between Taiwan and Taiwanese communities in China (associated with the IT industry as outlined by Saxenian 2006), and between the Philippines and several South East Asian countries (seen in the movement of Filipino domestic workers). Adopting a wider perspective, Hewison and Young (2006) outline the substantial movement of workers in many lower skilled occupations across most of the region. Most have to travel by air, relying on a variety of arrangements in employment contracts to meet the cost of their travel.

Domestic travel cannot be overlooked in the assessment of Asian air travel. This is revealed in studies of tourism where domestic travel is less expensive, does not require visa approval and passport ownership, and can be repeated perhaps several times a year. Similarly, in most countries there is a domestic element of business travel where staff move around organisations and make contact with clients, flows that again may be recurring. The latter aspect has been researched in the US, where the location of producer service jobs has been connected to domestic air transport flows (Debbage and Delk 2001). In Australia, domestic travel between Sydney and Melbourne has been linked to the respective roles that those cities play in the national economy (Fuellhart and O'Connor 2012). Air travel to visit friends and relations will similarly have a significant domestic element. Hence it is not surprising that five Asia-Pacific nations (China, Japan, Australia, India and Indonesia) are ranked in the 10 largest domestic markets in the world by Airport Council International (2010).

The importance of intra-regional air transport links has been recognised before, but just in parts of the region, as in the triangle connecting Bangkok, Singapore and Hong Kong (O'Connor 1995; Rimmer 2003), North Asia (Oum and Lee 2002) and Australia (Fuellhart

Table 11.1 **Number of seats available on domestic and intra-Asia-Pacific city pairs (millions)**

	1980	1990	2000	2010
Domestic	131.953	227.284	449.064	803.712
Intra-Asia-Pacific	44.124	81.702	151.899	261.348

Source: OAG 2012.

Table 11.2 **Asia-Pacific cities in a global city classification**

GaWC category	Cities in the region (in rank order)
A+	Tokyo, Shanghai, Hong Kong, Singapore, Sydney.
A	Beijing, Mumbai, Kuala Lumpur, Seoul, Jakarta.
A-	Melbourne, New Delhi, Bangkok, Taipei.
B	Manila, Bangalore, Guangzhou, Ho Chi Minh City, Auckland, Chennai, Karachi, Brisbane, Calcutta, Perth, Shenzhen, Osaka.

Source: GAWC 2010.

and O'Connor 2012). O'Connor and Fuellhart (2013) have shown how an increase in links within the region have re-shaped air transport flows out of Australia, but a continental scale perspective that incorporates intra- regional as well as domestic movements between cities (following approaches like Zook and Brunn (2005) in Europe, and Derudder et al. (2007) in the US), have not been applied to the Asia-Pacific.

This chapter will provide that perspective. The aim is to describe and account for the geography of air transport, via a focus on the domestic and intra-Asia-Pacific air traffic between the region's cities. The attention to domestic and intra-Asia-Pacific traffic is justified by the data in Table 11.1, which shows there are three times as many seats available on the domestic services as on the intra-regional services, and the domestic services are growing a little faster.

The approach will identify the main inter-city routes, the most important cities and airports, and also expose the changes that have occurred in their ranking. The first and second ranked global cities identified by the size of their business services sector (GAWC 2010), and confirmed by Shin and Timberlake (2000) and Mahutga et al. (2010), and displayed in Table 11.2, will play an important role in the pattern.

Data and Approach

As noted above, the focus of the research is that collection of countries spread around the Indian and Pacific oceans. The approach uses data from the Official Airline Guide (OAG) on the sum of seats available in scheduled services between airports within the region for the years 1980–2010. To simplify the analysis, the data are analysed in five-year intervals, with an emphasis upon the 1990–2010 period. For the analysis of airports, data on passengers moving through each airport are as provided by the Airport Council International. For the cities where there was more than one airport, the data were summed to create a single figure for the city. The role of these multiple airport regions will be discussed in more detail below.

Inter-City Domestic Routes

The spatial distribution of the top 50 inter-city domestic links in the region in 2010 is shown in Figure 11.1. These 50 links account for 26 per cent of the 803 million domestic seats available in that year, and while there are routes in almost every country in the region, six spheres of traffic are most prominent: those within China, Japan, South Korea, India, Indonesia, and Australia. The links are more intense in countries with higher income levels (best seen in the dense network in Japan, as well as Australia and S. Korea), and where long travel distances are a consideration (as in India, China, Indonesia, and Australia). Within most countries the domestic links are concentrated around one of the top ranked global cities acting as both economic and transport hubs (Shanghai, Beijing, Tokyo, Sydney, and Jakarta) or are links between the first and second ranked cities within a country (Manila-Cebu, Hanoi-Ho Chi Minh City, Delhi-Mumbai, Bangkok-Chiang Mai). This is very apparent in the Chinese network where the map shows second ranked cities such as Shenzhen, Guangzhou, Chengdu, and Xiamen are linked to Shanghai and/or Beijing. Exceptions can be seen in Japan, where the largest link is between Tokyo and Sapporo[2] (the link to Osaka is the second most important in that country), in South Korea, where the busiest link is between Seoul and the tourist island of Jeju[3] and in Malaysia, where connections to the eastern part of the country, rather than to the second largest city (Penang), are the most prominent (Hong Kong and Singapore are excluded from this analysis).

There are only two direct connections between lower ranked cities (i.e. in the A- and B category in Table 11.1). These are between Guangzhou and Chengdu in China and Melbourne and Brisbane in Australia. This finding suggests the importance of air links in most nations that involve connections with the top command and control and political centres. It also shows the influence of hub and spoke networks in most domestic air networks, as discussed elsewhere in this volume.

The Size and Intensity of Domestic Links

While the geography of the heaviest travelled links show strong connections to the most 'important' cities in the region in terms of raw numbers of seats, an assessment of the number of seats per departing link versus the number of links themselves provides additional insight into the nature of the geography of inter-city air travel. Of the top 200 departing cities for domestic air travel in 2010 displayed in Figure 11.2 the median number of departing links was 12 and the median number of seats per link was slightly more than 174,000. These median values are plotted in Figure 11.2 as reference dimensions; selected data on the measures from cities in China, Japan, India, Indonesia, and Australia (accounting for about 72 per cent of links and 85 per cent of seats in the top 200) are plotted relative to these values.

---

2   Tokyo-Sapporo is the largest air transport link because it is the only major intercity pair in Japan where high-speed rail service is slower that air transport.
3   High-speed rail dominates other city pair markets, such as Seoul-Busan.

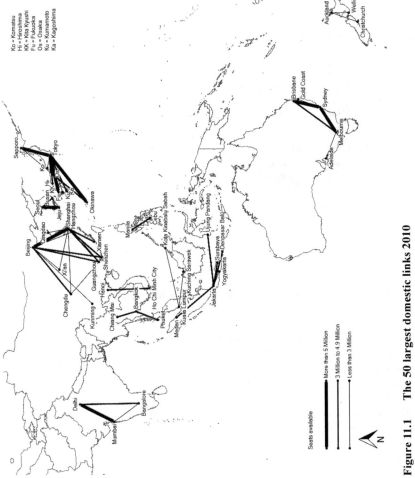

Ka = Komatsu
Hi = Hiroshima
KK = Kita Kyushu
Fu = Fukuoka
Os = Osaka
Ku = Kumamoto
Ka = Kagoshima

Seats available

━━━ More than 5 Million
━━ 3 Million to 4.9 Million
── Less than 3 Million

N

Figure 11.1   The 50 largest domestic links 2010

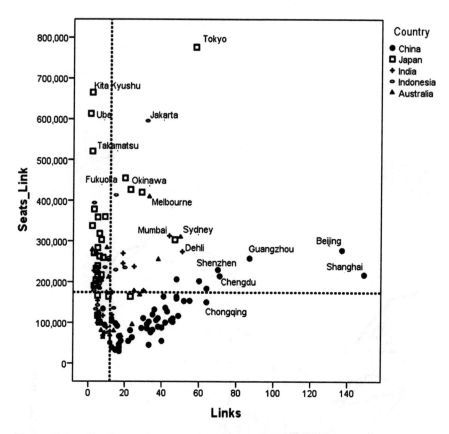

Figure 11.2   Number and average size of domestic links 2010

The results of the plot are quite remarkable, and several primary findings emerge. First, as expected, there are a large number of cities clustered around the median values for both links and seats per link. However, three additional groupings of cities are evident, largely grouped by country. In Japan most of the inter-city links are well above the overall seats per link median even though they generally have a low (and in a number of cases lower than the median) number of total links. This finding points to a high intensity of air service activity, as is captured by the very prominent position of Tokyo along with Fukuoka, Okinawa, Kitakyushu, Ube, and Takamatsu. Four of these cities require sea crossings to reach Tokyo and the other is at the extremity of Honshu, so that air services are probably the principal means of travel.

In sharp contrast to the Japanese cities are the dimensions of the air services at Chinese cities. Chinese cities tend to have many links, seen in the position of Shanghai and Beijing, along with four other large Chinese cities, in the right hand side of the figure. However, average seats per link are half those of the main Japanese cities. This outcome is no doubt related to the lower average income levels in China, along with a well-developed (and recently improved) rail network across the country, resulting in a lower propensity to fly. It may also reflect different sized aircraft used in the two countries; data are not at hand to explore that dimension. A third group of cities, mostly in Indonesia, India, and Australia, is prominent in the top right hand quadrant of the graph, with slightly higher figures than the median on both links and seats per link. Jakarta's role as the focus of Indonesian domestic travel is confirmed by its very large number of seats on flights and an above median number of links. As in Japan, many of the domestic services involve crossing from one island to another, so air services are important.[4] In addition Indonesia has one of the Asia-Pacific region's major tourist destinations – Bali – which may influence the passenger numbers from Jakarta. Delhi and Mumbai (as well as Chennai, Hyderabad, and Kolkatta) have more seats per link than most of the departing Chinese cities, although the number of links is lower. This suggests the Indian domestic system is less well developed than that of China, although its links are used more intensively. The Australian cities of Sydney, Melbourne, and Brisbane also have higher than median values on the reference measures. That may reflect Australia's deregulated domestic system that has experienced substantial passenger growth, to be explored in more detail below. Their position also confirms Sydney's major national economic role and its international gateway function, which stimulates domestic links. Melbourne operates at greater intensity with fewer links, suggesting its connections are mainly on the trunk routes of that country.

This analysis of the region's main domestic links shows there is a strong concentration in most countries. That concentration reflects the pull of the major cities, especially the higher ranked global cities, but in addition underlying geography (especially the need for island connections, as well as the need to cover long distances), income levels and the national commitment to provide and regulate air services influence the structure and intensity of the network of inter-city links. To some extent high speed rail services (in Japan and S. Korea) have had an effect on a few inter-city air services, but across the whole region this is not yet a major factor.

Intra-Asia-Pacific Links

While the discussion of domestic patterns provides insight into the ways in which the regional air networks of countries are constituted, an examination of intra-Asian transport provides a broader view of the ways places are connected through trade, immigration, tourism and the like. Airlines on intra-Asia-Pacific city links only carried a quarter of the seats available on domestic links, an outcome that reflects in part the domestic focus of deregulation. Putting the size difference to one side, the intra-regional links have an even more concentrated geography. That is expressed in two ways. First, the top 50 links in 2010 (Figure 11.2) account for over half of all the seats available, and a small number of places have very significant roles in the overall pattern.

An examination of Figure 11.3 shows the very substantial concentration of the major inter- city air traffic links along the Pacific Rim of East Asia, with an array of smaller links extending south to connect Bangkok, Kuala Lumpur, Singapore, and Hong Kong with the cities of Australia. Only one link to South Asia is included among the top 50. The strong Pacific Rim corridor reflects the many economic ties in trade and investment between countries of North and South East Asia. Closer study confirms that the region's cities ranked in Table 11.1 are the key nodes in this set of links, one group in North Asia

---

4   Japan's 4 main islands are all connected by fixed link tunnels and/or bridges and by high-speed rail.

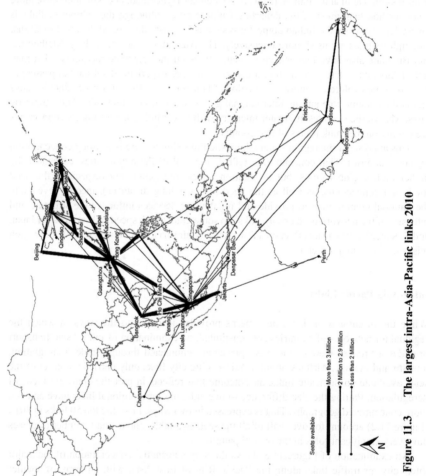

Figure 11.3   The largest intra-Asia–Pacific links 2010

Seats available

More than 3 Million
2 Million to 2.9 Million
Less than 2 Million

N

and a second in South East Asia. In North Asia connections between the top ranked global cities of Tokyo, Beijing, and Shanghai anchor a complex set of connections which include some links to second ranked cities such as Osaka, Nagoya, and Qingdao. In South East Asia the long- established triangle of air traffic between Bangkok, Hong Kong, and Singapore lies at the heart of a set of connections with several second ranked cities such as Jakarta, Kuala Lumpur, Penang, Manila, Taipei, and Kaoshiung. Ho Chi Minh City is unique in this respect as it has links to Bangkok, Singapore, and Hong Kong.

There are only a few links between the North and South East Asian clusters that figure in the top 50 busiest routes. These are Bangkok–Seoul and Singapore–Tokyo. Overall the majority of routes converge on Hong Kong, underscoring its fundamental role in the region's intra-Asia-Pacific air transport. Similarly, the pull of the major cities is such that cross-regional links between second ranked cities are not common with Bangkok–Kuala Lumpur, Bangkok–Guangzhou and Jakarta–Kuala Lumpur as the only examples.

These inter-city links illustrate that intra-Asia-Pacific connections in trade, investment, and social and community ties generate air traffic that in most countries is superimposed upon the concentrated domestic pattern, in particular reinforcing the roles played by the major cities in each nation. The involvement of lower ranked cities seen in domestic flows (especially in China and Japan) is not replicated here.

The Size and Intensity of Intra-Asia-Pacific Links

Similar to the analysis of domestic travel, the assessment of links and seats per link on intra-Asia-Pacific transport showed interesting patterns (Figure 11.4). Because of the smaller number of overall links, we analysed the top 100 departure cities (accounting for about 97 per cent of all seats) which had a median of about 13 links and 69,000 seats per link. The arrangements differ somewhat from those evident in the domestic analysis. First, there are a large number of cities in the upper right hand quadrant. The high number and large average number of seats per link at Hong Kong, Singapore, Tokyo and, at a lower level, Shanghai and Seoul, reiterate the importance of the business centres as a focus for air transport. In addition, the intra-Asia-Pacific links of these cities are stimulated by their hub status with major flag carriers, which consolidate and distribute passengers from around the world.

The effect of the region's geography can be seen in the high number of links from Taipei, Bangkok and Kuala Lumpur (and, at a lesser level, Ho Chi Minh City, Manila and Jakarta) as many inter-city journeys from these cities are short, less than many domestic flights in China, India and Australia. However, the average number of seats on these links is very high, confirming that social, cultural and economic ties between the nations of South East Asia generate high levels of traffic even between second ranked cities.

A different effect is at work in the case of Chennai and Perth. Both have few links, but very high average seats per link. Coincidentally, as shown in Figure 11.3, both have a link to Singapore that is among the top 50 in the region. Both are closer to Singapore than the larger cities within their nations and both have a special function: Perth as a gateway to the Australian mining industry, and Chennai as gateway to rapidly developing southern India. In contrast, Macau has as many city links as Shanghai, but one quarter the seats available on those links. This too is a special case, as many of the links accommodate tourism.

When the domestic and intra-regional connections identified above are overlaid it is clear that there is a very concentrated geography of air transport in the region, focused upon global cities. The second ranked cities that are engaged in these networks usually have a connection to the dominant city, either as a domestic or inter-regional link. However a

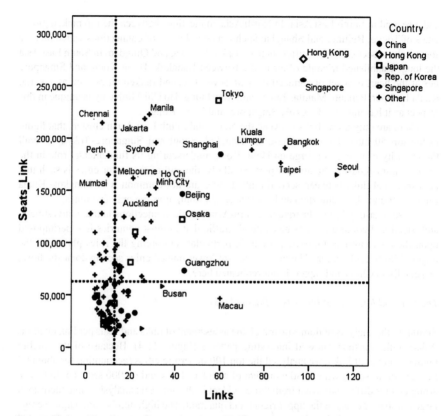

Figure 11.4   Number and average size of intra-Asia-Pacific links 2010

number have connections with one another, and also some links that by-pass major hubs have been identified. Those examples could be an indication that there will be increased dispersal of air traffic beyond the major cities in the immediate future.

A Regional Hierarchy of Airports

The region's airports emerged in the immediate post-World War II years and included cities that were colonial administrative centres as well as places connecting the region to Europe. That heritage can be seen in 1980 (Table 11.3), where Australian cities were also prominent, reflecting that country's economic development at that time.

Some of those cities remain significant today, but the important insight in the data is the effect of economic development trends on the region's airport development. That can be seen in the association between the level of air traffic and the global and world city rank (from Table 11.1) shown in the column for 2010. All but one of the region's top 10 airports in that year were ranked in the GAWC A category in the global hierarchy, whereas of those ranked 11–20, six were in category B or not ranked at all. That effect can be seen also in Tokyo's top rank over the last 25 years, consistent with the importance of the Japanese

Table 11.3   The hierarchy and global rank of the region's 20 busiest airports, 1980–2010

Rank	City	1980 Pax (000)	City	1990 Pax (000)	City	2000 Pax (000)	City	GAWC rank	2010
1	Tokyo	20623	Tokyo (MAR*)	52738	Tokyo (MAR)	83791	Tokyo (MAR)	A+	98026
2	Osaka	14740	Osaka	20600	Osaka (MAR)	40894	Hong Kong (MAR)	A+	81310
3	Sydney	8420	Hong Kong	18668	Seoul	36727	Beijing	A	73948
4	Hong Kong	6813	Singapore	14406	Hong Kong (MAR)	36150	Shanghai (MAR)	A+	71876
5	Singapore	6292	Bangkok	14329	Bangkok	29616	Seoul (MAR)	A-	51171
6	Melbourne	6145	Seoul	13878	Singapore	28618	Bangkok (MAR)	A-	45793
7	Jakarta	4840	Sydney	11227	Sydney	25755	Jakarta	A	44355
8	Bangkok	4590	Bombay	7968	Beijing	21691	Singapore	A+	42038
9	Bombay	4433	Melbourne	7618	Shanghai (MAR)	20641	Guangzhou	B	40975
10	Manila	4331	Jakarta	7419	Fukuoka	19615	Sydney	A+	35991
11	Seoul	3557	New Delhi	5407	Taipei	18681	Kuala Lumpur	A	34087
12	Brisbane	2975	Karachi	4942	Sapporo	18019	Busan		33605
13	Karachi	2955	Cheju	4845	Melbourne	14987	Osaka (MAR)	B	29141
14	Delhi	2828	Busan	4831	Kuala Lumpur	14732	New Delhi	A-	28531
15	Auckland	2463	Brisbane	4539	Guangzhou	13135	Mumbai	A	28137
16	Wellington	1432	Perth	2259	Manila	12764	Melbourne	B	27731
17	Christchurch	1370	Calcutta	2164	Bombay/Mumbai	11322	Manila	B	27135
18	Kuala Lumpur	1357	Denpasar Bali	2128	Naha	11234	Chengdu		25805
19	Calcutta	1307	Adelaide	2047	Brisbane	10981	Taipei	A-	25114
20	Perth	1253	Islamabad	1820	Nagoya	10889	Kunming		20193

Note: * MAR stands for Multiple Airport Region. The component airports are identified in Table 11.4.
Source: ICAO Civil Aviation Statistics of the World 1986; ICAO The World of Civil Aviation 2001; Airport Council International, *World Air Transport Reports 2000,* 2005, 2010.

economy over this period. Seoul's steady rise in rank, and the emergence and rise in ranking of Shanghai and Beijing, and later Guangzhou, relate to the development of S. Korea, and later China. Similarly the prominence of Bangkok, Singapore and Jakarta, as well as the rise in the position of Kuala Lumpur in the hierarchy, further illustrate how regional economic expansion of that part of the region has been felt in air traffic. The emergence of these countries seems to have had the effect of lowering the relative position of several Australian and New Zealand cities (Brisbane, Perth, Adelaide, Wellington, and Auckland), while Sydney (though an A+ ranked city) now has a middle order position in the airport hierarchy.

The hierarchy of airports in 2010 also provides more insight on the intensity of concentration in the region's air transport geography. Four of the five busiest cities (Tokyo, Seoul, Beijing, and Shanghai) are located within a 1,000 km radius in the north of the region; Osaka, Fukuoka, and Sapporo add to that concentration. Hong Kong, with the addition of Guangzhou to the west and Taipei to the east, reinforces a significant east-west axis across the region. Then in South East Asia, there are another three cities in the top 10 located close together (Singapore, Jakarta, and Kuala Lumpur). The presence of two Indian cities high up in the hierarchy is consistent with the prominent domestic links in that country.

Multiple Airport Regions

Multiple airport regions are a prominent feature of today's air transport (O'Connor 2003). As detailed in Table 11.4, Tokyo was the first city to build a second airport. The planning and construction of Narita, hamstrung by political opposition, has never reached its planned size, and still operates under flight restrictions. As can be seen in the table, Narita is primarily an international airport. In contrast, the original Tokyo region airport, Haneda, which is considerably busier than Narita, is predominantly a domestic airport, although it has embarked upon expansion under new regulatory arrangements to allow more international flights, many from nearby North Asian countries (Donohue 2006; Lieshout and Matsumoto 2012).

The construction of the new Kansai airport was planned to provide extra capacity in the Osaka region as the older Itami airport was constrained by its locational surroundings (Edgington 2000). Here the outcomes have been similar to the Tokyo region where the new airport has specialised on international traffic. Here, too, the traffic levels at the old airport continued to grow, while those at the new airport have slowed (O'Connor and Fuellhart 2010). A third airport in the region – Kobe – has also been built largely for domestic operations. New airports in Shanghai and Seoul followed soon after those built in the two Japanese cities. In Seoul, the new Incheon airport has accommodated international traffic, while in Shanghai, Pudong has international as well as (much larger) domestic passenger movements. In Bangkok, the new airport was almost a complete replacement for the original Don Muang, and now has large international and domestic traffic.

The case of Hong Kong is an unusual inclusion here, where the airports included (Hong Kong, Guangzhou, and Shenzhen) are close together and Loo (2008) has shown there are strong connections in the movement of airline passengers between them. The new Hong Kong airport was a replacement for a central city airport, which was de-commissioned. As the airports are in different political jurisdictions across mainland China and the Hong Kong SAR, all of Hong Kong's traffic is classified as international, although those passengers travelling through Hong Kong to and from China might be seen as 'domestic'. Shenzhen, when seen as a second airport, has mainly a domestic role. These data illustrate that the

Table 11.4   Multi-airport regions in the Asia-Pacific

City and airports and year of opening of second airport		Number of passengers ('000)				Passengers by origin/destination ('000), 2010	
		1990	2000	2005	2010	Domestic	International
TOKYO	Haneda	40188	61079	63282	64211	60328	3880
	Narita 1986	21664	28883	31451	33815	1652	32163
OSAKA	Itami	16821	17627	18948	14788	14778	0
	Kansai 1994	n/a	17337	16278	14353	3687	10436
SHANGHAI	Shanghai	n/a	12364	17797	31298	30327	971
	Pudong 1999	n/a	5841	23720	40578	26285	14100
HONG KONG	Hong Kong 1998	n/a	29728	40268	50348	50348	n/a
	Shenzen 1991	n/a	6422	15740	26713	26285	843
	Macau 1995	n/a	3239	4250	4249	4249	n/a
SEOUL	Gimpo		17092	13448	17566	14405	3160
	Incheon 2001		21057	26223	33605	529	32949
BANGKOK	Don Muang		32182	38985	3009	2993	14
	Suvarabhumi 2006				42784	9836	31417

Source: ICAO, OAG 2012.

extra capacity of multi-airport regions (much of it designated for international connections), have been central to the concentration of air traffic in the global cities of the region.

The Deregulation of Asia-Pacific Aviation

The geographic outcomes analysed above reflect some changes in the regulation of the air transport industry in the region. However, those changes have been slower and more locally focused than the experience of North America and Europe as 'the deep historical linkages between the state and the airline industry (that) have given the industry a strongly political flavor ... remain significant today' (Bowen 1997: 129).

For most countries the basic objective of initial regulation was the creation and protection of flag carriers to provide air transportation within a nation, and (via bilateral negotiations) on international routes, to assist the national economy, often with a special emphasis on the tourism industry. This policy was commonly expressed in decisions to create separate national and international carriers, limit new entry of rivals, control slots at airports and limit fifth freedom rights (Findlay and Goldstein 2004).

As Tretheway (1997: 71) observed 'many countries have not allowed their bilateral air services agreements to keep pace with the economy, and changes are usually reactive rather than proactive'. That early observation is well illustrated in several current observations. First, six airlines in a list of 16 'largest airlines in developing Asia' identified by Findlay and Goldstein (2004: 40) are still 100 per cent government owned and another six have more than 50 per cent government ownership. Second, regulation 'dominates most intra-Asian markets' (Fu et al. 2010: 33). Third, '... only a limited number of Air Service Agreements (just over 15 per cent) have incorporated open route schedules and that, although over half of the agreements allow for open 3rd and 4th freedom rights, the vast majority of them (over 70 per cent) enforce restrictions on 5th freedom rights' (Grosso 2008: 24).

However this situation is changing rapidly. Deregulation in aviation is a multi-faceted process, involving rights to routes, airport operations and ownership regulations among other things. For the current chapter it is the issue of rights to fly a route that is of particular interest as that can have a direct effect upon the scale of traffic on inter-city links, especially when it may involve the approval of operation by Low Cost Carriers (LCCs).

The Domestic Market

The most straightforward context for deregulation is within a domestic market. Here Australia and New Zealand have led the way in the region, deregulating airline operations in their respective domestic markets and privatising airports (Forsyth 2003; Freestone et al. 2006). That experience has been followed in a number of Asian nations, though with an emphasis upon South East Asia more than North Asia (Zhang et al. 2008). The overall effect has been to lift the share of seats available on (mainly domestic) routes in the Asia-Pacific region on LCCs from 11 per cent in 2001 to 19 per cent in 2010 (CAPA 2012). Research on S. Korea and Thailand shows these operations are overwhelmingly on city pairs in domestic markets. For example data assembled for S. Korea show LCCs have a 29 per cent share of domestic seats per week, whereas they have just 5 per cent of international seats available (CAPA 2012). In Thailand, the LCCs, accounted for 42 per cent of Thailand's domestic passengers in 2007 (Zhang et al. 2008)

In most countries, the effect of LCC operations on fares and route traffic has been significant on selected inter-city pairs. For example in S. Korea, LCC operation has stimulated tourism traffic to Jeju Island, even in the face of consumer scepticism of the airlines involved (Chung and Whang 2011). Competition of LCCs on two busy routes in Japan corresponded with an increase of 16.3 per cent in passengers between Tokyo and Fukuoka and by 9.4 per cent between Tokyo–Sapporo (Zhang et al. 2008).

One part of the region that has seen very significant change in domestic airlines and airport activity following changes to regulations is India, where deregulation began in 1986 (Mazumdar 2008). Here slow decision making, and a very negative policy on foreign investment, has limited change (Hooper 1997b). However, O'Connell and Williams (2006: 358) identified 'a three-fold increase in the number of scheduled airlines and a five-fold increase in the number of aircraft operated' and provide details of eight start-up airlines. The 2013 ranking of LCCs in the region (Airline Business 2013a) includes only four of these airlines.

The Intra-Asia-Pacific Market

The slower rate of intra-Asian deregulation was anticipated by Hooper (1997a) who suggested that most nations have been unwilling to allow new entrants that could undermine the commercial viability of their national carriers. Hooper's ideas are well illustrated in a case study of the drawn out negotiations and high level political interventions needed for Air Asia to be established in competition with Malaysia Airlines, a battle that has been justified, given its ranking as the region's second largest LCC in 2013 (Airline Business 2013a).

Change is now occurring at this level however, driven by cooperation between nations fostered by transport ministers and officials in ASEAN, and also in APEC. Although these organisations do not have the influence that the EU had in shaping European, and later

Europe–US, regulatory arrangements (as outlined by Button 1997), they do provide an institutional context for multi-lateral collaboration on transport issues, generally expressed in the context of economic development. A problem for the current chapter is that the membership of these organisations includes just a part of the Asia-Pacific region (in the case of ASEAN) or includes countries outside the region (in the case of APEC), and both exclude South Asia. Hence their progress will not be felt across the Asia-Pacific region as a whole, although their work may influence policy in non-member countries.

The Air Services Group of Transportation Ministers' Meeting of APEC provides a forum for aviation policy discussion in the Asia-Pacific region. The framework for the work of this group is a regional approach to deregulation based upon 'Eight Options for More Competitive Air Services with Fair and Equitable Opportunity' confirmed by APEC leaders in 1999 (Grosso 2008). A review of recent change suggests there has been 'increased 3rd/4th freedom capacity for existing routes, new 3rd/4th freedom routes (particularly into Chinese cities) and growth of low-cost carriers …' (APEC Transportation Working Group and The Australian Department of Transport and Regional Services 2007: 56). Zhang and Findlay (2011) have analysed the state of current Open Skies agreements. They find Australia is the most open country while China and Vietnam are the least open; Japan sits midway along that spectrum.

The ASEAN group of countries expressed a long term objective of an Open Skies arrangement in 1995 when Ministers signed a 'Multilateral Agreement on Air Services' (Forsyth et al. 2006; Ng 2009). As might be expected, progress has been uneven (Thomas et al. 2008: 15). As an example, Indonesian airlines have recently pressed for a slower rate of change (Decilya 2010). However, achievements do include new air service agreements between Cambodia, Laos, Myanmar, and Vietnam, put in place in 2003, between Singapore, Thailand, and Brunei Darussalam agreed in 2004, and the introduction of competition on the Singapore–Kuala Lumpur route.

These changes were felt in traffic on some inter-city links as seen in some short term case studies. For example, Ng (undated) shows a major increase in seats available on flights between Singapore and cities in Malaysia in little more than a year following the change in regulations, an outcome confirmed in a survey of a wider array of routes by APEC Tourism Working Group (2012). This increase is no doubt associated with lower prices; Damuri and Anas (2005) show that fares on the Bangkok–Singapore route, for example, have been cut to almost one third the original level following deregulation of carrier operation on that route.

Approaches to deregulation of airline operations on intra-Asian routes have been less successful in S. Korea, Japan, and China due to substantial differences in the policy stances taken by the three countries. Japan and China adopt a conservative approach in the interests of their carriers and airports, while S. Korea has been more open to deregulation. Hence although traffic growth in the sub-region has been rapid, this traffic is still controlled by carefully specified bilateral agreements. Yamaguchi (2011), for example found just 4 per cent of the 248 average daily flights between these countries in 2006 were operated by carriers from outside the region.

The aviation policy response in China is complex. There has been an openness to foreign investment in its aviation sector, which has allowed the upgrade of many of its airports, but a conservative view on carriers and routes that protects the vitality of its own airlines (Oum and Lee 2002; Williams 2009). One very significant change involved lifting the ban on direct flights between China and Taiwan, a connection previously made on a link from Taipei to Hong Kong (and more recently to Macau). The new regulations, applied in 2008, widened the links to seven Taiwanese airports and 21 Chinese airports, served by nine Chinese and five Taiwanese carriers. Lau et al. (2012) analysed data on passenger traffic following this shift and have found the most significant gains were recorded by Taiwanese carriers, and at Shanghai-Pudong and Beijing airports. In short, the regulatory change has completely changed the geography of traffic flows in this part of the Asia-Pacific region (although the Hong Kong–Taipei link is still by far the busiest intra-Asia-Pacific city pair).

The changes on routes between Taiwan and China have been replicated in the traffic on routes to Hainan Province where China allowed greater freedom to all foreign airlines in 2004. 'The effect of this unilateral Open Skies policy on the tourism industry has been tremendous. In 2002 Hainan Province received less than 400 000 overseas tourists but this figure had increased to about one million in 2008' (Zhang and Findlay 2011: 91).

Hence deregulation has been a major factor re-shaping the geography of air services within the region both in domestic and in some intra-Asian links. That has been felt in the operation of LCCs. A very recent global survey of these airlines has provided a ranking of the 75 largest carriers (Airline Business 2013a). This shows 31 based in the Asia-Pacific. However those 31 airlines account for just 25 per cent of the total traffic, as many of the Asia-Pacific carriers are in the middle or low rank positions. In fact only two (Lion Air (Indonesia) and Air Asia (Malaysia)) are ranked in the top 10 in the world in terms of passengers carried. In the future, if the pressure for deregulation in the intra-Asian context leads to further policy change, it is likely that some of these smaller airlines will begin to account for a growing share of global passenger movements. Much of that growth may be felt in the expanding LCC operations that are being spawned by the large full service carriers in the region. ANA, Japan Airlines, Singapore, Thai, Garuda, and China Eastern are following the Qantas-Jetstar model by creating and operating low cost divisions (Airline Business 2103b). That managerial structure may provide greater long term financial stability for these new airlines.

The Region's Airlines

The traffic at the region's airports, and the slow and uneven deregulation of the region's airline industry, is reflected in the traffic carried by the airlines in the region as displayed in Table 11.5. This shows that around one third of the top 100 airlines in the world ranked on revenue passenger kilometres in 2010 are based in the region. However, only one airline (China Southern) is in the top 10 and draws much of its traffic from the very large Chinese domestic market. The top 10 ranked global airlines include mainly the newly-merged mega carriers of the US, and the large established European carriers. Significantly these airlines operate in aviation markets that have experienced the fastest deregulation over the past few decades.

Asia-Pacific carriers are mainly in the second tier. In fact, six of the world's airlines ranked between 11 and 20 are based in the region. Many of these are among the region's oldest airlines. For example Qantas (established in 1922), Cathay Pacific (1946), Singapore Airlines (which was initially part of Malaysian Airlines established in 1947), Japan Airlines (1951) and All Nippon Airlines (1952) are prominent. The Chinese carriers date from the establishment of the Civil Aviation Administration of China in 1949; the current carriers (China Southern, China Eastern, and Air China), all created in 1987, are now among the largest in the region. Other earlier starters, such as Air India (1932), Garuda (1950) and Philippine Airlines (1941) have lost importance over time. Meanwhile, the effect

Table 11.5   Asia-Pacific airlines 2010

Rank in Asia-Pacific	Rank in world	Airline	Country	Pax traffic RPK (million)
1	9	China Southern	China	111328
2	11	Qantas	Australia	100727
3	12	Cathay Pacific	China	96588
4	14	China Eastern	China	93153
5	15	Air China	China	86194
6	16	Singapore Airlines	Singapore	84801
7	20	Korean Air	South Korea	60553
8	21	Japan Airlines	Japan	59740
9	22	All Nippon Airways	Japan	58413
10	24	Thai Airways	Thailand	55676
11	33	Malaysia Airlines	Malaysia	37838
12	41	China Airlines	Taiwan	32246
13	42	Hainan Airlines	China	32161
14	48	Virgin Australia	Australia	26895
16	49	Asiana Airlines	South Korea	26700
17	51	Air New Zealand	New Zealand	25829
18	54	EVA Air	Taiwan	23625
19	56	Shenzhen Airlines	China	23475
20	58	JetStar Airways	Australia	20493
21	59	Garuda Indonesia	Indonesia	20464
22	62	Philippine Airlines	Philippines	19816
23	63	Air India	India	19586
24	65	Vietnam Airlines	Vietnam	19088
25	67	AirAsia	Malaysia	18499
26	71	Lion Airlines	Indonesia	16784
27	72	Shanghai Airlines	China	16439
28	73	Xiamen Airlines	China	16216
29	75	Pakistan Int. Airlines	Pakistan	15657
30	76	Sichuan Airlines	China	15459
31	89	Kingfisher Airlines	India	12431
32	100	IndiGo	India	9588

of deregulation can be seen with new LCCs such as Virgin Australia and Jetstar mid-ranked and AirAsia, Lion, Kingfisher, and Indigo which are now counted in the world's top 100 airlines.

The major airlines in the region influence the activity at the region's airports, as many operate most of their routes from their home base. Hence the hierarchy of airports displayed in Table 11.3 has close links to the list of the region's airports in Table 11.5. Although there is not a direct correspondence, the top 10 airlines have home bases in nine of the top 10 airports. Jakarta is the only airport in the top 10 that does not have a top 10 airline; its prominence may reflect the influence of the fast growing LCC Lion Airlines. Other interesting outcomes can be seen in Tokyo, where its role as the base for two top 10 airlines (Japan Airlines and All Nippon Airlines) no doubt contributes to its top rank, while the rapid rise of Guangzhou in the hierarchy reflects the influence of China Southern, the region's largest carrier.

The Future

Increased Passenger Numbers

Boeing (2012) and Airbus (2007) suggest that Asia-Pacific will be one of the fastest-growing air transport regions in the world in the immediate future. These and other predictions are associated with the expected growth in the region's economy, maintaining and increasing business links within it, and also a rise in personal income, which is likely to be felt in increased travel (Gillen 2009). That thinking has led CAPA (2012: 5) to suggest North Asia is at a

> tipping point ... as GDP growth will reach levels that accelerate take up of international travel far sooner than the overall national averages would suggest. For China, these high growth levels are to be found along the east coast adjacent to its Japanese and Korean neighbours – making the conditions ripe for short haul international connections between regional centres.

To illustrate that effect, the implications of higher levels of participation in air travel have been explored. These involve the consideration of a change in travel by just 1 per cent of the population, in particular in the three most populous nations in the region, China, India, and Indonesia. Two measures are presented. In the first, the calculations apply the Australian rate of passengers carried per head of population, which at 2.27 is ranked sixth in the region; this is a high income country where deregulation has been substantial in both domestic and international services. The second measure uses the Japanese rate of passengers carried per head of population, which is ranked tenth in the region. Japan is a high income country where deregulation has been partially applied, and also high speed rail systems are mature. These measures are then applied to the 1 per cent of each country's population to produce a high and low estimate of the additional passenger traffic as if that cohort's air travel frequency had changed to a level like that in Australia or Japan. Results are shown in Table 11.6.

In China (where the current passenger-per-head-of-population ratio is a low 0.17) a change in air travel to the Australian level by 1 per cent of the population would increase passenger numbers by 30 million, which would be a more than 10 per cent increase on the current air transport activity in that country. A change to the lower Japanese level of air travel would add 9 million additional passengers. If the changes in travel were adopted by say 5 per cent of the Chinese population, the new passenger numbers are very significant: 150 million in the first case and 45 million in the second. In the case of India, the smaller scale of the current industry (one-quarter that of China) means that a shift in air travel behaviour will have very major effects on the local industry. An unlikely shift to an Australian level of travel by 1 per cent of the population would increase total passengers carried by 28 million, a 50 per cent increase on current activity. In Indonesia, the effect is smaller, as (relatively speaking) the population is smaller; as each 1 per cent of the population adopts

Table 11.6   Potential change in air passenger traffic in China, India and Indonesia

| Country | Current passengers per head of population | Population 2010 (m) | Additional passengers if 1% of population travelled at: | | Total passengers carried by nation's airlines in 2010 (m) |
			Australian pass/ head rate (2.27) (m)	Japanese pass/ head rate (0.74) (m)	
China	0.17	1331.380	30.6	9.8	229.062
India	0.05	1207.740	28.3	8.9	54.446
Indonesia	0.16	237.414	5.5	1.8	27.421

Source: World Bank Data. Air Passengers Carried and Population 2010, http://data.worldbank.org/.

the Japanese level of air travel, an additional million passengers are added to the industry. Calculations not shown here indicate that a shift to the Japanese level of passenger traffic would add around a half million new passengers in Thailand and over a million in Pakistan and Bangladesh for each 1 per cent of the population. The interesting issue is where will that growth actually be felt?

Two Scenarios on the Future Geography of Air Traffic

The main finding of the research reported here is that, to date, both domestic and intra-Asia Pacific air services have been concentrated around a few cities and along some narrow corridors. Major cities have coped with this trend by constructing additional airports. Looking to the future it is possible to consider two scenarios. The first recognises the deep foundations of the current trends, and predicts an extension of them, while the second outlines a possible change to a more dispersed pattern.

Maintaining a Concentrated Geography

The future geography of Asia Pacific transport geography is likely to remain concentrated for three reasons. First, urban settlement is concentrated in large cities and their surrounding mega city regions in most countries. The majority of future additional air travellers that emerge as incomes grow are most likely to be living in these prosperous parts of the nations of the region. Hence the existing structure of airports will be the main focus of additional demand.

Second, hub-and-spoke arrangements are important to the technical operation of both full service and LCCs. These are important not only in domestic services but also in longer-haul intra-regional services. Several of the largest cities have multiple airport capacity, allowing expanded hub and spoke operations by a wide array of airlines. A continued preference of global airlines for links to these large hubs will maintain their roles.

Third, it should be recognised that the rate of change in regulation may limit new route and carrier development, thus slowing the expansion of air services beyond existing city pairs. The implication of this scenario is the pressure it will create on already congested infrastructure of airports and air traffic control in many parts of the region.

Toward a Dispersed Geography

There was some indication that the future geography of air transport in the region could be more dispersed than it is today. That will occur with a likely increase in the number of passengers as incomes rise, and the expansion in the number of LCCs on both domestic and intra-regional routes as deregulation proceeds. Those changes will be felt in an extension of air services to smaller cities, taking advantage of the regional airports identified by Chang (2010). Some will become regionally important hubs (following the recent experience of Kuala Lumpur and Guangzhou). This outcome is likely to be most apparent in the big markets in China and India, where distances between regional cities favour the use of air travel. In China high speed rail is likely to have an important effect on the shorter inter-city markets, thus consolidating the role of air transport on the longer regional routes.

The dispersal effect might be reinforced as more direct services are provided between second ranked cities across the region, and in particular between second ranked cities in North Asia and South East Asia. The implication of this scenario is a need for additional airport and air traffic control capacity outside the major cores and corridors. In the not-too-distant past the region responded to an expansion of air transport with a major airport construction effort. It is likely a further round of construction will be needed.

Further Research

To enrich the insight of these scenarios calls for a wider review of the factors relevant to the air transport geography. One very important aspect will be a closer study of the airlines, and the aircraft they use, which will enable a more accurate understanding of the inter-city pairs, and the potential location of new services. A second will be closer analysis of international services. To date these activities have been seen as focused upon the major hubs, as a reflection of global city activities. However, it will be important to understand if new aircraft, new airlines and new regulatory arrangements allow international connections to be made with the many currently second-ranked cities across the region.

Acknowledgements

The authors acknowledge the generous assistance of Ben Derudder, Candida Gago Garcia, and Lei Zheng for help in accessing the data used in this chapter, and Tom Storme for drawing the maps. The advice of Andy Goetz on our approach was also important to the creation of the chapter.

References

Airbus. 2007. *Flying by Nature: Global Market Forecast 2007–2026*. Toulouse: Airbus Corporation.
Airline Business. 2013a. *Low Cost Carrier Traffic: The Top 75 Low Cost Carriers*, June, 38–39.
Airline Business. 2013b. *Low Cost Carrier Overview: Asia Partners on Low Fares*, June, 32.
Airport Council International. 2010. World Air Transport Report. Geneva: ACI.

APEC Transportation Working Group and The Australian Department of Transport and Regional Services. 2007. Liberalisation of Air Services in the APEC Region, 1995–2005. Singapore: The Asia Pacific Economic Cooperation Secretariat.

APEC Tourism Working Group. 2012. Destination APEC 2020: A Conference on Enhancing Tourism and Air Connectivity in the Asia Pacific Region Conference Synthesis and Proceedings. APEC Publication Number 12-TC-04.1 Singapore: Asia Pacific Economic Cooperation Secretariat.

Athukorala, P. and Hill, H. 2010. Asian Trade and Investment: Patterns and Trends, in Athukorala, P. (ed.) *The Rise of Asia: Trade and Investment in a Global Perspective.* London/New York: Routledge, pp. 11–58.

Boeing Corporation. 2012. Current Market Outlook 2012–31. Seattle: Boeing Corporation. Available at: http://www.boeing.com/commercial/cmo/pdf/Boeing_Current_Market_Outlook_2012.pdf (accessed 25 January 2013).

Button, K. 1997. Developments in the European Union: Lessons for the Pacific Asia Region, in Findlay, C., Chia, L.S., and Singh, K. (eds) *Asia Pacific Air Transport. Challenges and Policy Reforms.* Singapore: Institute of South East Asian Studies, pp. 170–180.

Bowen, J. (forthcoming). Spatial Patterns in Commercial Aircraft Size in Asia-Pacific, 1998–2012. Market Growth, Liberalization, and Sustainability, in Duval, D. (ed.) *Air Transport in the Asia Pacific.* Farnham: Ashgate.

Bowen, J. 1997. The Asia Pacific Airline Industry: Prospects for Multi-Lateral Liberalisation, in Findlay, C., Chia, L.S., and Singh, K. (eds) *Asia Pacific Air Transport. Challenges and Policy Reforms.* Singapore: Institute of South East Asian Studies, pp. 123–153.

Boyd, M. 1989. Family and Personal Networks in International Migration: Recent Developments and New Agendas. *International Migration Review* 23: 638–670.

CAPA Centre for Asia Pacific Aviation. 2012. North Asia LCC and New Age Airlines. Report Series Issue 2. Sydney: Centre for Asia Pacific Aviation. Available at: http://centreforaviation.com/reports/files/25/LCC%20North%20Asia%20Report%2009AUG12%20FINAL.pdf (accessed 23 January 2013).

Chung, J.Y. and Whang, T. 2011. The Impact of Low Cost Carriers on Korean Island Tourism. *Journal of Transport Geography* 19: 1335–1340.

Chang, Y.C. 2010. The Development of Regional Airports in Asia, in Posterino, N.M. (ed.) *Development of Regional Airports. Theoretical Analyses and Case Studies.* Southampton: WIT Press, pp. 53–76.

Cochrane, J. 2008. *Asian Tourism: Growth and Change.* Oxford: Elsevier.

Damuri, Y.R. and Anas, T. 2005. Strategic Directions for ASEAN Airlines in a Globalizing World. The Emergence of Low Cost Carriers in South East Asia. Regional Economic Policy Support Facility Project No. 04/008. Singapore: ASEAN Secretariat. Available at: http://www.aadcp2.org/uploads/user/6/PDF/REPSF/04–008-FinalLCCs.pdf (accessed: 15 January 2013).

Decilya, S. 2010. Airlines Want Government to Limit Air Deregulation. *Tempo Interactive,* 19 November 2010. Available at: http://www.tempointeractive.com/hg/nasional/2010/11/19/brk,20101119-292918,uk.html (accessed: 6 January 2013).

Debbage, K.G. and Delk, D. 2001. The Geography of Air Passenger Volume and Local Employment Patterns by US Metropolitan Core Area: 1973–1996. *Journal of Air Transport Management* 7: 159–167.

Derudder, B., Witlox, F. and Taylor, P.J. 2007. United States Cities in the World City Network: Comparing Their Positions Using Global Origins and Destinations of Airline Passengers. *Urban Geography* 28: 74–91.

Donohue, J.A. 2006. Room to Breathe in Tokyo. *Air Transport World* 435: 60–62.

Edgington, D.W. 2000. City Profile: Osaka. *Cities* 17: 305–318.

Edgington, D.W. and Hayter, R. 2000. Foreign Direct Investment and the Flying Geese Model: Japanese Electronics Firms in Asia Pacific. *Environment and Planning A* 32: 281–304.

Findlay, C. and Goldstein, A. 2004. Liberalisation and Foreign Direct Investment in Asian Transport Systems: The Case of Aviation. *Asian Development Review* 21: 37–65.

Forsyth, P., King, J. and Rodolfo, C.L. 2006. Open Skies in ASEAN. *Journal of Air Transport Management* 12: 143–152.

Forsyth, P. 2003. Low-Cost Carriers in Australia: Experiences and Impacts. *Journal of Air Transport Management* 9: 277–284.

Forsyth, P. and Dwyer, L. 1996. Tourism in the Asian-Pacific Region. *Asian-Pacific Economic Literature* 10: 13–22.

Freestone, R., Williams, P. and Bowden, A. 2006. Fly Buy Cities: Some Planning Aspects of Airport Privatisation in Australia. *Urban Policy and Research* 24: 491–508.

Fu, X., Oum, T.H. and Zhang, A. 2010. Air Transport Liberalization and its Impacts on Airline Competition and Air Passenger Traffic. *Transportation Journal* 49: 24–41.

Fuellhart, K. and O'Connor, K. 2012. Air Services at Australian Cities: Change and Inertia 2005–2010. *Geographical Research*, DOI: 10.1111/j.1745-5871.2012.00762.x.

GaWC. 2010. The World According to GaWC. Global and World City Project, Loughborough University. Available at: http://www.lboro.ac.uk/gawc/world2010.html (accessed: 12 December 2012).

Gillen, D. 2009. International Air Passenger Transport in the Future. Discussion Paper No. 2009–15, 18th International Transport Research Symposium of the OECD. Madrid, November. Available at: http://www.internationaltransportforum.org/jtrc/discus sionpapers/DP200915.pdf (accessed: 23 January 2013).

Grosso, M.G. 2008. Liberalising Air Passenger Services in APEC. Working Paper. Sciences Po and Groupe Economie Mondiale. Available at: http://www.gem.sciences-http://www.gem.sciences-po.fr/content/publications/pdf/GelosoGrosso_Air%20pas senger_122008.pdf (accessed: 8 January 2013).

Grubesic, T.H., Matisziw, T.C. and Zook, M.A. 2008. Global Airline Networks and Nodal Regions. *GeoJournal* 71: 53–66.

Hewison, K. and Young, K. (eds) 2006. *Transnational Migration and Work in Asia*. London/New York: Routledge.

Hooper, P. 1997a. Liberalising Competition in Domestic Airline Markets in Asia – The Problematic Interface between Domestic and International Regulatory Policies. *Transportation Research Part E: Logistics and Transportation Review* 33: 197–209.

Hooper, P. 1997b. Liberalisation of the Airline Industry in India. *Journal of Air Transport Management* 3: 115–123.

IATA. 2010. Asia Pacific: Challenges and Opportunities – Intra-Asia Market Eclipses North America as World's Largest. Montreal. Available at: http://www.iata.org/pressroom/pr/Pages/2010-02-01-01.aspx (accessed: 12 December 2012).

Lau, Y.Y., Lei, Z., Fu, X. and Ng, A.K.Y. 2012. The Implications of the Re-Establishment of Direct Links Across the Taiwan Strait on the Aviation Industries in Greater China. *Research in Transportation Economics* 35: 3–12.

Lieshout, R. and Matsumoto, H. 2012. New International Services and the Competitiveness of Tokyo International Airport. *Journal of Transport Geography* 22: 53–64.

Loo, B. 2008. Passengers' Airport Choice Within Multi-Airport Regions. MARs: Some Insights from a Stated Preference Survey at Hong Kong International Airport. *Journal of Transport Geography* 16: 117–125.

Ma, L.J.C. and Cartier, C. (eds) 2003. *The Chinese Diaspora: Space, Place, Mobility and Identity*. Lanham, MD: Rowman and Littlefield.

Mahutga, M.C., Ma, X., Smith, D.A. and Timberlake, M. 2010. Economic Globalisation and the Structure of the World City System: The Case of Airline Passenger Data. *Urban Studies* 47: 1925–1947.

Mazumdar, A. 2008. Some Limitations to the Success of the Low-Cost Carrier Business Model in India. *World Review of Intermodal Transportation Research* 2: 84–100.

Ng, J. 2009. The Impact on Airports in South East Asia: What Deregulation Means. Available at: http://ardent.mit.edu/airports/ASP_exercises/2009%20reports/Deregulation%20in%20SE%20Asia%20Ng.pdf (accessed: 8 January 2013).

OAG. 2012. Published Non-Stop Passenger Departures Scheduled Seats by Origin and Destination. Customised Matrix. OAG Aviation Solutions Schedules Database.

O'Connell, J.F. and Williams, G. 2006. Transformation of India's Domestic Airlines: A Case Study of Indian Airlines, Jet Airways, Air Sahara and Air Deccan. *Journal of Air Transport Management* 12: 358–374.

O'Connor, K. 1995. Airport Development in South East Asia. *Journal of Transport Geography* 3: 269–279.

O'Connor, K. 2003. Global Air Travel: Toward Concentration or Dispersal? *Journal of Transport Geography* 11: 83–92.

O'Connor, K. and Fuellhart, K. 2010. Air Services at Second Ranked Cities: Decline or Growth? in Sumalee, A., Lam, W.H.K., Ho, H.W. and Siu, B. (eds) *Transportation and Urban Sustainability*. Proceedings of the 15th International Conference of the Hong Kong Society for Transportation Studies, 687–694.

O'Connor, K. and Fuellhart, K. 2013. The Asia Pacific Region and Australian Aviation, in Duval, D. (ed.) *Air Transport in the Asia Pacific*. Farnham: Ashgate.

Oum, T.H. and Lee, Y.H. 2002. The Northeast Asian Air Transport Network: Is There a Possibility of Creating Open Skies in the Region? *Journal of Air Transport Management* 8: 325–337.

Rimmer, P. 2003. The Spatial Impact of Innovations in International Sea and Air Transport since 1960, in Chia, L.S. (ed.) *South East Asia Transformed. A Geography of Change*. Singapore: Institute of South East Asian Studies, pp. 287–316.

Saxenian, A.L. 2006. *The New Argonauts: Regional Advantage in a Global Economy*. Cambridge, MA: Harvard University Press.

Shin, K.H. and Timberlake, M. 2000. World Cities in Asia: Cliques, Centrality and Connectedness. *Urban Studies* 37: 2257–2285.

Smith, D.A. and Timberlake, M.A. 2001. World City Networks and Hierarchies, 1977–1997: An Empirical Analysis of Global Air Travel Links. *American Behavioral Scientist* 44: 1656–1678.

Thomas, I., Stone, D., Khee-Jin Tan, A. et al. 2008. Developing ASEAN's Single Aviation Market and Regional Air Services Arrangements with Dialogue Partners, Regional Economic Policy Support Facility Project No. 07/003. Singapore: ASEAN Secretariat. Available at: http://www.aviation.go.th/doc/public/REPSF%2007003%20Final%20Report%20120608.pdf (accessed: 4 January 2013).

Tretheway, M. 1997. Impediments to Liberalisation in Asia Pacific International Aviation, in Findlay, C., Chia, L.S. and Singh, K. (eds) *Asia Pacific Air Transport. Challenges and Policy Reforms*. Singapore: Institute of South East Asian Studies, pp. 65–73.

Williams, A. 2009. *Contemporary Issues Shaping China's Civil Aviation Policy, Balancing International with Domestic Priorities*. Farnham: Ashgate.

Winter, T., Teo, P. and Chang, T.C. (eds) 2009. *Asia on Tour. Exploring the Rise of Asian Tourism*. Abingdon: Routledge.

Yamaguchi, K. 2011. Cross-Border Integration in the Northeast Asian Air Transport Market. *The Pacific Economic Review* 16: 47–63.

Yueh, L. (ed.) 2009. *The Future of Asian Trade and Growth. Economic Development with the Emergence of China*. Abingdon: Routledge.

Zhang, A., Hanaoka, S., Inamura, H. and Ishikura, T. 2008. Low-Cost Carriers in Asia: Deregulation, Regional Liberalization and Secondary Airports. *Research in Transportation Economics* 24: 36–50.

Zhang, Y. and Findlay, C. 2011. Quantifying the Impacts of Structural Reforms on Air Traffic Flows in APEC Economies, in Findlay, C. *The Impacts and Benefits of Structural Reforms in Transport, Energy and Telecommunications Sectors*. Publication Number APEC#211-SE-o1.1. Singapore: APEC Policy Support Unit, 88–102. Available at: http://publications.apec.org/publication-detail.php?pub_id=1113 (accessed: 3 February 2013).

Zook, M.A. and Brunn, S.D. 2005. Hierarchies, Regions and Legacies: European Cities and Global Commercial Passenger Air Travel. *Journal of Contemporary European Studies* 13: 203–220.

Zook, M.A. and Brunn, S.D. 2006. From Podes to Antipodes: Positionalities and Global Airline Geographies. *Annals of the Association of American Geographers* 96: 471–490.

Chapter 12
Geographies of Latin American Air Transport

Gustavo Lipovich

Introduction

The Latin American airline market has experienced strong growth in recent years. Within a context of intensification of liberalisation and privatisation processes, its evolution was characterised by supply growth in the number of flights, available seats and available seat-kilometres, simultaneously with a deep market concentration in business and geographical terms. The analysis of such dynamism and its trends shape the aim of this chapter.

Historical Review of Air Transport in Latin America

The first airplanes arrived in Latin America and the Caribbean (LAC) during the first decade of the twentieth century and dazzled the crowds at various aerial exhibitions in open spaces. Soon, as also happened in other regions of the world, air transport was mainly used for mail and very little passenger distribution. The significant remoteness of the developed world, the great geographical extent of the region and the substantial areas of some individual Latin American countries formed the ideal environment for fast development of air transport that was provided mostly by foreign airlines and pilots. The first routes connected to Europe and North America with different points in LAC, and highlighted multiple scales of destinations due to the limited flight range of the airplanes of that time. Without much delay, the local enthusiasm for airplanes and the positive projection of aviation activity stimulated the training of Latin American pilots. Thus, Latin American aviation history features the main pioneers and developers, such as Alberto Santos Dumont (Brazil), Jorge Newbery (Argentina) and Jorge Wilstermann (Bolivia), among many others.

Quickly, the existence of local pilots who acted simultaneously with foreign pilots and the strong interest of states to develop sovereign air transport resulted in the creation of the first Latin American airlines whose operations were heavily subsidised by governments. Thus, it was possible to connect via air the capital and major cities, as well as remote locations in the Amazon, Patagonia, jungles, Mexican deserts, the Gran Chaco, and insular areas that were poorly connected by other transport modes. In the first generation of airline markets, the European situation was emulated by creating regional airlines covering complementary routes or flag carriers, among which were: Avianca-Colombia (1919), Mexicana de Aviación (1921), Lloyd Aéreo Boliviano (1925), VARIG-Brasil (1927), Aeroposta Argentina (1927), LAN Chile (1929), Cubana de Aviación (1930), Aeronaves de México (1934), PLUNA-Uruguay (1936), LACSA-Costa Rica (1945), and Compañía Panameña de Aviación (1947). Latin American air transport development was also accompanied from the industrial point of view by the creation of aircraft factories such as Talleres Nacionales de Construcciones Aeronáuticas (TNCA) de México (1919), Fábrica Argentina de Aviones (FAdeA) (1927), and Empresa Brasileria de Aeronáutica

(EMBRAER) (1950). Moreover, between World War II and 1950, the airline market reached a high level of institutionalisation taking into account the local advancements in air law as well as the participation and adherence of different countries to the Convention on International Civil Aviation: Nicaragua (1945), Paraguay, Dominican Republic, Peru, Argentina, Mexico and Brazil (1946), Chile, Venezuela, Bolivia, Guatemala, El Salvador and Colombia (1947), Haiti (1948) and Cuba (1949).

After 1950 and until the 1990s, the Latin American airline market usually developed in a setting in which state flag carriers covering domestic, regional and inter-oceanic routes co-existed with other airlines of national, provincial or private owners which mainly operated domestic networks and in some cases regional ones. The constant political fluctuations explain the many processes of nationalisation and emergence of private airline experiments, although in those years rate regulation systems and market protection were mostly applied.

Liberalisation and Privatisation

Undoubtedly, one of the central features that allowed the development of new production models and flexible accumulation processes is related to political action in favour of trade liberalisation, privatisation, downsizing of the state, decentralisation and other policies which promote the private sector. Transport was an ever present element in economic rationalisation reforms that took place around the world. The economic rationalisation model as applied to transport basically consisted of two dimensions – liberalisation and privatisation – that operated in tandem. Privatisation without regulatory changes lead to private monopoly situations, while liberalisation without privatisation promoted state capitalism and the maintenance of inefficient public monopolies (Graham 1995: 52). Indeed, transport in Latin America had to learn to adapt to liberalising policies (Figueroa 2005: 42).

Of course, the airline market was not immune to the economic rationalisation process and, in fact, is a sector that has always anticipated and led liberalisation applications prior to other transport modes and other economic sectors, both in domestic and international bilateral or multilateral markets (Freestone et al. 2006: 493). Among the distinguishing features of air transport that led to airline market liberalisation prior to other transport modes or economic sectors were assumptions of lower relative sunk costs and greater ease to open new routes. It was believed that air transport was a sector which would adhere more closely to the *contestable market theory* which claimed that markets could approximate perfect competition even with a small number of companies operating. According to the theory, if a route is operated by a single airline, it must continue to maintain competitive prices because an increase in rates would immediately stimulate the entry of a new competitor in the operation of that route as a result of the relatively low costs of entry and exit in the market (Vowles 2000: 121–122). If a market is perfectly contestable, then there is no need for government regulation, the market would regulate itself. By categorising airline markets as perfectly contestable, their liberalisation could become a successful example to follow for other transport modes and other economic activities.

Again, scientific justification alone would not be enough to convince all countries of the world about liberalisation benefits on the airline market, so it needed a political stimulus. Indeed, the Federación Internacional de Trabajadores del Transporte (1988: 7) found that 'organizations such as the IMF and World Bank are already exerting pressure on governments in Africa, Latin America and Asia to deregulate their aviation networks'.

The pressures to expand ideas about the advantages of liberalisation occurred even before verifying the results of the development of the airline market in this context. There really was uncertainty about whether the market was perfectly competitive and contestable, because of limited empirical evidence.[1] Sector workers opposed the airline market liberalisation due to the inevitable business concentration that would result from this process, where the interests of a few private corporations would guide the fate of this important activity worldwide (Federación Internacional de Trabajadores del Transporte 1988: 2).

With liberalisation, the concept of the *flag carrier* went into crisis, and government action on the airline market was weaker than ever. Airlines were clearly identified with national states prior to liberalisation (Biplan 2004), but changes in policy gradually weakened the symbolic significance of the airlines in the construction of national identity (Raguraman 1997: 254). Air transport geography was also being restructured from the interrelation – sometimes antagonistic – of deregulation, globalisation and national interest forces, leading governments to implement aerocommercial strategies – frequently in an inept way – that applied neoliberal economic principles while trying to minimize the negative impact on the national interest (Graham 1995: 3).

In addition to airline market liberalisation, privatisation was another substantial and closely linked component. Privatisation of state airlines would promote the creation of more competitive market-oriented companies to increase efficiency and promote service quality to users, reduce state involvement in public enterprises, and permit capital injection in companies that needed investment in a context of strong expansion of airline markets (Doganis 2006: 224). State airlines had many features and vicissitudes which would not have been compatible with a highly competitive market. VIASA (Venezuela) and Aerolíneas Argentinas were sold to Iberia. This Spanish company carried out a questionable management strategy that led to the bankruptcy of the first and the Argentine government had to rescue the second against the danger of closing. The Brazilian airline VASP bought Ecuatoriana de Aviación and Lloyd Aéreo Boliviano in 1995. Both companies went bankrupt soon after. AeroPerú was sold to Aeroméxico and subsequently went broke. Aeroméxico and Mexicana were sold together by the Mexican government under what was called the Cintra Group, but Mexicana went bankrupt. PLUNA, the Uruguayan state airline, was sold in 1994 to VARIG and went broke. Then it was resurrected by private capital and went broke again. LAPSA, the Paraguayan company, was sold to Brazilian TAM. Privatisation also hit Latin American airports (see Lipovich 2008 and Rico Galeana 2008).

The year 2005 marked the end of VARIG, the largest state airline in Latin America, which was later acquired by GOL. In perfect harmony with other privatisations, merger and acquisition processes that took place in Latin America since the late 1980s were intended to bring an end to the model based on quasi monopolies of state companies. Indeed, since that time, the Latin American airline market experienced many expected changes as a result of applied neoliberal policies. Participation of private airlines in the market was increased, competition was intensified, the linkage of these companies to the largest global airline alliances was stimulated, domestic markets were deregulated, and more open bilateral and multilateral agreements were signed, among other impacts. While an absolute open regulatory framework has not been reached between the Latin American markets, it is undeniable that there is a strong liberalising current within the region.

---

1   In fact, contestability theory was later shown not to work in practice in the airline industry, as actual entry was required to keep fares low (Levine 1987; Goetz 2002).

However, it should be noted that in recent years there were countercyclical cases featured by a number of countries headed by developmentalist, protectionist and populist governments, which managed the re-nationalisation, creation or strengthening of new state airlines in Argentina (Aerolíneas Argentinas and Austral), Bolivia (Boliviana de Aviación), Ecuador (TAME) and Venezuela (CONVIASA) in order to ensure air connectivity and the employment continuity of aeronautical workers. In the airport sector, Bolivia even re-nationalised its airports, while the Argentine State was incorporated as a minority partner in the concessionaire Aeropuertos Argentina 2000.

On the other hand, the Comisión Latinoamericana de Aviación Civil (CLAC) is forming an Open Skies Multilateral Agreement for CLAC Member States, already including a number of countries such as Chile, Colombia, Guatemala, Panama, Paraguay, Dominican Republic and Uruguay, subject to the reservations made by each country. Supposedly, this agreement would encourage Latin American integration and expanded opportunities for air services.

Although today some sectors consider that the process of airline liberalisation in Latin America is not enough and needs to quickly reach a level of full liberalisation, there are not too many researchers who find positive results of liberalisation from a Latin American perspective. Indeed, it is important to analyse the results of airline market dynamism in relation to a number of elements that are linked and interact cyclically in a context of increasing liberalisation, such as corporate concentration, geographic concentration of supply, and monopolisation levels of the market. This phenomenon can be termed as the *endogenous airline cycle of corporate oligopolisation and of primate territorial structuring* (see Lipovich 2010: 154–184). The methods used to reveal this phenomenon are linked exclusively to the evolution of airline market supply in Latin America, using the OAG databases as a key source. These databases are constructed from the information contained in the flight schedules of airlines and are abundant in detail, however, do not capture all service. In the case of Latin America, the data contained in the OAG databases comprise 98.57 per cent of the total available seat-kilometers (ASK) offered. Although the data do not cover the entire universe, they are quite representative.

The Evolution of the Latin American Airline Market

In the period 2003–2012, the total number of available seats in Latin America and the Caribbean increased by 50.43 per cent from 275.5 million available seats in 2003 to 414.5 million available seats in 2012 (Figure 12.1). While supply growth exceeded the world average registered in those years (42.48 per cent), it was lower than in other regions such as the Middle East, Asia-Pacific and Africa. The percentage of available seats in the Latin American airline market grew from 9.76 per cent in 2003 to 10.30 per cent in 2012 of all available seats worldwide.

Beyond the generalised growth of the Latin American airline market supply, analysis of the changes experienced between 2007 and 2012 revealed that the number of flights increased from 2.9M to 3.5M (+20.0 per cent), and available seats-kilometres (ASK) increased from 617.7M to 792.8M (+28.3 per cent). However, the number of Latin American and foreign airlines with services in this region was reduced by -19.6 per cent from 204 in 2007 to 164 in 2012. Therefore, it is possible to affirm that the major supply growth was not accompanied by market diversification in business terms. Thus, the analysis reveals some specific trends that characterised the evolution of the Latin American airline

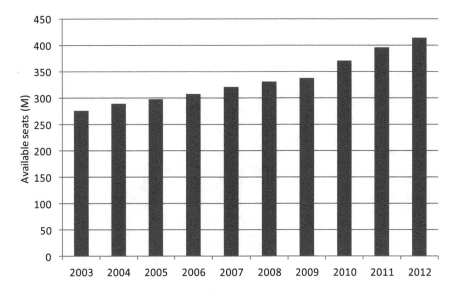

Figure 12.1   Available seats in Latin America (2003–2012)
Source: Elaborated with OAG Facts data 2010.

market: market business concentration, geographic concentration of supply, and changes in levels of monopolisation.

In order to inquire about the existence or absence of monopolisation and geographic concentration, it is possible to use several methods that are based on different concepts and analysis variables. Of course, the results of using each method can provide various corollaries, showing that some formulas are more conducive than others in their ability to express, as nearly as possible, the vagaries of the airline market which is becoming ever more complex and where the adoption of entry barriers to competition have novel configurations that are becoming more commonly used.

Airline Concentration

The more traditional, quick and easy methods to assess whether the airline market is becoming increasingly monopolistic can be included under the concept of business concentration which takes into account the market shares corresponding to the operation of the different airlines. Usually, airlines are categorised separately if the ownership differs among them. In this case, the market share of the subsidiary airlines is integrated with parent airlines in the calculations. Dennis (2007: 23) and Goetz (2002: 1) argued that concentration increases are mainly due to the market entry barriers imposed in the era of liberalisation. That is, the evolution of the free airline market generated the erection of entry barriers as a reaction. Governments did not lead the process, but barriers emerged as a result of the airlines' strategies to face an open competition environment. Hanlon (2007: 113) stated that business concentration is a direct and foreseeable result of airline market liberalisation. The concentration results of Latin American airline markets for 2012 are shown in Figure 12.2.

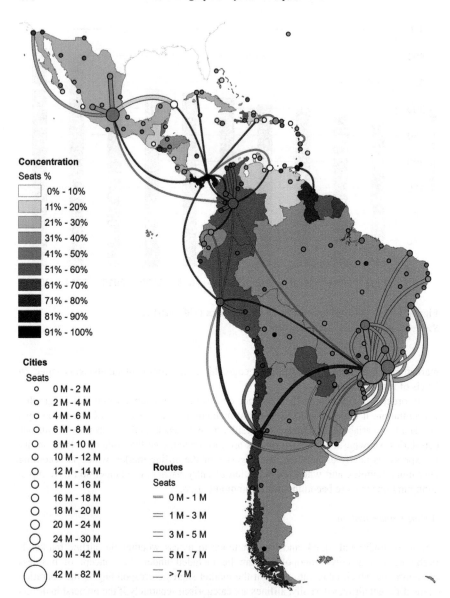

Concentration

Seats %

☐	0% - 10%
☐	11% - 20%
☐	21% - 30%
☐	31% - 40%
☐	41% - 50%
☐	51% - 60%
☐	61% - 70%
☐	71% - 80%
☐	81% - 90%
☐	91% - 100%

Cities

Seats

o	0 M - 2 M
o	2 M - 4 M
o	4 M - 6 M
o	6 M - 8 M
O	8 M - 10 M
O	10 M - 12 M
O	12 M - 14 M
O	14 M - 16 M
O	16 M - 18 M
O	18 M - 20 M
O	20 M - 24 M
O	24 M - 30 M
O	30 M - 42 M
O	42 M - 82 M

Routes

Seats

=	0 M - 1 M
=	1 M - 3 M
=	3 M - 5 M
=	5 M - 7 M
=	> 7 M

Figure 12.2   Airline market and geographic concentration in countries, cities and the top 30 domestic/regional routes of Latin America by seat capacity (2012)

Source: Elaborated by processing OAG database.

Table 12.1   Airline concentration in Latin America (2007–2012)

2007			2012		
Airline	**ASK (M)**	**ASK (%)**	**Airline**	**ASK (M)**	**ASK (%)**
American Airlines	65,458	10.60%	LATAM Group	134,184	16.92%
TAM Linhas Aéreas	48,890	7.91%	American Airlines	71,630	9.03%
Air France-KLM	41,824	6.77%	GOL	50,768	6.40%
LAN Group	32,982	5.34%	Air France-KLM	49,519	6.25%
Iberia	30,091	4.87%	IAG (British-Iberia)	47,972	6.05%
GOL	28,994	4.69%	Avianca-TACA	39,615	5.00%
Continental Airlines	24,775	4.01%	United Airlines	35,591	4.49%
Delta Air Lines	24,739	4.00%	Aeroméxico	30,352	3.83%
Aeroméxico	23,860	3.86%	Delta Air Lines	27,465	3.46%
Mexicana de Aviación	23,207	3.76%	Copa Airlines	27,094	3.42%
Others	272,914	44.18%	Others	278,642	35.15%

Source: Elaborated by processing OAG database.

A first approach to the analysis of market concentration is given by the number of companies offering their services in the Latin American market. Thus, in 2012, there were 40 fewer airlines than in 2007, during a period of intensification of air transport liberalisation policies. During the same time, the seat supply grew by over 29 per cent while the number of airlines decreased more than 19 per cent. Given this situation, it is arguable that monopolisation generated sufficient barriers to block the entry of new airlines in a growing market.

This disparity in the evolution between higher market growth and the smaller number of airlines resulted in an increase in the average number of flights, seats and ASK offered by each airline. Thus, airlines on average have grown in size, but of course, not all had a significant increase, and some airlines experienced declines.

However, for Morrison (2005: 409) the use of number of companies as a variable is not the most suitable for measuring market business concentration, as it is more appropriate to use market share of these companies. Additionally, the ASK variable could be more appropriate than the number of available seats in some cases. It is also possible to compare the market share held by the largest airline, the two largest companies, the three largest ones, etc. The choice in the number of companies to consider is absolutely subjective and changes can be very different. Table 12.1 shows the situation of ASK business concentration for two different periods (2007 and 2012).

In this case, and based on the ASK, 10 airlines were involved in 55.8 per cent of the airline market supply in 2007, while in 2012, this figure stood at 64.8 per cent. Corporate concentration can be easily distinguished if a trend line of the partial sums of the airline market shares were displayed cumulatively for all cases. Thus, when using this technique for comparative purposes and overlaying the two trend lines in the same figure, it will be verifiable that trend lines imply different surface areas and/or different curvatures indicating whether certain cases have higher or lower monopolisation levels. Consequently, the results become more explanatory. Similarly, the target variable could be flights, available seats or ASK, each providing additional levels of explanation.

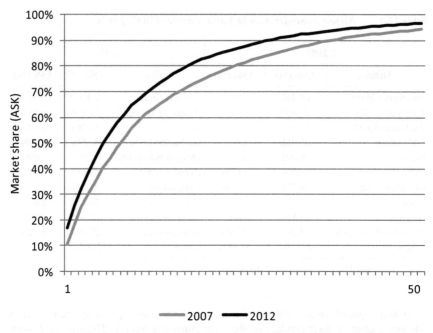

Figure 12.3   Airline market concentration in Latin America (2007–2012)
Source: Elaborated by processing OAG database.

Figure 12.3 presents the data of the ASK market share of each airline and it includes the top 50 companies. The results show the presence of a supply concentration process. That is, the growth of airline supply in Latin America was not uniform for all companies, but there are airlines which grew proportionately more than others. In addition, it is possible to highlight the market growth of Latin American multinational airlines (Multi-Latin airlines) in relation to the foreign ones.

Airline Centralisation

Because of the technological and regulatory nature of the airline market, the formation of alliances between companies is more complex than in any other transport mode. Airline alliances are an undisputed product of liberalisation, according to Wang and Evans (2002: 48–49) and Iatrou and Oretti (2007: 20). Regulatory features that prompted the formation of airline alliances were the open skies agreements that granted antitrust immunity (Stober 2003: 111) and the restrictions associated with the ownership and effective control of airlines. According to Gámir and Ramos (2002: 127–128), there are other causes that stimulated the formation of alliances in addition to those related to cost reduction and service expansion, such as connecting traffic between partners, improved quality of service, increase of alternative itineraries, inclusion in Global Distribution Systems (GDSs) and mutual participation in frequent flyer programs. The large number of alliances demonstrates the natural oligopolistic tendency present in air transport. Companies seem unwilling to compete with each other, but practice collusion strategies through a cooperative evolution (Shaw 2007: 114). These collusion actions are realised in strategic alliances with different commitment levels between companies. Airline alliances range from code-share agreements to total fusion, through schedule coordination, network coordination, strategic cooperation, joint route operation and/or share exchange (Cento 2009: 39).

It is sometimes difficult to discern oligopolistic structures in airline markets because of arrangements such as code-share agreements, blocking seats, or franchises. These complex functions are very different from other modes and industries, where arrangements such as these may not exist or where the structure is different. For this reason, the traditional business concentration concept is limited in trying to express the reality of the airline market. Beyond the existence of mergers, acquisitions, bankruptcies, and subsidiary airlines, there are many agreements between companies with differentiated capital formation, as if they were multiple self-regulated businesses, but acting as one corporation. They set prices, frequencies, operations, etc., and may or may not share capital stock. In addition, in each agreement it is very probable that the decisions of a specific actor prevail against the others by its greater operational scale. This leads to a greater exercise of centralised market power over different constituent elements. For this reason, from now on, the *corporate centralisation* term will be used to refer to this process. Business concentration is a more limited process that does not reflect the totality of centralisation power.

To illustrate the difference between business concentration and corporate centralisation, it is valuable to cite an example provided by Doganis (2006: 98) for the case of SAS in Copenhagen. The author tries to explain the market power of SAS in its main hub by differentiating between on the one hand, operations of the parent company SAS and its subsidiaries (which conforms to the more precise business concentration concept), and on the other hand by operations of other airlines that have a code-share with SAS or are in the same global airline alliance (which conforms to the more inclusive corporate centralisation concept). There is a gross difference between both concepts. While SAS had direct management of its own company and its subsidiaries, with its partners it could develop cooperation measures influencing schedules, frequencies, prices, etc.

The Latin American airline market has not been kept outside of joint exploitation agreement processes. The three largest global airline alliances (oneworld, SkyTeam and Star Alliance) together accounted for nearly 55 per cent of total ASK offered in the region in 2007, and that figure grew to over 67 per cent in 2012. The airlines included in the three major global alliances with operations in Latin America in 2012 were:

- Star Alliance (28.0 per cent of the Latin American ASK): TAM Linhas Aereas, United Airlines, COPA, AVIANCA, TAP Portugal, Lufthansa, TACA, Air Canada, Continental Airlines, South African Airways, Turkish Airlines, Aerogal, Swiss, TAM Transportes Aéreos Mercosur, Singapore Airlines, Air China, Isleña Airlines and AeroPerlas.
- oneworld (20.8 per cent of the Latin American ASK): American Airlines, LAN Airlines, Iberia, British Airways, Air Berlin, LAN Ecuador, LAN Argentina, Qantas Airways and LAN Perú.
- SkyTeam (18.5 per cent of the Latin American ASK): Air France, Aeroméxico, Delta Airlines, Aerolíneas Argentinas, KLM, Air Europa, Alitalia, Aeroflot, and Korean Air.

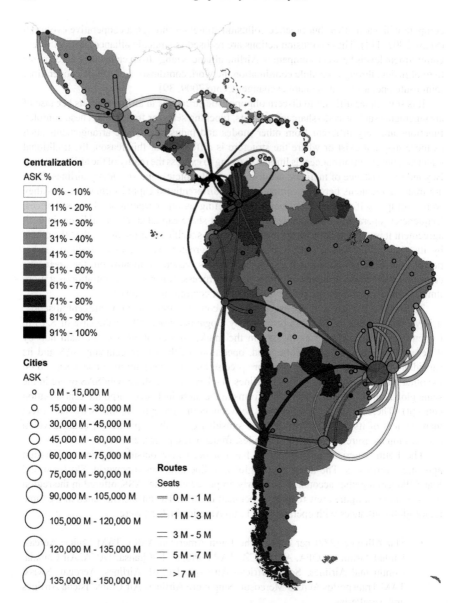

Figure 12.4   Airline market and geographic centralisation in countries, cities and the top 30 domestic/regional routes of Latin America by available seat kilometres (ASKs) (2012)

Source: Elaborated by processing OAG database.

In 2012 the more centralised markets in Latin America were Chile, Peru and Paraguay (under the influence of LATAM), Colombia and El Salvador (with a strong presence of Avianca), and Panama (a market dominated by Copa Airlines). Consequently, the main hubs of these countries and their major routes also experienced high centralisation levels (see Figure 12.4).

Because of their large sizes and the relative difficulty for an airline to reach very high centralisation levels in them, the two largest Latin American markets – Brazil and Mexico – still had moderate centralisation situations in 2012. LATAM centralised over 47 per cent of Brazil's ASK, while the amount of ASK centralised by Aeromexico was 31.6 per cent due to the significant influence that US airlines have on the international network of Mexico.

For other markets, such as Argentina, Bolivia, Ecuador and Venezuela, where it is easier for a high airline centralisation level to be produced, the strongly pro-growth strategies of Multi-Latin airlines were hampered by the application of re-nationalisation, and building and strengthening of state airline policies that were accompanied by market protectionism rules.

While calculating corporate centralisation has the advantage of generating results much more explanatory for the competition logics established by airlines in the contemporary world, these also could be characterised as insufficient from other points of view. Thus, it is convenient to analyse the spatial consequences of corporate centralisation processes.

Geographic Concentration of Flows

One of the main airline strategies to reduce costs and exploit economies of scale, economies of agglomeration, and economies of density, was to concentrate flights in operational bases, regardless of whether they fulfil the role of distribution or connecting flight centres. Different airlines install their own hubs and depending on the magnitude of them and the extent and density of their networks, they may have more than one hub. In a market liberalisation process with a corporate centralisation trend, the number of operational bases tends to decrease while the average size tends to be larger, and different airline hub-based networks tend to overlap each other to compete openly. Since some cities in Latin America have multi-airport systems, by grouping the values of the airports serving the same city, it is possible to appreciate the variability in the geographical service concentration.

Figure 12.5 exposes a slight but continuous process of geographical service concentration measured in ASK. In this sense, it is possible to affirm that the concentration level for the largest nodes is quite high, where the top 15 cities account for approximately 60 per cent of the ASK. The levels are more dispersed among the rest of the nodes. Results demonstrate that between 2007 and 2012, a slight intensification of primacy occurred due to the higher concentration level of the most important cities, while the trend reverts for the rest of the nodes. Clearly, the simultaneous coexistence of primate and homogenisation processes of the network was expressed.

Brian Graham (1998: 102) stated that during liberalisation, the spatial patterns of flows are maintained due to certain inertia, and there is no incentive to change. Territory seems to be the determinant of air transport, more so than the structuring effect that airline markets have over the territory. Nevertheless, state policies generated in order to relate transportation and regional development are aimed at providing acceptable levels of connectivity and accessibility to the regions (Vreeker and Nijkamp, 2005: 508). At the same time, airline market liberalisation policies may have led to increased air connectivity ensuring inclusion of nodes throughout the network (homogenisation) but also increased differentiation in accessibility terms (primacy and hierarchical dominance). According

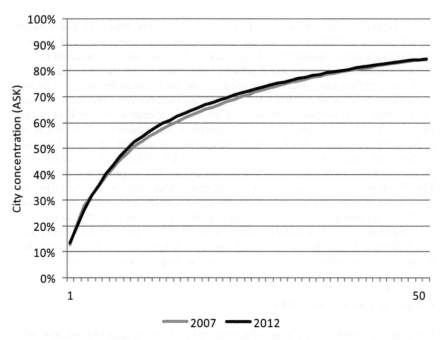

Figure 12.5   Geographic concentration of ASK in Latin America by city (2007–2012)

Source: Elaborated by processing OAG database.

to Rodrigue et al. (2006: 12), new transportation developments can result in territorial segregation through the reinforcement of some nodes at the expense of others, thus contradicting development policies that encourage balanced accessibility. In the case of the Latin American airline market, the growth of liberalisation was accompanied by an increase of between 20 per cent and 30 per cent of air transport activity based on a variety of measures between 2007 and 2012. However, the rise in these rates was offset by a reduction in the number of nodes within the airline market network. The network had 549 nodes in 2007, while in 2012 the number of nodes was 510. In the Latin American case, the network did not expand; it only was intensified in prime locations.

The increase in airline market primacy for fewer cities within the Latin American network also led to service concentration on a smaller number of routes that increased their relative hierarchical rank. That happened especially on those routes that link the major hubs that survived from the processes of bankruptcies, mergers and acquisitions and intensified their nodal importance. Similarly, the remaining routes homogenised their relative situations in the network. Thus, the routes linking the most hierarchical cities between them tend to experience scenarios of higher competition among airlines, which generates more service and cheaper prices. Usually, the trend is opposite for the other routes which are absolutely monopolistic markets or with a high centralisation of supply. The strong resulting rate differences stimulate the demand in the most hierarchical routes and intensify the hierarchical geographic imbalances and the airline markets network primacy. In turn, strong price competition prevailing in hierarchical markets encourages declining profit margins of airlines, and the application of cross-subsidies from monopolistic routes to the routes with competition. Then, when the price war ensues, new bankruptcies, mergers and acquisitions occur and lead to further market concentration.

The Geographic and Commercial Structure of the Latin American Airline Market

Given a scenario of growing airline market liberalisation, the processes of business concentration, corporate centralisation, geographic concentration of hubs, geographic concentration of flows, and the geographic imbalance of low/high fares, the Latin American airline market is subject to a vicious cycle of business monopolisation and geographic concentration of air transport.

The business and geographical concentration and centralisation of airline markets can be measured in terms of units offered – available seats – or distance-related units – available seat-kilometres (ASK). Both variables may reflect very different situations due to the characteristics of each market. While ASK may be a more explanatory variable than the available seats, it is important to consider both because of the presence of fixed and variable costs in airline markets. Table 12.2 presents the importance of the different Latin American airline markets in relation to both variables, while the levels of concentration and centralisation of various airline markets are illustrated in Figures 12.2 and 12.4.

The major national markets in Latin America are Brazil (by far), Mexico, Argentina, Chile, Peru and Colombia. In the case of major urban markets in the region some cities of the countries just mentioned are highlighted (see Table 12.2). In this sense, the primacy of Sao Paulo compared to other cities is noteworthy. Sao Paulo is the largest city in Latin America, and the economic centre of the largest country of the region. At the next level, it is possible to find Mexico City, Buenos Aires, Rio de Janeiro, Lima, Santiago and Bogota. Among the most important cities from the point of view of their airline markets, those with a higher level of centralisation, or single-carrier domination, are the Multi-Latin airline hubs: Panama City and Copa Airlines (84.19 per cent of ASK), Santiago and LATAM (72.11 per cent), San Salvador and Avianca (71.04 per cent), Guayaquil and LATAM (66.18 per cent), and Bogota and Avianca (65.19 per cent). Among cities with lower centralisation levels it is possible to include those whose airline market is oriented to the movement of tourists, such as Cancun (16.50 per cent), Punta Cana (17.93 per cent) and Montego Bay (21.75 per cent).

Similarly, in 2012 a total of 2,493 routes were operated of which 63.7 per cent were offered in a fully monopolistic way. Table 12.3 contains the top 10 domestic, regional and intercontinental routes. Considering the available seats, the most important routes for each of these categories were Sao Paulo–Rio de Janeiro, Sao Paulo–Buenos Aires and San Juan–Miami. On the other hand, the main routes for each category based on the ASK were Sao Paulo–Recife, Sao Paulo–Buenos Aires and Buenos Aires–Madrid. This last route has the highest ASK for Latin America.

Between the routes listed in Table 12.4, which comprise the most important in Latin America in the different categories, it is possible to highlight the presence of absolutely monopolistic routes as: Sao Paulo–Santiago (LATAM), Santiago–Panama City (Copa Airlines) and Sao Paulo–Lima (LATAM). Moreover, most of the routes according to the ASK in 2012 had a high degree of centralisation. Among these are: Lima–Santiago (LATAM, 80.40 per cent), Buenos Aires–Miami (American Airlines, 77.15 per cent), Sao Paulo–Bogota (Avianca, 72.68 per cent), Lima–Madrid (Iberia-IAG, 72.52 per cent) and Sao Paulo–Paris (Air France-KLM, 72.41 per cent).

Table 12.2   Available seats and ASK in the Latin American countries and dependencies (2012)

Country/dependency	Seats	Country/dependency	ASK (M)
Brazil	161,819,663	Brazil	262,913
Mexico	72,495,266	Mexico	136,130
Colombia	35,171,011	Argentina	68,182
Argentina	25,212,958	Chile	45,657
Chile	20,503,989	Peru	44,596
Peru	19,373,087	Colombia	42,403
Panama	13,951,716	Dominican Republic	35,253
Venezuela	12,085,154	Panama	31,624
Puerto Rico USA	11,652,988	Puerto Rico USA	22,387
Ecuador	11,440,504	Venezuela	22,166
Dominican Republic	11,145,596	Cuba	21,233
Costa Rica	6,543,644	Ecuador	15,290
Jamaica	5,755,819	Costa Rica	12,868
Cuba	5,513,354	Jamaica	12,681
Bahamas	5,511,370	El Salvador	8,176
Bolivia	4,503,835	Guadeloupe	8,162
El Salvador	4,413,268	Martinique	7,640
Trinidad & Tobago	4,124,919	Barbados	7,503
Guatemala	3,098,749	Trinidad & Tobago	6,134
Uruguay	3,010,368	Aruba	5,730
Guadeloupe	2,935,679	Uruguay	5,235
Aruba	2,681,886	Bolivia	5,013
Honduras	2,669,970	Bahamas	4,863
Curacao	2,650,502	Guatemala	4,857
St Maarten	2,579,547	St Maarten	4,534
Barbados	2,508,549	Curacao	4,186
Virgin Islands USA	2,416,055	Saint Lucia	3,210
Martinique	2,113,359	Virgin Islands USA	3,102
Haiti	1,724,370	Antigua & Barbuda	2,903
Nicaragua	1,563,905	Honduras	2,642
Cayman Islands	1,549,007	Haiti	2,577
Paraguay	1,511,344	French Guiana	2,575
Antigua & Barbuda	1,464,453	Surinam	2,277
Saint Lucia	1,367,626	Bermuda	2,248
Belize	1,361,108	Paraguay	1,976
Bermuda	1,143,992	Nicaragua	1,918
Turks & Caicos Islands	951,070	Cayman Islands	1,640
Guyana	847,209	Turks & Caicos Islands	1,422
Bonaire	704,316	Bonaire	1,171
Grenada	572,960	Belize	1,108
French Guiana	553,705	Guyana	1,102
Saint Kitts & Nevis	539,536	Grenada	658

Country/dependency	Seats	Country/dependency	ASK (M)
British Virgin Islands	527,553	Saint Kitts & Nevis	471
Surinam	522,482	Dominica	144
Saint Vincent & The Grenadines	376,926	British Virgin Islands	79
Dominica	339,117	Saint Vincent & The Grenadines	74
Anguilla	114,359	Anguilla	19
Montserrat	29,130	Montserrat	1

Source: Elaborated by processing OAG database.

Table 12.3   Available seats and ASK in the top 30 Latin American cities (2012)

City	Seats	Concentration	City	ASK (M)	Centralization
Sao Paulo	81,874,734	38.97%	Sao Paulo	147,932	51.57%
Mexico City	41,150,178	40.72%	Mexico City	71,181	46.72%
Rio de Janeiro	40,182,990	42.21%	Buenos Aires	66,038	41.82%
Bogota	29,633,550	59.32%	Rio de Janeiro	61,797	40.99%
Brasilia	24,191,370	44.58%	Lima	44,242	53.30%
Buenos Aires	23,021,348	37.42%	Santiago (CH)	43,833	72.11%
Lima	18,277,765	53.00%	Cancun	37,576	16.50%
Santiago (CH)	17,593,572	69.95%	Bogota	35,741	65.19%
Belo Horizonte	16,483,617	41.65%	Panama City	31,250	84.19%
Cancun	15,230,057	14.49%	Brasilia	29,506	49.52%
Panama City	13,898,395	81.81%	Caracas	20,943	26.68%
Salvador (BR)	13,594,862	45.42%	San Juan (PR)	20,663	34.66%
Curitiba	11,727,567	47.73%	Punta Cana	18,513	17.93%
Porto Alegre	11,348,345	45.54%	Salvador (BR)	16,253	38.56%
San Juan (PR)	10,824,979	35.17%	Recife	14,620	45.09%
Caracas	10,110,871	16.81%	Fortaleza	13,218	53.67%
Recife	9,949,922	37.84%	Belo Horizonte	13,178	31.26%
Guadalajara	9,365,107	32.22%	Havana	12,884	42.67%
Fortaleza	8,692,356	46.14%	Guadalajara	11,665	40.44%
Quito	8,438,726	31.31%	Porto Alegre	11,107	41.91%
Monterrey	8,018,915	31.56%	San Jose (CR)	10,781	31.78%
Medellin	7,046,884	56.42%	Santo Domingo	10,254	26.46%
Belem	6,259,785	41.01%	Tijuana	9,715	63.14%
Guayaquil	6,151,668	41.51%	Montego Bay	9,213	21.75%
Florianopolis	5,809,675	44.64%	Guayaquil	8,987	66.18%
San Jose (CR)	5,731,082	32.46%	Manaos	8,335	55.53%
Vitoria	5,136,982	40.37%	San Salvador (ES)	8,176	71.04%
Manaos	4,780,550	46.09%	Pointe-a-Pitre	8,134	35.03%
Cali	4,778,416	65.98%	Fort-de-France	7,640	36.12%
Tijuana	4,762,817	69.49%	Bridgetown	7,503	35.31%

Source: Elaborated by processing OAG database.

Table 12.4   Available seats and ASK in the top 10 Latin American routes (2012)

Domestic route	Seats	Concentration	Domestic route	ASK (M)	Centralisation
Sao Paulo–Rio de Janeiro	14,000 363	46.61%	Sao Paulo–Recife	5,619	49.83%
Sao Paulo–Brasilia	5,620,407	46.33%	Sao Paulo–Salvador	5,563	43.01%
Sao Paulo–Porto Alegre	4,985,347	41.81%	Sao Paulo–Fortaleza	5,145	50.47%
Sao Paulo–Curitiba	4,821,682	42.93%	Mexico City–Cancun	5,094	37.38%
Sao Paulo–Belo Horizonte	4,783,134	44.93%	Sao Paulo–Rio de Janeiro	5,093	46.13%
Mexico City–Cancun	3,915,068	37.22%	Sao Paulo–Brasilia	4,833	46.56%
Bogota–Medellin	3,841,846	61.37%	Sao Paulo–Porto Alegre	4,264	41.61%
Sao Paulo–Salvador	3,841,250	42.96%	Mexico City–Tijuana	3,294	43.09%
Mexico City–Monterrey	3,683,837	41.52%	Rio de Janeiro–Brasilia	2,750	54.83%
Quito–Guayaquil	3,179,298	47.97%	Mexico City–Monterrey	2,592	41.55%
Regional route	**Seats**	**Concentration**	**Regional route**	**ASK (M)**	**Centralisation**
Sao Paulo–Buenos Aires	2,493,985	43.92%	Sao Paulo–Buenos Aires	4,217	44.38%
Buenos Aires–Santiago	1,980,203	63.68%	Lima–Santiago	3,212	80.40%
Lima–Santiago	1,295,234	80.40%	Buenos Aires–Lima	2,839	56.61%
Buenos Aires–Rio Janeiro	1,175,610	34.92%	Sao Paulo–Mexico City	2,796	56.45%
Sao Paulo–Santiago	1,069,778	100.00%	Sao Paulo–Santiago	2,775	100.00%
Bogota–Quito	952,060	87.51%	Buenos Aires–Rio Janeiro	2,332	34.98%
Buenos Aires–Lima	906,551	56.61%	Buenos Aires–Santiago	2,224	63.68%
Bogota–Panama City	852,245	67.15%	Santiago–Panama City	1,985	100.00%
Bogota–Lima	687,853	70.58%	Sao Paulo–Lima	1,935	100.00%
Panama City–San Jose	667,961	77.08%	Sao Paulo–Bogota	1,917	72.68%

Intercontinental route	Seats	Concentration	Intercontinental route	ASK (M)	Centralisation
San Juan–Miami	1,929,336	52.61%	Buenos Aires–Madrid	8,980	55.28%
San Juan–New York	1,825,835	41.44%	Pointe-a-Pitre–Paris	7,623	35.33%
Bogota–Miami	1,137,681	35.74%	Fort-de-France–Paris	7,084	35.11%
Nassau–Miami	1,132,510	41.19%	Sao Paulo–New York	7,024	55.59%
Pointe-a-Pitre–Paris	1,129,612	35.33%	Lima–Madrid	6,356	72.52%
Caracas–Miami	1,061,879	53.93%	Sao Paulo–Miami	6,332	59.91%
Santo Domingo–New York	1,057,398	50.06%	Mexico City–Madrid	5,662	65.37%
Fort-de-France–Paris	1,034,629	35.10%	Buenos Aires–Miami	5,600	77.15%
Mexico City–Miami	1,033,493	45.33%	Sao Paulo–Madrid	5,586	65.69%
San Juan–Orlando	999,541	55.31%	Sao Paulo–Paris	5,583	72.41%

Source: Elaborated by processing OAG database.

The liberalisation and privatisation processes of the Latin American airline market were a key factor in the sustained growth of air service. In part, these processes created the conditions that allowed the growth of multi-Latin American airline consortiums to claim a significant market share in the region (after several bankruptcies of badly privatised state airlines had occurred), thus relegating the position that the US and European airlines had occupied in the past. Overconfidence in the success of private business models, including mismanagement of formerly state airlines, enabled the internationalisation of private interests that led to the formation of the multi-Latin airlines. These companies supported the opening of markets in order to gain substantial market shares and not to compete forever.

With the public air services network in the hands of purely economic interests, the optimistic consolidation process – or market concentration in a more classical version – emphasises the spatial distribution of services in increasingly few but strong cities. These results are expressed in Latin America with geographical situations featuring both an increasing emphasis on primate cities and a simultaneous homogenisation, albeit with fewer service nodes. The experiences of a return to protectionism and state management of airlines, combined with some modern techniques of airline market strategies, have slowed the trends of continental private oligopolies forming, thus recovering the design and generation of airline policies from the state for productive and social purposes. The state policy approach aims to look beyond the financial statements of an aviation company when determining the characteristics of air connectivity, accessibility and mobility. Latin America is experiencing a moment when very different models co-exist simultaneously. Surely, any comparative analysis should take into account these issues that go beyond the financial statements so that the assessments can be more holistic.

Conclusions

In recent years, Latin American airline markets experienced an important supply growth simultaneously with the deepening adoption and implementation of neoliberal policies that favour the opening of the domestic, regional and international markets. However, supply growth was oriented towards a trend that reinforces and increases market share by a few large airlines. This growth in the concentration level occurred as a result of bankruptcies, mergers and acquisitions in order for the surviving airlines to consolidate their market positions and remain competitive. Beyond the concentration levels achieved, joint exploitation agreements resulted in high levels of collusion and strategic alliances that led to reducing individual firm management and decision-making, in what could be termed a process of corporate centralisation.

These phenomena of concentration and centralisation were used as shields to survive in the competitive environments of liberalised airline markets, and resulted in a geographic concentration of supply. In Latin America, despite the market growth experienced in recent years, the air service supply in the most important countries, cities and routes was concentrated further. The geographic distribution of airline market supply was characterised by contraction in relative terms.

While pressures to liberalise the Latin American airline market continue, there are fewer companies able to offer a large supply. These operators are nucleated to avoid competition, the supply is concentrated incrementally in certain national and city territories, and the services offered by a single carrier in a strict monopoly way are very significant. In those countries where the airline liberalisation policy trend was reversed by revaluing market protectionism and statism – as in Argentina, Bolivia, Ecuador or Venezuela – these phenomena had inverse outcomes or they were much more tenuous.

Indeed, the phenomena analysed throughout the chapter reinforce and verify the existence of linked processes of corporate centralisation and geographic concentration of commercial aviation flows in a positive feedback that strengthens these processes. The Latin American airline market, which in 2012 accounted for 10.3 per cent of the global supply of available seats, shows that airline market liberalisation results in this chain of events which established a more concentrated primate hierarchical structure from both the corporate and territorial points of view.

Dedicatory

To Cristina Barbot (1953–2012) of the University of Porto, Portugal, due to the immense dedication and affection she used to transmit her knowledge of the airline market all over Latin America to inspire us. Hasta siempre.

Acknowledgements

I want to recognise the effort and perseverance of Leticia Dall'Ospedale in making the maps included in this chapter.

References

Biplan, P. (2004). Les compagnies aériennes entre la nation et la mondialisation. *Hérodote* 114: 56–70. La Découverte, France.

Cento, A. (2009). *The Airline Industry. Challenges in the 21st Century.* Germany: Physica-Verlag Heidelberg.

Dennis, N. (2007). Competition and Change in the Long-haul Markets from Europe. *Journal of Air Transportation* 12(2): 4–26.

Doganis, R. (2006). *The Airline Business.* 2nd Edition. London: Routledge.

Federación Internacional de Trabajadores del Transporte (1988). *Boletín de la Aviación Civil.* Federación Internacional de Trabajadores del Transporte.

Figueroa, O. (2005). Transporte urbano y globalización. Políticas y efectos en América Latina. *EURE* 31(94): 41–53.

Freestone, R., Williams, P. and Bowden, A. (2006). Fly Buy Cities: Some Planning Aspects of Airports Privatisation in Australia. *Urban Policy and Research* 24(4): 491–508.

Gámir, A. and Ramos, D. (2002). *Transporte aéreo y territorio.* Barcelona: Editorial Ariel.

Goetz, A. (2002). Deregulation, Competition, and Antitrust Implications in the US Airline Industry. *Journal of Transport Geography* (10)1: 1–19.

Graham, B. (1995). *Geography and Air Transport.* Chichester: John Wiley & Sons.

Graham, B. (1998). Liberalization, Regional Economic Development and the Geography of Demand for Air Transport in the European Union. *Journal of Transport Geography* 6(2): 87–104.

Hanlon, P. (2007). *Global Airlines. Competition in a Transnational Industry.* 3rd Edition. Amsterdam: Butterworth-Heinemann.

Iatrou, K. and Oretti, M. (2007). *Airline Choices for the Future. From Alliances to Mergers.* Aldershot: Ashgate.

Levine, M.E. (1987). Airline Competition in Deregulated Markets: Theory, Firm Strategy, and Public Policy. *Yale Journal on Regulation* 29: 393–494.

Lipovich, G. (2008). The Privatization of Argentine Airports. *Journal of Air Transport Management* 14(1): 8–15.

Lipovich, G. (2010). *Los aeropuertos de Buenos Aires y su relación con el espacio metropolitano. La inserción del subsistema aeroportuario Aeroparque-Ezeiza dentro de la lógica del mercado aerocomercial y de la estructuración urbana.* Tesis Doctoral. Facultad de Filosofía y Letras, Universidad de Buenos Aires, Buenos Aires.

Morrison, S. (2005). *Deregulation of US Air Transportation,* in Button, K. and Hensher, D.A. (eds) *Handbook of Transport Strategy, Policy and Institutions.* Amsterdam: Elsevier, pp. 405–420.

OAG (2010). *OAG Facts December 2010. Frequency and Capacity Trend Statistics.* OAG. UBM Aviation.

Raguraman, K. (1997). Airlines as Instruments for Nation Building and National Identity: Case Study of Malaysia and Singapore. *Journal of Transport Geography* 5(4): 239–256.

Rico Galeana, O. (2008). The Privatisation of Mexican Airports. *Journal of Air Transport Management* 14(6): 320–323.

Rodrigue, J-P., Comtois, C. and Slack, B. (2006). *The Geography of Transport Systems.* London: Routledge.

Shaw, S. (2007). *Airline Marketing and Management.* 6th Edition. Aldershot: Ashgate.

Stober, A. (2003). Who Soars in Open Skies? A Review of the Impacts of Anti-Trust Immunity, and International Market Deregulation on Global Alliances, Consumers, and Policy Makers. *Journal of Air Transportation* 8(1): 111–133.

Vowles, T. (2000). The Effect of Low Fare Air Carriers on Airfares in the US. *Journal of Transport Geography* 8(2): 121–128.

Vreeker, R. and Nijkamp, P. (2005). *Multicriteria Evaluation of Transport Policies*, in Button, K. and Hensher, D.A. (eds) *Handbook of Transport Strategy, Policy and Institutions*. Amsterdam: Elsevier, pp. 507–525.

Wang, Z. and Evans, M. (2002). The Impact of Market Liberalization on the Formation of Airline Alliances. *Journal of Air Transportation* 7(2): 25–52.

Chapter 13
Geographies of Middle Eastern Air Transport

Khaula Alkaabi

Introduction

This chapter focuses on the rising importance of the air transport systems of Middle East nations. Six of these countries are members of the Gulf Cooperation Council (GCC), which represents the economic engine in the region: Bahrain, Qatar, Kuwait, Oman, Saudi Arabia, and the United Arab Emirates (UAE). Despite the challenges faced by the global air transport industry (high oil prices, global financial recession), the Middle East aviation market has recorded outstanding overall traffic growth rates and diversification over the past years. The market is largely headed by the 'Big Three' Airlines: Emirates, Qatar, and Etihad. This chapter evaluates recent aviation growth by assessing the main carriers' business models, network and hub geography, major markets, main airports (e.g. Dubai, Jeddah and Doha), and socio-historical and political factors within the region. It finds that changes in the global economy, regional migration patterns, and strong national investment are magnifying the importance of the region as a global hub and local destination, though challenges remain.

Historical Evolution of Middle Eastern Air Transport

The centrality of the Middle East region across traditional trade routes connecting Asia to Europe has linked many Middle East cities with the world through linear transport networks (Hooper et al. 2011). Air transport services were introduced during the 1920s, mainly connecting major cities in Iraq and Egypt, like Basra, Baghdad, and Cairo (Hooper et al. 2011). Under the influence of colonialism and improved aircraft technology, air networks grew to service transcontinental routes as transfer points between England, France, and the Netherlands, and their colonial destinations in Asia and the Pacific (Hooper et al. 2011). After independence, a number of local governments adopted liberal policies and redeveloped existing airports to promote air services and traffic growth. For example, the Sharjah government (UAE) took over the Sharjah airport from British management in 1968 and expanded the airport in 1979.

The development of the Middle East air transport industry is largely tied to the discovery of regional petroleum-related reserves. In 2011, the Middle East holds about 54 per cent of the world crude oil reserves and 40.5 per cent of world natural gas reserves (OPEC 2012). Therefore, Middle East recorded a robust GDP growth of 500 per cent from 1991 ($297 billion) to 2011 ($1.7 trillion) (World Bank n.d.). Though also consumed, and thus a cost-factor, these locally available reserves have enabled Middle East governments and firms to invest substantially in new and existing air transport infrastructure.

Despite high oil prices, political disruptions, and the slow recovery of the global economy after the 2009 recession, the aviation business in the Middle East has recorded overall positive continuous growth rates in terms of air passenger and cargo traffic. Airlines in the Middle East received an annual revenue of about $1 billion in 2011 (CAPA 2012 March). Middle East air cargo recorded a robust increase of 8.2 per cent in 2011 and 14.1 per cent for the first 10 months of 2012, where the worldwide cargo market remained flat (Nelms 2013 January). The healthy growth in international traffic to/from the Middle East is largely possible due to the continuous growth in global networks and fleet capacity offered by GCC carriers (e.g. Emirates, Qatar Airways, Etihad), particularly on routes between the Americas, Europe, Australia, and Asia (Vespermann et al. 2008). However, some smaller airlines in the Middle East, like Bahrain-based Gulf Air, and Kuwait-based Kuwait Airways, have been hit by the Arab Spring wave. In 2011, Gulf Air recorded a loss of about $500 million partly driven by the violence in Bahrain and the heavy competition from Emirates, Qatar Airways, and Etihad Airways, which resulted in restructuring its route network and reducing fleet capacity (CAPA 2012 March). Moreover, Bahrain Air declared bankruptcy in February 2013. Yet overall, some Middle East countries continue to invest heavily in air transport.

Strategies of Major Carriers

This section addresses the relative cost position and business model of GCC region carriers. It summarizes their structured goals and the mechanisms they employ for creating value, delivering their services, and capturing the world passenger market.

Cost Position

By 2012, Emirates, a Dubai-based carrier since 1985, became the world's third biggest airline in terms of capacity (ASK) after United Airlines and Delta Air Lines, respectively (CAPA 2012 December). It has played a crucial role in highlighting the strategic central location of the Dubai hub on the world map. Despite impacts on global aviation performance from the 2009 global economic crisis, Arab Spring disruption, and high fuel costs, Emirates showed steady growth figures from 2009–2011, where it recorded a 23.7 per cent increase in passengers (27 million to 33.9 million) (Emirates Group 2012a). Qatar Airways (QR) is the second largest carrier in the Middle East in terms of served destinations, fleet size and RPK (Revenue Passenger Kilometres) (Table 13.1). It has operated since 1993, with a re-launch in 1997 from its Doha hub. From 2009 to 2011, QR recorded a 47 per cent increase in passenger volume (10.2 million to 15 million) despite political unrest and high oil prices (ATW 2010; Karp 2012). Etihad Airways, regionally is third in terms of network reach and fleet size. The airline carried 8.3 million passengers in 2011 across 81 destinations in 51 countries using 64 aircraft (Table 13.1). From 2009 to 2011, Etihad's passengers increased about 32 per cent (6.3 million to 8.3 million), and revenues rose 64 per cent (from $2.5 billion to $4.1 billion) (Etihad Airways 2012).

The ranking of the cost position of these 'big three' airlines is consistent with their relative RPK, which shows Emirates by far the leader, at about 153 million, nearly triple that of QR, and nearly four times that of Etihad. The big three carriers cost savings partly come from lower labour costs and the tax-free environment, which has made the region attractive to private investment. They take advantage of the abundance of lower-paid foreign-born workers, many originally from India and Pakistan. Possessing relatively open migration policies, the UAE and Qatar have some of the highest percentages of temporary foreign-born residents in the world, up to about 80 per cent for Qatar (Bowman 2007).

Table 13.1 Major legacy carriers and LCCs in the Middle East: Operating fleet and served destinations, 2011

Carriers	Est.	Hub airport	CP#a	Alliance	Average daily seats	Destin. served (#)	Operating fleet (#)	Total RPKb (m)
Emirates	1985	Dubai	13	–	154,228	122	169	153.264
Saudia	1945	Jeddah, Riyadh, Dammam	11	SkyTeam 2012	75,987	75	104	39.251
Qatar Airways	1993	Doha	11	Oneworld 2014	72,417	120	111	61.603
Etihad Airways	2003	Abu Dhabi	37	–	37,023	81	64	38.701
Iran Air	1946	Tehran	2	–	–	60	51	–
Gulf Air	1950	Bahrain	11	–	22,554	41	34	11.154
Royal Jordanian	1963	Amman	12	Oneworld 2007	12,215	55	33	8.400
Oman Air	1981	Muscat	3	–	16,799	42	26	8.457
Syrian Arab Airlines	1946	Damascus	–	–	230	4	21	–
Kuwait Airways	1954	Kuwait	5	SkyTeam 2012	9,853	37	17	7.429
Middle East Airlines	1945	Beirut	8		8,953	27	14	3.865
Yemenia	1961	Sana'a	2		6,035	30	13	1.815
Air Arabia	2003	Sharjah	–		19,466	62	24	9.603
Jazeera Airways	2004	Kuwait	–		–	–	7	–
Nas Air	2007	Riyadh	1		10,545	22	15	3.633
Sama	2005	Dammam	–		–	–	–	–
Felix Airways	2008	Sana'a	–		–	–	4	–
Flydubai	2009	Dubai	–		–	52	28	–
Wataniya Airlines	2009	Kuwait	–		–	–	–	–

Note: CP#a: Codeshare Partner Number; RPKb: Revenue Passenger Kilometres.
Source: AACO, Airline Websites, CAPA.

The investments in infrastructure and equipment, for example, in newer, more efficient widebody fleets with lower operating cost have created more competitive ticket pricing and improved profits. Moreover, the absence of night flying restrictions at Dubai, Doha and Abu Dhabi has been an added source of revenue.

Beyond the regional big three, the only major carrier is Saudia (SV, previously Saudi Arabian Airlines). In 2011, it gained a total RPK of approximately 40 million (Table 13.1) and drew over 54 million passengers (CAPA 2012 August). The liberalisation of the Saudi market in 2007 and the ending of SV monopoly contributed to these figures. Unlike the 'Big Three' carriers, SV services both domestic and international markets with 55.9 per cent and 44.1 per cent capacity (seats) share respectively from 27 May to 2 June 2013 (CAPA 2013). The international traffic is largely related to the massive infrastructure developments in the country that have attracted high movements of foreign workforce from the GCC, India, North Africa, China, and Southeast Asia. The carrier mileage strategy (Alfursan mileage program) and fleet strategy (replacing older 747 aircraft with more fuel-efficient and modern models including the Boeing 777, Airbus A380 and Boeing 787 Dreamliner) have stimulated travel demand further. Other smaller and more specialized airlines, like Royal Jordanian and Kuwait Airways operate on a much smaller cost basis. Carriers like Tehran-based Iran Air and Mahan Air have been hurt by limited funds and political tensions with the US and Europe.

Goals, Delivery, and Market Capture Mechanisms

Leveraging their enviable strategic location in the global economy, Middle East airlines and governments have set goals to meet demand by private and public investment on an unprecedented scale. They are very deliberately competing in traditional areas, like pricing, connection times, premium benefits, frequent flyer programs. Their strategies also include partnering with key segments that enjoy high visibility, like sports and medical organizations.

The leader, Emirates Airlines, provides a good example of the advantages that can come from a management structure focused on scale and investment. The airline has benefited from affiliation with the Emirates Group, a Dubai-based company with more than 50 subsidiaries (e.g. Dnata, Emirates Flight Catering, Emirates Holidays, and Emirates Engineering). In 2012, the Emirates Group employed about 68,000 workers in its various sectors, and provided its Emirates subsidiary with diverse services and training facilities, such as aircraft ground handling services, air catering services, tour and travel operator and event management, and freight forwarding and logistics services. The Emirates fleet strategy has focused on expanding its fleet capacity and seat density. It ordered 223 modern aircraft including 70 A350-900/1000 XWB, 69 Airbus A380, and 84 Boeing 777-300ER to support its network expansion strategy (Emirates Group 2012a). This newer and fuel-efficient fleet will allow Emirates to decrease fuel expenses and simplify its maintenance and crewing operations. Qatar Airlines has also invested in its fleet aircraft, which in 2011 numbered 111 aircraft, and had a relatively young average age of about four years (Table 13.1). The management and investment of Etihad Airways is guided by the fact that it is a joint public company. Etihad has made the move of investing in its IT infrastructure. For instance, in 2011 it signed a 10-year technology contract with Sabre Airlines Solutions to operate integrated software across reservations, marketing and inventory.

The GCC airlines also have adopted premium travel and mileage strategies designed to gain greater market competitiveness. Supplemented by an overall under-pricing strategy, Emirates offers premium travel services that have made it competitive with many European and Asian long-haul carriers, like Air France/KLM, Lufthansa and Cathay Pacific (Vespermann et al. 2008; Murel and O'Connell 2011). In addition, Emirates' mileage strategy through its Skyward frequent flyer program (6.2 million members in 2010) has attracted many passengers (Emirates Group 2011). To support QR's premium services strategy, it operates the world's only premium terminal exclusively devoted to its First and Business Class passengers at Doha Airport. Qatar was deemed best airline in the world by Skytrax in 2011 and 2012, partly due to its enhanced services. Qatar Air's expansion has been aided via its Open Skies strategies and codeshare agreements with many oneworld alliance members, like British Airways and Royal Jordanian. Using a business model similar to Emirates and QR, Etihad connects air traffic through its Abu Dhabi Airport hub. By the end of 2011, Etihad's partnering strategy has enabled it to acquire a 29.2 per cent stake in Air Berlin, and this has provided access to populous European markets (e.g. Germany, Spain, Austria, and Switzerland). Moreover, to support growth, the carrier's Etihad Holidays branch offers holiday packages in over 100 destinations.

The big three have also led the way in terms of arranging agreements in high impact segments, like sports promotion. Emirates has affiliated with sports organizations, like the London-based Arsenal Football Club in the English Premier League and FIFA World Cup. According to Emirates Chairman His Highness Sheikh Ahmed bin Saeed Al Maktoum, 'The Club has been an important enabler of the growth of our business over the last decade' (Emirates Group 2012b). Similarly, Qatar Airways has adopted this strategy by, for example, sponsoring the Barcelona Football Club in support of its Barcelona–Doha flights. Etihad has also sponsored sport clubs/events, including the Manchester City Football Club in the English Premier League.

The business model implementation for airlines beyond the big three differs given their focus on serving shorter-haul domestic and regional travellers interested in local employment, business and entertainment opportunities. With the exception of Saudia, which has been able to maintain both large-scale and a dual international/domestic passenger market, the remainder of the regional carriers beyond the big three cater mostly to local travel needs, and operate at a much smaller scale, equivalent to RPK's averaging around 7 million. Several low cost carriers (LCCs) have emerged offering more affordable travel and servicing medium and short-haul routes including: Air Arabia, Jazeera Airways, Nas Air, Sama, Felix Airways, Flydubai, and Wataniya Airlines (Table 13.1). Regional low cost travel was first introduced by Sharjah-based Air Arabia in 2003, to the benefit of medium/low income foreign labourers working in the GCC.

To summarize, the above targeted delivery and capture mechanisms have resulted in the dramatic growth in passenger traffic and profitability that the regional air transport system has enjoyed despite external economic and political pressures.

Network and Hub Geography

Emirates, with a fleet size of 169 aircraft in 2011 (Table 13.1), is the largest Middle East carrier, connecting over 33 million passengers from its Dubai hub to 122 destinations, particularly

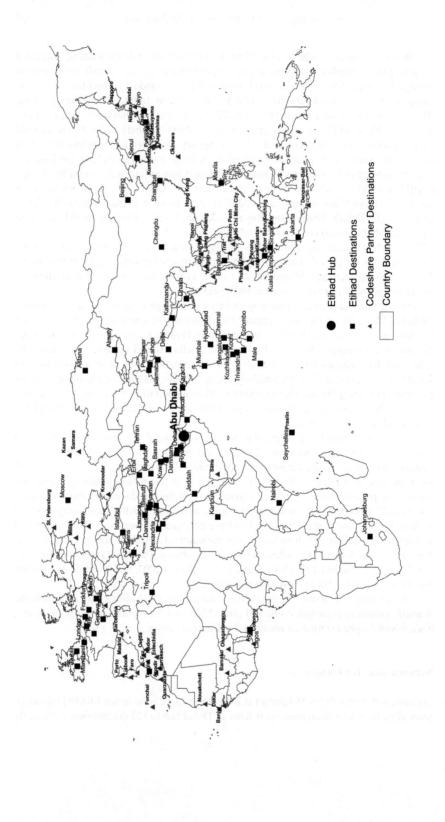

Etihad Hub

Etihad Destinations

Codeshare Partner Destinations

Country Boundary

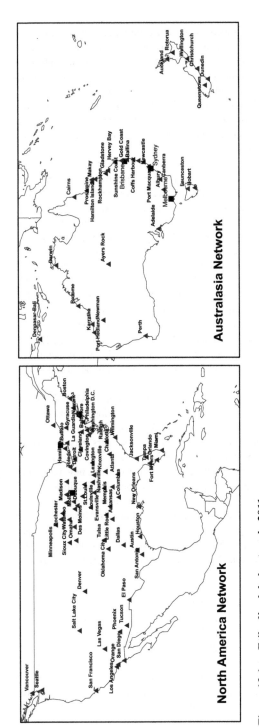

Figure 13.1   Etihad's global network, 2011
Source: Etihad Airways 2012.

between Europe, Australia, and the Indian Subcontinent. The central geographic location of Dubai, hub to populous markets within an eight-hour flight, has allowed Emirates to serve air traffic between east and west and facilitate trade shipment between north and south such as shipping perishables from Africa to Europe (Bowen 2010). Moreover, Emirates operates a number of long non-stop flights from its Dubai hub to the Americas including: Seattle, Los Angeles, San Francisco, Houston, Dallas, Buenos Aires, Rio de Janeiro and São Paulo. The 6th Freedom Rights made travel time via Emirates from Europe to North America inconvenient, so it sought 5th and 7th Freedom Rights to directly link these markets without transiting in Dubai (Vespermann et al. 2008).

Emirates' 'Kangaroo Route' restructuring exemplifies important air carrier strategies to increase competitiveness. A recent Emirates–Qantas partnership moved the Qantas hub from Singapore to Dubai airport in 2013. Such a major alliance will restructure the Kangaroo Route and enable both carriers to operate 98 weekly flights from Australia (e.g. Sydney, Melbourne, Adelaide, Brisbane, and Perth) to Dubai, and connect passengers from the Dubai hub to more than 30 European markets (Arabian Aerospace, 2012 September).

QR is operating the second largest network in the region with its Doha hub using 111 aircraft to connect passengers to 120 destinations in 70 countries worldwide in 2011 (Table 13.1). Passenger traffic increased at the Doha hub by 90.5 per cent from 2007 to 2011. The carrier has operated its longest non-stop flights from Doha to the Houston market (USA) with about 16 hours of travel time in 2009, and expanded its global network to 10 new markets in 2010. In 2011, QR launched services to seven new European destinations, and operated eight new routes to other global markets. In 2012, the carrier added 12 new destinations. The continuous expansion in the QR global network is largely supported with simultaneous growth in the fleet capacity and government interest to become a global aviation hub.

The third largest network in the region is operated by Etihad from its Abu Dhabi hub carrying over 8 million passengers across 81 routes in 2011. The growing air network and flight frequencies have boosted total air passenger traffic at Abu Dhabi airport by 78.5 per cent from 2007 to 2011. Etihad's busiest route by number of passengers was directed to Bangkok (transporting over 500 thousand people) in 2011 followed by London with more than 478 thousand passengers (Etihad Airways 2012). The delivery of six new passenger aircraft in 2011 has enabled Etihad to expand its network to five new destinations (Etihad Airways n.d.). Etihad's codeshare agreements with more than 30 airlines (e.g. American Airlines, Air New Zealand, Aer Arann, Malaysia Airlines, Sri Lankan Airlines, Turkish Airlines) have enabled it to expand its global network and access passengers to more than 200 markets in Europe, Australia and North America that are not directly served by Etihad such as Madrid, Lisbon, Boston, Miami, San Francisco, Perth, and Broome (Figure 13.1).

Despite well-established long-haul networks and hub services for Gulf carriers, there are sizeable markets largely underserved within the Middle East due to socio-political factors and uneven regulatory regimes that restrict air access to these markets. For instance, Iran's air passenger traffic limited growth (e.g. Mehrabad, Shiraz, Bandar Abbas airport recorded -0.02 per cent, -1.6 per cent, and -1.3 per cent growth from 2010–11, respectively) comes from governmental protective policy, influenced by a conflicting relationship with the US and international sanctions. However, the fast-growing local and expatriate populations are increasing demand. And this is true of the region as a whole, a boon to short-haul point-to-point travel. The gradual liberalization of the Saudi Arabia aviation sector, for example, has opened up the market to LCCs like Sama and Nas Air.

Table 13.2 International tourist arrivals and receipts by Middle East destination, 2009–2011

Destination	International tourist arrivals (000s)			Change (%) 11/10	Share (%) in 2011	International tourist receipts (US$ Million)		Change (%) 11/10	Total contribution to GDP (%) 2011
	2009	2010	2011			2010	2011		
Bahrain	–	–	–	–	–	1,362	–	–	12.7
Iran	–	1,518	–	–	–	–	–	–	5.3
Iraq	1,262	2,803	2,820	0.6	7.2	–	–	–	–
Israel	2,321	2,803	2,820	0.6	7.2	4,763	4,849	1.8	7.4
Jordan	3,789	4,557	3,975	-12.8	10.1	3,585	3,000	-16.3	20.6
Kuwait	297	207	–	–	–	241	199	-17.4	4.5
Lebanon	1,844	2,168	1,655	-23.6	4.2	8,012	–	–	25.1
Oman	1,524	1,048	–	–	–	775	–	–	6.8
Palestine	396	522	446	-14.5	1.1	667	–	–	–
Qatar	1,659	1,866	–	–	–	584	1,170	100	6.5
Saudi Arabia	10,897	10,850	17,336	59.7	44.0	6,712	8,459	26	5.3
Syria	6,092	8,546	5,070	-40.6	12.9	6,190	2,239	-63.8	16
UAE	6,812	7,432	8,129	9.3	20.6	8,577	9,204	7.3	14.4
Yemen	434	536	–	–	–	622	–	–	6.7
Total	37,327	42,053	39,431	-6.2	100	42,090	29,120	-30.8	–

Source: UNWTO 2012, WTTC n.d.

Major Markets

Movement toward a more diversified economy less reliant on oil revenues has led a number of Middle East countries to invest in tourism, and with it, expanded airline services (Dobruszkes and Van Hamme 2011). Tourist arrivals to the region have increased by 5.6 per cent (from 37.3 million in 2009 to 39.4 million in 2011) largely related to religious, leisure and business tourism, notably in Saudi Arabia, UAE, and Qatar (Table 13.2). Table 13.2 shows that Saudi Arabia attracted more than 17 million visitors with almost a 44 per cent market share of tourism to the Middle East in 2011, largely driven by Umrah and Hajj pilgrimages. With more than 1.8 billion Muslim inhabitants worldwide, the Saudi government is developing 69 properties to increase hotel rooms from 243,117 in 2011 to 262,049 rooms in 2016 (Alpen Capital 2012) and is spending about $80 billion on infrastructure development (e.g. airport expansions, Mecca-Medina Railway, and roads) to accommodate increased travel and facilitate tourism growth. The UAE is another major tourism destination in the region with an almost 21 per cent market share of Middle East tourist arrivals in 2011. More than 8 million tourist and business visitors to the country spend more than US$9 billion, a 14.4 per cent total contribution to GDP (Table 13.2).

Yet the Arab Spring has had a negative economic impact on the touristic sector of the affected countries. In 2011, tourism in Syria had decreased by 40 per cent (5.07 million international visitors, down from 8.5 million in 2010) and tourist revenues dropped by 63.8 per cent; Lebanon saw arrivals decline by 23.6 per cent (Table 13.2) over the same time span. Despite Jordan's relative political stability, its tourism sector, impacted by neighbouring countries, witnessed visitors decline by 12.8 per cent and tourist revenues drop by 16 per cent. Airlines like Syrian Arab Airliner and Royal Jordanian have suffered as travel demand dropped, resulting in their reducing fleet capacity and air networks.

Major City-Pairs

From the top 20 routes illustrated in Figure 13.2, 12 city-pairs within the region originate or end in Dubai. The busiest intra-regional route is Jeddah–Riyadh. Jeddah is a gateway to Mecca, while Riyadh is the Saudi capital and a major industrial city. Other main city-pairs in the region include: Dubai–Doha (ranked second), Dubai–Kuwait (ranked fourth), Dubai–Bahrain (ranked fifth), and Doha–Bahrain (ranked seventh). However, air traffic flow from Cairo to Jeddah, Riyadh, and Kuwait had dropped by January 2012 largely due to the socio-political unrest of Egypt's Second Revolution.

Outside the region, the biggest city-pair is the Dubai–London Heathrow route (ranked third), with a 6 per cent increase in weekly seat capacity by January 2012. Such air traffic flow has been largely shaped by Emirates' recent A380 deliveries and higher frequencies. Moreover, the large movement of South Asian labour and traders between UAE and India has stimulated further capacity on routes from Dubai to major destination markets in India and Pakistan. Medical and leisure tourism to Thailand has increased air travel flow on the Dubai–Bangkok route (Lunt et al. n.d.).

Major Airports

There are 37 civil airports located in the GCC, where Saudi Arabia operates 22 domestic airports and four international airports which account for about 86 per cent of total passenger traffic in the country in 2011 (Figure 13.3). The Middle East region has seen

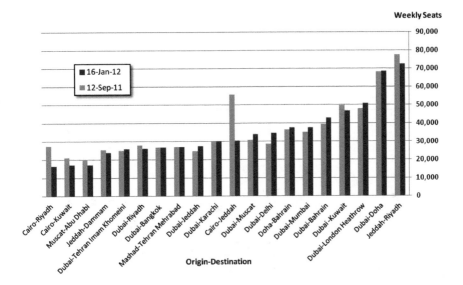

**Figure 13.2   Top 20 routes to/from/within the Middle East by weekly seats:
12 September 2011 vs. 16 January 2012**

Source: Data were extracted by the Author from CAPA 2011.

significant investment in airport infrastructure and facilities to accommodate travel demand and growing fleet capacity (also see Figure 7.1).

Dubai International is currently the busiest hub, with a 13.2 per cent increase in passenger traffic (50.9 million in 2011 to about 57.6 million in 2012), ranking it tenth among worldwide airports in terms of total passenger traffic in 2012 (ACI 2013). As the largest cargo hub in the region, it handled over 2 million tons in 2011, more than all other GCC airports combined (Table 13.3).

The second busiest airport in the region in terms of passengers is King Abdulaziz International Airport located in Jeddah, Saudi Arabia, accommodating 20.9 million passengers and moving 265,000 tons of cargo in 2011. This is mostly driven by the growth of Saudia and the low-cost carriers NAS Air and Sama Airlines (Table 13.3). The airport is experiencing a $7 billion expansion to quadruple passenger capacity from 20 to 80 million by 2035 (AMEinfo 2011). The government authority GACA has gradually privatized the aviation sector and awarded a total of $154.8 million management contracts to two foreign companies (Germany's Fraport and Singapore's Changi Airports International) to maintain growth.

Doha International Airport in Qatar is the third busiest airport in the region in terms of passengers (18.2 million passengers) and the second busiest airport in terms of cargo shipment (808,000 tonnes of cargo) in 2011. The airport is operated by Qatar Civil Aviation Authority (QCAA) and has one terminal with an over-capacity runway, largely occupied by Qatar Airways for international transit traffic. To cope with Qatar Airways' growth strategy, the government has spent over US$1 billion in infrastructure investment at Doha Airport including building three new terminals and expanding the premium terminal of Qatar Airways.

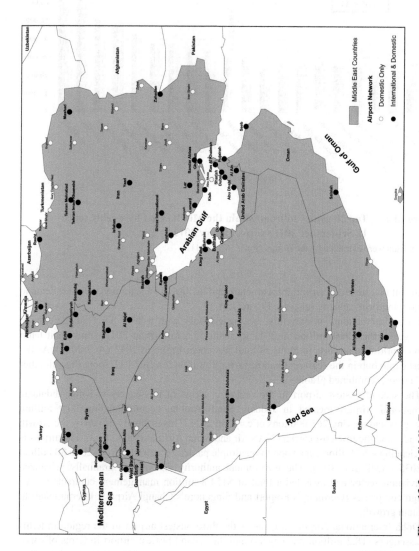

Figure 13.3   Middle East airports

**Table 13.3   Top 10 Middle East airports by air passenger traffic and
air cargo volume, 2011**

Pass. rank	Cargo rank	Airport (code)	Country – city	OA (#)[a]	Total pass. (000)[b]	Pass. share (%)	Total tonnes[c]	Cargo share (%)
1	1	Dubai (DXB)	UAE – Dubai	122	50,977	22	2,269,768	37.6
2	7	King Abdulaziz Airport (JED)	Saudi Arabia – Jeddah	56	20,925	9	265,629	4.4
3	2	Doha (DOH)	Qatar – Doha	46	18,202	7.8	808,099	13.4
4	8	King Khaled (RUH)	Saudi Arabia – Riyadh	43	15,432	6.6	263,886	4.4
5	10	Mehrabad (THR)	Iran – Tehran	7	13,238	5.7	109,568	1.8
6	5	Ben Gurion (TLV)	Israel – Tel-Aviv	60	12,978	5.6	296,700	4.9
7	3	Abu Dhabi (AUH)	UAE – Abu Dhabi	67	12,365	5.3	487,951	8.1
8	9	Kuwait (KWI)	Kuwait – Kuwait	61	8,542	3.7	195,820	3.2
9	6	Bahrain (BAH)	Bahrain – Muharraq	46	7,793	3.4	292,145	4.8
10	4	Sharjah (SHJ)	UAE – Sharjah	28	6,635	2.9	342,044	5.7
Total[d]					232,123,977	72	6,029,484	88.3

Note: [a] Operating airline number; [b] Total passenger includes the sum of commercial international and domestic enplaned and deplaned, and direct transit passengers counted once; [c] Total cargo includes the sum of commercial international and domestic loaded and unloaded freight, and total mail; [d] Total represents the sum of commercial passenger traffic/cargo tonnes for all listed Middle East airports at the ACI Annual Worldwide Airport Traffic Report 2012.
Source: ACI 2012, CAPA 2011.

The economic growth of the aviation sector in the Middle East has encouraged many GCC countries to spend billions of dollars building new airports to facilitate the aviation capacity growth. For example, 4 km from Doha Airport, the Qatari government is constructing the 'New Doha International Airport' at a cost of $15.5 billion. The new facility will have a passenger capacity of 50 million upon completion in 2016 to accommodate the new Airbus A380 superjumbo and become the central maintenance hub for Qatar Airways. Moreover, the Dubai government is spending $8.2 billion to build the largest airport in the world – the Al Maktoum International Airport, near Jebel Ali Free Trade Zone (Nelms, 2013 January). The Dubai government is also developing the world's largest integrated logistic cluster – a $33 billion Dubai World Central (DWC) urban development – close to Al Maktoum airport. The airport is planned to accommodate 160 million passengers and 12 million tonnes of cargo a year and host the world's largest maintenance and overhaul centre (DWC n.d.). This project intends to establish Dubai as a hub for new superjumbo aircraft and long-distance flights, ultimately employing 750,000 workers within the airport and its service sectors (Hvidt 2009). A key challenge facing Dubai aviation growth remains the limited airspace capacity which increasingly demands that GCC governments cooperate to unlock no-fly zones in the region and free up more civil airspace (CAPA 2008 December).

Conclusion

The air transport sector in the Middle East, particularly in the Gulf States, is experiencing remarkable growth, consisting of added capacity to their national carriers' fleets, increased connectivity, and airports expansion. The central geographic location of the Middle East between Europe and Asia has enabled its carriers to transfer traffic between these markets, stimulating tourism activities into their hubs. Places like Dubai, Abu Dhabi, and Doha have developed multiple tourism projects to attract transit traffic to visit the region.

Even though Middle East hubs traditionally are not an origin-and-destination market, their central geographic location, cooperative administration policies, slot availability, efficient airport services, competitive landing fees, and the growing domestic market has enabled them to service 5.8 billion people within eight hours of flight time. As cargo hubs servicing supply chain management, Dubai, Doha, and Abu Dhabi airports experience 8–10 per cent of entering cargo staying in the region, while the rest is transferred to other distant cargo centres.

The successful integration of Middle East air transport within global air transport networks and economies is highly indebted to the strategies and business models linked to heavily oil-financed government and public–private GCC investments. The strategy includes aggressive infrastructure expansion, liberalized flying partner agreements like Open Skies, and global sports event sponsorship. However, maintaining political stability in the region is one of the challenges facing continued progress in the aviation and tourism sectors, where some countries have already experienced substantial reduction rates in revenues for both sectors during the Arab Spring. Other challenges include unlocking airspace and maintaining capacity to keep up with not only global trans-world traffic, but increasing regional passengers serviced by low-cost carriers.

References

AACO. (n.d.), Member Airlines. Retrieved January 6, 2013 from http://www.aaco.org/Member_Airlines.
ACI. (2012), *ACI Annual Worldwide Airport Traffic Report*.
ACI. (2013), Preliminary 2012 World Airport Traffic and Rankings. Retrieved May 25, 2013 from http://www.aci.aero/News/Releases/Most-Recent/2013/03/26/Preliminary-2012-World-Airport-Traffic-and-Rankings-.
Alpen Capital. (2012), GCC Hospitality Industry. Retrieved March 2, 2013 from http://www.alpencapital.com/downloads/GCC%20Hospitality%20Fourth%20Draft_04October_Final.pdf.
AMEinfo. (2011), Massive Airport Projects Underscore Growth in Middle East Aviation Sector. Retrieved January 22, 2013 from http://www.ameinfo.com/267112.html.

Arabian Aerospace. (2012), Emirates and Qantas Sign 10-Year-Deal as Aussies Move in to T3. Retrieved May 25, 2013 from http://arabianaerospace.aero/emirates-and-qantas-sign-10-year-deal-as-aussies-move-in-to-t3.html.

ATW. (2010), World Airline Traffic Results 2009. Retrieved January 13, 2013 from http://atwonline.com/sites/atwonline.com/files/misc/ATW%20World%20Airline%20Report%20010_0.pdf.

Bowen, J. (2010), *The Economic Geography of Air Transportation: Space, Time, and the Freedom of the Sky*. London: Routledge.

Bowman, J. (2007), UAE Flatly Rejects Citizenship for Foreign Workers. *Arabian Business*. Retrieved June 5, 2013 from http://www.arabianbusiness.com/uae-flatly-rejects-citizen ship-for-foreign-workers-122627.html.

CAPA. (2008), UAE Looking to Address Increasingly Crowded Airspace. Retrieved May 25, 2013 from http://centreforaviation.com/analysis/uae-looking-to-address-increasing ly-crowded-airspace-4446.

CAPA. (2011), The Middle East's Biggest Air Routes: Intra-Regional City Pairs Dominate. Retrieved March 3, 2012 from http://centreforaviation.com/analysis/the-middle-easts-biggest-air-routes-intra-regional-city-pairs-ominate-58762.

CAPA. (2012, August), Saudi Arabia Reports Strongest Passenger Growth in a Decade as Market Prepares to Expand. Retrieved February 4, 2013 from http://centreforaviation.com/analysis/saudi-arabia-reports-strongest-passenger-growth-in-a-decade-as-market-prepares-to-expand-80470.

CAPA. (2012, December), United Ends 2012 as World's Biggest Airline, Emirates Third. Turkish and Lion Air the Biggest Movers. Retrieved January 8, 2013 from http://centreforaviation.com/analysis/united-ends-2012-as-worlds-biggest-airline-emirates-third-turkish-and-lion-air-the-biggest-movers-93047.

CAPA. (2012, March), Middle East Regional Carriers have Profitable Outlook for 2012. Retrieved January 24, 2013 from http://centreforaviation.com/analysis/middle-east-regional-carriers-have-profitable-outlook-for-2012-70718.

CAPA. (2013), Profile-Airline-Saudia-Schedule Analysis. Retrieved May 28, 2013 from http://centreforaviation.com/profiles/airlines/saudia-sv.

Dobruszkes, F. and Van Hamme, G. (2011), The Impact of the Current Economic Crisis on the Geography of Air Traffic Volumes: An Empirical Analysis. *Journal of Transport Geography* 19: 1387–1398.

DWC. (n.d.), Al Maktoum International Airport. Retrieved January 1, 2013 from http://www.dwc.ae/project-details/al-maktoum-international-airport/.

Emirates Group. (2011), Annual Report 2010–2011. Retrieved January 12, 2013 from http://www.theemiratesgroup.com/english/facts-figures/annual-report.aspx.

Emirates Group. (2012a), Annual Report 2011–2012. Retrieved January 12, 2013 from http://www.theemiratesgroup.com/english/facts-figures/annual-report.aspx.

Emirates Group. (2012b), Emirates and Arsenal Agree New £150 Million Sponsorship. Dubai, Emirates.

Etihad Airways. (n.d.), Our Airline Partners. Retrieved December 27, 2012 from http://www.etihadairways.com/sites/etihad/global/en/planatrip/Pages/partnerairlines.aspx.

Etihad Airways. (2012), Annual Report 2011. Retrieved January 13, 2013 from http://www.etihadairways.com/sites/Etihad/Etihad%20Images/Resources/annual-report-2011-en.pdf.

Hooper, P., Walker, S., Moore, C. and Al Zubaidi, Z. (2011), The Development of the Gulf Region's Air Transport Networks – The First Century. *Journal of Air Transport Management* 17: 325–332.

Hvidt, M. (2009), The Dubai Model: An Outline of Key Development-Process Elements in Dubai. *International Journal of Middle East Studies* 41: 397–418.

Karp, A. (2012), QA Invited to Join Oneworld. *ATW*. Retrieved January 13, 2013 from http://atwonline.com/airline-finance-data/news/qatar-airways-invited-join-oneworld-1008.

Lunt N., Smith R., Exworthy M. et al. (n.d.), Medical Tourism: Treatments, Markets and Health System Implications: A Scoping Review. *OECD, Directorate for Employment, Labour and Social Affairs*. Retrieved May 24, 2013 from http://www.oecd.org/dataoecd/51/11/48723982.pdf.

Murel, M. and O'Connell, J.F. (2011), Potential for Abu Dhabi, Doha and Dubai Airports to Reach their Traffic Objectives. *Research in Transportation Business & Management* 1: 36–46.

Nelms, D. (2013), Middle East Cargo Bucks the Global Trend. *Aviation Week & Space Technology*. Retrieved February 19, 2013 from http://www.aviationweek.com/Article.aspx?id=/article-xml/AW_01_21_2013_p41-35610.xml.

OPEC. (2012), Annual Statistical Bulletin. Retrieved February 26, 2013 from http://www.opec.org/opec_web/static_files_project/media/downloads/publications/ASB2012.pdf.

UNWTO. (2012), UNWTO Tourism Highlights, 2012 Edition. Retrieved February 26, 2013 from http://mkt.unwto.org/sites/all/files/docpdf/unwtohighlights12enlr_1.pdf.

Vespermann, J., Wald, A. and Gleich, R. (2008), Aviation Growth in the Middle East – Impacts on Incumbent Players and Potential Strategic Reactions. *Journal of Transport Geography*, 16: 388–394.

World Bank. (n.d.), DATA: GDP (current US$). Retrieved May 25, 2013 from http://data.worldbank.org/indicator/NY.GDP.MKTP.CD.

WTTC. (n.d.), Economic Data Search Tool. Retrieved February 28, 2013 from http://www.wttc.org/research/economic-data-search-tool/.

Chapter 14
Geographies of Air Transport in Africa: Aviation's 'Last Frontier'

Gordon Pirie

Introduction

Colonial Africa occupied a significant place in the overseas ambitions and itineraries of European airlines in the 1930s. Immediately after World War II, entry of American carriers into Africa seemed set to elevate the continent's position on the world airline map. Yet, as the reach, capacity and speed of commercial flying increased in the second half of the twentieth century, Africa's prominence on the world airline map declined.

Thirty years ago, after two decades of growth faster than the world average, air transport to, from and in postcolonial Africa accounted for 2.7 per cent of global aviation ton-kilometres (Taneja 1988). Twenty years ago Africa accounted for 3 per cent of international scheduled air traffic and 5 per cent of the world's registered civil aircraft (Endres 1995; Graham 1995). A decade later these shares had changed little. By then Africa's insignificant position was also evident in its tiny share of world commercial aircraft leases and slight participation in computer reservation systems (Goldstein 2001).

In 2011 Africa remained the world's smallest air traffic market, accounting for 2.8 per cent of global revenue-passenger-kilometres and 3 per cent of revenue-tonne kilometres; the continent had 3.6 per cent of the world aircraft fleet (African Airlines Association Annual Report 2012). Yet, despite the continent's small and stable world share, commercial air transport activity there is far from stagnant – it is a vital contributor to economic activity. Moreover, air transport in Africa is forecast to grow faster than the global average until 2030, and the industry is expected to be a key driver of regional economic development.

Africa's slight share of global air transportation is surprising in relation to the size of the continent (the world's second largest after Asia), the lengthy distances between economic centres and capital cities, and the weakness of overland transport. But, in the absence of a prosperous middle class, few Africans have had sufficient discretionary income to afford air travel. And, aviation does not lend itself to the high-bulk, low-value agricultural and mineral exports on which African economies have relied for so long. In addition, the continent's location on the world map in relation to concentrations of people and commerce elsewhere has meant that Africa was rarely even a mid-flight refuelling stop when aircraft had shorter ranges: Dakar and Cairo were exceptions on the Europe–South America and Europe–Asia routes for a time.

The structure and geography of Africa's commercial air transport was fixed strongly by its roots in the 1930s during colonial projects to assist European commerce and administration. Intra-Africa air links were not a priority like air services on a North–South axis with colonial powers in Europe, nor did they outshine airline geographies of post-war labour migrancy and religious travel between Africa and Europe and the Middle East. These legacy geographies are now tilting more heavily eastwards to the Gulf and Asia-Pacific regions. There are also indications that South African dominance of aviation markets in Sub-Saharan Africa is declining, and that intra-African air transport may increase.

The following analysis places African air transport activity in the context of contemporary world aviation and examines the geographies of air transport in the continent at intercontinental, continental, and domestic scales. The chapter also reflects on route innovation, hubbing patterns and connectivity deficits. It notes airline and airport investment geographies, and comments on low-cost carriers. The impact of global airline alliances and mega-carriers is considered alongside the regional developmental priorities of air transport for trade and tourism. The presentation draws on diverse publications. The mass of numerical information is not always compatible or consistent, and can be baffling; it can date rapidly, and should be taken as signifying trends.

African Air Transport

Africa's modest involvement in global air transport can be measured in various ways. Orders for aircraft and spares, navigation equipment, and aviation fuel are small by world standards. Africa is reckoned to represent 3 per cent of the GDP generated by the world's air transport industry, and 12 per cent of the global jobs in commercial air transport, including those in tourism which depend on air transport (Air Transport Action Group 2012). In terms of the aggregate distances flown by paying passengers (revenue passenger-kilometres), in 2007 Africa had less than 1 per cent of the global air service market despite having more than 12 per cent of the world's population (Schlumberger 2010). Airports Council International data show that Africa accounted for less than 3 per cent of global passenger traffic and less than 1 per cent of global airfreight in the year June 2011–June 2012.

Expressed differently, Africa's 12 per cent share of world population is serviced by only 3.9 per cent of all scheduled air service seats in the world. By contrast, the population of North America and Europe combined, which is roughly equal to that of Africa, has access to approximately 54.6 per cent of global seat capacity. In terms of annual available seat kilometres (ASKs) per person, each North American has access to around 5,083 ASKs, whereas each African nominally has access to 154 ASKs, 33 times fewer. On the same basis, Latin Americans and Asians have nearly four times more access to air service than Africans (World Economic Forum 2011).

The small scale of civil aviation in Africa can be presented and grasped in yet other ways. Satellite images and computer-reconstructed flight paths for Earth as a whole depict Africa's remoteness from the most intensive air traffic corridors.[1] One click on the 'Flightradar24' application for mobile data devices reveals in real time the paucity of flights over Africa relative to Europe and the Persian Gulf States.[2]

No less strikingly, a 2009 report noted that air traffic capacity in all of Sub-Saharan Africa (roughly 72 million seats in 2007) was only marginally larger than the capacity available at Madrid's airport (approximately 69 million). The combined domestic traffic for all Sub-Saharan African countries at the time (28 million seats) was just over twice the overall aircraft seat capacity handled at the French city of Nice (13 million). All markets combined in both North and Sub-Saharan Africa had about 122 million seats; in the United

---

1 For example http://globaia.org/en/anthropocene/gts.jpg and http://openflights.org.
2 http://www.flightradar24.com. Bradley Rink provided the pointer. Sparse land distribution of aircraft tracking signal receptors in Africa tells its own story.

States flights through Atlanta alone offered roughly 104 million seats in 2007. The air traffic at John F. Kennedy International Airport in New York exceeded intercontinental traffic in all of Africa in both 2001 and 2004 (World Bank 2009).

Despite Africa's small share of world commercial aviation activity, in recent years the rate of growth of air transport in the continent has been among the highest in the world, albeit off a low base from which percentage gains are easiest made. Whereas traffic grew by 18 per cent elsewhere between 2001 and 2007, total African traffic soared nearly 40 per cent; Sub-Saharan traffic grew as much as 47 per cent (World Bank 2009). At the time, Africa ranked third for growth behind the Middle East and the Asia-Pacific regions. Expressed differently, between 1998 and 2009 the compound annual growth rate of air traffic in Africa was 6.5 per cent. After peaking at 146 million passengers in 2008, the global economic slowdown reduced the number moving through the major African airports on all African and foreign airlines to 136 million in 2009 (World Economic Forum 2011). Substantial declines in North Africa in particular followed the 'Arab Spring' uprisings of 2010/11: Afriqiyah Airways and Libyan Airlines shut down. Passenger traffic on African airlines dropped from 61 million in 2010 to 56 million in 2011 (AFRAA Annual Report 2012).

The presence, profile and performance of airlines in African countries affect all air service provision and use. Toward the end of the first decade of the twentieth-first century there were four countries (Central African Republic, Niger, Lesotho, and the Western Sahara) without any known indigenous air service operators. Twenty-five African countries had only (small) private airlines.[3] Twenty countries subsidised their carriers using public funds or by obtaining government-directed advantages such as airport privileges for the flag carrier.[4] Five African countries (Egypt, Ethiopia, Kenya, Morocco, and South Africa) had dominating state-owned carriers (Schlumberger 2010). In 1996 Kenyan Airways became the first African airline to be privatised; Air Tanzania followed in 2002 (Debrah and Toroitich 2005; Irandu 2008). Cross-airline shareholding (KLM owns 27 per cent of Kenya Airways) and contracting management to overseas airlines and consultants have been popular strategies for strengthening African carriers.

The register of airlines in Africa shows high turnover. Thirty-one ceased operations between 2001 and 2007 in Sub-Saharan Africa. The total capacity lost was nearly 8 million seats. In time, after service hiatus that disrupted business and leisure travel and planning, the loss was more than reversed, 34 new market entrants collectively offering approximately 15 million seats. In the same interval in North Africa, new airlines provided 1.4 million seats, nearly twice the seat capacity that had been lost (660,000 seats) (Bofinger 2009).

Management difficulties explain many African airline troubles. In 2010 and 2011, 16 (50 per cent) of the state-owned airlines belonging to the African Airlines Association (AFRAA) lost their chief executive after less than one year in office (AFRAA Annual Report 2011). In South Africa's relatively mature airline industry, the SAExpress regional carrier lost four financial executives in the 2011/2012 financial year, and the government subsequently fired the airline's entire board (*Business Day* (Johannesburg), 14 August 2012). The disgruntled Board of South African Airways resigned *en masse* later that year. Turmoil

---

3 Botswana, Burkina Faso, Burundi, Chad, the Democratic Republic of Congo, the Republic of Congo, Côte d'Ivoire, Equatorial Guinea, Eritrea, Gabon, The Gambia, Ghana, Guinea, Guinea-Bissau, Liberia, Nigeria, Rwanda, São Tomé and Principe, Senegal, Sierra Leone, Somalia, Swaziland, Togo, Uganda and Zambia.

4 Algeria, Angola, Botswana, Cameroon, Cape Verde, Comoros, Djibouti, Libya, Madagascar, Malawi, Mali, Mauritania, Mauritius, Mozambique, Namibia, Seychelles, Sudan, Tanzania, Tunisia and Zimbabwe.

has also been evident elsewhere in southern Africa's 'airline graveyard', in Malawi, Zambia and Zimbabwe (*Economist* (London), 23 April 2013). Following impoundment of aircraft at least twice, in January 2012 Air Zimbabwe was placed under judicial management with a debt of $140m, including unpaid staff salaries. Across the continent as a whole, 37 airlines launched in the decade 2002–2012; 37 failed (Heinz and O'Connell 2013).

Corporate bankruptcy and other disruptions aside, past growth in African air transport is forecast to continue, in keeping with the anticipated growth of economies, cities and tourism in the continent. The expansion is expected to arise largely from demand for intra-African flights as regional economies become more intertwined. One view is that air travel will mimic patterns elsewhere during equivalent economic development. If comparative ratios between population size and air travel are any indication, Africa's population, bigger than that of China, should be generating close to 150 million passengers instead of the 15 million intra-Africa passengers counted in 2011. By 2040, Africa will be home to one in five of the planet's young people and will have the world's largest working-age population (Ohaeri 2012). Job mobility and aeromobility are anticipated to grow together. Urbanisation is expected to concentrate in second-order cities, and to support hub-and-spoke services.

The world's airlines and aeronautical manufacturers are gearing up for African growth. One sign is that four African airlines have become members of two global airline alliances in which partnering is intended to open and secure new markets by inter-lining: South African, Egyptair, and Ethiopian belong to Star Alliance; Kenyan is a member of SkyTeam. Another sign is the spurt of air transport trade shows and conferences on the continent. Events held in 2012 included a third successive annual conference on airports and development in Africa, an International Civil Aviation Organisation (ICAO) seminar on regional runway safety, and meetings convened by Airports Council International. On the back of recent double-digit growth of air cargo from Asia to Africa (featuring freight such as telecoms equipment), the 2013 calendar included an Air Cargo Africa meeting in Johannesburg.[5]

Also in 2013, the Airport Cities World Conference was held on African soil for the first time. The venue was close to O.R. Tambo International Airport (Johannesburg), the busiest on the continent, and the centrepiece of a self-proclaimed 'aerotropolis'.[6] For only the third time in Africa, the (69th) IATA Annual General Meeting and World Air Transport Summit were held in Cape Town.[7] There, the IATA Director General declared that 'nowhere is the potential for aviation greater than in the continent of Africa' (IATA 2013).

The attraction to Africa is not just aircraft sales and airline service provision for an industry, which, by late 2012, was said to transport 67 million people annually on 762,000 flights connecting Africa's 371 commercial airports. The attraction is also using aviation to stimulate much-needed economic growth: toward the end of 2012 IATA reported that those flights created jobs for 6.7 million Africans and generated $67.8 billion in associated economic activity.[8] Other jobs away from aviation may also be created by the aeromobility of business executives who, by mid-2013, had flown with the booming Swiss-based for-hire business jet company, VistaJet, to or from 136 different airports in Africa (*BBC News*, 18 September 2013).

5   http://www.stattimes.com/aca2013.
6   http://www.globalairportcities.com.
7   http://www.airportexpansionafrica.com; http://www.globalairportcities.com; http://www.aci-africa.aero.
8   http://www.iata.org/pressroom/speeches/Pages/2012-09-03-01.aspx.

The ICAO forecasts a 10 per cent growth rate for the intra-African aviation market in the near future, and over 8.5 per cent in the medium term. Strong traffic growth is anticipated on Africa–Middle East routes (over 6.5 per cent) and on Africa–North America routes (around 6 per cent). The comparatively 'mature' routes to Europe are expected to have the least increase in African passenger demand (World Economic Forum 2011). Another forecast is that passenger numbers in Africa will more than double from 67.7 million in 2010 to 150.3 million in 2030, with revenue passenger kilometres growing at an average annual rate of 5.1 per cent. Cargo volumes are projected to rise at a similar rate of 5.2 per cent per annum (Air Transport Action Group 2012).

Low cost airlines are expected to generate some of the growth in air traffic in Africa. By 2013 the penetration of low-cost airlines in Africa had been less than in any other world air traffic market, with less than 10 per cent share of 52 million continental passengers in 2012.[9] The record of low-cost airlines in Africa is poor (Amankwah-Amoah and Debrah 2009). In South Africa, 11 budget airlines sprouted and then closed down after deregulation in 1992. 'Velvet Sky' lasted a year before it was liquidated in March 2012; it operated one aircraft for domestic service, and used two older aircraft for luxury charter services into Africa. The ambitious launch of a low-cost air service that would replace arduous and dangerous taxi trips between Johannesburg and a remote rural region stalled promptly. The South African-based carrier '1-time' had won the World Travel Award for best low-cost carrier in Africa for the fourth year in a row before it went into liquidation in November 2012. Only a short while previously it had partnered with Harare-based 'Nu-Aero' to launch Zimbabwe's first low-cost airline 'Fresh Air' on a Johannesburg–Victoria Falls service (*Business Day* (Johannesburg), 3 August 2012).

Explanations for the failure of low-cost carriers in South Africa's comparatively well-developed air transport market vary from high fuel prices and the high costs of operating older aircraft to government meddling in favour of South African Airways and its own five-year-old, low-cost 'Mango' offshoot (*Daily Maverick* (Johannesburg), 28 August 2012). Hoping to become the first pan-African low cost carrier, newly launched 'Fastjet' bid for the assets of defunct '1-time' before tying up with another South African company (headed by the South African President's son) to host 'Fastjet' operations in South Africa starting in May 2013.

In a flurry of press coverage, Tanzania-based 'FastJet' made its first flights from the coastal capital, Dar es Salaam, to Mwanza and Kilimanjaro in late 2012. A lot of the excitement was about the one-third shareholding in the airline by the founder of Britain's 'easyJet', Sir Stelios Haji-Ioannou. In a turn of phrase reminiscent of colonial engagement with the continent, he remarked that Africa was aviation's 'last frontier' (*African Business Review*, 10 July 2012). He had in mind the untapped niche market for affordable flights away from mainstream inter-city routes. 'FastJet' is not the first low-cost airline tried in East Africa. In Kenya, Flamingo Airlines failed a decade ago and was absorbed into Kenya Airways. Also in Kenya, 'OneJetOne', backed by Chinese money, failed in 2009 (*African Business*, 13 December 2012). Now a more powerful parent, Kenyan Airways, is minting 'JamboJet' as its own low-cost subsidiary. Research into sustainable business models in the African airline operating environment, however, casts some doubt on the viability of low-cost variants (Heinz and O'Connell 2013).

In neo-liberal circles and developmental discourse, the anticipated growth of aviation based in and serving Africa is taken as welcome news for a generally poor continent:

---

9   Amadeus Air Traffic Travel Intelligence, 16 April 2013.

the hope is that aviation will deepen and spread economic development by opening up trading markets and by providing direct and indirect employment, not least in the tourism sector (World Economic Forum 2011). Estimates are that in 2007 air transport directly employed more than 150,000 people in Africa and contributed US$3.5 billion to GDP. This productivity was about four times higher than the average across all African economies. Indirectly, the air transport industry supported jobs for approximately 300,000 people in Africa. The aggregate 450,000 jobs would have contributed approximately US$10 billion to GDP in 2007. Air transport is calculated to have supported 3 million jobs in African tourism in 2007, contributing some US$22 billion to continental GDP (Oxford Economics 2008).

In South Africa alone, air transport is reckoned to contribute 2.1 per cent of the Republic's GDP and to support 227,000 jobs (1.7 per cent of the workforce). Including the sector's contribution to the tourism industry, these figures rise to 3.1 per cent of South African GDP and 343,000 jobs, or 2.6 per cent of the workforce. The jobs are generally highly productive: the annual value added by each employee in air transport services is over four times higher than the South African average (Oxford Economics 2011).

If correct, the predicted role of aviation in African development is tantalising. One forecast is that by 2026 air transport could directly provide jobs for some 700,000 people, making a GDP contribution of US$25 billion. It will support an additional 4 million jobs and US$77 billion of GDP in the tourism sector (Oxford Economics 2008). Forecasts for 2030 show 7.3 per cent real GDP growth due to air transport creating 879,000 new jobs in aviation (Air Transport Action Group 2012). The tourism spin-off is particularly significant in Africa because approximately 20 per cent of all tourism-related jobs there (675,000 in 2004) are supported by international visitors arriving by air, compared with only 4 per cent (310,000 jobs) in North America (Schlumberger 2010), for example.

Whether or not these long-range forecasts will prove correct, they are shaping aviation planning and investment. What is certain is that the geography of employment and GDP leveraging will occur unevenly across Africa; the biggest winners may be places that already have initial investment and operating advantage. The skewed benefits of all past transport investment have every chance of recurring in aviation, favouring prevailing economic and political interests (Daley 2009). Enlightened national action is essential, for example to protect small-scale horticulturalists from multinational corporations which want to monopolise fruit, flower and vegetable airfreight exports to Europe from Addis Ababa and Nairobi. Aligning tourism and aviation is also important: Mozambique's fly-in tourism industry, for example, is under-developed partly because airfares (in 2006) on the protected national carrier were 163 per cent higher on the Johannesburg–Maputo route than for the same distance flown within South Africa (Myburgh et al. 2006).

Intercontinental Air Transport

By volume (number of seats and number of flights), overseas routes to and from Africa account for less than half of the continent's air traffic. Forty-two per cent of Africa's air traffic was on inter-continental routes in 2011. By contrast, domestic (in-country) traffic accounted for 32 per cent, and cross-border traffic within Africa for 26 per cent (AFRAA Annual Report 2012).

Europe has always been Africa's most significant intercontinental air transport market. It remains so (Figure 14.1). In 2011 Europe accounted for more than half (56 per cent) of African overseas traffic. The Middle East routes operated by airlines such as Emirates,

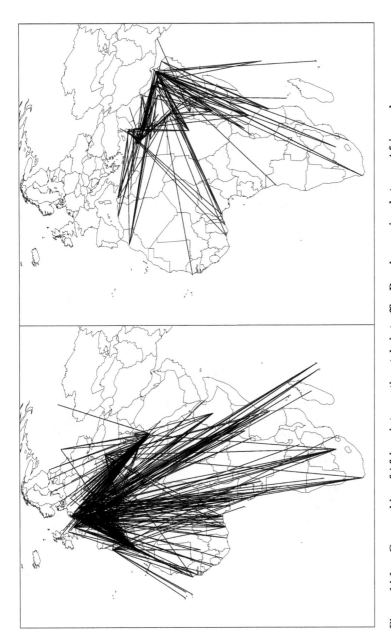

Figure 14.1   Geographies of African intercontinental air traffic: Regular services between Africa and Europe/the Middle East (early 2012)

Note: Threshold = 10 flights per month.
Source: OAG and Frédéric Dobruszkes.

Figure 14.2   Geographies of African intercontinental air traffic: Transatlantic and transpacific regular flights from Africa (early 2012)

Note: Threshold = 10 flights per month.
Source: OAG and Frédéric Dobruszkes.

Etihad and Qatar carried 14 per cent of Africa's intercontinental traffic in 2010; that share leapt to 24 per cent by 2011. The Asia-Pacific (4 per cent in 2011) and North American (1 per cent in 2011) routes (Figure 14.2) are minor channels of business, diplomatic and tourism traffic (AFRAA Annual Report 2012).

In overseas markets, non-African airlines carry most passengers and cargo; African carriers lifted only 36 per cent of the continent's intercontinental traffic in 2011. In the previous decade, African airlines lost 16 per cent capacity to foreign airlines. More of the traffic loss was to Middle Eastern than to European airlines (AFRAA Annual Report 2012). Turkish Airlines' rapid entry into African skies (its Africa destinations almost doubled in number to 33 during 2012) staunched the declining European carrier share. African airlines have a larger slice of the North American market where they account for 41 per cent of the traffic and Middle East airlines carry 34 per cent. African carriers hold the majority (72 per cent) of weekly seats and flights for direct Asia services (AFRAA Newsletter January 2012).

During 2012, African airlines carried the overwhelming bulk of traffic within the continent, and a lesser but majority share of traffic between Africa and Asia (80 per cent) and Africa and North America (Table 14.1). Foreign airlines had the largest and approximately equal share of European and Middle East flights and seats, with the European market being double the size.

Of the African airlines that service the inter-continental market, five are dominant: Royal Air Maroc, Egyptair, Ethiopian, Kenya Airways and South African Airways. Operating from their respective hubs at Casablanca, Cairo, Addis Ababa, Nairobi and Johannesburg, Africa's 'big five' are constantly exploring ways to anchor themselves more firmly in growing markets. Presently, those in India and China are particularly alluring as sources of business and inter-governmental traffic. The absence of any prominent West African overseas airline is striking: the region's airline activity fractured and declined sharply after the demise of several carriers, including Air Afrique, the 40-year-old federal West African airline (2002), Nigerian Airways (2003) and Ghana Airways (2004) (Goldstein 2001; Amankwah-Amoah and Debrah 2010, 2013). An all-night prayer vigil in 2003 failed to exorcise evil spirits thought to be cursing Ghana Airways (Asamoah-Gyadu 2005).

Economies of scale in aircraft and spares purchase achieved by the world's largest airlines help explain why foreign carriers dominate Africa's inter-continental market. Even the biggest African airlines (South African, Kenyan, Ethiopian) are minnows compared with the likes of British Airways and KLM (and their broader holding companies), and with Emirates. Mega-carriers have considerable extra leverage over the prices of new aircraft, spares and fuel. The European and Middle Eastern airlines also have the advantage of strong hubs that feed their Africa networks with plentiful traffic. A considerable number of passengers are transfers from airline alliance partners, and many travellers are committed to carriers by frequent-flyer loyalty schemes, airport terminal preferences, and airline reputation.

Non-African carriers have also had another commercial advantage: crudely labelled 'operating efficiency', the average passenger load factor in African airlines in 2011 was 68 per cent compared with the global average of 78 per cent. Africa is the only region in the world where this load factor for home airlines is less than 75 per cent (AFRAA Annual Report 2012). A combination of poor aircraft selection, weak traffic monitoring and sluggish aircraft sale or route re-deployment explains some inefficiencies. Relatively high fares might also explain some under-utilisation: aircraft operating costs are higher in Africa, partly because of higher fuel, maintenance and insurance costs (World Bank 2009). In a capital intensive business there are very few ways of reducing airline operating costs safely.

Table 14.1   Geographies of Africa air passenger market share, January–December 2012

	African airlines				Other airlines			
	Flights	% African airlines	Seats	% African airlines	Flights	% other airlines	Seats	% other airlines
Intra Africa	906533	96%	88536230	92%	42214	4%	7634643	8%
Africa–Europe	64958	40%	10862093	35%	98653	60%	20292343	65%
Africa–N. America	2892	51%	795889	54%	2828	49%	679072	46%
Africa–M. East	30249	40%	5599714	37%	46227	60%	9435362	63%
Africa–Asia	7743	80%	1981649	80%	1933	20%	506359	20%
Total	1012465	84%	107775575	74%	191855	16%	38547779	26%

Source: AFRAA.

Ownership of African airlines is often thought to be a reason for their underperformance. Approximately half of Africa's 54 countries have a national airline with at least 51 per cent state ownership. The financial conditions and operating abilities of the majority of these mostly small airlines are a cause of concern. Most are subsidised operations with large losses. Few are able to negotiate favourable unit input costs when ordering for only small businesses (World Bank 2009).

Exclusion of many Africa-based airlines from European Union skies is no reason why African carriers do not service destinations there more frequently. The African airlines forbidden from flying to and from Europe because they fail to meet ICAO safety audits are generally small operators and are registered in countries where traffic could not sustain direct European service, at least not from a second-string carrier. In April 2012, in its sixth year, the EU 'banned list' barred 284 airlines in 24 countries worldwide from flying into Europe. Seventeen countries were African. Effectively, a third of all African nations hosted airlines on the banned list. The Democratic Republic of Congo (36 airlines) topped the list. Sudan (14), and Mozambique and Angola (13 each) were next.[10] The exclusions are contentious: their consistency and purpose has been queried, and the reputational damage done to all African airlines has been noted.[11] The EU has even been accused of conspiratorially keeping African carriers on the list so as to expand European airline operations into the continent (Chingosho 2012a).

Within the general picture of less dominant Europe–Africa ties, and foreign carriers predominant on overseas routes collectively, the most important air traffic generators in Africa are in the extreme North and South of the continent. African countries fringing the Mediterranean (Morocco, Tunisia, Algeria, Egypt) account for most of the air traffic between

---

10 Others were São Tomé and Principe (10), Benin Republic (8), Gabon (7), Sierra Leone (7), Republic of Congo (5), Ghana (1), Rwanda (1), Djibouti (1), Zambia (1), and Mauritania(1).

11 http://www.iata.org/pressroom/speeches/Pages/2012-09-03-01.aspx.

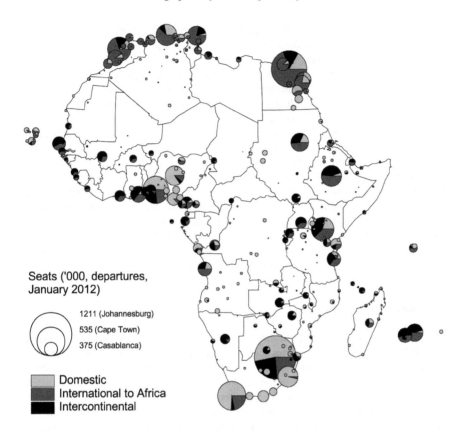

Seats ('000, departures, January 2012)

1211 (Johannesburg)
535 (Cape Town)
375 (Casablanca)

Domestic
International to Africa
Intercontinental

Figure 14.3   Departing aircraft seat availability at African airports in January 2012, showing allocation to domestic, cross-border and intercontinental destinations

Source: OAG and Frédéric Dobruszkes.

Europe and Africa, principally for tourism (Figure 14.3). Addis Ababa, Lagos, Nairobi and Johannesburg have a big share of the remaining overseas traffic. Three of the only Sub-Saharan routes with capacity exceeding 1,000 seats per day[12] connect Johannesburg with Dubai, Harare, and London. More than a third of the 75 busiest routes in Sub-Saharan Africa involve Johannesburg (World Economic Forum 2011).

The continued prominence of South African Airways, if not Johannesburg and South Africa, in Africa's inter-continental air transport market is not assured. Compared with its Kenyan and Ethiopian rivals, South Africa's flagged airline is an end-of-line carrier that suffers from extreme distance between its main intercontinental city-pairs, and from its inability to intercept passing traffic. This geographical handicap has been aggravated by

12   More than 300 intra-Asian routes offer more than 1,000 seats per day (World Economic Forum 2011).

airline management troubles, and by decades of government protection, rescue and subsidy which have done little to make the airline more nimble and commercially aggressive.

Cosseting the quasi-monopoly flagged airline in some immediate national interest has been extremely costly, and may well be eroding national image and competitiveness. A 2006 study of the indirect benefits of open market air transport in Southern Africa found that airfares on liberalised routes had declined by an average of 18 per cent, with significant economic benefits. In cases where a low-cost carrier entered the market, airfares were generally 40 per cent lower than before liberalisation. Estimates were that full liberalisation across Southern Africa would increase passenger volumes by 20 per cent, increase employment, carry more than 500,000 additional foreign tourists, and accordingly boost spending by more than US$500 million. Taking into account the multiplier effect on the Southern Africa economy as a whole, it was estimated that this spending would increase the region's GDP by about US$1.5 billion, a growth of 0.5 per cent. In addition, 35,000 jobs in the tourism industry and an additional 35,000 jobs in the overall economy would be created (Myburgh et al. 2006). Additional research is needed to tease out any circumstantial evidence about post-liberalisation fares, to test the projections published in 2006, and to incorporate other and more refined impact measurements.

Continental Air Transport

Albeit with variations at different airports (Figure 14.3), cross-border traffic between airports in different African countries accounts for approximately a quarter of air transport in the continent. The distribution of air traffic plying solely between African countries is concentrated heavily at two extremities. Southern Africa takes the lion's share at 29 per cent. North Africa accounts for 21.5 per cent of cross-border traffic on the continent. The remaining traffic is divided between West Africa (16 per cent), East Africa (14.2 per cent) and Central Africa (5.1 per cent). Air service within the latter, vast eight-state region (including Chad, both Congos and Angola) is infrequent and multi-stop.

Within each of the five regions, air traffic is quite localised: between-region flows account for only 14.2 per cent of all African air traffic (World Economic Forum, 2011). Strikingly – and taking geography literally – there are just three flights a week each way between Africa's two biggest cities, Cairo and Lagos. By comparison, there are 350 between India's largest metropoles, Mumbai and Delhi (*The Independent* (London), 28 November 2012).

International traffic within Sub-Saharan Africa grew at an annual average of 6.5 per cent between 2001 and 2007, more rapidly than intercontinental traffic (6.3 per cent). Traffic between Southern Africa and North Africa increased by 25 per cent annually. Africa's principal airline hubs – Johannesburg, Nairobi, and Addis Ababa – handled 36 per cent of cross-border air traffic in Africa. In 2007, national carriers dominated traffic within Sub-Saharan Africa: South African Airways, Kenya Airlines, and Ethiopian Airlines accounted for 34 per cent, 74 per cent, and 86 per cent, respectively, of the international Sub-Saharan traffic passing through their hubs (Bofinger 2009).

Despite the overall growth in cross-border air traffic, the number of city pairs served in Sub-Saharan Africa dropped by 229 between 2001 and 2007. Connectivity declines were greatest in West and Central Africa (the Central African Republic had only one flight per week in November 2007) and in Eritrea and the Seychelles islands. Landlocked countries from Mali to the Central African Republic, and many small-market coastal countries in the region (Gambia, Benin, Togo, Cameroon, the Republic of Congo, and Gabon) also lost international links. Namibia and Botswana were among the 15 countries that lost connectivity (Bofinger 2009). Many African airline geographies were evidently vulnerable to traffic decline, route alterations, airline fleet changes or political interference.

Weak airway connectivity in Africa manifested in more than half (51 per cent) of the 660 regional and domestic city-pairs in Africa being served by fewer than five flights per week in July 2011. A mere 3 per cent were served by 50 or more weekly flights (Chingosho 2011). In 2010 only 16 per cent of Africa's routes were operated on a daily schedule; 600 others were served less regularly. One estimate of the shortfall was that although there were 751 non-stop markets served in Africa, there was potential to add a further 386 regional routes, including 70 to and from the continent's major airports (*Airline Business*, 24 March 2010). Recent projects aiming to create and tap traffic include a six-country federal airline for Central Africa (being set up with Air France-KLM holding a 34 per cent stake). Other ambitious launches are Korongo Airlines operated by Brussels Airlines in the Democratic Republic of Congo, Air Cote d'Ivoire (Air France-KLM holding 20 per cent), and Gambia Bird (90 per cent German owned) (*Aviation Week*, 27 May 2013).

From both a business and a post-colonial political perspective, improving air connectivity between African countries is imperative. Arguably it is at least symbolically more important to Africa's future than continued development of overseas services. This is a useful reminder in relation to recent research which implies that a key register of air transport progress in Africa is the degree of the continent's direct air linkages with world capital cities on other continents (Pirie 2010; Otiso et al. 2011; Bassens et al. 2012).

After being excluded from African skies during apartheid, South African Airways has been a conspicuous exponent of inward 'Africanisation' (Pirie 2006). In 2002, in an effort to strengthen its presence and service in its home continent the carrier bought a 49 per cent shareholding in Tanzania's national carrier when it was privatised. A decade on, after targeting mineral rich and developing markets across Africa, the airline serves 38 destinations on the continent (*CAPA Aviation Analysis*, 4 December 2012). In August 2012 it turned its back on 20 years of direct flights between Cape Town and London (selling one of its three valuable early morning slots at Heathrow) in favour of serving closer markets – and arguably more strategic 'Afropolitan' markets – in West Africa where a gap in continental airline service had emerged. British Airways promptly doubled its daily direct Cape Town–London service, snatching some traffic that would otherwise have to re-route through Johannesburg.

The decline of air connectivity in Africa in the first decade of the twenty-first century resulted, in part, from liberalisation measures first provided for in 1988 (via the Yamoussoukro Declaration) and then echoed and reinforced in 1999 (Goldstein 2001). Years of mismanagement and high staff turnover in some airlines precipitated restructuring and some staff poaching (Amankwah-Amoah and Debrah 2010; Amankwah-Amoah and Debrah 2011a; Amankwah-Amoah and Debrah 2013). Liberalisation marginalised many weak carriers, some of which ceased operation, for instance, Air Tanzania, Nigerian Airways and Cameroon Airlines. But liberalisation also helped stronger airlines such as the flagged airlines of Ethiopia, Kenya and South Africa. It was possible for them to start serving routes abandoned by collapsed carriers by using their comparative geographical advantage near the centre of the continent (in the case of Ethiopia and Kenya), by using their individual financial, commercial and managerial strengths, and by exploiting their access to inter-continental markets to feed regional services (Figure 14.4). Simultaneously,

**Figure 14.4   The geographical advantage of Nairobi over Johannesburg for direct
air services**

Note: Isolines (of increasing width) show range of places reachable from Nairobi (dashed lines) and
Johannesburg (solid lines) within 4, 6 and 7 hours flying time (equivalent to an in-day 10- 14- and 16-
hour aircraft turnaround, with 2-hour stop).

Source: Drawn by Philip Stickler.

networks were consolidated by phasing out some low-density routes and focusing on routes
to and from hubs at Addis Ababa, Nairobi and Johannesburg (Schlumberger 2010).

Air traffic between East and West Africa is growing. In the evolving airline service
map, Kenyan Airways' routes to 45 African destinations in 2012 stand out (*CAPA Aviation
Analysis*, 16 April 2012). Previously, in January 2010, ASKY airlines, based at Lomé,
Togo, made its first revenue-earning flight as a feeder to Ethiopian Airlines. The parent
retains a 40 per cent stake in ASKY. Shortly, the launch was overshadowed by an air crash
involving one of ASKY's aircraft, keeping the spotlight on safety compliance and training
issues in Africa (*Air Transport World*, July 2010).

The effect of liberalisation on Africa's thinly trafficked, long-sector air routes was always open to doubt. Yet there is some evidence that competitive practices on previously monopolised routes have reduced ticket prices and enhanced frequencies. This was the case in East Africa on services connecting Nairobi to Cairo, Entebbe and Harare (Irandu 2008). As on inter-continental flights, belly cargo capacity was effectively increased by more frequent flights, enhancing export of fresh fish, vegetables, fruit and flowers.

Other instances of liberalisation also show positive effects, according to one research group. After moving from multiple designation of carriers and increasing daily flights from 4 to 14 in 2000 on the Nairobi – Johannesburg route, full liberalisation led to a 69-fold increase in passenger volumes. Liberalisation of the Johannesburg – Lusaka route in 2006 led to an average 35 per cent drop in ticket prices across all fare classes, and a 38 per cent increase in passengers. The effect translated into an additional 6,300 tourist arrivals per year in Zambia, and an additional income of about US$8.9 million per year from tourism. New entrants to the liberalised South African domestic market created an 80 per cent growth in passengers between 1994 and 2004. The introduction of low-cost air service to one of the poorest regions of the country was followed by 52 per cent passenger growth and a 13 per cent increase in visitor numbers (Myburgh et al. 2006).

Domestic Air Transport

In-country air traffic in Africa is far from insignificant, albeit there are some states without any registered airlines. At the other extreme, in a highly developed internal market (Figure 14.3), the Johannesburg–Cape Town route in South Africa ranked ninth busiest in the world in 2011 (tenth in 2012), flying 4.5 million passengers (4.4 million in 2012).[13] Air traffic within the boundaries of Sub-Saharan African states had the fastest annual growth rate (12 per cent) of all Sub-Saharan African traffic between 2001 and 2007. By then, South Africa and Nigeria accounted for 72.5 per cent and 10.5 per cent respectively of scheduled domestic services in Sub-Saharan Africa (Bofinger 2009).

Domestic air traffic growth has not been distributed evenly. For example, annual increases in domestic traffic in Nigeria reached as high as 67 per cent, whereas there was an absolute decline in traffic in about half of African countries between 2001 and 2007. In North African states, domestic air travel declined by more than 3 per cent; measured in seat-kilometres the domestic market there is about one-fifth the size of Sub-Saharan Africa. In both regions, the number of city pairs has been declining: traffic has consolidated along key routes and locations have been dropped from domestic networks. The most dramatic reduction in city pairs occurred between 2001 and 2004, with an overall loss of 207 routes in Sub-Saharan Africa (137 outside South Africa, Nigeria and Mozambique) and 32 in North Africa. Many of these losses are attributable to the collapse of regional carriers (Bofinger 2009).

Liberalisation of domestic air transport regulations in African countries has been happening to various degrees for the past 20 years. New airlines have been started, many licensed to fly new routes. Success has been erratic in all African regional markets. In 2007, one provider, usually the state airline, served 54 out of 286 domestic routes in Africa. One strategy has been for flag carriers to subcontract thinner routes to private operators

---

13   *Economist* (London) [online], 14 May 2012; Amadeus Air Traffic Travel Intelligence, 16 April 2013.

(Bofinger 2009). In Nigeria, the geographical effects of deeper liberalisation varied. At first, in the mid-1980s, the process reduced the number of domestic routes from 63 to 15; 40 per cent of services performed by monopoly Nigerian Airways had been operated solely for political reasons (Akpoghomeh 1999). Subsequently, many small private airline operators (as many as 35 at one time) started flying more diffuse routes. With strong ethnic affiliations, new carriers established themselves in secondary towns; Lagos' share of annual total domestic passengers declined from 45 per cent to 36 per cent between 1986 and 2006 (Daramola and Jaja 2011).

Airport provision is a critical element in the emergence of domestic air services: international gateway airports handle cross-border passenger and freight traffic adequately but expansion of domestic services to many provincial towns in Africa is hampered by inadequate airport infrastructure. There were approximately 3,000 airports in Africa toward the end of the first decade of the twentieth century. In Sub-Saharan African countries in 2006, the number ranged nationally from 728 in South Africa to 2 in São Tomé. Of the total, 37 per cent (1,018) were commercial airports; the remaining 63 per cent were airstrips. The number of commercial airports across Africa ranged from 195 in South Africa to one in São Tomé. Other top nations as regards commercial airports were Kenya (172), Zimbabwe (129) and Botswana (101). Ten countries had 20 or fewer commercial airports (Chen and Addus 2007).[14]

Only a small fraction of Africa's unevenly spread airports (Figure 14.3) handle scheduled services, and that proportion fluctuates in part due to seasonality. In November 2007, an estimated 280 airports throughout Africa (371 in 2012)[15] received scheduled services. Confirming shrinking air connectivity, the number of African airports with scheduled services declined between 2001 and 2007. A fifth of 179 airports examined cursorily in Sub-Saharan Africa were in poor condition; 4 per cent were in marginal condition (Bofinger 2009).

Construction of new airports in Africa, and improvement or extension of existing runway, apron and terminal facilities has occurred with a mixture of rationality, opportunism and naïveté. There was considerable investment in South African airports before the 2010 World Cup football tournament there; an entirely new international airport was built for Durban (*Airports International*, June 2010). The expansion of Victoria Falls International Airport is underway as the resort town faces a major facelift ahead of the United Nations World Tourism Organisation General Assembly in 2013 (*Herald* (Harare), 8 May 2012). In the tiny, impoverished kingdom of Swaziland, the 12-year, $1 billion construction of Sikhuphe International Airport 80 km from the capital, Mbabane, appears to have been little more than 'a royal vanity project' (*Mail and Guardian* (Johannesburg), 4 May 2012).

There, as elsewhere, chasing after status and development has been associated with hasty and dubious contracting and project implementation. In February 2010, 1,300 families were evicted from the site of a new terminal at Julius Nyerere international airport in Dar es Salaam. They protested without success that compensation undervalued their land assets by 50 per cent and that the enabling eviction act was obsolete. Their forced relocation 36 km away brought hardship and no third terminal: the contract with a Chinese firm was ended after it was found that a parallel oil rights exploration grant had been made improperly. Simultaneous Chinese investment in Air Tanzania appears to have been less

---

14   Cameroon, Cape Verde, Gabon, Ghana, Mauritania, Mauritius, Sao Tome, Senegal, Seychelles, and Uganda.

15   http://www.iata.org/pressroom/speeches/Pages/2012-09-03-01.aspx.

problematic (*Guardian* (London), 2 March 2012). With project income and enhanced trade in mind, China (currently the largest infrastructure financier in Africa, and a significant generator of business and engineer passenger air traffic to and from Africa) has shown interest in building airport facilities or is actually constructing them, especially in resource-rich countries. The list includes airports at Luanda, Lusaka, Nairobi, Juba (South Sudan), Accra, Nigeria (four terminals) and Sierra Leone (*Africa Report*, 15 October 2012). A Saudi Arabian firm is constructing Dakar's new airport.

Efforts to enhance the efficiency and capacity of African airports have focused on (re)construction. Varieties of privatisation have occurred at a dozen or so airports since 1996 (Mills 2011).[16] Operating concessions have been awarded at others.[17] The Nigerian government opted for a full public–private partnership model to design, build and operate a new terminal at Lagos. The remainder of Nigeria's 22 commercial airports are 'embarrassingly lacking' in passenger and cargo handling facilities (Babalakin 2008). In the Republic of Congo, airport privatisation has occurred at Brazzaville, Pointe-Noire and Ollombo (Janecke 2010). Some concessioning has also occurred at Nairobi's Jomo Kenyatta International Airport (Irandu and Rhoades 2006a, b).

Airport efficiency may yet become an even more significant consideration in air transport connectivity in Africa, whether domestic or cross-border. If low cost airlines are to succeed, slick airport operations are essential. The rapid aircraft turnaround on which low-cost airlines depend requires efficient aircraft and passenger handling on the ground. Ineffective on-line ticketing and unpredictable access to airports on congested roads could hamper low-cost airline operations. More generally, the shortage of low-tariff secondary airports in African cities may be an obstacle to proliferation of low-cost services.

Conclusion

As on other continents, the geography of commercial air transportation in Africa is complex and dynamic. Myriad local, regional and international political and economic decisions and organisations affect provision of airlines and airports, route development, and regulation of airline rights. Tracking the consequences exhaustively is difficult.

Broadly, air transport geographies are emerging that focus on serving African air passenger and freight travel markets and economies by capitalising on the continent's locational and economic advantages, not least for fly-in tourism. Air transport in Africa remains a minor element of global aviation, but it is buoyant and is set to develop a profile more in keeping with the continent's commercial and political leanings and standing. Improving air connectivity within the continent is essential. Sensing first-arrival airline business opportunities, and new aircraft and allied equipment markets, the aviation industry is paying more attention to prospects in Africa. As on any frontier, there are uncertainties and risks.

Besides Africa's overseas air transport markets where Europe's historic share is being reduced by Asia-Pacific growth, Africa's distinctive continental air transport sub-markets are in the North, East and South of the continent. Each region is served by strong hubs and dominant carriers. Air traffic in the Arab Africa belt remains more of a Southern European

---

16   Cameroon, Côte d'Ivoire, Ghana, Kenya, Madagascar, Mauritius, South Africa (4), Tanzania.

17   Service concessions at airports in Algiers, Abidjan, Libreville and Kilimanjaro; a terminal concession at Yaoundé and Cairo.

than an African sub-market. In Sub-Saharan Africa, the West African and Central African zones are poorly served. Despite the emergence of low-cost airlines, this geographical unevenness may yet worsen as airline economics tilts advantages the way of established airports and airlines. Already, an orientation toward China and India threatens to marginalise the western side of Africa. There, Accra, Lagos, Abuja and Dakar will contest for trans-Atlantic and regional air traffic gateway primacy. In East Africa, Addis Ababa and Nairobi (and their home airlines, Ethiopian Airlines and Kenya Airways), will exploit their locational advantage as alternative traffic hubs to those in the Persian Gulf. Johannesburg is likely to remain the regional hub in Southern Africa.

Reorganising African aviation around dominant hubs but away from nation-based, flag-carrying airlines may be one way of creating more robust and durable air transport geographies on the continent. The prospects of hitching successful region-wide feeder services to inter-continental services have already caught the attention of Emirates. Possibly sensing a back-door acquisition, the CEO of Kenya Airways told the AFRAA 44th Annual Assembly in Johannesburg in November 2012 that Africa's big three airlines, Ethiopian, Kenyan and South African, should merge: 'we are lambs at the gate', he said balefully (*African Aviation Tribune*, 13 December 2012). But, as has been noted elsewhere (Goldstein 2001; Amankwah-Amoah and Debrah 2011b), and as the AFRAA Secretary General conceded days later at the Second Africa Aviation Law Conference in Nairobi, pan-African airline co-operation has a weak record (Chingosho 2012b). Beyond code sharing, the 'fit' and resource that African airlines can offer each other is unclear, and four African airlines' affiliations to global airline alliances are not likely to be given up easily.

The future of air transport geography across the continent seems set to resolve itself into a four- or five-hub and airline tussle (Ssamula 2012; Ssamula and Venter 2013). At those hubs and elsewhere, the rhetoric and practice of aviation-led development in Africa needs careful costing, monitoring and balancing against the industry's social and environmental consequences.

References

African Airlines Association [AFRAA]. 2011. *Annual Report 2011*. Available at: www.afraa.org.

African Airlines Association [AFRAA]. 2012. *Annual Report 2012*. Available at: www.afraa.org.

African Airlines Association [AFRAA]. 2012. *Newsletter, January 2012*. Available at: www.afraa.org.

Air Transport Action Group. 2012. *Aviation: Benefits Beyond Borders*. ATAG: Geneva.

Akpoghomeh, O.S. 1999. The Development of Air Transportation in Nigeria. *Journal of Transport Geography* 7(2): 135–146.

Amankwah-Amoah, J. and Debrah, Y.A. 2009. The Emergence of Low-Cost Airlines in Africa: A Preliminary Analysis of Internal and External Drivers. S. Davis and K. Ibeh, (eds) *Contemporary Challenges to International Business*. Basingstoke: Palgrave Macmillan, pp. 218–231.

Amankwah-Amoah, J. and Debrah, Y.A. 2010. The Protracted Collapse of Ghana Airways: Lessons in Organizational Failure. *Group and Organization Management* 35(5): 636–665.

Amankwah-Amoah, J. and Debrah, Y.A. 2011a. Competing for Scarce Talent in a Liberalised Environment: Evidence from the Aviation Industry in Africa. *International Journal of Human Resource Management* 22(17): 3565–3581.

Amankwah-Amoah, J. and Debrah, Y.A. 2011b. The Evolution of Alliances in the Global Airline Industry: A Review of the African Experience. *Thunderbird International Business Review* 53(1): 37–50.

Amankwah-Amoah, J. and Debrah, Y.A. 2013. Air Afrique: The Demise of a Continental Icon. *Business History* 55(7): 1–30.

Asamoah-Gyadu, J.K. 2005. 'Christ is the Answer': What is the Question? A Ghana Airways Prayer Vigil and its Implications for Religion, Evil and Public Space. *Journal of Religion in Africa* 35(1): 93–117.

Babalakin, B. 2008. Developing and Improving Air Traffic into Africa: The Role of Private Sector Investment in Aviation Infrastructure. US–Africa Infrastructure Conference, Washington, DC.

Bassens, D., Derudder, B., Otiso, K.M. et al. 2012. African Gateways: MeasuringAirline Connectivity Change for Africa's Global Urban Networks in the 2003–2009 Period. *South African Geographical Journal* 94(2): 103–119.

Bofinger, H.C. 2009. An Unsteady Course: Growth and Challenges in Africa's Air Transport Industry. Background Paper No. 16. Washington, DC: World Bank.

Chen, D.Y. and Addus, A.A. 2007. Growth in Air Transportation of Sub-Saharan African Nations. 48th Annual Meeting of the Transportation Research Forum, Boston, MA.

Chingosho, E. 2011. Air Transport Market Trends in Africa. Airline Business Seminar on Connectivity in Africa, Nairobi, Kenya, 19–21 July. Nairobi: AFRAA, p. 5.

Chingosho, E. 2012a. EU Operational Ban of African Carriers. ICAO African Ministerial Meeting on Aviation Safety, Abuja, Nigeria.

Chingosho, E. 2012b. Strategic Alliances: The Need for Collaborations and Partnerships: Africa Dilemma. Second Africa Aviation Law Conference, Nairobi, Kenya, 5–6 December 2012.

Daley, B. 2009. Is Air Transport an Effective Tool for Sustainable Development? *Sustainable Development* 17(4): 210–219.

Daramola, A. and Jaja, C. 2011. Liberalization and Changing Spatial Configurations in Nigeria's Domestic Air Transport Network. *Journal of Transport Geography* 19(6): 1198–1209.

Debrah, Y.A. and Toroitich, O.K. 2005. The Making of an African Success Story: The Privatization of Kenya Airways. *Thunderbird International Business Review* 47(2): 205–230.

Endres, G. 1995. Airlines in Sub-Saharan Africa. *Travel and Tourism Analyst* 5: 4–23.

Goldstein, A. 2001. Infrastructure Development and Regulatory Reform in Sub-Saharan Africa, the Case of Air Transport. *World Economy* 24(2): 221–248.

Graham, B. 1995. *Geography and Air Transport*. Chichester: John Wiley.

Heinz, S. and O'Connell, J.F. 2013. Air Transport in Africa: Toward Sustainable Business Models for African Airlines. *Journal of Transport Geography* 31: 72–83.

Irandu, E.M. 2008. Opening Up African Skies: The Case of Airline Industry Liberalization in East Africa. *Journal of the Transportation Research Forum* 47(1): 73–88.

Irandu, E.M. and Rhoades, D.L. 2006a. Challenges of Sustaining Growth in African Aviation: The Case of Jomo Kenyatta International Airport. *World Review of Entrepreneurship, Management and Sustainable Development* 2(4): 362–374.

Irandu, E.M. and Rhoades, D.L. 2006b. The Development of Jomo Kenyatta International Airport as a Regional Aviation Hub. *Journal of Air Transportation* 11(1): 50–64.

Janecke, H.-D. 2010. Managing and Delivering an Airport Privatisation Programme: Case Study of the Republic of Congo. *Journal of Airport Management* 5(1): 10–18.

Mills, G. 2011. *Why Africa is Poor*. Johannesburg: Penguin.

Myburgh, A., Sheikh, F., Foandeiro, F. and Hodge, J. 2006. *Clear Skies Over Southern Africa: The Importance of Air Transport Liberalization for Shared Economic Growth.* Woodmead, SA: ComMark Trust.

Ohaeri, R. 2012. International Finance Institutions and the Future of Africa's Air Transport Development. *Aviation Business Journal* 15 August.

Otiso, K.M., Derudder, B., Bassens, D. et al. 2011. Airline Connectivity as a Measure of the Globalization of African Cities. *Applied Geography* 31: 609–620.

Oxford Economics. 2008. *Aviation: The Real World Wide Web*. Oxford: Oxford Economics.

Oxford Economics. 2011. *Economic Benefits from Air Transport in South Africa*. Oxford: Oxford Economics.

Pirie, G.H. 2006. 'Africanisation' of South Africa's International Air Links, 1994–2003. *Journal of Transport Geography* 14: 3–14.

Pirie, G.H. 2010. Trajectories of North-South City Inter-Relations: Johannesburg and Cape Town, 1994–2007. *Urban Studies* 47: 1985–2002.

Schlumberger, C.E. 2010. *Open Skies for Africa: Implementing the Yamoussoukro Decision*. Washington, DC: World Bank.

Ssamula, B. 2012. Comparing Air Transport Network Operations in Sparse Networks in Africa. *Research in Transportation Business & Management* 4(October): 22–28.

Ssamula, B. and Venter, C. 2013. Application of Hub-and-Spoke Networks in Sparse Markets: The Case of Africa. *Journal of Transport Economics and Policy* 47(2): 1–19.

Taneja, N.K. 1988. *The International Airline Industry*. Lexington: DC Heath.

World Bank. 2009. *Air Transport Challenges to Growth*. Washington, DC: World Bank.

World Economic Forum. 2011. The Africa Competitiveness Report 2011. Geneva: World Economic Forum.

Conclusion

Andrew R. Goetz and Lucy Budd

The Big Picture

In the nearly 20 years since the publication of *Geography and Air Transport* by Brian Graham (1995), global air transport has grown considerably but also experienced several shocks which have significantly altered the industry and its operations, with concomitant effects on people and places throughout the world. The geographic patterns of global air transport activity have been changing as a reflection of economic, social, cultural, demographic and political dynamics as well as unprecedented challenges from financial, security, and environmental concerns. Through the contributions of a distinguished group of air transport scholars, this book has shed new light on the emerging geographies of air transport in the early twenty-first century.

The airline industry has always been highly sensitive to economic fluctuations, but the first decade of the twenty-first century witnessed two economic catastrophes that resulted in massive financial losses for the world's airlines. The economic turmoil in the 2001–2006 period coincided with the effects of the 9/11 terrorist attacks in the US, wars in Afghanistan and Iraq, heightened security measures, the SARS outbreak, and rising fuel prices, which together resulted in huge financial losses for the global airline industry, amounting to over US$42 billion. Another period of severe financial turmoil occurred as a result of sharply rising fuel prices and the fallout from the global economic crisis of 2008–2009, resulting in over US$30 billion in losses to airlines. While the global airline industry rallied in 2010 to register robust profits of US$19.2 billion, its profits since then have been more modest, with a net post-tax margin of just 1.2 per cent in 2012 (IATA 2013).

The brunt of the negative economic impact has been felt mostly in the US, Europe, and Japan while secondary impacts have occurred in other countries and regions (Dobruszkes and Van Hamme 2011). In Chapter 3, John Bowen compares how the top global airlines have changed since the 1990s, showing that US and European full-service carriers are still the largest in the world, but have maintained their positions only because of megamergers. In the US, Delta's merger with Northwest created the world's largest airline as of 2011, which then relinquished the top position to United in 2012 due to its merger with Continental, which in turn will be replaced by American in 2014 as a result of its recently-consummated merger with US Airways. Likewise, the merger of Air France and KLM created the third largest airline in 2011, while the merger of British Airways and Iberia resulted in the world's fifth largest airline. The largest growth, however, has been for airlines in the Middle East and Asia-Pacific regions, especially 7th-ranked Emirates Airline (ranked 48th in 1998), 9th-ranked China Southern (35th in 1998), and 13th-ranked Air China (42nd in 1998). The shifting geographies of air transport activity can also be revealed by comparing activity changes in the world's busiest airports. Anne Graham and Stephen Ison show in Chapter 6 the relative decline of airports in the US and Europe, and the rise of airports in Asia-Pacific, especially Beijing, Jakarta, Bangkok, Singapore, Guangzhou, and Shanghai, as well as the meteoric rise of Dubai in the Middle East.

A major focus of air transport research in the 1990s was the impact of revolutionary shocks from deregulation, liberalisation, and privatisation policies enacted first in the US, then Europe, followed by other world regions. These policy changes continue to have dramatic effects on air transport, especially upheaval among the pre-existing full service carriers (FSCs) and the rapid growth of new low-cost carriers (LCCs). While every world region has been affected by these policy changes, some regions have embraced sweeping reforms and experienced dramatic changes, while others have more selectively adopted or resisted these new policies. In the US where the policy shifts first began, Sean Tierney shows in Chapter 9 that the reconfiguration among FSCs, and their alliances with smaller regional carriers, has resulted in a more consolidated industry, while LCCs, led by pioneer Southwest Airlines and more recent upstarts like JetBlue, have carved out a substantial market share at many US airports. Frédéric Dobruszkes in Chapter 10 documents the impacts of EU air transport liberalisation, the consequences for the FSCs, and the remarkable rise of LCCs, especially Ryanair and easyJet. Expansion of the EU to include countries in Central and Eastern Europe together with expanded LCC service there and in other more peripheral regions have altered geographic patterns of mobility, tourism, development, and migration throughout Europe. While the Asia-Pacific region as a whole has been less aggressive in adopting liberalisation policies, Kevin O'Connor and Kurt Fuellhart point out that some countries such as Australia, New Zealand, Thailand, S. Korea, and several others have experienced notable effects from deregulation including significant LCC expansion. The extremely rapid growth of air transport in China derives not so much from embrace of international deregulation policies but from its own distinctive model of development, and is a direct reflection of its rising position in the global economy and its enormous investments in airport and air transport infrastructure.

Turning to other world regions, Gustavo Lipovich points out in Chapter 12 that liberalisation and privatisation processes in Latin America have led to numerous bankruptcies and subsequent consolidations. This resulted in the disappearance of many formerly state-owned airlines and the emergence of multinational Latin American airline consortia such as LATAM (composed of LAN (Chile) and TAM (Brazil)) and Avianca (composed of Avianca (Colombia), TACA (El Salvador), and other subsidiaries). At the same time, some Latin American countries, such as Argentina, Bolivia, Ecuador and Venezuela, have re-nationalised, created, or strengthened new state airlines as a reaction to previous liberalisation policies. In addition to China, the other big story of remarkable growth belongs to the Gulf region of the Middle East, featuring its 'big three' airlines: Emirates, Qatar, and Etihad. Khaula Alkaabi in Chapter 13 documents the phenomenal growth of these three airlines serving mainly international traffic between Europe and Asia through their geographically well-positioned hub airports in the United Arab Emirates (Dubai and Abu Dhabi) and Qatar (Doha). Similar to China, these airlines are controlled by state-owned corporations and benefit from protective domestic state policies, but have also taken advantage of a liberalising international air transport environment that favours open skies and expansive 6th freedom rights (see Chapter 2 by Debbage and Chapter 7 by Derudder and Witlox, this volume). While the smallest of the major world air transport regions, the air transport market in Africa is one of the fastest growing. According to Gordon Pirie in Chapter 14, most airlines in Africa remain state-owned or controlled, including the 'big five' of Royal Air Maroc, Egyptair, Ethiopian, Kenya Airways (privatised in 1996, but the

Kenyan government still holds the largest ownership share) and South African Airways, while LCCs have not penetrated the market as much as in other world regions.

In the 1990s, globalisation had become a major topic of popular discussion and scholarly inquiry, especially in geography and air transport, and it has only increased in importance. The clearest manifestation of globalisation in the airline industry was and still is the creation and expansion of global airline alliances. As Brian Graham (1995: 101) noted at the time, 'the world-wide response to liberalisation and deregulation has been the formation of strategic alliances at regional, national, and global scales'. Keith Debbage in Chapter 2 charts the progression of international regulatory arrangements from a regime of restrictive bilateral air service agreements conducted in the wake of the Chicago Convention of 1944 to a regime of increasing 'open skies' agreements in the 1990s and 2000s. Airlines responded to changing international air service agreements by forming global alliances, and the consolidation of the top three alliances (Star, oneWorld, SkyTeam) is one of the major trends of the last two decades. As John Bowen points out, these three alliances as of 2012 have grown to include 50 airlines and now account for 40 per cent of global seat capacity. The expansion of global, as well as regional, alliances has increased accessibility to previously remote cities and regions, as documented by Ben Derudder and Frank Witlox in Chapter 7. At the same time, major world cities such as London, New York, Tokyo, and Paris at the top of the urban hierarchy have continued to be the major centres of the global air network, based on air transport connectivity. The most notable cities moving up the global air transport hierarchy have been Beijing, Shanghai, Hong Kong, Seoul, and Dubai.

Air transport is itself a product of remarkable technological achievements that have produced revolutionary breakthroughs in the ability to move people and freight farther, faster, more efficiently, more safely, and more comfortably over time. Lucy Budd in Chapter 1 charts the historical progression of air transport development, noting how technological improvements, many of which originated from military and security imperatives, have altered the geography of air transport activity. As first noted by O'Connor (1995) and discussed in more detail by Budd, Derudder and Witlox, and O'Connor and Fuellhart in this volume, air transport networks have changed over time in response to technology, policy, and demographic shifts from multi-stop linear networks to concentrated hub-and-spoke networks. Major players in this technological evolution have been the leading aircraft manufacturers, represented today by Airbus and Boeing, which have developed new wide-body aircraft such as the huge capacity A-380 and fuel-efficient B-787 Dreamliner, as well as narrow-body aircraft such as the A320 neo and B737 MAX. As John Bowen documents in Chapter 3, these aircraft are the latest entries to set new standards of performance in size, fuel efficiency, reduced emissions and noise, and passenger comfort. The experience of travelling by air is one of the subjects discussed by Peter Adey and Weiqiang Lin in Chapter 4 who explore the social and cultural geographies of air transport. Reconceptualising the spaces of air transport, including air space, the space of the aircraft, and the space of the airport, provides new perspectives of and appreciation for human experiences in air travel mobilities.

A major concern in air transport has been its sustainability, based on the concept as developed originally by the Brundtland Commission report in 1987 (World Commission on Environment and Development 1987) and reiterated by the Rio conference in 1992, balancing the economic, environmental, and social equity dimensions of development. While transport as a whole is subject to concerns about its use of petroleum, carbon emissions, and local air quality, even more pressing concerns have been raised about the sustainability of air transport. As Tim Ryley in Chapter 5 and Christopher Paling,

Paul Hooper and Callum Thomas in Chapter 8 document, the environmental impacts of air transport are even more considerable than other transport modes, especially its high rate of petroleum-based fuel use per passenger-kilometre, and its rapidly-growing output of greenhouse gas emissions. These realities of contemporary air transport cast a shadow over its future sustainability in a world of ever-increasing fuel prices and international efforts to limit and reduce greenhouse gas emissions. Air transport possesses many desirable transport characteristics especially its ability to move people and goods rapidly and safely over both land and water, which makes it a vital transport mode for economic development and international interconnections. Progress in aircraft technology and economic regulatory reforms have resulted in lower average airfares and greater accessibility to a wider segment of human society. The growth of low-cost carriers, in particular, have enabled many people to access the benefits of air transport for the first time. But increased air transport use causes disproportionately negative impacts on the global and local environment, including noise and air quality impacts on neighbourhoods near major airports, as well as the need for more airport and airspace capacity. The challenge for air transport involves properly mitigating the negative effects of its use, while being able to tap its considerable strengths as a transport mode.

Geographies of Air Transport

Also since the 1990s, the geographical study of air transport has grown and become more diverse, encompassing new areas of inquiry generated from economic, urban, environmental, political, social, and cultural geography, as well as from transport geography itself. The most notable expansion has been in the area of 'mobilities' research, which is focused on the social aspects of mobility, including 'both the large-scale movements of people, objects, capital, and information across the world, as well as the more local processes of daily transportation, movement through public space and the travel of material things within everyday life' (Hannum, Sheller and Urry 2006: 1). As applied to air transport, Adey and Lin (this volume) explain how a mobilities approach emphasises 'the way air travel would shape societies, culture and politics, and the role societies could play in re-shaping aviation'. Engagement with the study of 'aeromobilities' and an appreciation for 'the "small", unanticipated and unintended emotions, affects, senses, urges and nuances of life in-the-air', contribute to the study of philosophically deeper and more diverse air transport geographies.

An appreciation for the diverse geographies of air transport also includes the comparative analysis of air transport dynamics involving different regions of the world. Historically dominated by developments in the US and Europe, air transport has grown and expanded to become a more global activity, symbolised by very strong growth in the Asia-Pacific and Middle East regions, as well as in Africa and Latin America. The largest airlines and airports are still predominantly in the US and Europe, and given the hierarchical position of important global cities such as London, New York, Paris, Chicago, Los Angeles, Washington, Frankfurt, and Munich, it is expected that air transport will continue to be strong in these regions. Nevertheless, economic pressures have resulted in a more varied geographical patchwork of growth and decline, where especially some US cities including Detroit, St Louis, and Pittsburgh have seen their relative air transport standing decline in response to economic and industry upheaval. At the same time, the growth of economies in the Asia-Pacific region, facilitated through both established and emerging global hub cities such as Tokyo, Hong Kong, Shanghai, Beijing, Singapore, Seoul, and Sydney, has been the key factor behind rapid air transport growth in this dynamic region. While Japan, China, Australia, Singapore, South Korea, and Thailand have led the way and other large countries such as India and Indonesia are poised for take-off, most other countries in the region have rudimentary levels of air transport development. The same can be said for the Middle East, Latin America, and Africa, although the stunning aviation growth of several Middle East Gulf States, especially the United Arab Emirates and Qatar, is globally significant and dwarfs development in most of the other countries of that region. A notable exception is that of Turkey which straddles both the Middle East and Europe, and boasts one of the largest airlines in the world (Turkish Airlines) and one of the world's largest airports (Istanbul). The growth of air transport development in Turkey is also globally significant, both in terms of its domestic growth as well as international linkages between Europe, the Middle East, and Asia, as well as developing connections to Africa. Air transport in specific Latin American countries such as Brazil, Mexico, Chile, Argentina, Colombia, and Peru has outpaced others in the region, while South Africa, Egypt, Ethiopia, Kenya, Morocco, and Nigeria are the clear air transport leaders in Africa.

Yet another approach through which to study the diverse geographies of air transport is through the concept of scale, and the appreciation of geographical expressions of air transport at the global, national, local, and micro levels. While much of the foregoing discussion emphasised the global scale of analysis, there are important geographical manifestations at the national or regional level for larger countries. Taking the US as a prime example, the internal geography of the country has shaped and been shaped by the development of air transport. The economic fortunes of cities like Atlanta, Chicago, Dallas-Ft Worth, Denver, Los Angeles, Miami, and New York have been influenced by their roles as domestic air transport hubs and/or international gateways, leading to a strong air transport orientation in their metropolitan economies (see Derudder and Witlox, this volume). Related economic activities in tourism, trade, logistics, and producer services have benefitted from the high degree of air transport service available in these places. Cargo hubs such as Memphis, Anchorage, and Louisville have benefitted as well from their air transport activities. At the other end of the scale, declining cities, such as Detroit, Cleveland, Pittsburgh, St Louis, and Buffalo have seen their share of air transport activity drop, further reinforcing their downward slide. At the local scale, airports have influenced growth patterns through related economic activity and land use changes. The airport city, or 'aerotropolis', concept has cast the relationship between airports and urban development in a new light, emphasising the transformative potential of coordinated airport and urban development. As discussed by Graham and Ison (this volume), existing and developing airport city/aerotropolis projects in Hong Kong, Incheon, Kuala Lumpur, Beijing, Dubai, and other cities are affecting the urban structure of these places. In other cities where airports have become surrounded by urban development, concerns over increased airport activity, congestion, and noise impacts threaten the continued growth of air transport operations in these places. At the micro scale, as Adey and Lin (this volume) suggest, the use of and perceptions associated with airport space have led to a 'cultural economy' approach to the study of airports, which adds another dimension of analysis to existing narratives concerning the operation and use of airports. Another micro-space that previously has not been a major focus of geographic research is the enclosed space of the aircraft as experienced by 'entubulated' passengers and workers.

Future Air Transport Geographies

While much of this conclusion has focused upon changes in the geographies of air transport over the past 20 years, this final section casts an eye to the future, and suggests possibilities for the study of future air transport geographies. Twenty years from now, the geographies of air transport will undoubtedly be different due to technological, economic, political, and demographic changes. Many of these effects are already 'in the pipeline' and will become more apparent over time.

Since air transport is itself a product of remarkable technological advancements from the twentieth century, it is expected that the twenty-first century should yield significant improvements, especially in the continued applications of information technology and greater operational efficiencies (see Bowen, this volume). Each generation of aircraft produced by Airbus and Boeing has been able to fly farther and more safely, using less fuel per passenger-mile. One of the sustainability challenges for future aviation technology is the development of aircraft that can be powered by renewable fuels. Reliance on petroleum-based jet fuel is accompanied by numerous vulnerabilities that threaten the sustainability of air transport. Development of commercially-viable aircraft powered by renewable fuels that do not contribute to global greenhouse gas emissions or local air pollution, while reducing noise, will help greatly to mitigate the negative environmental impacts of air transport. If advances such as these can be developed, it may be possible to revisit the era of supersonic air transport which ended with the grounding of the Concorde in 2003. The geographic effects of higher speed and longer distance air service should be a natural topic for future research. Likewise, commercial space travel, currently in its infancy, may also grow and become a topic for future geographic research.

In the economic and political realms, the rapid growth of China and other countries of Asia-Pacific has greatly affected the global profile of air transport. These growth trends are expected to continue into the future, with China likely to assume a leadership position in air transport similar to that of the US and Europe. As conveyed in the chapter by Debbage (this volume), the geopolitical and international policy aspects of air transport have historically been dominated by the US and Europe, but they will likely be joined by China in this sphere of influence. The further development of the Chinese military and commercial aircraft industry will challenge the dominance of Boeing and Airbus. Chinese airlines will continue to expand their domestic air services as incomes rise. They will also expand international air services to those places where significant connections will be forged based on strategic geopolitical and economic concerns, especially access to natural resources. An area that will continue to be problematic involves airspace sovereignty, such as the current dispute between China and Japan over contested islands in the East China Sea. While military and security issues have not been a major focus of geographical air transport research in the past, Budd, Debbage, and Adey and Lin in this volume all mentioned this topic as an area of growing interest.

There is a certain inevitability associated with demographic change, since we already have a good idea of where populations will be greater 20 years from now. The growing populations of countries in Africa, Asia, Latin America, and the Middle East should result in increased air transport activity in those places, subject to parallel economic growth. While the US, Europe, and more developed countries of the Asia-Pacific region will see their relative share of population continue to decline, their relative share of air transport activity will probably not decline to the same degree due to foundational economic strength and existing air transport infrastructure investment. There will likely be a more even distribution of air transport activity in the future across the major world regions, but it will still be dominated by the leading global and world cities in each of these regions. Urbanisation will continue to increase, and emerging secondary cities in rapidly growing areas will replace those that were once significant but are now in a process of long-term decline. At the local scale, airports and their environs will continue to be major nodes of urban activity connected by rail and other transit to high-density, mixed use centres throughout their metropolitan areas.

In the next iteration of this book, it will interesting for future air transport scholars to document how the geographies of air transport differ from those of today. There will be new philosophical and methodological perspectives to guide this research, and unforeseen developments that will have great effects on these future geographies of air transport.

References

Dobruszkes, F. and Van Hamme, G. 2011. The Impact of the Current Economic Crisis on the Geography of Air Traffic Volumes: An Empirical Analysis. *Journal of Transport Geography* 19: 1387–1398.

Graham, B. 1995. *Geography and Air Transport*. Chichester: John Wiley & Sons.

Hannum, K., Sheller, M. and Urry, J. 2006. Editorial: Mobilities, Immobilities, and Moorings. *Mobilities* 1(1): 1–22.

IATA. 2013. *Annual Review 2013*. [Online: International Air Transport Association]. Available at: http://www.iata.org/about/Documents/iata-annual-review-2013-en.pdf [accessed: 10 December 2013].

O'Connor, K. 1995. Airport Development in Southeast Asia. *Journal of Transport Geography* 3(4): 269–279.

World Commission on Environment and Development. 1987. *Our Common Future*. Oxford: Oxford University Press.

Index